Politics in the Sudan

Peter K. Bechtold

The Praeger Special Studies program—
utilizing the most modern and efficient book
production techniques and a selective
worldwide distribution network—makes
available to the academic, government, and
business communities significant, timely
research in U.S. and international economic, social, and political development.

Politics in the Sudan

Parliamentary and Military Rule in an Emerging African Nation

PRAEGER SPECIAL STUDIES IN INTERNATIONAL POLITICS AND GOVERNMENT

Praeger Publishers   New York   Washington   London

Library of Congress Cataloging in Publication Data

Bechtold, Peter K
    Politics in the Sudan.

    (Praeger special studies in international politics
and government)
    Includes bibliographical references and index.
    1. Sudan—Politics and government. I. Title.
DT108.7.B4   320.9'0624'04   76-6466
ISBN 0-275-22730-8

PRAEGER PUBLISHERS
111 Fourth Avenue, New York, N.Y. 10003, U.S.A.

Published in the United States of America in 1976
by Praeger Publishers, Inc.

Printed in the United States of America

For my Mother and Father

PREFACE

The material for this book has been gathered intermittently during a period of more than ten years, which included five separate visits to the Sudan totaling approximately two years. The most recent journey concluded in January 1975, and the writing was completed a few months thereafter.

Most of the field research was conducted in the capital area, although I was able to visit all provinces at least once. The people whom I met, and the great and small adventures I encountered, have been among the most memorable and rewarding experiences of my life. I know that I will always be indebted to my many wonderful Sudanese friends, not only for their help and hospitality, but also for the many lessons about the art of living which they unknowingly imparted to me. It is impossible to name them all here; in any case, they know my feelings and that, in a larger sense, this book is dedicated to them.

I was able to draw on many authors for historical and anthropological perspectives, but the bulk of this book is based on my own field work. This applies in particular to the material on parliamentary elections for which I compiled most of the tables in the text personally, sometimes entirely on my own, and at other times combining data from publications of the various election commissions. I was very fortunate to have received "observer" status from the commission in 1965/66, and I am grateful for this permission and the opportunity to gain an unusual insider's view.

Maps 4.1, 4.2, and 7.1 are derived from personal photographs of large maps that were published by the 1958 and 1965 commissions, although the graphic depiction of electoral gains in the latter case is my own. Map 5.1 is reprinted from the frontispiece of the Autumn 1958 issue of the Middle East Journal and portions of Chapter 8 are taken from an article in the same publisher's Winter 1975 issue; in both instances the Journal's authorization is gratefully acknowledged.

I wish to record my gratitude to Professors Morroe Berger and Carl Brown of the Near East department at Princeton University who read the first version of the manuscript and gave me valuable substantive comments as well as encouragement, and to Professor John Anthony of SAIS, Johns Hopkins University, who helped me greatly to improve one particular chapter. I also want to thank the Graduate School of the University of Maryland for financial assistance during one summer of writing and to Provost Mary F. Berry of the Division of Social and Behavioral Sciences for her moral support and for procuring a travel supplement. I am also grateful to the many other unnamed individuals, including my family, who helped me intellectually or personally over the years. However, responsibility for the final version of this book must remain my own.

CONTENTS

LIST OF TABLES, FIGURES, AND MAPS

GLOSSARY

Transliteration of proper and place names from Arabic presents inherent difficulties because of regional variations, popularizations by the Western media, and also inconsistency on the part of local users. For those reasons most scholarly organizations such as the Middle East Institute and the Middle East Studies Association have opted for the standard of the Library of Congress transliteration method. Unfortunately, Sudanese usage differs so greatly from that method that its strict application might create more confusion than clarity. This problem is compounded by the fact that most Sudanese scholars, including those cited in this book, have published major works while using highly personalized transliterations of their own names. Because it seems hardly appropriate to challenge a native scholar on the spelling of his name, or the native English language editors on their usage, this writer decided to retain local spellings in the body of this volume. The table below, which contains some of the more common names, is presented in the hope of alleviating any potential confusion and inaccuracies.

Popular Spellings	Library of Congress Method
Abbas	'Abbās
Abboud	'Abbud
Abdallah, Abdullah	'Abdallāh
Abdel-Khalig	'Abd al-Khāliq
Abdel-Rahman	'Abd al-Raḥmān
Abou Zeid	Abū Zayd
Ahmed	Aḥmad
Ali	'Alī
Ansar	Anṣar
Anyanya, anya'nya, nya'nya	———
Atbara	'Aṭbarah
Awadallah	'Awaḍallāh
Babikir	Bābikir
Bahr el-Ghazal	Baḥr al-Ghazāl
Beshir	Bashīr
Cairo	al-Qāhirah
Darfur	Dār Fur
Daoud	Dāwud
El-Azhari	al-Azharī
El-Fasher	al-Fashir
El-Mahdi	al-Mahdī
El-Obeid	al-Ubayyiḍ

Popular Spellings	Library of Congress Method
El-Tayeb	al-Ṭayyib
El-Turabi	al-Turābī
El-Zein	al-Zayn
Faisal	Fayṣal
Farouq, Farouk	Fārūq
Gaafar, Jaafar, Ja'far	Ja'far
Gezira	Jazīrah
Hashim	Hāshim
Hassan	Ḥasan
Hussein, Hussain, Hassain	Ḥusayn
Ibrahim	Ibrāhīm
Imam el-Hadi	Imām al-Hādī
Ismail	Ismā'īl
Jebel Nuba	Jabal al-Nūbah
Khartoum, Chartoum	Khurṭūm
Kheir	Khayr
Kordofan	Kurdufān
Mahgoub, Mahjoub	Mahjūb
Mahmoud	Maḥmūd
Maamoun, Ma'Moun	Ma'mūn
Mansour	Manṣūr
Mohammad, Mohammed, Mohamed	Muḥammad
Nasser	Nāṣir
Nimeiri, Numeiri	Numayrī
Omdurman	Umm Durmān
Omer, Omar	'Umar
Osman	'Uthmān
Qaddafi	Qadhdhāfī
Sadig, Sadiq	Ṣādiq
Shafieh	Shafī'
Sheikh, Shiekh	Shaykh
Sudan	Sūdān
Umma	Ummah
Wau	Wāw
Zarroug, Zarrouq	Zarrūq

INTRODUCTION

A book on contemporary Sudanese politics should have several aims: to identify the major actors and components of the Sudanese political system, to examine the ways in which these interrelate and interact, to isolate and illuminate the chief public issues of recent years, and to analyze system performance, that is, the ways in which Sudanese have dealt with their various problems, the degree to which these problems have been successfully resolved, and the existence of conditions making for political stability or instability in the country.

To approach these tasks, it will be necessary to blend historical description with comparative analysis, in full recognition of the risk that purists among both historians and political scientists may be perplexed from time to time. For the benefit of those readers who might care to know, this author will go on record as believing that historical analysis and cumulative theory building in political science are not only compatible intellectual pursuits, but are, in fact, interdependent to the point where even limited success in either area has become unthinkable without dependence on the other. For those reasons, fair amounts of descriptive materials have been included in Parts I and II, for the record as it were, because there does not exist as yet a systematic treatment of Sudanese politics since independence, to the author's knowledge.

Methodologically, this study will be based on a political culture approach—if labels are necessary—modified to suit both Sudanese conditions and the author's predilections. Emphasis will be on process and behavior rather than formal institutions and chronology of political events. Nevertheless, it should go without saying that the former cannot be adequately understood without paying considerable attention to the latter as well.

Sudanese political history makes a fascinating subject for study. The country itself is a veritable microcosm of all of Africa. It occupies the largest territory of any state on the continent, and within its borders it harbors a variety of peoples who represent—in pure form and in mixtures—every racial community to be found in Africa at large. In ethnic, geographic, and political terms, the Sudan constitutes a crossroads of Africa. As such it has been and continues to be the object of foreign interests with geopolitical, economic-exploitative, and cultural-ideological designs. These different forms of imperialism, and the Sudanese reaction, have markedly influenced public affairs during the last century. They are primarily responsible for the development of slave raids and trade in the southern portion of the country more than one hundred years ago—the seeds of the contemporary Southern Problem. They have indirectly caused the emergence of the Mahdist rebellion in the 1870s, one of the first successful national liberation movements in modern times. They have characterized Anglo-Egyptian rivalry during the condominium period of the first half of this century, and are primarily responsible for the changing foreign policy postures of postindependence Sudanese governments.

On the domestic level, Sudanese politics presents a varied study in political instability and contrasting styles of rule. Since independence on January 1, 1956, the Republic of Sudan has experienced three major self-proclaimed revolutions, and the format of government has twice changed between parliamentary democracy and military rule.

Actually, the Sudanese have had effective control over their political destiny as early as 1953, when the Anglo-Egyptian Agreement of February 12 provided for the election of a Constituent Assembly, whose members were charged with deciding upon the future constitutional status of the country. For that reason the period covered in this book will begin with 1953, even though the Sudan was technically still a condominium at that time. A British-style parliamentary democracy lasted until November 17, 1958, when a group of army officers, headed by Lieutenant General Ibrahim Abboud,[*] established a military regime and dissolved all political parties by decree. The junta remained in power until it in turn was overthrown in the wake of the October 21 Revolution in 1964.[1] Following a short transitional period leading up to parliamentary elections, the new government returned to the multiparty system of the pre-junta years. This arrangement lasted until May 25, 1969 when, once again, a group of military officers led by Colonel Ja'far el-Nimeiri proclaimed a new revolution and outlawed all other organized political activities.

These events are quite astounding in themselves; even more astounding is that each of the three abrupt changes has been accomplished with an almost complete absence of bloodshed and that each was enthusiastically supported by the great majority of people aware of its occurrence. Moreover, on each occasion revolutionary leaders and supporters alike vowed to "have learned the lessons of history and never to return to the corruption and/or tyranny of the past." The new leaders proceeded to espouse views and to support a number

---

[*]Sudanese place and proper names have been transliterated in accordance with popular usage rather than the more rigorous Library of Congress method. For alternate spellings, refer to the Glossary.

of policies that appeared to be radically different from those of their predecessors, especially in the field of foreign affairs and in the large-scale arrests and trials of members of the previous regimes.

Yet, we may observe that on balance none of the three revolutions of 1958, 1964, and 1969 accomplished very much,[*] despite some radical departures in policies and despite the enthusiastic initial support given to them by the public. For more than 17 years government in the Sudan had been based on a transitional constitution, even though committees and assemblies have been charged since 1954 with setting up a permanent constitution. And during the first 15 years of independence, no regime had made substantial progress toward, or even concentrated its efforts on, the three major problems facing the country: economic development, social change, and the rebellion in the southern provinces. It took two years of serious domestic disorders, culminating in a short-lived coup d'etat in mid-1971 to force a reevaluation of political priorities on the part of the regime of President Nimeiri; yet credit must be given to his administration for perceiving the urgency of these three issue areas and for subsequent actions of at least moderate success. Thus, a settlement with southern rebel leaders was effected in March 1972, and the agreement on regional autonomy for the South permitted the finalization of a permanent constitution on May 8, 1973.

But the fact remains that, for most years since 1953, conditions in all three problem areas have deteriorated, albeit at somewhat varying rates. This simultaneous deterioration was among the chief reasons for the outbreak of revolutions at the three different points in time. In this sense, the failures of the three first governmental regimes in the Sudan are quite similar; in the end, the failures of each of the once hailed revolutions led to the return to systems that the revolutions had set out to destroy.

But why should this be so? Why should essentially opposite political systems and at times opposite policies yield similar results? Why did the self-proclaimed revolutionary leaders twice return to governmental formats that previously had failed to meet the specific requirements of Sudanese conditions? Conversely, why was the

---

[*] This does not mean that they accomplished nothing of value, but it implies that the attribute "revolution" should be reserved for fundamental rather than incremental changes. As indicated, the Nimeiri regime has made the most progress toward fundamental changes, relatively speaking. Yet one could argue that many of these accomplishments could come about only after the realignment of political forces away from the original composition of the May 1969 leadership, and a concomitant shift of policy priorities.

democratic leadership unable or unwilling to avoid past mistakes that had already once brought about the demise of parliamentary democracy? Finally, what are the prospects of stability and progress for the new rulers?

These are the major questions for which I will attempt to provide some answers in Part II through an evaluation of political developments during the periods of parliamentary government and military rule. The peculiarities of governmental changes have presented a considerable organizational problem. In principle, I prefer a thematic to an historical approach in order to facilitate the reader's understanding of patterns and trends in military politics, for example. Yet, for the benefit of historical continuity the materials in Chapters 5 through 8 have been presented in fairly chronological order, and include analyses of the rulers' performances for the four respective historical periods. Comparisons of the effectiveness of the various regimes in critical issue areas, and the efficacy of different political systems under Sudanese conditions, have been reserved for Chapters 9 and 10, whereby new criteria for cross-regime comparisons were applied to avoid repetition of earlier analytical evaluations.

In order to place the historical and comparative analyses into the proper contexts, the first part of this book introduces the reader to environmental and cultural forces that have affected the political behavior of the individual Sudanese, and to the roles that traditional and modernizing elements have played, and continue to play, on the level of group dynamics.

It is evident that such a broad range of topics necessarily precludes detailed treatment of any; therefore this study should be seen as a modest attempt to survey and analyze those basic forces that have shaped Sudanese politics in recent years. The only apparent exception involves the relatively extensive coverage of parliamentary elections in Chapters 5 and 7. The materials in Chapter 4 and the Appendix have been added in order to illuminate the social setting and general atmosphere for elections and the specific issues and electoral behavior of Sudanese in undoubtedly the most interesting constituency. This was done in part because parliamentary elections in the Sudan have been unusually open and fair by African and Middle Eastern standards;[2] as such they constitute a major hallmark of Sudanese politics and deserve special recognition. In part also, this author believes that a relatively detailed study of electoral politics can reveal much about political trends over time, and probably more about the interplay of significant social, economic, and political forces than any other issue.

The following four major issue areas have been selected for special attention throughout this volume: the domestic political process, the status of the national economy, foreign affairs, and the Southern Problem.* These four issues have constituted the major tasks facing all Sudanese governments, both colonial and native, throughout the last century. They are, of course, interrelated to different degrees and the policies regarding one of them will affect all the others. Nevertheless, the special focus of this book demands that the main emphasis by far should rest on an analysis of domestic politics; thus, we shall have to await more comprehensive studies of the other subjects by competent scholars.

Finally, an observation about the dynamics of the situation is in order. It is a truism that few things in life are as pervasive as change. Perhaps the major problem of politics in Africa and the Middle East has been the phenomenon of widespread and fundamental changes affecting all aspects of life. The need to cope with these changes in some viable manner is a monumental task for all political systems in the area; many have failed to master that task and Sudanese governments have been prominent among them. Reasons for failure have been many and varied and will be shown in subsequent chapters. However, one very prominent factor deserves to be highlighted, that is, a factor that characterizes today's political drama, and that runs like a thread throughout Sudanese public affairs: factionalism. It is my basic contention that politics in the Sudan, and especially the degree of political stability there, is today a function of the same basic forces—a particular form of factionalism—as it has been since the decade prior to independence. For that reason it is necessary to take a close look at the component factors that shape Sudanese factionalism and its relationship to the formation and subsequent activities of political organizations, and its effect upon the conduct of democracy as well as military rule.

We shall begin by looking at the ways in which environment and demography have contributed to factionalism in the Sudan.

---

*Although the North-South conflict has received wide attention in the foreign press as well as scholarly works, it will be treated here only as one of several problems that have persistently confronted the various Sudanese regimes. There will also be no evaluation of such specific items as the Addis Agreement of March 1972 or the performance and composition of the Southern Regional Assembly in Juba.[3]

NOTES

1. The rise and fall of the Abboud regime has been previously discussed by this author in a short article, "The Military in Sudanese Politics," Africa Today 15, no. 2 (April-May, 1968): 23-25, and in much greater detail and depth by Ruth First, The Barrel of a Gun: Political Power in Africa and the Coup d'Etat (London: Penguin, 1971), Part V.

2. A comparative analysis of the parliamentary elections of 1953, 1958, and 1965 is contained in a detailed study by Peter K. Bechtold, "Parliamentary Elections in the Sudan" (Ph.D. diss., Princeton University, 1968). The study also examines the relationships of elections to effective political participation and to democracy in the Sudan.

3. The interested reader is referred to such volumes as William Deng and Joseph Oduhu, The Problem of the Southern Sudan (London: Oxford University Press, 1963); Beshir Mohammed Said, The Sudan: Crossroads of Africa (London: The Bodley Head, 1965); Mohammed Omer Beshir, The Southern Sudan: Background to Conflict (London: C. Hurst, 1968); Oliver Albino, The Sudan: A Southern Viewpoint (London: Oxford University Press, 1970); Francis M. Deng, The Dynamics of Identification: A Basis for National Integration in the Sudan (Khartoum: Khartoum University Press, 1973); Ministry of Foreign Affairs, Peace and Unity in the Sudan (Khartoum: Khartoum University Press, 1973); Dunstan Wai, ed., The Southern Sudan and the Problem of National Integration (London: Frank Cass, 1973); Cecil Eprile, War and Peace in the Sudan 1955-1972 (London: David E. Charles, 1974); Robert O. Collins, The Southern Sudan in Historical Perspective (Tel Aviv: Shiloah Center, 1975); Mohammed Omer Beshir, The Southern Sudan: From Conflict to Peace (London: Barnes & Noble, 1975); and numerous shorter treatments in books and scholarly journals.

MAP OF THE SUDAN

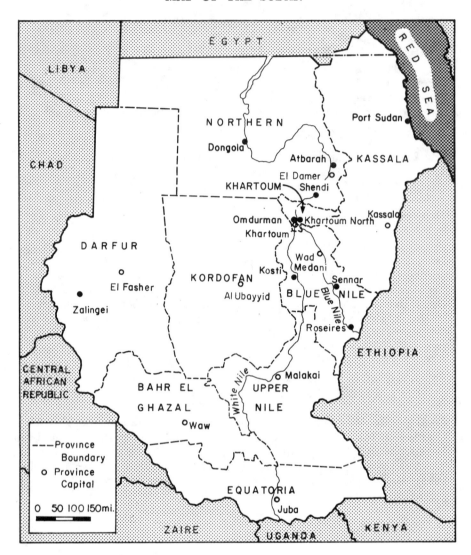

In the Sudan as elsewhere, actors in the political process are many and varied: governmental and other official institutions, various public associations, social groups, and individuals. All of these interact with one another and modify each other's behavior in turn. Moreover, all actors are influenced to various degrees by their multifarious environments. Hence, our analysis must include such factors as demographic and geographic variables, economic conditions, foreign influences—both current and historical, material and cultural, supportive and antagonistic. In addition, it is a truism that mass, group, and individual behavior has been and continues to be affected by such phenomena as political heritage, tribal and social customs, religious norms, and so on. In other words, the above items—by no means an exhaustive list—may be viewed as inputs into the political process that together produce as one of several outputs our basic unit of analysis: Sudanese political man.

Accordingly, the initial chapter of this book will be devoted to brief surveys of land and people in the Sudan, economic opportunities and limitations, various factors contributing to social and political conditions and to the cultural heritage, and the impact of foreign affairs.

LAND AND PEOPLE

Scholars and social philosophers alike have observed from time immemorial that man's behavior is in large measure a product of his environment. Anyone who has ever deliberated the merits of walking as little as 80 yards to a government office under the blazing late morning sun in Khartoum, or as much as 80 miles

to the nearest polling booth at election time in Western Kordofan, will
heartily agree with that learned observation.

But there is more to our assumption than considerations of discomfort and inconvenience. Throughout history, natural barriers have
tended to divide and isolate peoples from one another, just as fertile
plains have tended to bring them together both physically and culturally.
Thus, the spread of Islam, for example, is thought to have been contained by geographic barriers that were considered to be unfavorable
to the Arab milieu, such as rainforests in both Europe and Africa.

Moreover, a glance at contemporary states in the Middle East
suggests that demographic and cultural variables appear to be correlated to an astounding degree with relatively high governmental
stability. In other words, such states as Tunisia, Egypt, and Saudi
Arabia, with basically homogeneous societies—in terms of ethnic,
religious, and geographic cleavages—have experienced much more
stable rule than such states as Syria, Iraq, Sudan, with very heterogeneous societies. In fact, if one were to place all roughly 20 independent states of the region from Morocco to Iran and Turkey to
Sudan upon a continuum on the basis of societal cleavages, one would
discover a remarkable degree of correlation between homogeneity of
the population on one hand and governmental stability on the other,
virtually regardless of the format of government involved, for example,
single party, multiparty, monarchical, and so on.

While this interesting hypothesis cannot be pursued further in
this study, a few relevant comments should not be omitted. First,
regime control over a population is clearly a function of physical
accessibility, among other things, both in terms of space and communications. Second, in societies where personal loyalties are predominantly to primary and secondary groups, the relative absence of
ethnic and religious cleavages will make much easier the building of
a communal-national esprit, as well as consensus and legitimacy for
one set of rulers, compared to societies with multiple and frequently
reinforcing cleavages. As we shall see immediately below, the Sudan
is unfortunately burdened by disadvantages on both counts. In fact,
the most apt capsule description of the country and its people might
well be: almost infinite vastness and variety.

The Setting

The Republic of the Sudan is the largest state in Africa and
covers an area of almost one million square miles. It stretches
between latitude 4° North and 22° North and between longitude 22°
West and 38° West; the Sudan shares borders with Egypt and Libya

in the North, Chad and the Central African Republic in the West,
Zaire, Uganda, and Kenya in the South, Ethiopia in the East, and faces
Saudi Arabia across the Red Sea.

The country exhibits a variety of geographical features from the
desert expanses in the North to the flat plains of the heartland and to
the rolling hills and mountain ranges along the western, southern,
and eastern borders. Similarly, there is a variety of soils from sandy
to tropical and a wide range of vegetation in direct proportion to the
amounts of annual rainfall, beginning with desert scrubs in the northern region and becoming both lusher and thicker in concentration as
one moves southward, featuring steppe, savannah, bush, and thick
jungle, respectively.

Yet amid all this variety two factors predominate the geographical
features of the Sudan: (1) the vastness of all regions; vast cotton
fields, vast deserts and vast swamps alike, making communications
an overwhelming problem; (2) the river Nile. It is hard to overestimate the importance of that river to the peoples who inhabit the
countries through which it flows, both as a giver and taker of life, a
natural barrier to expanding armies and raiding tribesmen, and an
object of international conferences and treaties. The Nile does exude
a certain undefinable magic to all who come into more than fleeting
contact with it; it attracts both nomads and pilgrims from West Africa
to settle along its banks, and it apparently casts a magical spell over
those who have lived there and who cannot bear to leave it for any
length of time, in accordance with the ancient proverb that "He who
has drunk from the River, shall return."*

Climatic conditions almost completely regulate the affairs of
daily life. The Sudanese rises with the sun and normally begins work
at 6 o'clock in the morning. He retires around 2 P.M.,† when the heat
has reached its maximum, very rarely under 100°F in the shade, in
a country where shade rarely can be found except inside buildings.
Shortly before sunset, social activities including politicking begin and
may last until late at night. The outside observer frequently cannot
help but feel that, for various reasons, after-five activities are
approached by the Sudanese with much more vigor, enthusiasm,
charm, and skill than those during working hours.

Another regulating factor of daily affairs is the annual rainy
reason. This affects substantially all who live in the rain belt except
those in the capital. Because of the virtual absence in the country of

---

* In Sudanese colloquial man sharab min an-nil birjah.

† The only exceptions are office-workers; civil servants arrive
later at their desks and leave earlier, while business employees
usually work a few additional hours in the evening.

all-weather roads, towns and smaller settlements are cut off from
one another because of the sheer impossibility of moving any vehicles
through the mud. Even rail services are heavily curtailed because of
the frequent washouts along the old-fashioned narrow-gauge tracks.

As one moves farther south in the country, the length of the rainy
season increases, and all communications come to an absolute stand-
still. Plains turn into swamps, and swamps and rivers into immense
lakes.

In contrast to the sedentary sector, the nonsedentary population
welcomes the arrival of the southern trade winds bearing humidity.
During the rainy reason the low reserves in the water holes and
baobab trees are replenished, the scorched central plains sprout
forth with tall green elephant grass at an incredible speed, and the
nomads once again change directions in their wandering patterns in
pursuit of pastures.

Administratively, the Sudan is divided into provinces that, in
turn, are subdivided into various local councils. During the early
1970s, a broad administrative reorganization took place for the stated
aim of bringing people and government closer together through decentralization. As a result there are 15 provinces at present and almost
4,500 local councils. These numbers are likely to be increased as
soon as the reorganization extends to the southern region.[*]

This new arrangement supersedes the Local Government Ordinance of 1951, which had been in effect for almost twenty years. This
period was surely one of the most formative in Sudanese history, and
even at the turn of 1975 it is apparent that many Sudanese still find
it difficult to adjust to the recent administrative changes. Because
the material in this book covers most of that period, it is both useful
and necessary to explain the old system briefly.

During the 1950s and 1960s the Sudan was divided into nine
provinces, of which six—Northern, Khartoum, Blue Nile, Kordofan,
Darfur, and Kassala—are considered to be northern and the remaining
three—Upper Nile, Bahr el-Ghazal, Equatoria—are southern. The
local councils ranged from four to eighteen in number per province,
totalling 84 in all, and they constituted the smallest units of local
government staffed and supervised by the central government.

-----

[*]During 1974 the larger northern provinces were subdivided as
follows: Northern into Northern (Capital Dongola) and Nile (El-
Damer), Blue Nile into Blue Nile (Damazin), White Nile (El-Dueim),
and Gezira (Wad Medani), Kordofan into North Kordofan (El-Obeid)
and South Kordofan (Kadugli), Darfur into North Darfur (El-Fasher)
and South Darfur (Nyala). Earlier, Kassala Province was subdivided
into Kassala (Kassala Town) and Red Sea (Port Sudan).

In March 1976 the following reorganization took place in the South:

In each province there has been a Provincial Administration composed of a commissioner (governor), a Province Council, and Province Authority. He is "responsible to the minister of Local Government for the good government in the province, is the head of all government officials within the province, and is responsible for coordination and reporting on the activities of government units."[1] The Province Council, formerly responsible to the Council of Ministers (Cabinet), now to the Province Commissioner, is a "body corporate, composed partly of representatives elected by Local Government authorities in the Province and partly of members of the Province Authority and other members directly elected or appointed whenever elections become an impracticable possibility. The Province Authority consists of Head Representatives of Ministries functioning in the Province."[2]

Since the new law took effect in 1971, these province councils were augmented by 34 area councils, 225 rural councils, 79 city councils, 3,392 village councils, 590 district councils, and 158 other councils for smaller commercial units. Members of local councils have generally been two-thirds elected by popular vote and one-third appointed by province authorities. It is noteworthy that, since 1971, women were given a 25 percent representation in all new councils in order "to insure the role of women and their democratic rights which were guaranteed by the law."[3]

During colonial times and more than a dozen years after independence, this form of local government has been complemented by the so-called "native administration." We shall return to this topic in greater detail in Chapter 3; suffice it here to identify its practice as the former official recognition by the Sudan government of various tribal leaders as native administrators in their own tribes or subtribes.* These positions authorize the holders to execute limited functions of the kind that are usually associated with the duties of a civil magistrate in Western countries. Although the tribal leaders receive a modest salary from the Ministry of Local Government, and although that ministry officially confirms their appointment, they are actually elected by the members of their administrative units. We may distinguish between three types of tribal leaders: (1) the <u>sheikh</u>, who normally presides over a village or a "quarter" in a larger town; (2) the <u>omda</u>, who is responsible for a number of sheikhdoms comprising a district similar to a county in Western countries; and (3) the <u>nazir</u>, or paramount chief, who rules over a large tribe and

---

Eastern Equatoria (Juba), Western Equatoria (Yambio), Jonlei (Bor), Upper Nile (Malakal), Lakes (Rombek), Bahr el-Ghazal (Wau).

* This practice has been reviewed by the Nimeiri regime and has been abolished for the most part.

enjoys considerable overt and covert powers and whose position
approximates that of a grand chieftain among American Indians.

The capital of Sudan is Khartoum, which is situated at the juncture of the Blue and White Niles and which derives its name from
that location. (Khartoum means elephant trunk; the location of the
old city near the river junction resembles the shape of an elephant
trunk when viewed from above.) Actually Khartoum constitutes only
one-third of the complex known as the Three Towns, the other two
being Khartoum North and Omdurman. All major government offices
and head offices of large firms are located in Khartoum, and the vast
majority of the foreign population lives there, including naturalized
immigrants and their descendants. Khartoum North is developed as
an industrial area, while the "real" Sudanese capital is Omdurman
on the west bank of the Nile. Omdurman has been described as the
largest native capital in Africa: This refers to the fact that virtually
no foreigners reside there. All truly prominent families in the
northern Sudan either live in Omdurman or have relatives living
there. Politicians and big businessmen commute daily to Khartoum.
If it is possible to think of a country as having a heart, then the heart
of the Sudan is surely Omdurman.[*]

Population

The population of the Sudan is estimated as approximately 16
million inhabitants as of 1975. (The last published population census
of 1956 is hopelessly outdated; this figure was taken from a 1975
World Bank estimate.) As Map 1.1 reveals, they are distributed
unevenly, with a fairly heavy concentration along the Nile and in the
Gezira[†] (from 20 per square kilometer to over 100 per square kilometer), while the desert regions of the northwest and northeast are
virtually uninhabited. The average density is 5 per square kilometer
in the country as a whole.

Three modes of living exist in the Sudan. According to updated
estimates, 15 percent of the population live in urban centers and 72
percent are settled farmers. The remaining 13 percent are nomads.
However, these figures do not portray the patterns of livelihood
accurately. The 72 percent settled farmers should be subdivided

---

[*] It may be significant that the generally recognized basic Arabic
colloquial is not called Sudani or Khartoumi, but Omdurmani.

[†] The area between the White and Blue Niles, north of the
Sennar-Kosti railroad line.

MAP 1.1

Population and Tribal Groups

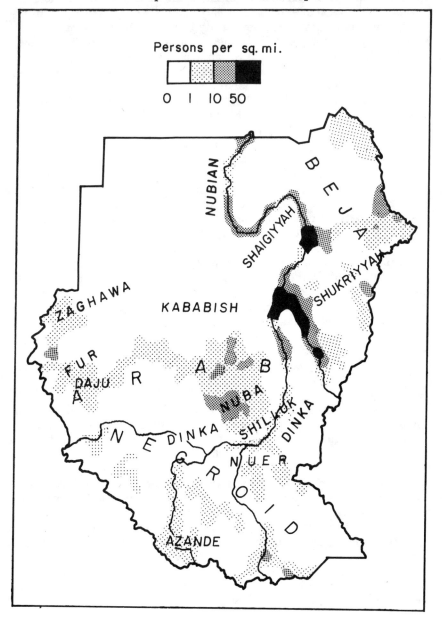

9

into at least three different categories that would reflect the actual patterns more properly. (Unfortunately, accurate statistics about the relative sizes of the three groups are again unavailable. One can assert with reasonable accuracy that members of the first group live predominantly near rivers, especially in the North, those of the second may be found in most of the South, and the seminomads inhabit mostly fringe areas in central Sudan near, but not directly by, water sources.) There are, of course, a large number of cultivators, those who own their own parcels of land, and those who work in any of the several agricultural schemes, of which the Gezira is the largest and best known. These cultivators may live partly off their own produce, but are likely to market their surplus crops on a regular basis.

The second group consists of sedentary types who live in a subsistence economy of the most primitive type: They hunt and fish for their own livelihood and, in some cases, their women may grow small amounts of local cereals to complement the protein-rich diet. Others—in parts of the South—merely camp under fruit trees that need no upkeep. They may own some small livestock as a form of security for future contingencies, but rarely use such livestock except for payment in personal affairs—bride-price or blood money.

Finally, there is a considerable sector of seminomads. These are clans who live part of the year in established settlements, which they use as a home base for the migrations that some of them—grown youths and young adults—make during the rest of the year in search of pastures for their livestock.

Ethnicity

Ethnically, the Sudanese represent a cross section of all Africans. Some are Arabs, some Hamites, and some Negroid-Africans, yet most are a mixture of two or of all three. Some authoritative sources claim that there are 597 tribes in the Sudan comprising 56 tribal groups.[4] For the purpose of this study it will suffice to make only two major distinctions, which are also the ones that most Sudanese consider to be important: (1) the North-South split, and (2) the main (rival) groupings within these two major regions.

The northerners are simply almost all inhabitants of the northern provinces. They are overwhelmingly Muslim (Sunni) and have an acceptable command of the Arabic language. These two factors have shaped a certain degree of identity among northerners and have created a kind of common cultural heritage resembling that of other Arabs yet remaining distinctly Sudanese.

The main ethnic groups in the North that exhibit fairly strong tribal cohesiveness and act as political pressure units are the Nubians (originally Hamites), the Beja of the eastern region (also Hamitic), various Arab tribes occupying the whole central belt, for example, Kababish, Ja'aliyin, Baqqara, and others, and remnants of earlier peoples, the most important ones being the Fur in the West, and the Nuba in the mountains of Kordofan. It should be clearly understood that in all cases, family and clan loyalties exceed attachments to subtribe and tribe. Moreover, the previously mentioned cultural identity among northern Sudanese should not be overestimated. For many reasons members of one tribe continue to be extraordinarily suspicious of members of all other tribes wherever they may be encountered. And it not at all untypical that, for example, the Beni Amer of the Hadendowa (a major subdivision of the Beja group) experience greater communality toward their cousins in (foreign) Eritrea than toward the Ja'aliyin along the Nile.

Historically the Southern Sudanese—those living south of latitude 10° north—have been protected by various geographical and climatic barriers from invasions. The difficulty of the terrain has led to a scattering of larger tribes into smaller units, all with their own languages or dialects. The Southerners may be classified into these three categories: (1) Sudanic (clusters of tribes living west of the Nile), (2) Nilo-Hamitic (the peoples of the southern Nile Valley, for example, Bari and Latuka). (3) Nilotic (inhabitants of the rivers and swamps in the heart of the south). Of these, the latter are the most important for our purposes, as their three main tribes—Dinka, Nuer, Shilluk—are collectively the largest in the South, politically the most dynamic, and as far as the central government has been concerned the most troublesome.

Many Southern tribes have close consanguineous affinities with tribes in Ethiopia, Kenya, Uganda, and Zaire, as the international boundary in the South and East is nowhere an ethnic one. (This is also true in the West except that here many rivalries exist among tribes, resulting in raids over disputed territories.[5])

The degree of cultural identity found among northerners does not exist in the South.[6] The horizons of virtually all but a very few educated southern tribesmen are the limits of their own tribal group, usually their own clan. Everybody else is outside those limits, a potential rival and enemy, and hence not to be trusted. Tribal clashes were fairly common in the very recent past, and only during the last two decades has a new element been introduced in southern consciousness: a feeling of common animosity toward the "new imperialists"—the "Arabs" from the North, who have supplanted the British in their functions as colonizers in the South (in the eyes of the southerners). They are considered to be worse than their predecessors;

while the British exuded at times a paternalistic air, the northern administrators have been cast as exploiters.

While it is true that southerners have been united in their intense dislike of northerners, it is also true that this feeling appears to be—for the time being at least—the only unifying bond.[*]

Religion

Religious cleavages in the Sudan are almost as pronounced as ethnic ones and, in terms of political impact, probably more damaging. The development of these patterns will be discussed in greater detail in a subsequent chapter; suffice it to identify the major groupings here. On the most basic level we may distinguish among Muslims, Christians, and Animists.

Although about 98 percent of the northern Sudanese are Muslims of the Sunni variety, this apparent homogeneity is misleading. Islam in the northern Sudan is based on tariqah, an "organization of religiously minded people united by a common faith in the peculiar spiritual virtue of some particular teacher who acts as intermediary between the follower and the Deity."[7] There have existed and continue to exist a great number of turuq (plural of tariqah) in the northern Sudan.[8] However, the two major ones are the mahdiyyah (followers of the house of Mahdi, also known as ansar) and the khatmiyyah. The existing suspicion and distrust between members of these two sects can hardly be overstated, and we shall return to that phenomenon shortly.

With the exception of a few expatriates and naturalized immigrants in the northern towns, all Sudanese Christians are southerners. Although exact figures are impossible to come by, it is estimated that they number approximately one-quarter million, about one-tenth of the population in the three southern provinces. Of these, roughly four-fifths are Roman Catholics and the remainder Protestants. The significance of these figures lies in the fact that Roman Catholic southerners have received considerable support—moral and material—from the Vatican as well as from fellow Roman Catholics in neighboring countries in their struggle against perceived northern domination.

---

[*] Certain southern politicians will take violent exception to this statement; yet documentable evidence, such as the continuance of raiding, tribal clashes, and so on, tends to support the assertion.

The overwhelming number of southern Sudanese are animists,* or spiritualists who may worship a variety of deities, but especially venerate ancestral spirits. These spirits are reincarnated in successive generations of rainmakers or spiritual chiefs, in whom the function of spiritual and temporal authority may be combined, according to Professor Mohammad Omar Beshir. He adds a rather relevant observation with regard to the possible impact of animism on southern political action: pagan religions are tribal religions and do not provide a basis for united actions by several tribes, and the influence of the rainmaker or spiritual chief is, therefore, confined to his own tribe.[9]

Education

Education has spread throughout the country at a very rapid pace. Before independence there were 633 elementary schools (199 of these for girls), 149 intermediate schools (21 for girls), and 24 secondary schools (8 for girls), about half of them being government schools.[10] Various surveys indicate that prior to the 1953 elections literacy in the country was estimated near 2 percent. This figure has risen sharply since, due mostly to the establishment of adult education centers and the accelerated growth of the educational establishment. During the academic year 1973/74, 1,387,277 students were enrolled in the public education system, 31 percent of them girls.[11] On the average, enrollment in all types of schools has doubled approximately every five years. It would be correct to state that free education is available to anyone who desires it (at least at the primary level throughout the northern Sudan†). In the case of certain nomadic tribes whose leaders have not been convinced of the need for educating their children, the government has tried to lure these children to schools by providing free room and board, clothing, and some expense money.

---

*There are also a few thousand Muslims.

†Secondary schools are still hard to find in remote areas, which means that most eligible students must be willing to live away from home as boarders. The public school system throughout the southern region still suffers from the disruptions during the periods of civil strife (1955-72), when nearly all schools there were closed down.

For those who pass a series of competitive examinations, university level education is available at three government institutions and one private institution.*

In the area of social development, we encounter the same overwhelming variety as elsewhere. The spectrum ranges from sophisticated urbanites to naked swamp dwellers. It may be of interest that a number of reputable "Africa hands" have labeled certain portions of the South—especially the Sudd region—as the most backward part of all Africa. While the northern part of the country is generally more advanced along all conventional indices of modernization than its southern counterpart, some areas in the North also suffer from extreme poverty and backwardness. As recently as June 9, 1970, the current regime has sponsored a "campaign against nakedness" in the Nuba Mountain region of Kordofan.[12]

The major distinction, however, in terms of social development—here intended as a compound variable including education, detribalization, and secularism—and political sophistication is between urbanites and rural peoples. It is a striking experience to travel just a few miles east of Khartoum into any rural settlement, a passage from an atmosphere of international airport, taxis, cinemas, foreign embassy personnel with their concomitant noise, tension, and excitement to one of rural tranquility, unsurpassed hospitality, and conservative-traditional customs. In the political realm, one can sense the pulse of the nation's capital, not only in the numerous administrative offices, but also in the apparently continuous political debates, in private or in public, in the sensationalism of the mass media, and as a breeding ground of new political movements. In rural areas, political action means basically a demonstration of loyalty to one's acknowledged leader.

What, then, are the effects of environmental and demographic variables on life in the Sudan? Geographic configurations and climate have set economic limitations on different regions and have thereby substantially prescribed the lifeways of their inhabitants. Demographic variety has produced a highly heterogeneous society deeply divided along ethnic, religious, geographic, cultural, occupational, and almost every other conceivable line. There emerges a resultant pattern that resembles a mosaic of rich variety framed by imposing environmental restrictions. As it is, however, the requirements of a modern nation-state necessitate frontal attacks on environmental and demographic constraints. Among the chief tasks confronting

---

*Khartoum University, Cairo University (Khartoum branch), Khartoum Technical Institute, and the new Islamic University. In addition, there are several teachers' training colleges.

Sudanese governments have been efforts to develop, broaden, and diversify the economy, to ameliorate historic rivalries and channel political and social resources into nation building and to improve the overall system of communications. We shall return to the former topics in subsequent chapters, and conclude this section with a few comments about the latter.

Communications constitute perhaps the greatest obstacle to modernization of the overall economy as well as the political system. Whether the problem is shipment of essential goods overland or contacting a political figure out in a province, it may require at least several days and possibly weeks of exhausting travel over "roads"[*] that resemble either corrugated-iron tracks, or spurs through sand dunes. Only the sturdy, old-fashioned Bedford Lorry seems able to conquer these, not so much because of its adaptability to surface conditions, but because it is invariably loaded with fifty or more passengers who by sheer pooling of physical strength can extricate the vehicle from whatever sand or mudhole it may be stuck in. The absence of repair shops in but a few large centers increases the difficulties, and it is a testimony to the skill and imagination of the local drivers that the vehicles are moving at all.

Railroad and steamer services exist but in insufficient quantity. The railroad is burdened by an old-fashioned narrow-gauge track that reduces maximum speed to 40 m.p.h., by the absence of a second track for passing trains, except in stations, thus causing delays at virtually every stop, and by the unpredictability about arrival and departure of any particular train, notwithstanding the official schedule.

Air communications have increased considerably since independence, but for reasons of commercial solvency flights to provincial centers are limited to a few times per week.

It is possible to write volumes on the state of communications in the Sudan; but it may suffice for the reader's understanding of the situation to cite just one example: In the Jebel Marra region of Darfur many kinds of Mediterranean fruits are grown on terraced fields, from strawberries to citrus fruits to mangoes, yet much of the harvest is spoilt, because the fruits cannot be transported to the nearest population centers in Kordofan in less than three full days, a period entirely too long in the absence of any kind of cold storage or refrigeration facilities in an exposure of heat of up to 135°F.

---

[*]By early 1975 there was still only one paved highway in the entire Sudan, aside from paved roads in a few of the larger towns, namely the Khartoum-Wad Medani Road.

CULTURAL HERITAGE

Few reasonable men will deny that individual political behavior
is frequently influenced by various ostensibly nonpolitical factors,
such as social customs, group values, religious norms, historical
experiences, and so on. Indeed, some scholars have developed new
methodological techniques for examining the influence of socialization,
of political culture, and others, on political action. And while the complexity of these phenomena tend to make an already unwieldy subject—
politics—even more unwieldy, it is nonetheless incumbent upon the
student of political process to consider at least the more prominent
aspects of what might be called cultural heritage.

In the case of the Sudan, we shall survey the influence of tribal
and other social customs, religious beliefs, and political heritage[*] on
the public behavior of average Sudanese. Within the framework of this
study it is, of course, impossible to quantify "influence" and
"average" in any precise fashion; that task is left to sociologists and
others who are yet to discover the vast research possibilities in
Sudan. We shall have to be satisfied with a series of generalized
observations, in the hope of elucidating some relevant characteristics
of Sudanese behavior.

Customs

Group loyalties form an integral part of Sudanese behavior patterns. Social ties are most pronounced toward family, clan, locality,
and tribe, in that order. One might add that religion inevitably reinforces these ties. In other words, it is virtually unheard of that
members of the same family or tribe adhere to different religious
beliefs; in fact, such deviance would not be permitted.

Within one's own group, relations are based on mutual trust and
a sense of brotherhood that takes even explicit forms in verbal dis-
course as well as in caring for a deceased "brother's" relatives.
Equal to the strength of these bonds are mistrust and sometimes
hostility for all outsiders. The phenomenon is, of course, still rather
common in this part of the world, and it accounts largely for the
extent of localism and particularism in public affairs. As such it
constitutes one of the major obstacles to effective nation building.

---

[*]Political heritage will be treated separately in the third section
of this chapter.

While this condition persists to some extent throughout Africa, it is particularly severe in the Sudan, given the size of the country, the multiplicity of tribal groupings, and the acute problems of communication.

Authority in Sudanese clans rests in the person of the male head of the household, who is usually treated as a sort of family patriarch. His authority in personal matters is almost boundless, and not infrequently conflicts with the expectations of the younger, more educated generation. A rather extreme example of this condition is portrayed by the following incident that took place—on excellent authority— about the year 1950 in the Blue Nile town of el-Hassaheissa.

One Friday morning, while the male members of the extended family were assembled in the courtyard of the family compound (hosh) as usual, the household head decided to discuss the subject of marriage and inquired about the number of unmarried boys and girls in the family. The answer was, ten and eight, respectively. After eliminating the two youngest boys, the sheikh began to match up the remaining eight boys and girls, being careful, of course, that each matched couple was made up of first- or second-degree cousins. As it happened, so the anecdote goes, Ali and Ahmed, both well-educated and employed as teachers in nearby Wad Medani, discussed their "assignments" and indicated to each other a preference for exchanging brides. They approached the sheikh and requested that Ali be matched with Fatima and Ahmed with Suad rather than as had been originally proposed. The old man listened to their request and then ruled that he had spoken and that there was no need to reopen the subject.

This decision may seem unreasonable to many, especially since no damage would have resulted from exchanging Fatima and Suad. The point, however, was that a reversal of decision would have undermined the sheikh's authority in the eyes of some (especially his own) people, and respect for traditional authority should outweigh personal considerations. As it happened, the two young men maintained that respect and accepted the ruling. I should hasten to add that this particular occurrence is no longer representative of any but the most rural areas.

As paradoxical as it may seem, this form of authority relationship coexists with a tradition of decision making in public matters by some form of popular consent. Whether an issue is relevant to the fortunes of clan or tribe, the individual always had—and still has— access to the actual decision-making body or person. It is true that the elder makes the final decision regarding family affairs, the sheikh for the village, the nazir for the tribe (where still applicable); and on the surface, this process has all the trimmings of authoritarian, willy-nilly behavior. However, if one disregards the structure of this process in favor of the actual functioning, an important point

emerges: access is available to virtually all levels. If any individual—
no matter how low his personal status—desires to state his point of
view on an issue, he will always have a chance to be heard; and if he
is at all serious, his opinion will be considered. This form of access
is in evidence even at the national level, where large crowds of
individuals—many of them laborers and nomads—mill around the
Republican Palace* waiting to petition the head of state in person. If
they stay long enough, they will invariably be heard, no matter how
insignificant their problems may appear to be to the statesman. It
has been inconceivable to the Sudanese that freedom of expression is
curtailed in any form; and it is this author's contention that one of the
chief reasons for the downfall of the military regime in 1964 was that
the regime had begun to act like a military one, that is, access by the
common man to the governing authority had been cut off. The current
military regime under General Nimeiri seems to be walking a tight-
rope in this regard by outlawing political parties (except its own) and
curtailing freedom of speech, yet encouraging "public discussions"
of governmental policy.

In a survey study of Sudanese ethics the Norwegian philosopher
Tore Nordenstam found that the following were perceived as traditional virtues: courage, generosity, hospitality, honor, dignity,
respect, and self-respect.[13] The findings conform to this author's
unsystematically gathered field observations. Of particular interest
to the political analyst is the extent to which notions of honor, dignity,
and respect affect social behavior in conflict situations. On one side
of the coin we may notice deference to traditional and legitimized
authority, respect for the elder's judgments and decisions. On the
other side, one sees persistent attempts at maintaining that authority,
even in the face of evident mistakes or of subjective ignorance. This
then usually results in the employment of various face-saving techniques that may be harmless at best, yet not infrequently demand
substantial expenditures of time and energy. This sort of thing is
unfortunately not limited to traditional settings such as tribal councils,
but has been transferred to many facets of daily life. This author is
reminded of his almost daily observations of one particular and well-
known senior government official—who must remain unidentified, of
course—who spent perhaps 90 percent or more of his time on image
projection, face saving, and fence mending, and at best 10 percent
on planning or executing policies. It was little wonder that, during
the roughly 18 months of observation, stagnation seemed to abound
in the particular agency headed by this individual. On the other hand

_____

*Now titled Peoples' Palace, the official residence of the head
of state, which overlooks the Blue Nile.

one must acknowledge the payoff from this sort of behavior: our man survived several civil service purges by revolutionary regimes, many attacks by his various enemies, and has amassed considerable wealth as of this writing.

In another context, honor and self-respect require the protection of one's family from potential disrespect from outsiders. Of particular importance is the safeguarding of the reputation of female family members,[14] a concern that has led to a kind of overprotection that is no longer cherished by the growing masses of educated Sudanese women. This overprotection has taken the form of various social restrictions that, in turn, have become focal points of attraction for the growing Sudan Women's Association in the northern Sudan. It is worth noting that concerted efforts by that group almost succeeded in bringing about the electoral defeat in 1965 of well-known conservative candidates by a leading communist who advocated a loosening of many of the social restrictions (see Appendix for details). The nature and extent of these restrictions may be illustrated by the following examples:

Some Sudanese have reported that in the mid-1950s "no Sudanese woman would call her husband by his own name. Today, [among young people], their wives call them by their names. Sometimes they will eat with them on the same table. And this, of course, did not happen in the old families. . . ."[15]

To this day most young girls have no say in the selection of their husbands; these and many other decisions are made for them by the male head of the family (after the actual groundwork of personal contact and negotiation has been carried out by other close relatives). Despite gradual changes in social customs, women still experience a kind of second-class citizenship; they are unable to meet male guests in their own house, must use a separate gate to their courtyard that leads to a separate women's section of the compound, and in many cases still walk in the streets about 15 feet behind their husbands.[*] An indication of the subdued role of women is the somewhat hilarious case of one of this writer's best friends, a highly educated and successful import-export businessman, whom I asked one day in jest if his wife would not mind his being late for dinner practically every day (he is one of the few Sudanese who regularly works overtime in his office). He asked me how it was possible for his wife to mind, and when I suggested that she might get angry and hit him with some instrument such as a hammer, he replied in all earnestness that this would be quite impossible since he had not bought her a hammer.

---

[*]This latter practice is becoming more scarce, especially in urban areas; the others are still widespread.

Those girls who managed to join public life in positions such as secretaries are still expected to behave in traditional manners; for example, they should not look up from their typewriters or files in the presence of outsiders. It is most interesting to note that these girls seem to lose much of their shyness as soon as the male Sudanese leave the room; they smile readily at foreigners and engage in pleasant conversations until the boss or male colleague returns, at which time they revert to their previous frozen pose. The author had various opportunities to discuss this phenomenon with a number of young Sudanese girls who were secretaries in offices or students at the university. Although mine was a very limited sample, it was nevertheless enlightening to hear the rather outspoken, definite, and well-formulated views of these girls, who all admitted to sympathies for the communist candidates in elections. They seemed obviously delighted to talk to anyone who took an interest in their personal problems and who treated them as equals. They all emphasized that it was quite impossible for them to talk to their menfolk about the subjects that we discussed; moreover, they did not expect their fathers to understand their problems or even bother listening to them.

Sudanese men are most reluctant to discuss the subject of women with any strangers, including close friends. At the few times when I was able to direct the conversation toward that topic in connection with elections, it was remarkable to observe the inability of these often highly educated men to understand simple psychological processes regarding their women. For example, my suggestion that the exposure of Sudanese girls to Egyptian magazines and Egyptian and Western films, in which women are depicted as enjoying great social freedom, would affect the mentality of those girls and make them susceptible to the slogans of anyone who promised similar liberties, was dismissed as inapplicable to Sudanese conditions. Just the same, certain Egyptian actresses had become heroines for many Sudanese girls, who told me about their admiration for these actresses because of their "free life."

Religion

In the Sudan, religion as an institution is more powerful as an influence on political behavior than as a belief system. While religious beliefs are obviously important to the practitioner, their substantive contents seem to have relatively less influence on his public conduct than their associated sociocultural aspects. Thus, one almost never encounters religious discrimination in the Sudan or, for that

matter, much public debate of a theological nature of the sort that is
rather common in Western countries. Even the North-South conflict
has been more of a clash between relatively alien cultures and between
unequally developed regions than a struggle between Muslims and
Christians, as it has been described most erroneously by several
non-Sudanese observers (see below). In what way, then, do religious
affiliations affect the political behavior of Animists, Christians, and
Muslims in the Sudan?

Animist beliefs are basically localized. Rainmakers, witch doctors, ancestral spirits, venerated bushes, or animals have meaning
only for a small local group. Consequently, conceptions of belonging
to a larger movement do not develop, thereby limiting the possibilities
for unified action at a politically significant level.

Among southern Christians institutional influences most clearly
outweigh theological ones. Missionary settlements afforded not only
facilities for religious indoctrination, but also for medical treatment,
education, and emergency food relief. Over the years, Christian
mission schools have provided most southern political leaders, whose
attitudes seem to reflect more a sense of antipathy toward northerners
(also Muslims in this case) than a sense of doctrinal conviction. In
this regard it seems fair to say that missionary attitudes have reinforced those of British colonial administration in the South, namely,
to convey to southerners a feeling of greater affinity with peoples of
neighboring countries than with northern Sudanese. Perhaps it is
unfair to impugn southern Christians for the apparent shallowness of
their religious commitment, especially in view of the scarcity of
clerical guidance available to them. Nevertheless, the fact remains
that today, at least, doctrinal influences on public conduct appear to
be negligible.

This is not at all the case with Sudanese Muslims. For one thing,
Islam has generally been credited with being an effective barrier to
the intrusion of communism or similarly perceived atheistic doctrines.
Recent Sudanese history includes several cases of violent anticom-
munist outbursts by militant Muslim groups that were supported or
condoned by much of the rest of the silent majority. For another,
Islam is taken rather seriously by its adherents throughout the northern Sudan; in fact, if it were possible to devise a scale of piety for
all Islamic countries, one would think that Sudanese Muslims would
rank very near the top. This impressive degree of religious commitment facilitated the political influence of a number of local "saints"
throughout the last few centuries. Even today a few families remain,
whose members are thought to have been blessed with barakah—a
special form of grace—and who command massive popular followings.
This source of local support does, however, have the disadvantage of
contributing to factional rivalries, as we shall see throughout the

book. One group with substantial influence, based upon national and supranational rather than local ties, is the Muslim Brotherhood, which has continued to gain in importance since its establishment after World War II, despite the need to operate underground from time to time.

Finally, one should not forget to point out the role that Islam has played and continues to play in creating close bonds between the Sudanese and the rest of the Arab world. Although these bonds reinforce a sense of communality in a general way, one cannot ignore their simultaneous divisive potential. Recent examples have been the late King Faisal's attempts to forge an "Islamic alliance" against "progressive/atheistic" regimes (with Sudan caught in the middle), the transnational activities of Muslim Brethren against regimes unsympathetic to their cause, and the sporadic support of Sudanese governments for the Eritrean Liberation Front, despite the Sudanese-Ethiopian agreement to respect each other's national integrity and to refrain from aiding each other's rebel forces.

POLITICAL HERITAGE

Among the most difficult aspects in placing a contemporary problem into historical context are the decisions about where to begin and which facets to include. This is no different in our case. I propose to select two developments: The Mahdist revolt in the 1880s and the role of the civil service in the rise of Sudanese nationalism in this century; the former, because it constituted the first successful nationalistic anticolonial movement in the Sudan's modern history, and the second because the demands for self-determination were articulated most effectively by the native intelligentsia, which consisted almost exclusively of civil servants. Their demands eventually led to the establishment of various political organizations that, over time, pressured the colonial administration into sharing and finally surrendering political control to the Sudanese. In the latter portion of this section we shall try to survey the major steps in this evolutionary process; but first we shall take a look at the Mahdist revolt and the subsequent establishment of the condominium.

The Mahdist Revolt

The so-called mahdiyyah is in itself rather complex. As a movement it filled religious and temporal needs; as a state it was an experiment in political development and economic regression.[16]

Originally, it was centered around the person of Mohammad Ahmad al-Dongolawi (or Dongola) who proclaimed himself to be the Mahdi* openly on June 29, 1881 at Aba Island in the White Nile. He soon acquired a large and rapidly growing following who helped him to amass a series of astounding victories over Egyptian-Ottoman governmental forces and eventually to set up a Mahdist state in 1885. This state lasted until 1898,† when the mahdist armies were defeated by an Anglo-Egyptian expeditionary force under Lord Kitchener.

Reasons for the spectacular success of the Mahdi are manifold and complementary: personal charisma, visionary qualities, and organizational skills of the man himself, millenarian predilections on the part of many Sudanese Muslims, deep-seated resentment by the natives over the extraordinarily oppressive policies of the foreign rulers, and conspicuous ineptitude in military and administrative matters by these same rulers.

The significance of the mahdiyyah—throwing off the colonial yoke—was rekindled by various leaders in the twentieth century. Even more impressive than the aspect of national liberation, a substantively negative objective, was the unification of hitherto feuding and warring native factions, initially under the Mahdi's guidance and later culminating in the creation of the Mahdist state, a substantively positive objective.

But not all Sudanese tribes and groupings—not even all Northern ones—supported the mahdiyyah. Many followers of the great rival tariqah, the khatmiyyah, refused to join, and, in fact, aided the Egyptian campaigns. It is not at all coincidental that khatmiyyah leaders, and their future political organizations, are said to have served as mouthpieces for Egyptian interests in the Sudan for almost the last one hundred years, while Mahdists and their descendants have traditionally opposed Egyptian interests and allied themselves with the latter's antagonists.

For ordinary Sudanese citizens living in the postindependence era, the meaning of the mahdiyyah is essentially twofold: On one hand, the religious followers—also known as ansar—continue to constitute a very sizable force in domestic politics. The ansar are perhaps the single most powerful group in terms of number and

---

*The "rightly guided one," a sort of messianic figure who is expected to return near the end of time and to establish God's (Allah's) kingdom on earth.

†Even though Mohammad Ahmad died in June 1885, about one-half year after the conquest of Khartoum. He was succeeded as head of the new state by the Khalifah, Abdallahi Mohammad Turshain (1846-1899).

intensity of loyalty and must be reckoned with as such by both supporters and opponents.

On the other, the Mahdi has provided the Sudanese people with an authentic folk-hero along the lines of a Peter of Russia, an Ataturk, or a Simon Bolivar—a source of national pride and symbol of incipient nationhood regardless of one's particular background or political persuasion.[17]

The Anglo-Egyptian Condominium

After the defeat of the Mahdist armies by an Anglo-Egyptian expeditionary force under Lord Kitchener's leadership it became necessary for the victorious partners to reconstruct the governmental and administrative apparatus for the Sudan. This was accomplished by setting up the so-called Anglo-Egyptian Condominium on January 19, 1899. In theory, this meant that Egypt and the United Kingdom were to share the burden of administration in the Sudan. However, in practice virtually all positions of importance, from governor-general to district commissioner, were in the hands of the British, especially from 1924 on, when Egyptian influence in the Sudan was significantly curtailed after the assassination of the governor-general, Sir Lee Stack, in Cairo, and local unrest among followers of one Ali Abdel-Latif in the Sudan.

Not surprisingly, the Sudanese viewed their country as a British colony, although most British officials there took pains to explain that they were employees of, and foremost loyal to, the Sudan government. They could even point to a few instances where the interests of the colonial administration clashed with those of the United Kingdom. (Such cases were rare, but did occur due to the unusual constitutional setup of the Sudan government.) Even though they were British subjects and therefore naturally products of British culture, they desired to be viewed as Sudan government employees. Not many Sudanese were convinced by this line of reasoning; nevertheless, it must be said that most men in the Sudan service were highly qualified for and equally devoted to their difficult task. Several experienced scholars have asserted that the Sudan Service attracted some of the top graduates of British universities, who considered an assignment in the Sudan as a great challenge. One consequence of this attitude was that these civil servants were unusually sympathetic to the various plights of the indigenous people, tried hard to improve their living conditions, and in the process developed strong paternal attitudes toward the Sudanese people. (As contrasted by their relations with Egyptians, whom the British never seemed to care for very much.)

Almost at the beginning of this century the Sudan civil service began to take in nationals at the lower ranks; but it was not until the late 1930s that senior administrative posts became accessible to qualified Sudanese. If one remembers that virtually all top-educated men graduated into civil service positions, and if one considers the usual structural limitations of a colonial service, it is easy to visualize how Sudanese bureaucrats began to experience at least two major kinds of frustrations: one, inability to rise beyond a certain rank, just because of their nationality; and two, inability to pursue creative approaches or ideas because of the usual limitations of bureaucratic compartmentalization and its various consequences. While the latter condition may be said to hold in almost any bureaucracy, it is nevertheless particularly painful to a member of the native elite. In the words of a highly respected and very experienced Sudanese former civil servant:

> Unlike bureaucracies in developed countries, the colonial
> civil service does not attract the "prototype bureaucrat,"
> an organization man who tries to fit in, but the top brains
> among the colonized. These men experience a variety of
> frustrations: For one thing, they tend to feel that they are
> in the best position to assay a given problem in their own
> country, yet their advice may not be given much weight.
> For another, new ideas and intellectual direction are most
> likely to be spawned by these men; yet their official func-
> tions do not permit them to follow through on these ideas
> or on new approaches in a creative manner. This situation
> is reinforced by the fact that the colonial power wants to
> maintain the status quo and, hence will tend to suppress
> new ideas as radical. Consequently, it is not at all sur-
> prising that frustrated bureaucrats become politicians.
> In our country, virtually all politicians are former
> bureaucrats.[18]

It would be a gross exaggeration to insist that all Sudanese civil servants felt frustrated in the above manner. Nevertheless, it is reasonable to assume that a large number of them did in fact feel that way and did express their feelings informally, and that most of the remainder was susceptible to any movement that appealed to these frustrations. Such a movement gradually emerged and mani-fested itself in the establishment of the so-called Graduates' Congress during the summer of 1937. Subsequently, many Sudanese civil serv-ants joined the congress.

The Graduates' Congress

As the name implies, this body was an association of graduates; in reality membership was open to all Sudanese who had attended schools of a standard higher than elementary.[19] About 1,200 joined out of roughly 5,000 who would have qualified for membership at the time.[20]

Originally the congress was conceived as a forum for the growing number of educated and semieducated Sudanese, who tended to congregate in the capital and who began to consider themselves as the native intelligentsia. Since almost all of these graduates were absorbed by the bureaucracy, the congress assumed the dual function of speaking in the interests of both the educated and the civil servants. The members established their headquarters at a club in Omdurman, with considerable financial aid from Egyptian sources; ever since, the primary center of political activities—overt and underground— had found a home.

The significance of the Graduates' Congress in the evolution of self-government is twofold: one, it constituted an active body whose members made up the political vanguard in the nationalist movement; and two, it was the first organization in the Sudan that regularly employed the device of free elections for office: in this case, for membership in the congress' Executive Council. As it turned out, the first demands for general elections throughout the Sudan were voiced by leaders of this same body.

The explanation for the use of elections in the Graduates' Congress may be found in the orientation of the members. They were aware of their colonial status, but desired to be treated as equals. A natural reaction was for the considerable number of higher civil servants, who had either spent some time in the United Kingdom in their training programs, or who had been closely exposed to British ways, to imitate the British model for regulating club affairs. The reason why members of the intelligentsia called for general elections will be discussed below.

Of all things that educated Sudanese found objectionable in the colonial administration, the item that probably caused the greatest displeasure was the policy of indirect rule. While we cannot be concerned here with all the consequences of that policy for Sudanese history, we can nevertheless consider its effect on the opinions of the Sudanese intelligentsia. Indirect rule meant, in fact, a bestowal by the Sudan government of certain administrative and judicial powers upon tribal authorities in the provinces. To the educated, this indicated that they were being by-passed—despite their training and education—in favor of uneducated chiefs who had made a deal with the colonialists to maintain the status quo.

Thus, it is easy to see why it seemed to the young educated urbanites that the beneficiaries of indirect rule, the tribal chieftains, became interested in maintaining the status quo along with the colonialists. To the progressives, these chieftains became reactionaries and were suspected of betraying their compatriots. From now on, they must be fought along with the foreigners. To the colonial administrator, the progressives seemed like young half-educated radicals who, if given the chance, would destroy in their blind fanaticism most of what the colonial government had built up laboriously over the decades. Hence, they were to be kept away from power as far and as long as possible.[21]

This situation created unhealthy relationships. A son of a tribal leader studying at the university was torn between loyalty to his family on one side and the appeal of new attractive ideas on the other. The British civil servant found it more difficult than ever to collaborate with his subordinate, most likely a member of the congress. To the latter, his superior was foremost a Britisher; so if the British blocked the road to Sudanese political development, perhaps one ought to turn to the Egyptians for help. After all, the Egyptians in the Sudan were shoved aside by the British in a similar fashion as the Sudanese intelligentsia had been. Moreover, they were fellow Muslims and Arabs and would, therefore, understand the plights of the Sudanese much better.

Meanwhile, the Egyptians had various designs of their own on the Sudan, and they were only too anxious to involve themselves in the internal movements. They began (anew, from historical perspective) to support certain factions in the Sudan that were prepared to represent Egyptian interests.*

As the years passed by, through the 1930s and early 1940s, these basic conditions persisted and eventually led to a hardening of the fronts, since neither the Egyptian-Congress partnership nor the British-rural chieftains coalition attempted to reevaluate rigid

---

*Especially leaders of the khatmiyyah in the North and certain tribal chieftains in the South. The latter were invited to Cairo and feasted lavishly. The khatmiyyah is one of the two dominant sectarian movements in the North; its leaders have been allies of Egyptian governments for almost one hundred years and, some say, their mouthpieces in the Sudan.[22]

approaches. The various demands put forth by the Graduates' Congress[23] to allow the Sudanese wider participation in the formulation of public policy were virtually ignored by the Sudan government. The result was that the members of the congress, faced with their inability to produce measurable effects, split into various factions, all advancing mutually incompatible alternative approaches to the colonial problem. This situation led directly to the formation of political parties in the Sudan.

Emergence of Political Parties

The first body to organize itself in structure and function as a political party was the so-called Ashiqqa (blood brothers). This was a group of young men united by very close friendship and "common struggle," as they were fond of pointing out, and were led by one Ismail el-Azhari, an ambitious politician with important educational and religious assets.[*] El-Azhari's personal relationships with other leaders in the congress as well as his political maneuvers form highly complicated patterns and cannot be dealt with in detail here. Suffice it to say that el-Azhari surrounded himself with a select core of civil servants and some businessmen who were very loyal to him personally. He soon attracted followers from essentially these two social bases by emphasizing secular political issues. (In the context of recent Sudanese history "secular" means primarily independent from sectarian influences, a concept explained in more detail below.) The political slogan of the Ashiqqa called for independence from British rule through support of a "unity of the Nile valley" policy, leading to some form of political union with Egypt. This group formed the core of what was later to become the National Unionist party (NUP).

The Ashiqqa were urban-based and enjoyed the full support of the slowly emerging middle class in the towns as well as the native press. With the benefit of Sayyid Ismail's astute leadership they were able to dominate congress almost at will. (El-Azhari managed to "pack" important congress meetings with his own Omdurmani following by clever scheduling in such a way that members from the provinces found it virtually impossible to attend. Agenda and acceptable alternatives to the issues of the day had been decided on in advance and

---

[*] He was educated at the American University of Beirut, and his grandfather is considered to have been a Holy Man and the founder of the Azharite tariqah in the Sudan.

were in effect "ratified" by the attending members.) So it was not surprising that rural and tribal groups began to search for an organ to counterbalance the influence of the Ashiqqa. After some initial confusion, that organ was found in the Umma party, which came into existence in March 1945.

This dichotomy, urban-educated on one side and rural-tribal on the other, might have been relatively simple had it not been for a factor that we have ignored so far, but that cannot be ignored in any meaningful analysis of Sudanese politics for some time to come: the role of religion in general, and of sectarianism in particular.

The growth, spread, and present-day practice of Islam and its various turuq in the Sudan are described in an excellent book by J. S. Trimingham, Islam in the Sudan.[24] Suffice it here to identify the two prominent sects in the northern Sudan, namely the khatmiyyah, comprising the followers of Sayyid Ali el-Mirghani, and the mahdiyyah, mentioned previously, whose followers—called ansar—venerate the mahdi and his descendants. The former are located mainly in the North and the East, while the latter can be found primarily in the western and central Sudan. At one time most Sudanese Muslims were strongly devoted adherents of either of these sects. With the spread of secular education and the slow penetration of Western culture in the country, the allegiances of some Sudanese (especially civil servants and businessmen) to either sect weakened, and were usually displaced by identification with the one nonsectarian movement available—the Ashiqqa, later the NUP. (Sudanese communists will be discussed below.)

However, it must be clearly understood that a former adherent of one sect, who had turned nonsectarian, would never completely lose his deep-seated mistrust for leaders and even followers of the other sect. The mistrust and dislike of one of these groups for the other cannot be overestimated and will remain, for some time, one of the biggest obstacles to political stability in the country. The roots of this cleavage are complex. There are theological, regional, and even some ethnic differences between the sects. But the single most important factor is probably historical rivalries between the houses of el-Mahdi and el-Mirghani, which date back to the last century. As already indicated, the latter group has been closely allied with Egyptian rulers for over one hundred years and received various forms of patronage whenever Egyptian influence in the country was dominant. Another important factor is that mirghanists abstained from the Mahdi's revolt against the Turkish-Egyptian occupation. Meanwhile, the ansar have been extremely suspicious of Egyptian designs for the Sudan and allied themselves with other forces that were wary of Egyptian policies.

Hence it is easy to see that by 1945 the position of Sayyid Abdel-Rahman el-Mahdi, the imam (leader) of the ansar, as patron of the Umma Party was the main obstacle that prevented that party from becoming the rural-based alternative to the Ashiqqa. Although the party represented provincial, tribal, and agrarian interests against the Ashiqqa, and had a large rural following, too, the Umma Party was nevertheless unacceptable to Sayyid Ali el-Mirghani, because of its identification with the house of el-Mahdi. In the process, Sayyid Ali began to support the Ashiqqa, though somewhat reluctantly because of their nonsectarian tendencies. This coalition of somewhat strange bedfellows never matured into an integrated union, but rather led to factionalism within the NUP and, years later, to a complete separation of the two groups.

With Sayyid Ali's decision, the Umma lost all non-Mahdist following. This new alignment made a certain amount of sense, not in terms of the conflicting social interests between the khatmiyyah and Ashiqqa, but because both groups promoted a "unity of the Nile valley" policy. Meanwhile the slogan of the Umma party became "Sudan for the Sudanese," that is, complete independence.

Various other minor parties came into existence, but these hardly deserved the trademark of party, because they were insufficiently organized, consisted only of a few individuals, and as a rule lacked a clear policy. Rather, they constituted factions that broke away from larger parties, usually because of personality clashes. Evidence of both their existence and impotence was provided by Congress elections in which nine "parties" unsuccessfully contested seats for office,[25] including the Anti-Imperialist Front, a cover-organization for the then small and clandestine communist movement in the Sudan.

Relations between the major parties and the Sudan government varied to some extent over the years. But in essence, the attitude of the condominium powers and their officials in the Sudan toward the parties was quite clear. Since the NUP slogan coincided with Egyptian policy for the Sudan, it stood to reason that the Cairo government would support the cause of the NUP morally. After World War II this moral support was supplemented very effectively by increasing material support, a fact about which the British, in London and in the Sudan, were less than ecstatic, particularly because Ashiqqa strategy entailed labeling British policy as imperialistic, and insinuated exploitive designs behind practically all actions of British officials in the Sudan Service.

This development had two immediate consequences: one, it made the Ashiqqa very popular among professional and radical groups in the urban centers,[26] and two, it alienated official and individual British opinion to the point where the Umma party received the unspoken endorsement and private sympathy of nearly all Britishers. In turn, the Ashiqqa were not about to let this relationship go unnoticed and made a point of labeling Umma people reactionaries and collaborators with the Imperialists, and they circulated rumors to the effect that the "British" Sudan government was intending to declare Sayyid Abdel-Rahman king of the Sudan. The prospect of such an event had the result of driving all non-ansar even closer to el-Azhari's organization, especially all followers of the khatmiyyah, who preferred anything to becoming subjects of a Mahdi king.

Meanwhile the Umma party leaders were quite prepared to cash in on their favorable status in British eyes. But they also had additional reasons for opposing any policy that might produce Egyptian sovereignty over the Sudan. There was the aforementioned rivalry with the khatmiyyah, whose leaders could certainly be expected to receive preferential treatment from the future government in the event of a union of Sudan and Egypt. Moreover, the Umma party was, of course, the political organ of the ansar; and it was the Mahdi and his followers who had fought against essentially Egyptian rule in the Sudan and had liberated the country from Egyptian influence. The bloody battles had been waged too recently to be forgotten already; it was quite clear during the 1940s and 1950s—and it is indeed to this day—that no love was or is lost between Egyptians and members of the mahdiyyah.

Evolution Toward Self-Rule

These relationships between native political organizations, the Sudan government and the condominium powers constitute the background for the evolution of direct participation by Sudanese in regulating the affairs of their own country. By "direct" is meant a form of participation going beyond mere administrative functions, as well as distinct from "indirect" participation through pressure groups, enlisting public opinion, demonstrations, and so on; in other words, active participation in the formulation of public policy. The essential difference between these two roles lies in the burden of responsibility for governmental policy and performance, which now came to be shared by Sudanese nationals along with foreign administrators.

The reader will recall the foundation of the Graduates' Congress in 1937 as an organization of educated Sudanese nationals. The congress performed many useful social and political functions during the following years. The outstanding event was the publication in 1942 of a memorandum that was addressed to the Sudan government and contained twelve demands by congress covering practically every

point of controversy during the 1940s right up to independence. The
most important of these twelve for our concerns are presented here:

1. The issue on the first possible opportunity by the British
and Egyptian Governments, of a joint declaration granting
the Sudan, in its geographical boundaries, the right of self-
determination, directly after this war; this right to be safe-
guarded by guarantees assuring full liberty of expression
in connection therewith; as well as guarantees assuring the
Sudanese the right of determining their natural rights with
Egypt in a special agreement between the Egyptian and
Sudanese nations.
2. The formation of a representative body of Sudanese to
approve the Budget and the Ordinances.
3. The carrying out of the principle of welfare of the
Sudanese and their priority to government posts as follows:
    a. By giving the Sudanese an opportunity to share
effectively in ruling the country; this is to be attained by
the appointment of Sudanese in posts of political responsibility in all the main branches of government.
    b. By limiting the appointments to government posts
to Sudanese.[27]

The immediate reaction of the Sudan government was to ignore
the memorandum officially and to warn the congress of further action,
if the members did not refrain from engaging in affairs "beyond the
authorized scope of the association." However, the government
realized that in the long run it would be advisable to create some
channels for including Sudanese opinion officially in the process of
shaping public policy. Toward this end the Advisory Council for the
northern Sudan was promulgated in late 1943, and had its initial
session in May of 1944. It consisted of twenty-eight members, of
whom twenty were "elected," eighteen were chosen by the six
northern province councils and two by the Sudan Chamber of Commerce; the remaining eight were appointed by the governor-general.
    The word "elected" is set in quotation marks to signify the
limited nature of the electoral franchise, as the candidates were
somewhat less than representative of Sudanese public opinion and
society as a whole. This argument is based on the following observations: In order to be members of the province councils the candidates had to be approved by the Sudan government. They were
elected not by popular vote, but by all members of the province
councils (normally tribal leaders and heads of government depart-
ments, such as province medical officer, province chief engineer,
and so on). The most extensive information about the composition of

the Advisory Council stems from a short article in the London Times,
which stated that ". . . included among the 28 members are the Nazirs
(grand chieftains) of the Hadendoa, Rizeigat, Gawama, Messiria, and
Shukria tribes, besides the Mek (king) of Fung Gism, two minor
shiekhs, three native leaders in the local administration, four native
officials serving or retired, four businessmen, and the senior native
officer of the Sudan Defense Forces . . ."[28]

This list clearly shows the extent to which council membership
was tilted toward rural interests and recipients of the benefits of the
indirect rule policy. As a consequence, congress and the urban press
attacked the Advisory Council as a collection of hayseeds and yes-
men.[29]

As time passed it became increasingly clear that this form of
native representation in the Sudan government was unsatisfactory.
As a result, an Executive Council and Legislative Assembly Ordinance
was promulgated on June 19, 1948.[30] The Executive Council was to
replace the Advisory Council; and it consisted of six Britishers and
six Sudanese.

The Legislative Assembly was to be "an organ with legislative,
financial, and administrative powers, consisting entirely of Sudanese."[31]
In the end, 75 Sudanese from all over the country were elected to
that body; and it has been suggested by some that this event marked
the beginning of true representation for the Sudanese in an assembly.
This is not correct.

Officially, among the 75 members, 10 were directly elected by
the towns, 42 by electoral colleges in rural areas, 13 by the southern
province councils, and 10 were nominated by the governor-general.

Let us consider the 65 "elected" members. Those who were
chosen by the southern province councils had the same kinds of qualifications as the members of the Advisory Council four years earlier.
The 42 electoral colleges in rural areas were made up of tribal
notables and a few government employees; in essence, they were
large-scale replicas of local councils. Given prevailing constellations
of power in rural Sudan (based on native administration, that is, in
the hands of chiefs) it was almost a foregone conclusion that the tribal
leader in the area would be elected. Regarding the cities it must be
pointed out that all "unity of the Nile valley" parties (with the
Ashiqqa in the forefront) boycotted the elections throughout the
country.[32] Since Ashiqqa strength was dominant in the towns, this
meant that in most urban constituencies the Umma party candidate
was elected unopposed. (Some sources insist that even the educated
members of the Umma party failed to turn out on polling day.) Since
in all subsequent general elections the NUP won over 90 percent of
the urban constituencies, it seems fair to assume that the victorious
candidates did not represent the genuine distribution of popular

sentiment, just as the members of the assembly on the whole did not reflect Sudanese political opinion accurately.

This is not to suggest that election by electoral college in the rural areas was not the best method of representation at that time, in view of the primitive state of the rural population, and in view of the fact that members of tribal organizations normally deferred decisions affecting public affairs to their tribal leaders and elders. The issue of determining the most practical system for electing representatives in an underdeveloped country like the Sudan will be returned to at some length in subsequent chapters. The point of importance here is that the 1948 elections for membership in the Legislative Assembly were not sufficiently representative, because of the limited suffrage in the overwhelming portion of the country, and because of the virtual absence of interparty competition. However, this is not to deny that these elections constituted a further step along the road to self-government, and that they provided those Sudanese who participated—as candidates and as voters—with an important experience about some aspects of the electoral process. Meanwhile, those who chose to remain aloof were at least in a position to gain the benefits of observing a heretofore unfamiliar phenomenon.

The Legislative Assembly experienced four years of much local unrest and hectic political maneuvering among the major Sudanese parties, Egypt, and the United Kingdom. The central issue was to determine the future status of Sudanese sovereignty, a question that had been avoided in the Condominium Treaty of 1899 as well as in the treaty between Egypt and the United Kingdom in 1936.

After much confusion and intrigue the matter was finally resolved by the Anglo-Egyptian Agreement of February 12, 1953, which provided the Sudanese with the opportunity to choose their future status themselves and, at least in theory, without foreign interference. The agreement called for general elections for a Constituent Assembly, which was to deliberate the future constitutional status of the Sudan by taking only one of two decisions: (1) that the Sudan shall be linked with Egypt in some form, or (2) that the Sudan shall have complete independence. The elections were to be supervised by a neutral international commission.

SOCIETAL CLEAVAGES

No historical survey—not even one as brief as this one—would be complete without a description of social trends. In the course of the last one hundred years Sudanese society experienced a series of transformations that significantly altered not only perceptions and attitudes, but even the configuration of power blocs. One can note, of course, many patterns that evolved over time; politically the most significant were a series of societal cleavages.

Urban versus Rural

One of the earliest took place between nomadic and settled groups and became especially influential in shaping political relations during the mahdiyyah. With the growth of settlements in riverine areas during the twentieth century, this particular dichotomy decreased in importance in favor of one between rural and urban populations. In both cases, each group had developed distinct lifeways and concomitantly distinct value systems; and by and large political orientations tended to follow and correlate with social orientations. Thus, during the mahdiyyah the major conflict was between the awlad al-balad (riverine settlers) and the nomads under baqqara leadership. Three-quarters of a century later the urban areas identified with secular political parties against the sectarian parties-oriented rural areas.

In addition to the above, the two most significant societal cleavages from contemporary perspective are those that developed along religious and ethnic-cultural lines. The former refer essentially to relations between non-Muslims and Muslims, and among Muslims between members of the mahdiyyah and khatmiyyah sects. The latter deal primarily with the growing split between northerners and southerners.

Religious Cleavages

Khatmiyyah-mahdiyyah antagonisms and subsequent political rivalries have already been mentioned elsewhere; suffice it to state here that these antagonisms have deep historical roots that can be traced to rivalries between competing turuq from about 1800 A.D. on, that they reinforced existing ethnic and geographic divisions, and that they resulted in a separation of northern Sudanese Muslims into two camps with virtually no connecting links. A modern manifestation of this rivalry was the eventual establishment by both sectarian movements of their own political organizations, namely the Umma party for the ansar, and the People's Democratic party (PDP) for the khatmiyyah, respectively.

Animists were viewed by both Muslims and Christians as primitive heathens living in spiritual darkness, whom it was a sacred

duty to convert to the true religion. The animists, in turn, have been
somewhat bewildered and bothered by the intrusions and conflicting
claims of the two proselytizing camps; by and large their attitudes
toward either have been colored by nontheological considerations,
such as fear of, or actual, conquest and/or domination by Muslims
on one side, and the provision of services (schools, health care, and
so on) by Christian missionaries on the other.

Relations between Muslims and Christians are more difficult to
ascertain. It seems fair to say that on a theological level prejudice
and discrimination appear to be surprisingly limited, and as usual in
Muslim countries, Christians are much more accepted and respected
as separate but equal worshippers of the same God than vice versa.
The fact that more than 99 percent of the Christians in Sudan are
either southerners or "foreigners," including naturalized immigrants,
clouds the analysis of reasons for the existing tensions between
Sudanese who are Muslims and those who are not.

Members of foreign communities, such as Greeks, Armenians,
Copts, and so on, have traditionally preferred their own associations
and have tended to lead as separate a life from the average Sudanese
as their business and social obligations have allowed them. This
form of voluntary isolation has naturally led to some feelings of
uneasiness, fueled by rumors born of mutual ignorance about each
other's psychological needs. In the past such isolation may have been
the logical outcome of colonial policy, which favored foreign minority
groups to some degree and which had interests in keeping alive perceived differences in education and social and religious customs.
More recently, however, the just requirements for nation building
plus the postindependence search for national identity have demanded
a much more thorough integration of diverse groups than these
national minorities have been willing to participate in. Although
Sudanese governments have generally been lenient toward these
groups and surprisingly slow in nationalizing jobs and resources,
some policies in that direction have been formulated recently and
have been interpreted as discriminatory on religious grounds—mostly
unjustified in the view of this author.

North-South Antagonisms

The second Christian minority group in the Sudan is southerners.
Here again, differences on religious grounds—such as between southern Christians and southern Muslims—appear to be minimal. The
major area of tension lies in relations between southerners and
northerners in general, and thus should be viewed not so much in

religious, but ethnic/cultural terms, although in this case the cleavages are reinforcing.

Latent fears, suspicions, and hostility between members of both regions broke out into the open in August 1955 when members of the Southern Defense Corps mutinied at Juba, Equatoria Province. In the disturbances that followed, 261 northerners and some 75 southerners were killed.[33] For most of the subsequent years an open rebellion has existed in various parts of the South, pitting the anya' nya* rebels against government soldiers. Tens of thousands of lives have been lost during that time span, the overwhelming number as a result of government military actions; several hundred thousand southerners have fled into neighboring countries. To compound matters, some rebel leaders proclaimed a separatist state—Azania—and received various forms of aid from such diverse foreign quarters as Roman Catholic relief organizations, some neighboring countries (albeit unofficially), and more recently, Israel.

The antecedents of this conflict go considerably beyond the Juba incident, however, and blame for the current malaise must be distributed among many contributing factors, some historical, some due to certain objective conditions, and some resulting from governmental policies, both colonial and postindependence.

Antagonisms between northerners and southerners can be traced at least to the period of slave raids one hundred years ago when several "northern" tribes had been contracted to conduct raiding activities in the South. As one would expect, many atrocities were committed in the process and memories of the events have been handed down from generation to generation. And although slavery and certainly slave raiding have long been abolished in the country, some hints of the past continue to haunt the descendants.

On the southern side, unrealistic fears of renewed subjugation were propagated especially among the many illiterates; on the northern side cultural superiority complexes and ridicule of southern customs sadly delayed possibilities for a rapprochement. (An indication of this phenomenon is that one can still hear an unhappily large number of northern children refer to southerners in their neighborhoods by the epithet abid—slave, this despite vigorous government efforts to prosecute guilty parties.)

Among the objective conditions are the very real differences between northerners and southerners in ethnicity and cultural identification. This statement should by no means be interpreted to suggest

---

*Sometimes spelled Anyanya, self-proclaimed southern freedom fighters whose name is derived from a poison, which can be obtained by crushing the head of the Gabon Viper.

that the two groups are monolithic in ethnic or cultural terms; as previously mentioned, such cleavages dissect both regions to an unfortunately high degree. Nevertheless, ethnic and cultural cleavages between northerners and southerners exceed existing ones within the regions to the extent that various governments during this century have considered this condition to be sufficiently serious to warrant some separate policies vis-a-vis the two regions. At any rate, the end result has been the development of patterns whereby northerners have oriented themselves primarily in the direction of the Arab world to the North and Northeast, whereas southerners have turned primarily inward and secondarily toward their consanuineous relations in neighboring countries to the South.

These rather natural developments have been complicated by geographic and climatic conditions that have made communications between regions unusually difficult, thereby inhibiting a possible rapprochement. In addition, these conditions also are responsible to some degree for the development of different life styles, ranging from such items as emphasis on subsistence hunting and fishing in much of the South to the widespread custom of nudity. The rather simple point here is that a list of antecedents for North-South conflicts cannot be limited to the actions or omissions of men and governments, but must include such items as swamps, the length of the rainy seasons, and the tsetse fly as well.

While there is very little that anyone could do about this latter problem, some argue that something could have or should have been done in another realm, namely the observable differences between the two regions as a whole in their respective stages of social and economic development. Although it is true that the northern Sudan is quite underdeveloped in both aspects from a worldwide perspective— we may, in fact, have here the two chief problems responsible for political instability and continuing unrest—the South, by comparison, is almost infinitely worse off on both counts; so much so, in fact, that it has been labeled by knowledgeable Africa hands as the single most primitive region of its size on the entire continent.

Some of these differences may very well be unavoidable because of the aforementioned limitations imposed by a very harsh environment. Others, however, result from deliberate and yet others from well-intentioned but ill-conceived policies on the part of various central administrations. This is not the place to investigate such policies in sufficient detail for satisfactory understanding, nor is it the purpose of this author to assess praise or blame to various parties; suffice it to identify a few major events and trends in outline form.[34]

British colonial policy until 1947 was designed to treat the southern Sudan as a separate entity, partly due to British recognition

of the distinctness of the region and of its backwardness on all counts
as contrasted to the North, but partly also because the Foreign Office
could not decide on the eventual fate of this area. Among the various
options pondered were unification with other territories in East Africa
and eventual independence; only after the 1947 Juba conference did
the colonial administration settle on a policy for a united Sudan.
Clearly, imperial considerations have outweighed Sudanese interests.

Among the consequences of colonial policy in the South were the
further division and deepening of cleavages between North and South,
resulting from such decrees as outlawing of the jallabiyyah—the
flowing Muslim gown popular throughout North Africa—the super-
imposition of English over Arabic as a lingua franca, and severe
restrictions placed on interregional travel and the proselytizing of
Islam. Concomitantly, Christian missionary activities were encouraged as part of a deal whereby missionaries were given considerable
latitude in the realms of religious indoctrination and general education
in exchange for performing some socialization services. The objective
here is not to challenge these policies on some normative grounds;
undoubtedly, most British officials were motivated by considerations
of the best interests of the southern peoples as they perceived them.
At the same time one must appreciate the northern interpretation
that saw this paternalistic attitude as an outgrowth of typical colonial-
imperial mentality, designed to keep the Sudanese people weak, backward, and divided.

Unfortunately for all concerned, postindependence regimes
headed and dominated by northern politicians were of little improvement over their predecessors. The civilian leaders, from Prime
Ministers Ismail el-Azhari (following the 1955 rioting) to Mohammad
Ahmed Mahjoub (until 1969) concentrated most of their efforts on
strategies designed to reap political benefits from their constituents,
and thus by and large failed to appreciate and meet southern grievances on their merits. The military juntas, headed by General
Ibrahim Abboud (1958-64) and General Ja'far Mohammad Nimeiri
(1969-   ) during his first two years in power tended to perceive the
Southern Problem in a like manner as the military leaders during
civilian regimes had and as most military leaders elsewhere are
wont to do, namely as a military or security problem, rather than a
complex socioeconomic-political one. For the sake of fairness it
must be stated that the Nimeiri regime had even then adopted the
most broad-minded approach of all to this vexing issue, and its
eventual success in bringing about the Addis Accords of 1972 over-
shadows earlier shortcomings.

Just the same, a few controversial actions can be identified.
When 800 civil service positions were "Sudanized" following independence, all but 4 went to northern bureaucrats. Recruitment and

employment figures have consistently favored northerners ever since
independence. The establishment of economic—especially agricultural—
schemes and of educational opportunities have similarly favored
northern regions in a manner disproportionate to the relative sizes
of the two regions and their populations. Finally, a matter of grave
concern and acute sensitivity to the southern leaders has been the
fact that virtually all security positions in their region—from governor
to military commander to police chief—have been staffed by northerners.* This writer is sympathetic to the northern response that
there simply were no qualified southerners available, and that all
those who were have in fact been appointed to positions of high
responsibility, a technically correct statement.

In this instance, if blame is to be assessed, it must be shared by
both British and northern administrators who did not do their utmost
to overcome this deficiency. As it was, southern rebels have been
no more impressed by sincere promises of remedying the situation
in the future than their militant minority colleagues in other parts of
the world. They wanted immediate action and have been understandably impatient with (technically correct) arguments about impracti-
calities.

Much of the foregoing survey of the roots of the Southern Problem
points to the tragic confluence of geographic, ethnic, social, and
historical factors beyond the direct control of man. And although
many sins of omission and commission have been perpetrated by
administrators and political leaders on all sides, the analyst is
tempted to attribute most to ordinary human failing rather than
malicious calculations as has been so frequently asserted.

Just the same, a most serious problem has persisted for seventeen crucial years, a problem that drained the country's very limited
resources and, worst of all, caused much human suffering. It has
also contributed to the political instability of Sudanese regimes, and
given the country an unfavorable image abroad.

Granted that economic, social, cultural, historical, and political
factors have all contributed to this crisis, one cannot help but feel
that the major obstacle to an earlier solution, as well as the prospects
for genuine accommodation even after the formal peace agreement of
1972, may depend primarily on psychological factors. This refers to
the very great degree of mutual mistrust by both parties of one
another and the consequent suspicion of the other side's real motive
whenever a potentially workable (and probably sincere) solution has
been suggested. This author had the opportunity to observe in person

---

*This policy was reversed by the Nimeiri government after the
March 1972 Addis Ababa Agreement.

that leaders of both sides more often than not seemed to speak on different levels of analysis about the same problem, and consequently failed to understand each other even in the most fundamental terms.

It appears that most southern leaders have developed a ghetto mentality and view themselves as a permanent minority that will always be exploited by the cunning northerners. The latter, in turn, have been unable, by and large, to place themselves at or near the southerners' level of perception, and hence lack the necessary empathy for their fears and inadequacies. It is to be hoped that the new arrangement of regional autonomy will permit both sides to free themselves of their respective anxieties. An old adage states that time heals wounds of the past. One can only hope that the basically congenial nature of both peoples will help them to move from hesitant reconciliation through increasing communication and mutual awareness to new levels of cooperation.

ECONOMIC FACTORS

In the eyes of many laymen and professional observers and, unfortunately, too many analysts as well, the relative underdevelopment or development of country X is mostly synonymous with economic development. This view is particularly widespread in the Third World countries among government officials and ordinary citizens alike. While social scientists may be justly offended by this simplistic correlation, their vexation does not alter the perception of the opinion holders and sadly, neither do their scholarly efforts.

For our purposes this phenomenon is relevant on two counts. First, rightly or wrongly—and I happen to think rightly—it establishes the primacy of economics in the public affairs of all societies and subsocietal units in which the basic requirements for a decent humane standard of living have not been made available to the preponderant portion of the social unit. Second, in these areas, and not these areas alone, governmental performance tends to be judged more in economic terms than on any other criterion. Consequently, political stability may be to a very considerable extent the function of economic performance by the rulers. To illustrate this point further, I wish to suggest a simple model that has been developed in the discipline of social psychology,[35] but that can be adapted successfully to elucidate the relationship between economic performance by the regime and political stability in the country.

A Model

Our basic assumption is that citizens—in groups of variable size—respond to the impact of public policy on their standard of living. What counts, then, is first of all the level of their perceived aspirations or expectations (e) over time. The expectations are measured against actual achievements or, more correctly, perceived achievements (a). The difference between perceived aspirations and perceived achievements at any moment may be called the "gap of frustration" (f).

It is postulated that the gap of frustration will always be positive; that is, an aspect of human nature seems to provide that man's hopes and expectations always exceed his accomplishments, if only ever so slightly. It is further postulated that, if this gap exceeds a certain size—which we may label "threshold of tolerance"—then the individual(s) in question will respond by demonstrating his (their) displeasure in some form, the ultimate of which is violent revolution. (In Figure 1.1, f' may be an acceptable gap, and f" unacceptable.)

At this point a number of observations are in order: First and most obviously, this model is applicable to many situations in life

FIGURE 1.1

Gap of Frustration Model

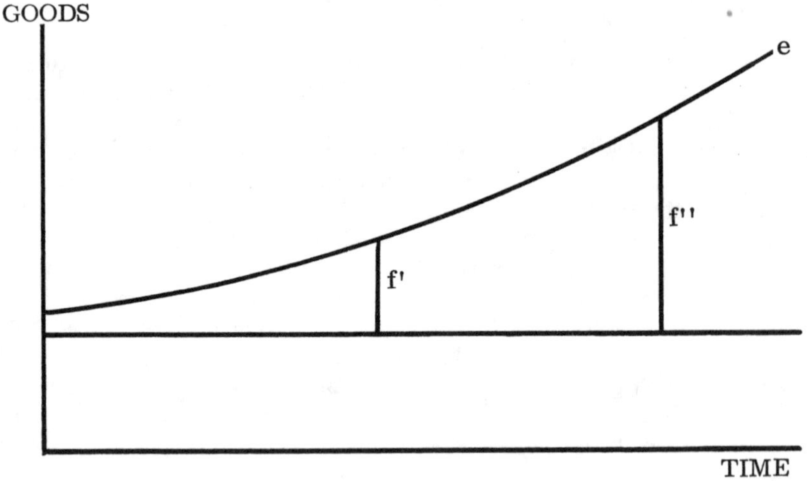

Source: Compiled by the author.

other than economic performance, for example, personal happiness, foreign policy, athletic performance, and so on. Second, measurements of e, a, and f require thorough and sound methodological techniques. Limitations of time and space do not permit elaborations on this theme; however, it seems reasonable to argue that, in principle, sound conceptual and quantitative devices can be developed for each individual problem.

Third, aspirations (e) are in most instances a function of economic opportunities. For that reason, we expect that e' in country x' may differ substantially from e'' in country x'' at the same point in time. While it is true that the so-called demonstration effect raises expectations at times beyond the level of feasibility, it is nevertheless the case in most countries that ordinary citizens exhibit a good deal of realism—and not infrequently, despair—in their assessments of economic opportunities. Thus a Sudanese peasant does not expect to live as well as his European counterpart; and moreover, a cultivator in Kordofan does not expect to achieve the same standards as his counterpart in Gezira.

Fourth, we should not expect a uniform threshold of tolerance. Some people, for example, Egyptians, seem to have become much more phlegmatic in this respect than others, for example, Syrians. This observation brings us to a very important point. It may be possible, and very instructive, to develop our model in X number of (country) cases and then compare the degree of coincidence between sizable gaps of frustration and antigovernment activities (riots, strikes, electoral defeat of incumbents, revolutions).

However, the analytical value of the model, and especially its predictability, will be considerably enhanced if populations are broken down into various groupings. For example, we may differentiate between four groups in society: the masses of rural destitutes, the urban proletariat (including unemployed and underemployed), the salaried middle class, and the upper class of wealthy businessmen, landlords, and other very influential figures.

Comparatively speaking, we notice at once that the relative sizes of these classes will vary substantially; for example, in Egypt the lowest stratum constitutes the majority of the population whereas in Lebanon it is markedly smaller. Figure 1.2 denotes an estimated breakdown for these four groups in the Sudan in 1953 and 1975. (Of course, there is some movement from rural poor to urban proletariat, and so on. In each sector, members in marginal areas may be about to either move upwards or drop to the next lower level.)

If we apply this breakdown by groups to our analytical model, we notice the effects of socioeconomic status upon economic and political perceptions. Taking for the moment some hypothetical

FIGURE 1.2

Stratification of Society

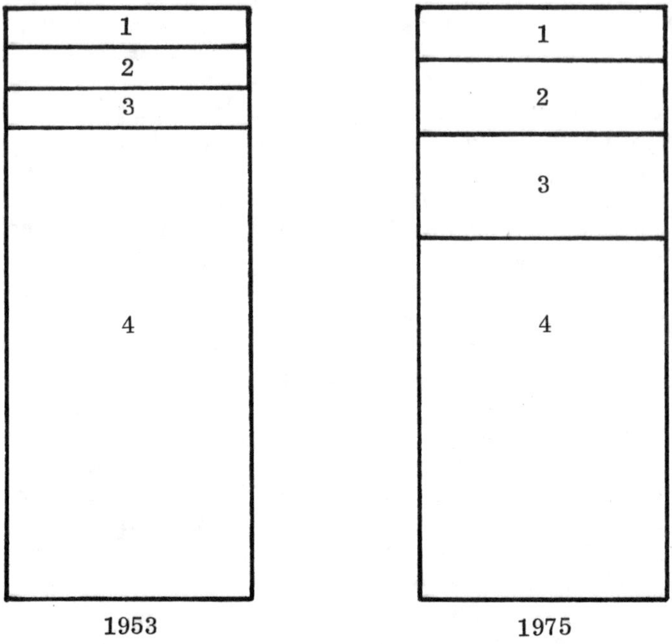

1953	1975

1 = upper class
2 = salaried middle class
3 = urban proletariat
4 = rural destitutes

Source: Compiled by the author.

averaged data from Africa and the Middle East, the model produces
the following results as shown in Figure 1.3.

In this idealized model, the frustration gaps for the upper- and
lowermost categories are comparably close throughout, albeit at
different levels. This merely suggests that the most wealthy achieve
what they expect in a nonsocialist setting, at least where property is
not sequestered; and that for destitute peoples, aspirations and achievements are so low as to be almost identical. Historically speaking, we
may notice that revolutions have rarely been started by the destitute
groups, perhaps because they were too ignorant, too physically weak,
or too occupied with ekeing out a living. The most sizable frustration

gaps appear in the middle sectors, and we may infer that the urban
proletariat, especially after exposure to better things in life, has
become available for political mobilization, whereas the salaried
middle class[36] will provide the activists and leaders for political
opposition. Naturally, not all members of that middle class will man
the barricades; many will be apathetic as elsewhere. Nevertheless,
it is this class that most likely will provide the intellectual leadership
for revolt or revolution and that will also provide those who will implement the ideas—likely a group of military officers. (Ready examples
are provided in Africa and the Middle East: Gamal Abdel-Nasser,
Abdel-Karim Qasim, Mu'ammar al-Qaddafi.) In some cases, one

FIGURE 1.3

Application of the Frustration Gaps to Four Classes

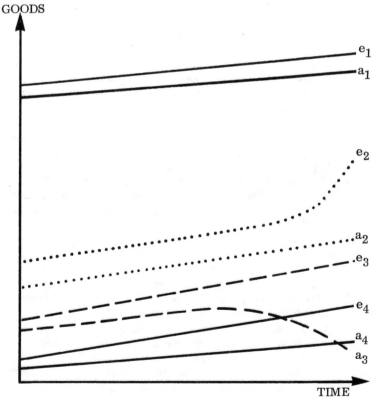

Source: Compiled by the author.

element of the middle class may topple another, as for example in
Iraq and Syria, almost with regularity. This phenomenon results from
widespread perception that the middle class sector has become stag-
nant and that overall progress is not being made relative to economic
and other potentials. Without discounting such external (to our model)
factors as political control and repression, we may, nevertheless,
speculate that the absence of similar turmoil in Egypt may reflect
the greater success of Egyptian propaganda in projecting an atmosphere
of progress in comparison with the aforementioned cases of Syria
and Iraq. What counts, then, is the degree of perceived mobility by
politically conscious members of the middle class on the one hand,
and the size of frustrated urban proletariats who are available to
support counter-regime activities on the other.

The Sudanese Economy

We may now proceed to apply this model to the Sudanese case.
First of all, however, we need to describe and examine those basic
economic conditions that exist in that country.

In the most capsule terms, the Sudanese economy has been characterized by the overwhelming share played by the agricultural sector,
and within that, the role of cotton as the one outstanding cash crop.

Fairly reliable statistics indicate that 85.6 percent of the Sudanese
labor force is engaged in agriculture, livestock production, forestry
and fishing. Manufacturing is a distant second with 5.1 percent, and
services follow with 4.6 percent.[37] A United Nations survey concludes
that "in few countries are men so preponderantly absorbed in primary
production . . . as in the Sudan." Unfortunately, the report continues,
"skills developed in farming and animal raising . . . have only remote
relevance to modern industrialization." Moreover, "existing skills
are not utilized by modern management techniques."[38]

Sudanese cultivators—somehow the terms "farmers" and
"peasants" seem equally inappropriate—can be divided into two
groups: the large masses engaged in subsistence "farming," and
those affiliated with the several government-sponsored agricultural
schemes, of which the Gezira is the largest and the most famous.[39]
Regarding the former, two leading Sudanese economists observed
that "the ease with which subsistence peasant farming and animal
breeding can be undertaken by nomadic and semi-nomadic people
limits their incentive to shift to the modern economy. As a result,
many new agricultural schemes find it difficult to induce enough
people to settle."[40] In fact, the relative underpopulation of the
country—in terms of physical size and available natural resources—

has brought about "a high ratio of consumers per potentially effective producers," hence a considerable share of economic productivity falls on children. (Approximately 20 percent of the agricultural labor force is under 15 years of age, and about 50 percent under 20 years of age.) This deprives them of chances for formal education in order to acquire those skills that are not possessed by present adult groups. As a consequence, there does not exist the degree of physical movement from countryside to urban areas that we can observe in most other Middle Eastern states.

Cultivators in agricultural schemes are much more organized, in both economic and political respects. Their work is directly supervised by government inspectors, their incentive for maximum output is substantial and, as a group, they form one of the most important sectors of the national economy. This is especially true of those engaged in the prestigious Gezira scheme who can point to an impressive history of economic productivity and political impact as a pressure group. The former can be better understood if one realizes that over the years the Sudan has derived roughly three-fourths of its foreign exchange from sales of cotton and cotton by-products. In addition, about 40 percent of government revenue is based on cotton sales, virtually all from the Gezira. Regarding the latter, it is noteworthy that the Gezira Tenants' Union may have been the single most influential pressure group in the country during the past quarter century. Although the overwhelming majority of Gezira tenants has been loyal to conservative political groups, notably those affiliated with the ansar sectarian movement, it is worth recalling that the Communist party of the Sudan—then known as Anti-Imperialist Front—gained a foothold in that region in the 1940s. (For more details, see Chapters 2 and 3.) At the time, this was probably the largest communist following on the African continent.

Other foreign exchange earners in addition to cotton are sesame seeds, ground nuts, camels and cattle, oil cake, hides and leather goods, and gum arabic. Although the last item amounts to 80 percent of world consumption, it, along with the other entries, is dwarfed by cotton in terms of magnitude. Because of this great dependence on cotton as the major cash crop, the state of the entire economy has been subject to the consequences of fluctuations in annual crop output and in world prices. The need for diversifying the economy has been realized by some Sudanese in high places, but relatively little action has been undertaken to exploit the country's considerable resources in animal husbandry and forests, as well as the latent potentials in

fruit production and cultivation of crops other than cotton on a larger
than token scale.*

It should be noted, however, that the Sudan is almost completely
self-sufficient in basic food stuffs. The country is fortunate to the
extent that no Sudanese should have to starve for many years to come,
for there exists a considerable surplus of fish, beef and mutton,
fruits, and basic cereals. This surplus could be tripled easily, given
adequate incentives in the private and public sectors. In this regard
the Nimeiri administration's decision of late 1974 to give top priority
to agricultural development is most welcome. In fact, the prospects
for agricultural growth have been judged to be so outstanding that
Arab and World Bank investors expect Sudan to become the region's
preeminent "breadbasket" for the last fifth of the century.

As already suggested, the nonagricultural sectors of the Sudanese
economy are comparatively very small and in a stage of underdevelopment. Manufacturing is limited to selected items in light industry.
Heavy construction is confined largely to communications projects
and to dams for hydroelectric energy and flood control. Consequently,
the industrial labor force is very small; nevertheless, it has been
quite effectively organized as part of the Sudan Trade Federation.
The federation has been extraordinarily active in both the economic
and political realms since 1948 when the Trade Unions Ordinance
permitted the organization of workers. The two single most prominent
subgroups have been the Sudan Railways Workers Federation and the
aforementioned Gezira Tenants' Union, which both proved to be fertile
grounds for leftist politicians and ideas.

Of course, economic, social and political conditions have changed
markedly over the years, especially, and at an accelerated rate, in
the period since independence. It is therefore rather difficult to
speak precisely about the interrelationships between economics and
political factors as outlined in the model above. Nevertheless, some
basic trends have persisted over the past fifty-odd years, and these
can be identified, if only in broad terms.

The upper class in the Sudan has been and continues to be extraordinarily small. Wealthy businessmen, landlords, and otherwise
influential families have never numbered more than a few hundred
at most. Part of the reason may lie in the absence of feudal rela-

---

*Happily, in late 1974 the director of the Gezira Board announced
a major shift in crop rotation and a sizable decrease in cotton cultivation in order to free land for large-scale food and fodder production.
A similar policy can be expected after the opening of the giant Rahad
scheme. Also, the Kenana sugar plantation will be one of the largest
in the world.[41]

tionships of the kind that could be found in Egypt, Iran, and India until recently. There has always been an abundance of land for anyone willing to settle and work it; moreover, strong egalitarian values of the Arab and African heritage apparently prevented economic subjugation of ordinary folk to privileged individuals. Another significant phenomenon is that those few Sudanese who may be described as wealthy have never acquired the kinds of tastes for imported luxuries that one may observe in countries to the north and south. Thus in private, Sudanese millionaires dress very much like everyone else— the jallabiyyah is a most attractive and practical costume worn by almost all northerners and many southerners—they eat virtually the same food, listen to the same music, and attend the same kinds of social events as do all but the lowliest citizens. As a result, the level of expectations among upper class families has been relatively limited in terms of consumption, except for a few amenities such as occasional foreign travel. Wealth became almost an end in itself, although some clearly realized its potential for acquiring political influence and power, too. If there existed a frustration gap among the rich, it had to do with nationalist-cultural notions rather than economic-political dissatisfaction. Some undoubtedly preferred the social and cultural amenities of Egyptian pashas and the like, but there were others who just as surely scoffed at those life-styles.

On the other end of the scale are the masses of subsistence dwellers in the North and South. With few exceptions, they appear to be a happy lot, and for good reasons. Basic foodstuffs are available to anyone who bothers to search for them; life's luxuries consist of such items as all-weather housing and the possession of goats or cattle for personal security. The majority of these people remain happy in their own environs and are literally blissfully ignorant of other standards of living. As long as the communications explosion has not reached them, their respective frustration gaps continue to be tolerably small.

The salaried middle class has been growing steadily in size and importance. It is mainly composed of civil servants and various professionals who live almost exclusively in urban areas. Politically speaking, this group has been the most active in recent history and has furnished leadership in the independence struggle, for political organizations and movements, as well as the three subsequent revolutions. Until recent years, this group could be economically satisfied—and politically mollified—through cooptation into the system. Civil service positions were readily available to qualified applicants and the market for skills in industry, business, or services was equally favorable. This condition no longer persists in that form, and we shall return to that issue in subsequent chapters. Frustration gaps among middle class members were primarily a function of

perceived political stagnation by individuals who saw and continue to
see themselves as vanguards in the struggle for national development.

Finally, the politically most volatile element is constituted by the
urban proletariat. This sector has been almost negligibly small until
the mid-1960s, when a combination of factors produced a significant
swelling in their numbers. Economic mismanagement in several
areas, the attractions of urban life to some "country relatives," and
the continued supply of school graduates who could not all be gain-
fully absorbed in the lagging economy, all combined to heighten
unemployment and disguised unemployment in the capital cities.
Together with the normal consequences of uprooted traditional life-
styles, this phenomenon planted the seeds of an urban proletariat
that had hitherto been unknown in Sudanese history. It was striking
to observe the availability of these groups for mass demonstrations
for or against any convenient policy or organization, be it the U.S.
Embassy, the Sudanese Parliament in 1965, the Dairat el-Mahdi,* or
the Communist party headquarters. It was primarily this group that
politicians were fond of pointing to whenever they advocated their
particular policies or solutions to national crises, as in the interest
of, and supposedly supported by, al-sha' b (the people) or al-jamahir
(the masses). As we proceed through our study of political and economic development in subsequent chapters, we shall need to pay
special attention to the latter two groups.

A discussion of economic factors and economic development
would not be complete without some observations about the human
element. Widespread and fundamental material progress cannot be
accomplished in a traditional society without a transformation of
individual attitudes and values to be more in line with modern concepts of resource-maximization, efficiency, and incentive for growth,
as distasteful as these may be to all who fear for the humane costs
of progress.

This author sensed an uncommon delight in the humane pace of
life, in the prevalence of values that seemed to elevate personal
relations over material comfort, and spiritual over physical content-
edness. All of this made the Sudan such a pleasant place to live in
and the Sudanese people such marvelous companions to be with. And
it was in this spirit that a Western-socialized individual could reconcile a certain amount of bureaucratic inefficiency and occasional
physical discomfort, and much of what is symbolized by the colloquial
phrase of ma'alesh.

---

*A family compound belonging to the Mahdi house until 1969 and
used for a variety of public affairs purposes.

Unfortunately for all concerned, the continuing and justifiable demands for modernization require the sacrifice of congenial styles and simple pleasantries for the sake of greater and more comprehensive efficiency. As it stands now, both goals are unmistakably clear to most Sudanese in high places. Their fundamental incompatibility has just begun to be appreciated, and the battle will be waged in the immediate future. One should like to hope that there will be only victors.

THE INFLUENCE OF FOREIGN AFFAIRS

As in most comparable cases, the prominent features of Sudan's environment have shaped the nature of her foreign relations to a significant degree, particularly since that country represents a crossroads of Africa in geographic and ethnic terms.

These two features of geography and ethnicity—while by no means exclusively responsible for foreign policy formulation and Sudan's international interactions—have, nevertheless, dominated the patterns of foreign affairs to such an extent that they lend themselves to central themes for grouping relevant influences.

On one hand geographic configurations have caused outsiders to view the Sudan with geopolitical, economic-exploitative, and more recently, cultural-ideological designs in mind. This has been true of the Egyptians almost from the beginning of recorded history, of the British since the end of the nineteenth century, and of late the two superpowers, the United States and the USSR.

On the other hand, the various ethnic cleavages in the country have led to political factionalism, as discussed in previous sections, and have indirectly affected the Sudan's relations with neighboring countries. Both the North-South cleavage and factionalism among dominant northern groups have influenced neighborly relations; in some instances as a result of overt interference in or exploitation by these neighbors of existing cleavages, and in others as a result of particular factions seeking various forms of support from across the borders.

The significance of geography and ethnic composition of the population as the two major determinants of Sudanese foreign relations lies in the fact that these conditions are objective or givens and unlikely to be altered by political events or the mere passage of time. Consequently, they constitute a sort of permanent parameter within which successive Sudanese regimes have to operate.

What follows is a broad overview of the ways in which these conditions have influenced the foreign policy goals and means of

major powers and of neighboring countries vis-a-vis the Sudan, and
of the reaction of Sudanese politicians and ordinary citizens in turn.

Egypt

From Sudanese perspective, especially in historical terms,
Egypt has occupied the position of a major power in the Nile basin.
From earliest recorded history onward, Egyptian rulers have sought
to control the headwaters of the Nile river, the most basic source of
livelihood for their states. An outgrowth of this major goal has been
periodic forays by Egyptian armies into the "land of the blacks"—the
meaning of the term Sudan. Some of these expansionist drives have
resulted in the subjugation of local rulers to Egyptian overlords,
others have led to direct occupation and annexation of what are today
Sudanese territories. From pharaohs to Mamluk kings to khedivial
rulers the most coveted objects were foodstuffs, certain treasures
such as gold and ivory, and soldiers and/or slaves for Egyptian
armies. In all these commodities the Sudan has been vastly richer
than Egypt, and vague notions about its potential resources—many as
yet unexploited—have held the imagination of Egyptian rulers throughout history. That Sudanese peoples have always been less advanced
by all conventional criteria of modernization than their northern
neighbors has given added incentives to the Egyptians for pursuing
their objectives in those southern provinces.

More recently, Egyptian policy had been forced to shift from
imperialism and direct intervention to what some scholars refer to
as "informal penetration," in order to maintain Egyptian interests.
Examples are (a) the exploitation of mahdiyyah-khatmiyya rivalries
resulting in Egyptian overt and covert support of the latter group to
the point that khatmiyyah leaders have been viewed by many as
mouthpieces of Egyptian interests in the Sudan throughout the twentieth century (see the section on political heritage above); (b) the
massive influx, especially during the condominium period, but prior
and subsequently as well, of Egyptian specialists, for example,
technicians, teachers, civil servants, who proceeded to spread their
own culture; and (c) since World War II the large volume of propaganda, directed primarily through the overpowering influence of
Egypt's communications media including radio, newspapers, films,
journals, and cultural exchange activities.

The United Kingdom

The second major power to affect Sudan's destiny has been the United Kingdom. For British imperial policy the huge Sudanese territory constituted a major link in the famous Cairo-to-Cape Town Axis scheme. To attain this goal and to thwart rival French designs in East Central Africa, the British embarked on a mad rush to head off French forces advancing eastward from French Equatorial Africa. The military confrontation took place at the village of Fashoda in 1899 in a showdown that saw the British victorious; for the next fifty-odd years they were intent on maintaining a dominant position in that area. Although the colonial status of the Sudan was formally that of a condominium (1898-1955), to be jointly governed by Egypt and the United Kingdom, the latter did in fact control almost all positions of real power and was viewed as the actual colonizer by the Sudanese people.

As such, the British exhibited normal interests in exploitation of natural resources and the development of a market economy, but not as extensively as their colleagues in North, West, and East Africa had done, nor as various local nationalists have asserted from time to time.

The colonial administration set up a number of agricultural development schemes, of which the Gezira Cotton Scheme is the most famous and has since served as a model for similar plans elsewhere. Furthermore, monopolistic import concessions were given to British firms and a few handpicked expatriate minority businessmen. Nevertheless, it would be unfair to accuse the British rulers of typical colonial exploitation. For one thing, the native market had never developed to the point where it could absorb British consumer products to any significant degree. For another, the establishment of agricultural schemes was primarily designed to keep the condominium fiscally solvent, not to feed the textile mills in Lancashire with raw materials, although the latter development did come about. In fact, if the colonial administration can be charged in this area at all, it should be charged with benign neglect, since the natural resources of the Sudan would have warranted a far greater intensification of development schemes than had been established. Rather it would appear fair to conclude that British development policy reflected mostly a paternalistic attitude vis-a-vis the Sudanese on the one hand, and an overriding emphasis on maintaining the status quo on the other.

Once the end of the condominium came in sight, attempts were undertaken to retain some influence for the British through strengthening commercial and cultural ties in the hope of creating some form of dependence. Meanwhile, in the political realm administration support for the pro-British Umma party was intended for the same purpose, a fact not at all lost on Umma rivals and especially on the budding native intelligentsia among the nationalists.

The United States and the Soviet Union

With the decline of the British Empire after World War II and the concomitant reductions in overseas commitments, the United States of America began to move slowly and somewhat hesitantly into areas of soon-to-be-created vacuums, particularly in the late 1950s and early 1960s.

From American perspective the Sudan occupied an important strategic position between such key countries as Egypt in the Middle East and Zaire and East Africa in sub-Saharan Africa. An illustration of this conception was the apparent success of U.S. influence that helped to sway the regime of President Abboud in prohibiting Egyptian "volunteers" from crossing Sudanese territory in an attempted intervention in the Congo crisis of the early 1960s. During the Kissinger years, however, Sudan seems to have been downgraded in U.S. strategic thinking both relative to, and together with, the rest of Africa.

The major instrument of U.S. policy in the Sudan has been foreign aid programs on a medium scale; the outcome was a mixed success at best, partly because of the lack of well-conceived (from a Sudanese perspective) projects, and partly because of rather mediocre performance in execution.

But just as important in an assessment of this policy is the perception of the host country. The Sudanese, as most Africans, are impressed neither by capitalism as symbolized by the United States nor by communism as symbolized by the USSR as models for political, economic, and social development. If anything, they tend to look to Yugoslavia as a model, a country that, significantly, had developed a certain degree of independence from the major cold war rivals, and that had adopted the moderate brand of socialism that appears to many African thinkers to be more appropriate for existing local social and economic conditions.

As we shall see in subsequent chapters, incidents of anti-Americanism in the Sudan increased throughout the 1960s, and culminated in the severing of diplomatic, and subsequently economic, relations following the 1967 Arab-Israeli War.

This series of events presented the USSR with a natural opening in the area. Soviet objectives seem very similar, albeit antithetical, to those of the United States, that is, to penetrate into the Muslim World and Africa, especially in a country of some geopolitical importance, with access to North, Central and East Africa, and the Red Sea.

Like the United States and her Western allies, Soviet policy, closely coordinated with those of East European states, emphasized economic, technical, and military aid. The Sudanese were naturally anxious to accept this aid, especially in view of the favorable terms available (in comparison to those from the West). This acceptance does not, however, indicate a proclivity for communism on the part of either the Sudanese regimes or ordinary citizens. And although the communist movement in the Sudan over the past twenty-five years has flourished more than perhaps in any other Middle Eastern and African nation, this relative success is contrasted by extraordinarily deep-seated antipathy towards communism on the part of the overwhelming portion of the country's population (see subsequent chapters). The 1971 announcement by President Nimeiri calling for a ''round-up'' and a ''crushing'' of the movement and its members only repeats earlier parallel instances and manifests the very tenuous position of Sudanese leftists.

At this time, Sudan's relations with Third World states are strictly functional and limited to trade and technical assistance programs. Most prominent in this category have been the Peoples' Republic of China, India, Kuwait, Libya, Syria, and most recently, the Lower Gulf states.

Relations with Neighboring States

As already suggested on preceding pages, certain effects of ethnic cleavages and tribalism have dominated Sudan's relations with her neighbors, especially the six adjacent non-Arab states. We may identify three distinct but related patterns:

First, several Sudanese tribes with consanguineous relations in Chad, the Central African Republic, and Ethiopia have periodically wandered back and forth across Sudanese borders. Usually these movements are related to the normal search for pasture by nomadic peoples; sometimes they result from evasive action during the seasons for tax collection and conscriptions, and every so often they may involve clashes emanating from raids, reprisals, feuds, or simply conflicts over pasture grounds and water holes. Especially when clashes involve the loss of life, which has happened not too infrequently, appeals for protection or retributions are made to the respective governments. These kinds of incidents then generate mini-crises along borders and temporarily sour relations. Unless patterns become one-sided and repetitive, the incidents are usually soon forgotten.

Second, like the Sudan itself, several of its neighbors have faced rebel insurgents who frequently escaped across borders and proceeded to operate from neighboring territory. Examples are the Eritrean Liberation Front, which has desired secession from Ethiopia, the Congolese Liberation Front in the 1960s, and active anti-regime rebels from Chad and Uganda. Most Sudanese postindependence governments have been sympathetic to these groups, and some have selectively given various forms of aid from time to time, ranging from havens of refuge to permission to operate from Sudanese soil to outright granting of facilities and direct aid. This sort of policy can, of course, become a double-edged sword, since all of the target states were in a position to grant, and periodically actually have granted, similar support to Sudanese anti-regime rebels. This situation has produced some grotesque results when, for example, in 1964-65 Sudan and Congo Kinshasa gave aid to each others' rebel forces. When the Khartoum government of Prime Minister Sirr el-Khatim el-Khalifah decided to permit airlifts of weapons to Christopher Gbenye's Congolese Liberation Army, most of the shipments were intercepted in transit by anya'nya rebels on the road south of Juba and were eventually used against the Sudanese armed forces.

Third, Sudan's relations with her southern neighbors have suffered considerably due to the effects and the deterioration of the problem of the South. Hundreds of thousands of southerners have fled across Sudan's borders into neighboring states, some merely to regroup, but most to remain at length as refugees. These refugees became a financial burden to their host countries and a great source of negative publicity for the Sudan. In general, the southern neighbors, as fellow black Africans, have been sympathetic to the rebels' and refugees' cause; what has prevented them from giving outright aid has been the restraining influence of the Organization of African Unity—which categorically opposes secessionist movements—plus the potential for Sudanese reprisals in view of minority problems in their own countries.

It must be added that all states involved have agreed to respect each others' territorial integrity and not to interfere in internal matters. The only neighbor who has been periodically suspected of possible territorial designs has been Uganda; but the likelihood of acquisition or annexation of Equatoria Province has diminished with the passing of years since the 1947 Juba Conference. Attitudes on this subject seem to have varied between Presidents Obote and General Amin; nevertheless, it seems most improbable that any Ugandan leader would do more than possibly dream about expansion.

A final factor, not to be overlooked, has been the clandestine entrance of Israel into this region. Exact dates and figures are difficult to ascertain and validate; but it is a known fact that Israeli support for anya'nya rebels increased considerably after the Sudanese government assumed a militant anti-Israeli posture following the June 1967 War. Israeli officers were said to have trained guerilla leaders for some time at bases in Ethiopia and Uganda, in which countries Israel maintained military aid missions. At the outset of the 1970s, some Israeli activities shifted into the southern Sudan itself.[42]

Finally, it remains to evaluate Sudanese reaction to the various influences of foreigners. Emerging patterns are obviously complex and subject to change depending on day-to-day events. Nevertheless, one can identify as dominant theme a general ambivalence by the Sudanese toward all of their partners in foreign relations.

Black African states have been viewed by southerners as potential allies, yet there has been dissatisfaction with the rather limited support received thus far; they have been suspected by northerners for these very sympathies, yet northerners are simultaneously conscious of their own Africanism in terms of blood ties and heritage.

The superpowers and their respective cold war allies are viewed as welcome donors of technical and economic aid, yet there is much wariness of being drawn into any cold war rivalries and confrontations, something the Sudanese want to avoid at any cost.

The British retain their role as excolonial overlords. On one hand they have been blamed for much of the current political instability in both North and South; on the other they have left behind not a few customs and values that have been embraced by Sudanese in public and private affairs.

Lastly, Egyptians have been viewed as the overpowering neighbor to the North requiring constant vigilance lest Sudan's independence be usurped. At the same time Egypt has been the gateway to the Arab world, a favored recreation and recuperation point for Sudanese abroad, and perhaps most importantly, the symbol of Arabism in short.*

---

*Significantly enough, reference to the northern neighbors in Sudanese colloquial is not as "Egyptians" but as "Arabs"; thus the Egyptian Social Club in Khartoum is officially known as the Arab Club, as contrasted with the Syrian Club.

CONCLUSION

It remains now to pull together the various influences discussed
in the preceding sections and to identify their combined effects upon
our key unit of analysis: Sudanese political man.[*]

The two dominant dimensions of our interest are attitudes and
behavior—individual as well as collective—by Sudanese toward a wide
variety of items, but particularly toward politics, society, and religion.
These influences or variables may be viewed as a series of successive parameters delimiting the scope and alternatives for Sudanese
in shaping attitudinal and behavioral patterns. Of course, the variables
are both complex and interrelated; hence the following threefold distinction must be understood as little more than a matter of analytical
convenience: environmental and demographic features, foreign
affairs, cultural and political heritage.

Environmental and demographic variables determine essentially
the patterns of daily life, such as customs, habits, economic opportunities and limitations, and different types of social behavior in
general.

Ethnic crossbreeding over the centuries has produced hybrid
peoples in the Sudan with an almost infinite variety of combinations
in terms of pigmentation, physical features, and racial origin. Yet
all of these exhibit admixtures of Arabism and Africanism in appearance and behavior; some knowledgeable and astute observers have
concluded that the Sudanese people seem to have been blessed with
the virtues of both cultures. Examples of hybrid behavior—appearance

---

[*] At this point a caveat of theoretical character is in order: The
above described influences are not only multiple and diverse, but
also tend to have different weights and targets. In the parlance of
vector analysis, the resultant (end product) is a function of the sums
of all vectors (factors, influences). Since each vector has two dimensions, that is, direction and magnitude, we have to be cognizant of
the fact that some influences may be more weighty than others, that
some might be reinforcing, others complementary, others over-
lapping and yet others conflicting, that is, two or more may cancel out.

It is my contention that this conversion process of factor inputs
can be delineated in a sufficiently rigorous manner to satisfy readers
with scientist inclinations. I will not oblige them here, however, primarily out of a calculated desire to minimize jargon and methological
considerations, and also out of some deference to that majority of
readers who are interested primarily in my substantive analysis of
Sudanese affairs.

is obvious to anyone—are especially prominent in the northern Sudan
and range from assimilated customs to religious conduct (many turuq
mix Muslim rituals with an African beat) to overt forms of socio-
political deportment. An illustration of this latter generalization is
that Sudanese tend to be much more action-oriented and less hypno-
tized by the spoken word than Arabs usually are; at the same time,
they also exhibit a higher degree of social and political sophistication
in comparison to most Africans.* One is reminded of parallel cases
of automobile accidents in Cairo and Khartoum. Whereas in the former
instance the observer is frightened by the intensity of verbal exchanges
and wild, threatening gesticulations but relieved to see the opponents
part after 20 minutes without any further damage done; in the latter
case he may be amazed to note the quick and decisive response: a
few words and then a hard right to the chin. I should hasten to add,
however, that it would be a grave injustice to depict the Sudanese as
a violence-prone people. In fact, there exists a great distaste for
political violence—as distinct from personal, including racial violence—
accounting in part for the virtual absence of bloodshed following the
past three revolutions. To inflict injury for political reasons is generally considered bad manners; on the other hand, it may be warranted
in order to protect one's honor. The point here is simply that by comparison to Egyptians, for example, Sudanese cannot be expected to be
as docile or willing to suffer lengthy perceived hardships without
resorting to some practical recourse.

In the economic realm opportunities are quite limited by Western
standards, but not as confined as in most countries of the region.
For one thing, physical and occupational mobility are not as restricted
by social or geographic origin as one might suspect; for another,
incentive for hard work depends primarily on individual initiative.
Except for strife-torn regions, starvation is not a major concern. If
anything, the sufficient availability of foodstuffs coupled with the
almost ascetic consumption habits of almost all Sudanese has
decreased the incentive for maximal exploitation of resources. As
individuals, many Sudanese seem to be content to work just as hard
as is necessary in order to get by (what would they do with amassed
wealth anyhow?); yet collectively, they expect a certain minimum
performance by their governments. If those standards are not attained

---

* I refer here to an appreciation of the complexity of most issues
and of the significant difference that a nuance might make in determining a particular outcome. This sort of statement is clearly relative; yet most objective observers will testify to the relatively more
advanced position of Arab civilization in comparison to Africa.

at local or national levels, the people have been ready to turn elsewhere.

From the perspective of geography, the vastness of the country
and the inadequate state of communications facilities explain the isolation of many areas from one another, and of most from the national
capital. Politically, this means essentially a lack of effective control
by the central government over most outlying areas and the concomitant autonomy enjoyed locally.

Another aspect of the vastness of the country and the relatively
sparse population is that the many nomadic and seminomadic groups
possess a relatively high degree of physical mobility. Once again,
these groups are practically isolated from the outside world and are
effectively supervised only by their local leaders. As a result, much
of the substance of politics in the Sudan is local politics, a fact that
cannot be overemphasized too much, and that is in sharp contrast to
Egypt, for example.

The previously mentioned diversity of peoples and multiplicity
of spoken dialects merely reinforces this situation. In addition to the
resulting high degree of local autonomy, it helps to shape patterns of
identification and perceptions of in- and out-groups. The dominant
social unit throughout the Sudan is the clan or extended family, in
terms of loyalty and identity more important than the tribe. The clan
is usually ruled by its oldest male member, whose authority over-
rules all other considerations, including those of educated adult sons.

This situation is, of course, not entirely static. Just as we can
observe some changes from traditional to transitional behavior in all
walks of life, although not uniformly permeating society, we can note
the gradual erosion of traditional forms of identification, more
rapidly among the young than the old, the educated than the illiterate,
those in or near urban centers than those in rural areas. However,
it would be a grave error to overestimate the very gradual nature of
this process.

Foreign affairs are comparatively less important as determinants of Sudanese political behavior than environmental or cultural
factors; nevertheless, some influences are discernible. These may
be distinguished according to origin, such as the introduction of new
cultural values, and direct contact with foreigners at home and
abroad.

Historically, Sudanese have encountered foreigners primarily
as conquerors and/or exploiters of Sudan's resources. Consequently, there has developed a healthy skepticism toward the designs
of all outsiders regardless of their explicit intentions. In the process
of social intercourse the Sudanese have naturally assimilated some
values of Arab, African, or colonial vintage; and they have exhibited
a proper appreciation for the various achievements and contributions

by foreigners. One example might be the importance attached to
properly constituted authority and to the formal elections of their own
leaders. Another might be the strongly held belief in the cherished
right to free expression, although origins of this belief might be difficult to ascertain inasmuch as they could derive equally well from
Arab, African, or British traditions. Nonetheless, the Sudanese
response has always been to emphasize the uniqueness of their own
experience, culture, and personality. And, in fact, the Sudanese have
never been afraid to assert their independence, in public or privately,
vis-a-vis outsiders or their own central governments. It is a hallmark of these very proud people that, while they will be incomparably
hospitable to outsiders of all descriptions, they will also not display
deferential obsequiousness.

Most ordinary Sudanese know foreigners only as local colonial
administrators or as assistance specialists. They tend to treat them
with respect for their technical expertise, but expect due consideration for local customs. Those Sudanese who have lived abroad extensively, especially as part of their vocational training, tend to have
formed rather definite opinions about the value and appropriateness
of foreign institutions. To illustrate, some have become "more
British than the British" to the point of drinking tea at five o'clock
sharp, others have become acutely anti-British, perhaps as a result
of adverse personal encounters. In any case, these individuals are
likely to translate their potential of considerable impact on public
policy due to the usually exalted positions of the persons involved.

Another related phenomenon is that these members of the native
elite are at least nationally, if not internationally, oriented and thus
frequently find it easier to identify with other foreign elites than with
their uneducated and untraveled fellow citizens. At a time of rising
consciousness about Arab and African nationalisms, these elite members then are likely to form the nucleus of progressive, nationalis-
tically oriented movements.

Cultural heritage is treated here as a residual category containing a myriad of influences, from which I have selected what appeared
to be the three most important, namely religion, authority patterns,
and factionalism.

As previously discussed, religion at the group level has contributed to divisiveness in the country at large, and between sectarian
movements in various regions. This has been a crucial element of
Sudanese politics precisely because religious affiliation tends to be
based on tribal and ethnic ties and thus to reinforce existing
cleavages.

On the individual level, religion has acted as a source of personal
strength—because of the high degree of piety especially among northerners—and of political strength, because of mutual support among

leaders and followers of a particular denomination in temporal as
well as spiritual matters.

Authority patterns might best be understood by examining the
Sudanese perspective on the relative legitimacy of traditional and
formal-legal authority. Holders of traditional positions of authority,
such as heads of a family, clan, tribe, or sect are respected as long
as the legitimacy of their social group is unquestioned. That is to
say, heads of families and clans are treated deferentially, regardless
of their competence. Tribal and sectarian leaders have usually been
accepted as legitimate as long as tribe and sect are viewed as such
and if their ascension to power conformed to traditionally established
patterns, such as election by an inner circle.

By contrast, legitimacy of formal-legal authority, such as the
regime in power, or elected representatives at local, regional, and
national levels is a direct function of their effectiveness. If they can
deliver the goods, they will be retained, be they traditional leaders,
parliamentarians, or members of a military junta; should they fail,
the body politic will look elsewhere—and has done so several times
in recent years—for more effective leadership. Most Sudanese seem
to perceive their relationship to formal-legal authority as participants
in a bargain: they will grant loyalty and legitimacy in return for
promised goods and services. If the regime cannot produce these
items, it has broken the bargain and effectively lost its legitimacy.
The difficulty with this rather admirable interpretation is, as we
shall see in subsequent chapters, that most Sudanese citizens and
political leaders have interpreted these goods and services from a
local rather than national perspective. Thus, it was possible to
purchase group support by providing some schools here and an agricultural scheme there, but national problems were too frequently
sacrificed for considerations of political expediency. Such policies
were facilitated, of course, by the single most dominant characteristic
of the political system, that is, the factional nature of Sudanese
society.

Factionalism in the Sudan, as noted previously, has dominated
the political history of the Sudan during at least the past thirty years.
It is the product of reinforcing cleavages along geographic, ethnic,
religious, and linguistic lines that has prevented the emergence of
a strong political grouping with majority support. Its effects upon
individual regimes and their policies will be examined in detail in
the remainder of this book. Suffice it here to note that, historically,
factionalism has been so deep-rooted in Sudanese society, that it
was impossible for a national front to be created, as was the case
in Morocco, for instance. Why? For one thing, the Sudan did not
have a king or any other person with sufficient charisma (or

barakah* as the case may be) to unify the various factions. For
another, the element of factionalism is symptomatic of Sudanese
behavior. For centuries, even in the days of the mahdiyyah, the
Sudanese were never united politically or militarily. Even then,
religious sectarianism was reinforced by racial and tribal cleavages.
Factionalism has come to pervade many aspects of life in the Sudan,
from struggle for political or economic power to patterns of identification. A good illustration is provided by the situation in soccer-
football, a sport that attracts the close attention of almost every male
Sudanese residing in settled areas. It is characterized by competition
between supporters of the two largest clubs, Merikh and Hilal. This
competition includes power struggles in the executive committees of
the association as well as partisanship in treating job applications.
It has been said that virtually every northern Sudanese male is either
a Hilalabi or a Merikhabi. The author has witnessed many times
during matches between, for example, visiting Czechoslovakian teams
and Hilal that supporters of Merikh hoped fervently (and gave expression to these hopes) that Hilal would be defeated by a terrible score,
because that would make Merikh look good relatively. And vice versa.
The thought of supporting the home Sudanese team against the invading
foreigners never seemed to occur to the fans. Factionalism seems
to fill a need. The author had many occasions to observe the functioning of a particular club or interest group where, by all logic, it would
seem to be to the advantage of every member to pull into the same
direction. Yet, when matters appeared to move smoothly, and especially then, someone "inevitably rose to create an artificial problem"
(a recurrent phrase used by introspective Sudanese) no matter how
ridiculous, and he would labor until the greatest imaginable state of
disharmony had been produced, totally oblivious to the material and
social costs to the group, including himself. A preliminary explanation for this type of behavior may be that patterns of identifications
are still localized in most aspects of life, a phenomenon that allows
the individual to find security only in very small groups, among his
"brothers," and that places the rest of the universe in the category
of outsiders.

---

*A form of grace, bestowed upon the recipient by Allah, and
recognized as such by a large share of the general population.

NOTES

1. Republic of Sudan, Central Office of Information, Sudan Almanac, 1965-66, p. 83.

2. Ibid., p. 84.

3. Sudanese Socialist Union, Documents of the First National Congress, January 1974, 25, Document No. C/1/2, p. 12.

4. For example, see Beshir Mohammed Said, The Sudan: Crossroads of Africa (London: The Bodley Head, 1965), p. 12.

5. For a fascinating account of the border problems in Western Darfur at the turn of the century, see A. B. Theobald, Ali Dinar, Last Sultan of Darfur (London: Longmans, Green Co., 1965).

6. For excellent discussions of Sudanese cultural identities, see Francis M. Deng, Dynamics of Identification (Khartoum: Khartoum University Press, 1973) and Muddathir Abdel-Rahim, "Arabism, Africanism and Self-Identification in the Sudan," Journal of Modern African Studies 8, no. 2 (July 1970): 233-49.

7. Mohammed Omer Beshir, The Southern Sudan: Background to Conflict (London: C. Hurst, 1968), p. 7.

8. For details and description, see the excellent study by J. Spencer Trimingham, Islam in the Sudan (London: Oxford University Press, 1949).

9. Beshir, op. cit., p. 7.

10. Republic of Sudan, Central Office of Information, Sudan Almanac 1956, pp. 136-37. For a comprehensive treatment of educational growth and policy, see Mohammed Omer Beshir, Educational Development in the Sudan, 1898-1956 (Oxford: Clarendon Press, 1969).

11. The Middle East and North Africa, 1975-76, 22nd ed., p. 646.

12. The Sudan News, June 9, 1970.

13. Tore Nordenstam, Sudanese Ethics (Upsala, Sweden: Scandinavian Institute of African Studies, 1968), passim.

14. For details, see ibid., pp. 92-105 especially.

15. Ibid., p. 221, 312-14.

16. For details of the Mahdiyyah period, see the excellent study by Robert O. Collins, The Southern Sudan (New Haven: Yale University Press, 1962); also Peter M. Holt, A Modern History of Sudan (London: Weidenfeld and Nicolson, 1961); and A. B. Theobald, The Mahdiyya: A History of the Anglo-Egyptian Sudan 1881-99 (London: Longmans, Green Co., 1951).

17. A stirring account of the greatness of the Mahdi is rendered by the recent Prime Minister Mohammed Ahmed Mahgoub in his book, Democracy on Trial: Reflections on Arab and African Politics (London: Andre Deutsch, Ltd., 1974), especially pp. 26-27, including a laudatory citation from Winston Churchill.

18. Daoud Abdel-Latif, in an interview with this author. He added that there is another reason for that fact, namely that in a colonized country political action is monopolized by foreigners, and that in such a system the highest posts for natives are those of medium-level, and later high-rank, bureaucrats. Because the bureaucrats are really politicians at heart, they tend to be highly individualistic in the execution of their tasks. Since independence, many civil servants have been known to countervene policies from the central government, should they disagree with them; if they are fired, they just become "politicians."

19. J. S. R. Duncan, The Sudan's Path to Independence (London: William Blackwood & Sons, 1957), p. 139. See also Mahgoub, op. cit., p. 40.

20. Ibid. Mohammed Omer Beshir, Revolution and Nationalism in the Sudan (New York: Barnes & Noble, 1974), reports the official founding of the congress on February 12, 1938, although graduates' clubs had been established as early as 1931. For a detailed discussion, see Chapters 7 and 9.

21. The general aspects of this policy are discussed by J. W. C. Dougall in an article entitled "Colonial Policy and the Christian Conscience," published in International Review of Missions 30, no. 120 (October 1941): 477-92, and quoted by Duncan, op. cit., p. 218. ". . . One obstacle (to the improvisation of our political systems so that colonial peoples share the responsibility as well as the duty of citizenship) arises from our preference for the tribal rather than the educated native. We often appear reluctant to give the younger and more progressive leaders a real share in central and local government. Indirect rule is admirable as a philosophy but it must somehow be supplemented or developed, if the connexion is to be made between Local Native Government and the Central Legislature . . ."

22. For details about these relationships, see P. M. Holt, A Modern History of the Sudan (London: Weidenfeld and Nicolson, 1961), passim.

23. For details see K. Henderson, Sudan Republic (New York: Frederick A. Praeger, 1965), pp. 82-83 and Beshir, Revolution and Nationalism in the Sudan, op. cit.

24. Trimingham, op. cit.

25. Henderson, op. cit., p. 90.

26. Including among students at then Gordon Memorial College, who voted 138-2 in favor of a "unity of the Nile valley" policy. See Salah el-Din el-Zein el-Tayeb, The Students' Movement in the Sudan 1940-70 (Khartoum: Khartoum University Press, 1971), p. 40.

27. K. Henderson, The Making of the Modern Sudan (London: Oxford University Press, 1953), pp. 540-41.

28. London Times, May 17, 1944.

29. Henderson, Sudan Republic, op. cit., p. 89.

30. Duncan, op. cit., p. 136.

31. Duncan, op. cit., p. 135.

32. In addition, leaders of students and workers organizations protested against the establishment of the Legislative Assembly. See el-Tayeb, op. cit., p. 53.

33. Beshir, The Southern Sudan: Background to Conflict, op. cit., p. 73, and Mohammed Omer Beshir, The Southern Sudan: From Conflict to Peace (London: Barnes & Noble, 1975), pp. 49-51.

34. The interested reader is referred to the scholarly study by Muddathir Abdel-Rahim, Imperialism and Nationalism in the Sudan (Oxford: Clarendon Press, 1969); and Henderson, Sudan Republic, op. cit., chapter 10 for the perspective of a former civil servant. See also, Said, op. cit.; Beshir, The Southern Sudan: Background to Conflict, op. cit., chapters 5-7, especially; Oliver Albino, The Sudan: A Southern Viewpoint (London: Oxford University Press, 1970), passim; William Deng and Joseph Oduhu, The Problem of the Southern Sudan (London: Oxford University Press, 1963), especially chapters 5, 6); and Cecil Eprile, War and Peace in the Sudan (London: David E. Charles, 1974). Among the best analyses are the recently published Robert O. Collins, The Southern Sudan in Historical Perspective (Tel Aviv: Shiloah Center, 1975) and Francis M. Deng, Dynamics of Identification, op. cit.

35. James C. Davies, "Toward a Theory of Revolution," in Macridis and Brown, eds., Comparative Politics, 3rd ed. (Homewood, Ill.: Dorsey, 1968), p. 631, originally published in the American Sociological Review 27, no. 1 (February 1962): 5-19.

36. For an excellent definition of this class, see Manfred Halpern, The Politics of Social Change in the Middle East and North Africa (Princeton: Princeton University Press, 1963), pp. 52-60.

37. Omar Mohammed Osman and Ali Ahmed Suleiman, "Economy of the Sudan," in The Economies of Africa, eds. Peter Robson and D. A. Lury (London: Allen and Unwin, 1969), p. 461.

38. United Nations, Population Growth and Manpower in the Sudan (New York: UN, 1964), p. 123.

39. For a detailed description of the Gezira scheme, see Arthur Gaitskill, Gezira (London: Faber, 1959).

40. Osman and Suleiman, op. cit., p. 445.

41. Middle East Economic Digest 13, no. 1 (January 3, 1975).

42. For details, see Jerusalem Post Weekly, March 30 and April 6, 1971.

2

THE GROUP BASIS
OF POLITICS:
TRADITIONAL ELEMENTS

It is axiomatic that any social system is composed of multiple elements. A proper understanding of the functioning of such a system requires that we examine its main components, and the way in which these interact. The group-theoretic framework associated with the well-known social scientists Arthur Bentley and David Truman, though commonly and successfully employed by many Western political analysts, has been found wanting by students of non-Western political systems because of marked differences in social, economic, and political conditions. Although such criticism seems fundamentally sound, it does not, by itself, argue against the utility of examining major groups or elements of the system as individual units. The next two chapters of this book are devoted to a study of these major elements in Sudanese politics, albeit only in survey form.

Identifiable groups in Sudanese society that have been significant participants in the political process can be divided into two basic categories: those based on primarily traditional forms of identification such as political organization in tribal groups, religious sects, and political parties, and those resting on relatively more modern class forms of identification such as the intelligentsia, the civil service, the mercantile sector, the military, and other professional associations.

Some may object that political parties constitute an integral part of a modern political system and should therefore be listed in the second category.[1] For our present purposes, however, political parties have been included in the first category, because we shall argue that political orientation in the Sudan has been highly correlated with membership in a given tribe, which in turn has been highly correlated with sectarian affiliation; and the most important Sudanese parties have either been outgrowths of sectarian movements or rallying points for those who did not care to align themselves

politically with either of the two major sects. For a start, the data
from our voting analysis clearly support these assertions; let us
therefore try to gain additional insights by examining political patterns in tribal structures, religious sects, and political parties. The
substance of our hypothesis suggests that we begin our inquiry with
an examination of the political organization of ethnic communities.

THE POLITICS OF LOCALISM

As previously mentioned, social ties in the Sudan are most pronounced toward family, clan, locality, and tribe, in that order. Membership in a given family or clan almost automatically means adherence to the same tariqah in the northern Sudan and generally to the
same animist cult in the southern region, although here the effects
of conversion to Christianity or Islam have altered the previous
uniformity of ethnic-religious congruence.

Several things account for the continued strength of clan and
tribal identification, more so than in almost all African and Middle
Eastern countries: the enormous heterogeneity of the society, the
rather limited social mobility caused in part by the relatively slow
penetration of educational growth into the hinterlands, but particularly by the overwhelming obstacles to more effective communications,
and the fact that marriage throughout the Sudan still units members
of the same clan or tribe in more than 90 percent of the cases. Predictably, social intercourse among different ethnic communities has
been greatest in the urban centers of the three capital cities, and in
Port Sudan, Wad Medani, El-Obeid, Atbara, Malakal, Kassala, in
probably that order. Yet it is significant that Sudanese who have
moved to these cities continue to maintain strong ethnic ties by
following a variety of patterns that may take the form of residing in
particular quarters,* congregating socially in the homes of fellow
tribesmen, joining social clubs established exclusively for certain
tribal groups;† and it is not at all unusual for a young man to meet
his future wife through her brother or cousin at such social gatherings.

---

*Frequently, residential quarters are thus designated, for ex-
ample, the Baqqara area, the Khatmiyyah, Danaqla, among others in
Khartoum North alone.

†For example, the Khartoum Province Shaiqiyyah Club, where
Shaiqi men originally from the Northern Province could spend most
of their evenings chatting, reminiscing, and playing social games.
The Nimeiri regime has closed down these clubs, in an effort to

It is interesting that education, while broadening individual horizons and creating a greater awareness of the richness of other ethnic communities and their customs and folklore, does not seem to diminish the strength of personal identification with and loyalty to one's clan or tribe. For example, it is common knowledge that appointment to a senior administrative position invariably entices the new executive to stock most available vacancies with relatives or other fellow tribesmen. This practice is sufficiently common that it has been followed in the government bureaucracy, private enterprise and higher education, and at the highest levels of academia.

To many outside observers this form of patronage may be not only excessive, but objectionable on ethical and administrative counts. It would be difficult to disagree with such critics; however, in fairness to all concerned, the reader should be made aware of the tremendous intraethnic pressures on a native son to support the causes of "his own." Another, only slightly related aspect of this same phenomenon, is the positive strength emanating from tribal solidarity that, in the case of Sudan, is invariably grounded in pride of past accomplishments—be they in the realms of the sword, the pen, the cattleman's stick, or the hoe—and embroidered by an unusually rich and diversified folklore.

Local politics in the Sudan is closely interrelated with local government as, indeed, in most other societies. The main forms worth identifying correspond to the three demographic categories of urban, rural settled, and rural nomadic life-styles. (For purposes of this short survey, seminomadic peoples will be treated in the same category as the nomadic ones.) Urban areas are exclusively administered by the civil service through the Ministry of Local Government in the various provinces. As already explained in Chapter 1, each province has a governor, each municipality a local council presided over by the town clerk or omda as the case may be, and each rural district a rural council executive presided over by a civil servant from the above mentioned ministry (formerly the district commissioner). In addition, each city quarter, rural village, hamlet, and nomadic section is coadministered by a sheikh (or his equivalent in the South). The sheikh is almost always elected by the peoples' elders, and serves for as long as he wishes. (In exceptional circumstances, government pressure may force a sheikh to resign before his normal retirement.) His main function is to serve as a communications link between the people and his regional superior, also as a tax collector and a sort of justice of the peace, who is expected to

---

minimize "tribalism," but many have been reopened or relocated under different auspices.

resolve minor disputes. In nearly all cases the sheikh can be expected
to know personally every inhabitant of his domain and to be astutely
conversant with the main concerns of his people.

This position is illustrative of one side of the kind of dual administration that has been in existence in the Sudan practically since the
inception of the Anglo-Egyptian condominium. It was intended to
parallel the local government civil service with a so-called native
administration. Originally designed by the British for administrative
and political expediency, this system has tended to enhance the power
of local chiefs, who quite naturally pursued conservative policies
commensurate with their positions and influence. This, in turn, has
been a thorn in the sides of the indigenous intelligentsia, who have
attacked the system of native administration as a major obstacle to
modernization in the country since the days of the Graduates'
Congress.

However, the real focus of this attack has rarely been the local
sheikh, but almost always the nazir (tribal chieftain). Although the
institution itself has been phased out progressively during the past
decade, the influence of nazirs on Sudanese politics cannot and must
not be overlooked, debatable as that influence may have been. It is
associated with such famous names as Abu Sin of the Shukriyyah,
Zubeir Hamad el-Malik of Dongola, and Ali el-Tom of the Kababish
in northern Sudan alone. These were giants among their own,
and no one who has ever met any of them, could possibly be unaffected
by their sheer presence. Over the years the number of nazirs has
differed: not every tribe has been ruled by a nazir, owing primarily
to size and status of the tribe. Furthermore, there have been differences among these leaders as well; in this brief survey we shall
limit ourselves to the most exalted form, namely those who have been
officially recognized as nazir umum (paramount chief). This title
meant, among other things, that the central government has conferred
certain administrative and especially judicial powers upon the title-
holder, and will offer him remuneration for these services.

Because of the tremendous number and variety of tribes in the
Sudan, it is impossible to cover all types of tribal politics here.
Fortunately, the reader can be referred to a growing number of good
anthropological studies that have increased our basic knowledge of
Sudanese tribes.[2] In the next few pages we will present examples of
the political organizations of a few selected tribes in northern and
southern Sudan in order to illustrate their diversity. The aforementioned Zubeir Hamad el-Malik has been nazir umum of Dongola
and was generally acknowledged as the most influential nazir of the
Northern Province. In many ways he has performed similar functions
and has earned similar stature as previous kings of Nubia, of whom

he is a descendant, as his name indicates.* He was known, admired,
and respected by his subjects, the inhabitants of towns and villages
in what is now the southernmost part of Nubia. Because these are
nearly all engaged in agriculture and settled within a rather confined
geographic area, administrative control has been technically easy
in Dongola.

A very different environment is that inhabited by the Kababish
nomads, who roam over an area of about 48,000 square miles in the
semidesert of northern Kordofan. The Kababish are subject to an
animal tax levied annually, which under the old system was collected
in cash by the section sheikh. He then handed the money over to the
nazir who presented the tax for the whole tribe to the rural council
executive at Sodiri (administrative center for Dar Kababish).† A
section usually coincides with a subclan. The section sheikh is
locally chosen, but has no power other than as tax collector and com-
municator between the nazir and the tribesmen.

This situation did not always exist, but was brought about by the
late Ali el-Tom. Ali had been most successful in unifying the various
tribes comprising the Kababish group, and well before his death in
1937 he had managed to deprive the various individual sections of
their local identity and their sheikhs of any independent power.[3] His
authority was passed on to the awlad fadlallah clan, who have formed
an elite nobility, from whom all sheikhs have been selected. They
are referred to as ahl as-sultah (people of authority) by ordinary
tribesmen. The most recent nazir umum has, among his functions,
been president of the highest local court in the district, and also the
ex officio deputy chairman of the Dar Kababish District Rural Council.
(The chairman is the local government inspector, a career civil
servant.)

In ethnolinguistic terms the number and variety of southern
tribes exceeds even those of northern Sudanese. According to official,
though dated, census figures, they range from the roughly two million
Dinka to a few dozen individuals. In keeping with the pattern of the
previous few paragraphs, our selection is not designed to be representative, but rather to illustrate variety.

The Azande form a group of tribes inhabiting portions of southern
Equatoria Province and northern Zaire, with a substantial population
living in the Sudan. Zande political authority is pyramidal in

---

*Malik means king. The kingdom of Nubia extended from south-
ern Egypt into the northernmost reaches of the Sudan along the Nile.

†The animal tax a few years ago amounted to 50 piasters per
camel, 40 piasters per horse, 10 piasters per sheep and so on.

organization. The hereditary avungura clan enjoys absolute authority vis-a-vis the commoners. Each Zande kingdom is divided into provinces, headed by a chief. Both the king or independent chief must be avungura.

Like the Azande, the Shilluk of the White Nile region near Malakal are predominantly agricultural and settled. The chief of a settlement is known as jago and derives from a special lineage. He is locally elected by a council of elders, but owes certain obligations to the reth (king). The reth rules as the supreme head of all Shilluk people. He also heads the royal clan (Kwareth), which is the largest of all clans and is based on patrilineal relations. After a king dies, a new reth is chosen by an electoral college.

The Dinka constitute a congeries of independent tribes spread over a vast area reaching into three provinces. Collectively, they form the largest tribal confederation in the Sudan, but have never been effectively united unlike their Nilotic neighbors, the Shilluk. In Kindaland the subtribe is the largest body politic with a recognized decision-making authority, and has traditionally been autonomous. The Dinka system features a diffusion of leadership roles: among the important figures are the "spear-chief"—a combination rain-maker and justice of the peace, the cattle chief (ban wut) and war leader, and the man of magic (ban de rap).

Our last example are the Nuer, a most extraordinary collection of tribes, who have acquired some fame of sorts in the social science literature because they seem to have no common organization or central administration.[4] This apparent anarchy persists down to the levels of districts and villages that have no formal headmen or councils. Only a group of elders provide leadership and advice for the community when required. Beyond them only a few recognized figures remain in Nuer society, such as the "leopard-skin chief," who possesses certain ritual, but few political powers. Yet despite this apparently unstructured organization, the Nuer did not collapse, but have proven to be resilient: When challenged by outsiders, neighboring tribes "coalesce to form a political system."[5]

If we wish to compare the political organization of our four southern examples, we note a steady decrease in the centralization of authority as we move from the Shilluk to the Azande to the Dinka to the Nuer.

As previously stated, the critics of native administration have blamed the considerable power and reactionary policies of local chiefs as major obstacles to social and political development for that great mass of Sudanese who inhabit rural areas. These arguments are well developed in F. M. Deng's excellent case study on Tradition and Modernization[6] in the Dinka culture, and can be considered as applicable to other tribal systems, though they were not intended as such by the author. He shows how the confrontation over modernization has been crystallized between the chiefs, who are generally illiterate, and the educated class. By training, the latter wants to impart its skills for the general welfare; but according to traditional standards, the educated class does not qualify for leadership (p. xxxv). Nowadays, the traditionalism of the tribal hierarchy has become even more centralized after it was equipped with the coercive powers of the modern state. And the more the uneducated chief feels threatened by the influx of new ideas, the more he resorts to his coercive powers.

After the October 1964 Revolution the first concrete steps were taken by the new government toward curtailing the powers of nazirs, but the eventual objective of phasing them out altogether was not accomplished until after the May 1969 revolution as part of the Nimeiri junta's policy of attacking all traditional political institutions. As it stands, their government subsidies have been cancelled and their official titles removed; but how can one legislate away social status and religious influence? All evidence so far suggests that the tribal chieftains continue to live among their people, continue to draw their respect for personal acumen, social status, and family wealth; and it does not require an extensive sample survey to realize that the nazir, because of familiarity to and with his own people, can still accomplish the management of local affairs more effectively than the new team of young university graduates sent by the Ministry of Local Government. What's more, is it not more significant than ironic that many close relatives, obviously endorsed by the chieftains, won seats in the recent elections to the Peoples' Assembly in 1974?

THE POLITICS OF RELIGION

In the first chapter of this book we have already referred to the roles of saints (tombs), holy men and ancestral spirits as rallying points for popular religion in the Sudan, and of the consequently localized nature of the various "denominations." We have also called attention to the distinction between private devotion and public behavior for the religious Sudanese, a point of considerable importance to our perspective.

We acknowledge, of course, that religion involves essentially a private relationship between the individual and the supernatural. But there is always a public manifestation to this relationship, when applied to the community of which the individual is a part; and this manifestation always has some effects on social forces, and frequently on political ones as well. Because the central objective of this book is to discuss political phenomena, we must limit our analysis to the public significance of religious behavior.[7]

While it is difficult to make many generalizations that hold for the numerous sects and cults throughout the Sudan, we can neverthe- less assert that the public significance of sectarian followings is greater in the Sudan than in most Arab or African countries. The cause for this phenomenon is probably that the religiously very heter- ogeneous society enhances the identity consciousness of individual groups. As a result, added weight is given to the concept of group membership, and it is readily observable throughout the country that the feeling of belonging to a given religious community seems to exceed in importance the substantive contents of its doctrines. Per- haps this explains why there are relatively few theological debates going on, even by Middle Eastern standards, and why, conversely, rituals and ceremonies play as important a role as they obviously do.

In order to become more specific it is incumbent to treat the predominantly Muslim and non-Muslim areas separately. In the southern Sudan we must again distinguish the Christians from the Animists. The former have developed relatively little cohesiveness, not only because they have been divided into Protestant and Roman Catholic denominations, but also because their conversions from pagan beliefs took place within individualized contexts. That is to say, one family or certain members of a family made personal deci- sions to convert to the new faith, unlike the more traditional con- texts, whereby entire tribes would embrace an Islamic tariqah or where a chief and his "medicine man" would control the collectivity of his clan or tribe by invoking the threats of evil spirits for any recalcitrant person. The political behavior of southern Christians therefore has been influenced primarily by their contacts with mis- sionaries and mission schools, resulting not so much in an awareness of commonality among southerners, as in a sense of distinctness from (and implied exploitation by) northern Muslims.

As regards the animists, religion would tend to influence their political behavior only in the sense that certain taboos set parameters for private and public behavior, and also in the aforementioned con- text where clan or tribal leaders may threaten the use of spiritual powers in order to gain intraclan support on local matters, and, in a few instances, to ensure voting support on larger issues.

To a certain extent this situation applies to much of the northern Sudan as well, albeit with different sets of parameters. But there is much more. The Sudanese, like other traditional Muslim societies, is characterized by a substantial fusion of religion and state in the community of believers. This means that a recognized religious leader has also acquired political influence among his followers by virtue of his barakah (divine blessing). This influence also pervades

social and economic relationships in addition to the religiopolitical
ones; in fact these relationships become mutually reinforcing to such
an extent that the entire community acts as a political bloc vis-a-vis
outsiders, and generally the only internal threat to its cohesiveness
results from competition over succession to leadership.

A glance at the various Sudanese turuq reveals the validity of
our hypotheses about the fusions of religiopolitical behavior. J. S.
Trimingham in his excellent analysis of popular religion in the Sudan
describes the histories and doctrinal peculiarities of ten major turuq
for the northern Sudan in some detail,[8] and in every instance the
founders of the tariqah, and most of their successors, were able to
translate their barakah into political support—and frequently into
economic benefit as well.

Even though only two have gained national prominence in Sudanese
politics, some of the minor turuq, such as the hindiyyah, isma'iliyyah,
or tijaniyyah, have managed to leave a mark on public affairs by
virtue of their leaders' distinguished records in high political offices.
The two major sects, in terms of political significance, have been the
ansar and the khatmiyyah, led respectively by the houses of el-Mahdi
and el-Mirghani, and therefore have sometimes also been identified
as the mahdiyyah (although this term refers more properly to a
historical period in the last quarter of the nineteenth century) and
mirghaniyyah. This latter form of identification is symbolic for their
emphasis placed on personal allegiance as opposed to doctrinal
commitment.

Originally the ansar were literally the "followers"[*] of Mohammad
Ahmed el-Dongolawi, the self-proclaimed Mahdi. But over the next
several generations ansar loyalty has been transferred to the Khalifah[†]
Abdullahi, and then to the Mahdi's posthumous son Abdel-Rahman and
his descendants. And although the mahdiyyah movement was not
strictly speaking a tariqah in the orthodox sense, but essentially
millenarian, it has developed or become Sudanized into such a sectarian movement for all practical purposes.

The khatmiyyah can lay claim to somewhat greater orthodoxy,
theologically speaking, but its organizational development tends to
parallel that of the mahdiyyah. It was founded in the early nineteenth
century by Mohammad Osman el-Mirghani, who proselytized throughout western Arabia and eastern Sudan. After his death the order in
the Sudan became effectively localized around Kassala. Its leaders

---

[*] The Arabic term ansar means "adherents, followers, disciples,"
and was first applied to the supporters of the prophet Muhammad in
Medina.

[†] An Arabic word meaning "successor," anglicized as Caliph.

decided to resist the mahdiyyah militarily and politically, and thereby
laid the foundations for a century of rivalries. An important hallmark
of khatmiyyah doctrine is the semidivine status of the Mirghani family
(the founder had claimed direct descent from the Prophet Muhammad),
from which all regional leaders had to be drawn. The most venerated
and politically most influential khatmi in the twentieth century has
been Sayyid Ali el-Mirghani (1879-1968).

In addition to the political, or community-power, base of barakah-
wielding patriarchs, economic dependencies tended to reinforce the
leader-follower relationships in both movements. Such dependencies
and relationships have taken two basic forms: One is the traditional
zakat, a kind of tithing, whereby nomadic followers may contribute
some livestock, and settled agriculturists portions of their crops.
For example, among the heavily khatmi Shaiqiyyah tribesman of
Northern Province, perhaps 80 percent have donated such items as
the fruits of one date palm. This is collected by the local khalifah
who looks after the Mirghani property in his district and who trans-
mits the contributions and property earnings to his master's headquarters. Some of the wealthier among the faithful may have donated
portions of, or entire, fruit and vegetable gardens to the Mirghani
estate or facilitated the purchases of suitable pieces of land so that
sizable gardens or plantations would be procured. Such plantations
and agricultural schemes constitute the second aspect of economic
interrelationships, in which numerous faithful may work as unpaid
or only nominally paid cultivators, whose main recompense is
physical closeness to the "annointed one" in the present, and promises of spiritual rewards in the hereafter. Over the years both
houses had acquired such large plantations, but especially good
examples are provided by the White Nile agricultural schemes in
and around Kosti. These, Abdel-Rahman el-Mahdi had managed to
build into an agricultural empire during the middle third of this
century through the judicious acquisition of agricultural licenses
and installation of diesel pumps. Some of these estates were as large
as 40,000 acres, subdivided into small parcels for cotton and millet
cultivation; their resident sharecroppers constituted a fertile recruit-
ing ground for Umma votes and ansar mobilization.[9]

After the Nimeiri regime came to power in 1969 it was determined to crush the sectarian movements. It recognized the Mahdi
family holdings as their fundamental power base, and proceeded to
confiscate most of the property. These developments frightened the
Mirghani house into initiating hurried and partially concealed sales
of some property to local residents, with very interesting results.
According to reliable sources, most potential buyers, who were of
course khatmi, refused to purchase the property despite unusually
low prices, simply because they could not reconcile themselves to

laying their hands on anything that in their view really belonged to the revered mirghanis.

From all this it is easy to see how sectarian leaders could maintain religious influence and political authority within their movements, why their policies remained conservative in outlook, and why their followers constituted more than merely a flock of the faithful, but potentially a base for social and political mobilization.

POLITICAL PARTIES

Just that kind of transformation of sectarian movements into political organizations has already been described in previous sections of this book with reference to the Umma Party and initial khatmiyyah support for the Ashiqqah. Here we shall only recapitulate that the Umma Party was the political organ of the ansar and came into existence in the early 1940s as a rural-oriented counterweight to the Ashiqqah (for details see Chapter 1). The Ashiqqah group, in turn, became the forerunner of the National Unionist party, and was thusly proclaimed prior to the 1953 elections. After several years of uneasy partnership, the khatmiyyah faction seceded from the NUP in June 1956 and proclaimed the Peoples Democratic party as its political organ.

Dur to the numbers of their followers, these three parties have managed to control Sudanese governments during periods of parliamentary rule; but they constitute by no means all.

The Communist party of the Sudan (CPS) has experienced turbulent conditions during the few years of its official existence, and we shall examine those experiences later in greater detail. The Muslim Brotherhood had a relatively late start in the Sudan and did not contest for power until after the October 1964 Revolution, when it organized itself into the Islamic Charter Front (ICF).

In addition, there have been a number of parties (more properly viewed as independents) with regional foci; if we eliminate those strictly local groups who emerged only for one election, obtained a minute fraction of the votes, and vanished immediately thereafter, we are left with the following: the Beja Congress in the eastern region, the Nuba Mountains Federation in the West, and the Southern Front and Sudan African National Union (SANU) in the South. Lastly, both the Socialist Republican party of the North and the Southern Liberal party contested the 1953 elections and obtained a number of parliamentary seats, but disappeared with the end of the first Constituent Assembly.

In the remainder of this chapter we will try to compare the organizational structures, ideological postures, bases of leadership and support, and general performances of these parties. Because of the variations in size, age, and orientation, it would be too unwieldy and often repetitive to discuss each party, one by one; rather it would seem to be more fruitful to divide them into the three categories of dominant tradition (NUP, PDP [DUP], Umma), radical (CPS, ICF) and regional (Beja Congress, Nuba Mountains Federation, SANU, and Southern Front).

The Dominant Traditional Parties

There can be no doubt that the Umma party, NUP, and PDP (as well as the DUP after the latter two's 1968 merger) have been dominant during periods of parliamentary rule: in the four national elections since 1953 they have always garnered upwards of 80 percent of the total vote and more than three-fourths of the assembly seats. For that reason alone they must occupy our special attention.

Organization

There has been little difference among the three parties in terms of their formal organizational structures. They all claimed to vest power in a 12 to 15 member Executive Council, which held regular meetings in their capital headquarters and which was to determine policy and also to serve as a link with the party apparatus in the provinces. In addition, they all publicized their views through their official newspapers, Al-Nil (Umma), Sawt al-Sudan (PDP), and Al-Alam (NUP), whose publication schedules were sometimes irregular, but which had almost the same circulations and media effects as the country's independent dailies.

Yet despite these close structural similarities there were real, substantive differences in the quality of the three organizations. It is probably fair to identify the Umma party as the most effective of the big three, if we consider the 25 years prior to the May Revolution and are not unduly distracted by periodic ups and downs. This is so because, on one hand, the party leadership was composed of ansar tribal leaders in addition to ranking Mahdi family members, and therefore contained strong elements of geographic representation; on the other hand the party was able to utilize the existing communications network of the ansar movement, which featured a tight hierarchical structure of province, district, and village committees. This aspect was very important in the political realm because the

original concept of a mahdiyyah had heavy political overtones to begin
with (that is, the establishment of a religio-political community under
a messianic figure), and therefore ansar membership connoted a
commitment to follow the military, political, and so on, edicts of the
Mahdi leadership. As a result, it is fair to say that ansar members
tended to be the most fanatically loyal to their movement and could
also be mobilized most easily of any.

On paper it may seem that the PDP should have had the very
same advantages as its western rival, but that was not to be. For one
thing the khatmiyyah movement, by not being messianic in character,
had fundamentally more limited objectives, emphasizing relatively
more localized and doctrinal aspects in comparison to the ansar.
As a result, its leadership tended to be more elitist in character,
and the followers less militant in action and, by implication, not
quite as easy to mobilize. Of course, another reason for the lesser
effectiveness of the PDP organization was its shorter history as an
autonomous party—two years before the Abboud coup, and about four
more years following the October 1964 revolution. Whereas the
ansar-Umma organization was characterized by clear objectives and
strong internal loyalties, its khatmiyyah-PDP counterpart appeared
vague and lackluster. This image can be traced all the way back to
the birth of its political organization when the ittihad al-khatmiyyah
(union) was established as a sort of transitional body between the
tariqah and the PDP. Its membership consisted of educated
mirghanists and it was in composition and orientation more similar
to the Graduates' Congress of old than to the Umma party/ansar
movement. A further point of difference lay in the relationships of
party leadership to the sectarian patriarchs, and hence in the resulting patterns of identification for the masses of followers. Until its
factional split during the past few years the Umma party had always
been associated with and presided over by the most prominent member
of the Mahdi house, while the khatmiyyah patriarch presented himself
merely as an advisory figure. And although there can be little doubt
that Sayyid Ali el-Mirghani's advice carried great weight in the PDP
and also for Sawt al-Sudan editors, the fact remains that he was
never as visibly identified with party affairs as Sayyid Abdel-Rahman
el-Mahdi by comparison. The PDP itself had been founded and presided over by Sheikh Ali Abdel-Rahman, the grandson of a famous
ulema leader and a well-known judge, who had also been a cofounder
of the Ashiqqah and the old NUP.

By all odds the NUP organization should have been the most
modern, if not also the most effective, of all parties in view of its
leadership's background and mass appeal. The party was the outgrowth of the more educated and secularized majority segment of
Graduates' Congress members, and it represented the young

Sudanese nationalists who had fought for political independence from the colonialists. By implication, it also opposed the latters' conservative allies in the rural Sudan and became the party of merchants, civil servants, and other professionals with consequently strong roots in the urban areas. Over the years the NUP managed to build up a reasonably effective organizational structure in the major cities of the northern Sudan but never in the countryside, and had to rely on khatmiyyah ties in the rural northern and eastern regions during the periods of alliance with that movement. The Executive Council at party headquarters in Omdurman was heavily dominated by an "old-boy" network, going back to the days of the Ashiqqah and the congress. They were mostly career politicians who depended on a well-functioning patronage system for support. Through astute placement of personnel, the party elders managed to gain substantial influence, if not outright control, of such key offices as Customs and Import-Export Control, with obvious benefits to the many big merchants on whose contributions the NUP depended for financial survival. But financial backing from a few wealthy men does not by itself guarantee electoral success; the rank and file must be first attracted and then mobilized in order to produce victory at the polls. And in this general area, the NUP never could live up to its promises. Its leadership under Ismail el-Azhari banked on automatic support from the growing educated middle class and on its presumed distaste for sectarian politics. This meant in effect that the NUP, except perhaps in 1953, was not thought of so much as a party with a specific and positive platform, but as an alternative to the less acceptable conservative and rural forces. This sort of strategy can succeed only as long as the rank-and-file perceives the contrast to the traditional forces as clear, and also the alternatives as highly undesirable. For many younger civil servants especially, these conditions no longer existed in the middle 1960s, when the Oxford-educated Sadiq el-Mahdi took the helm of the Umma party and el-Azhari's policies became increasingly conservative, while his political style resembled more and more the discredited old politics.

    Let us take a few moments to examine this style of Sudan's most successful civilian politician: While the British effectively ruled the Sudan, Ismail el-Azhari turned to their Egyptian rivals for support and proclaimed a nationalist policy that fired the imagination of all those who desired a speedy end to colonial rule. After the election victory the Egyptians had served his purpose and the task became to limit their influence in the country. When the time was opportune he came out for complete independence, a position on which he had settled privately prior to elections.[10] After the loss of the khatmiyyah section in 1956, he tried to broaden his political base by appealing to secular and "progressive" forces and attacked the conservative and

"reactionary" sectarian movements. However, not everyone was
taken in by this posture because, as his critics claimed, el-Azhari
behaved as though he were promoting a neo-tariqah with himself as
leader and patron, and his followers as the faithful believers in his
mission.[11] After the October Revolution of 1964, he suddenly found
himself thrust into the camp of those very same "reactionaries"
whom he had earlier attacked bitterly; he responded to the increasing
influence of the truly secular Front of Professionals by advocating
the establishment of an Islamic state in which "all alien ideas would
be combated and defeated." After the 1965 elections he took his
party into a coalition-government with the Umma in exchange for
being assured the position of Head of State. After the Umma prime
minister, Mohammad Ahmed Mahjoub, indicated that el-Azhari's
position was essentially titular (el-Azhari and Mahjoub both insisted
on heading Sudan's delegation to the meetings of the Organization of
African Unity and of the Arab heads of state, and the latter won out
temporarily), el-Azhari did not rest until Mahjoub had lost a vote of
confidence in the Assembly and was replaced by the very able Sayyed
el-Sadiq el-Mahdi. After the latter continued to gain in national stature by making some progress on the economic and political fronts,
especially toward a solution of the Southern Problem, el-Azhari
feared the aspirations of his young rival and threw his party's support
in the assembly behind the conservative Umma faction of the former
Prime Minister Mahjoub and, thus, caused the downfall of Sayyed
el-Sadiq.

The effects of all this maneuvering on NUP rank-and-file was
that the older generation by and large continued to support its leadership in a spirit of personal loyalty and admiration for past achievements, while the younger either drifted toward leftist groups who
now had become the "true nationalist" alternative to conservative
politics—or simply abstained from participating at the polls. In this
author's opinion the greatest shortcoming of the NUP organization
was that it could not adjust itself sufficiently to appeal to and attract
the substantial number of newly educated Sudanese, both male and
female, who were not prepared to vote for any radical or any sectarian party, but also felt indifferent toward the uninspired and old-
fashioned self-proclaimed party of the middle.

Appeal

Despite these partial shifts in sentiment, the NUP was able to
win more than 90 percent of the assembly seats in urban areas of
the North from 1953 to 1968. It had also built up a substantial following in the northern portion of the Gezira Agricultural Scheme
in Blue Nile Province. The only significant tribal support came

from the nomadic Kababish, who voted almost unanimously NUP in
all four elections; this phenomenon can almost certainly be attributed
to historical antecedents, especially because the Kababish do not
belong to the khatmiyyah: One century ago, only a few of their tribesmen joined the mahdiyyah, the others resisted; after the Mahdi's
military victories, many Kababish leaders were beheaded and the
tribes entered into a period of decline until the arrival of Ali el-Tom.

The sometime NUP partner PDP drew its main support from the
rural tribes in Northern and Kassala provinces, especially the
Shaiqiyyah, Bisharin, Amarar, Beni 'Amer and Shukriyyah, the latter
two having been the most forceful warriors of el-Mirghani in his
confrontation with the Mahdi one hundred years ago. Again we have
an example of contemporary political loyalties based on historical
alliances. This also accounts for the lone Umma support in Beja
territory, namely among the el-Tirik subtribe of Hadendowa. A comparable ansar island in basically khatmiyyah territory is Dongola,
the effective capital of Nubia, and the birthplace of the Mahdi. By
contrast, Umma strongholds are situated throughout the western
provinces of Darfur, Kordofan, and the White Nile region around
Aba Island and Kosti.

In terms of ideological postures there have been relatively few
policy differences among the big three, their own assertions to the
contrary notwithstanding. In domestic affairs, the Umma party has
been traditionally conservative: it favored an Islamic constitution, a
free enterprise system designed to attract private and foreign investments, and politically absolute independence for the Sudan, meaning
especially noninterference from Egyptian quarters. This latter item
has been the major policy difference for the PDP, which has traditionally acted as Egyptian mouthpiece in the Sudan, as explained in
Chapter 1. At times the PDP also flirted with socialist concepts
(early 1965) of the Castroite or Nasserite variety, reflecting leftist
factions within the party; but at other times it supported the conservative objectives of the Umma, thereby once again demonstrating
the rather vague and uncertain orientation of the party. The NUP
always tried to maintain a middle position between the two other
rivals, as regards its cautious policy toward Egypt and also its
cautious endorsement of a mixed economic system favoring private
businessmen. The NUP, as the self-proclaimed "only secular"
party, could not very well endorse an Islamic constitution; nevertheless, its leadership did not object to the Arabization and Islamization
of the southern provinces in the immediate postindependence years,
and its president, el-Azhari, often and publicly exclaimed his pride
in the Sudan's Arab and Muslim heritage—even in very forceful terms
during the 1965 Round Table Conference that had been designed to
reassure southern leaders of northern tolerance.[12] In this connection

it is intriguing that el-Azhari's grandfather, a celebrated sheikh al-islam in western Sudan, had become famous for his opposition to the Mahdi and his written opinion refuting the Mahdi's claim.[13]

Performance

Measuring party performance raises several conceptual difficulties, as any reader of the theoretical literature will acknowledge. Here we shall limit ourselves by choosing for our comparative inquiry the four items of decision making, party unity and discipline, recruitment, and effectiveness in elections.

To the extent that this author was able to gain information about the processes by which the diverse parties arrived at their respective policies, it appears that decision making was highly centralized in all three parties, whereby the individual presidents and a handful of close associates in the executive committees controlled most issues. In the NUP case, this group would include the recurrent ministers Ibrahim el-Mufti, Hassan Awadallah, Abdel-Magid Abu Hassabu and, before his death, Mubarak Zarrouq. President el-Azhari showed great skills in piloting his preferences through committee meetings, often by adjusting the agenda and time of sessions in such a way as to minimize the voting influence of dissenting committee members.

The PDP executive council similarly included a small number of prominent former ministers whose voices would carry more weight than those of the collective remainder; but even more influential was that of the khatmiyyah patriarch Sayyid Ali, who preferred to remain passively in the background, but retained an effective veto over all party and newspaper policies.

Of the three, the Umma party probably broadened its decision input base more than the others, because its president actively solicited the views of tribal chieftains in the countryside and of party notables in the capital. To be sure, the opinions of the imam (spiritual leader of the ansar) carried great weight, but not to the extent of veto power, especially in the 1960s. Also, there seemed to be relatively more room for intra-Mahdi family disagreements over particular policies, and also for the opinions of the Umma parliamentary group (consisting of elected members of Parliament from all over the country). While it would be inaccurate to speak of grassroots politics with reference to any Sudanese party, we can, nevertheless, conclude that the Umma maintained relatively more open channels for inputs and discussions—especially in the geographic sense—than the more autocratic PDPs and NUPs.

In terms of recruitment, all three parties failed to move beyond the first stage of mobilizing their "natural" clienteles in their respective localized strongholds. There seems to have persisted a

spirit of deference or, perhaps more accurately, hopelessness in the
prospects of making inroads in someone else's territory. As a
result, some portions of Blue Nile Province plus certain sectors in
the capital cities became the only areas of active party contests. It
is also interesting that the three parties made little more than token
efforts to organize supporters at Khartoum University and other
centers for potential new leadership; and it did not surprise any close
observers of the university scene that the traditional parties found
little resonance there.[*]

The degree of party unity was relatively similar for the three
core groups, if we compare them for the entire 1950s and 1960s.
Each party contained a conservative and a liberal wing, whereby the
conservative wings shared their commitment to traditional religion
and landed and mercantile interests. The liberal wings of the PDP
and NUP leaned more towards socialism, the first toward the
Egyptian variety and the second toward vague notions of Fabianism.
The liberal Umma faction represented a movement of mostly younger
educated persons with aims of turning the party from close identification with the imam and the past toward a more modern, nationalist
direction, perhaps similar in orientation to the Christian Democrats
of Western Europe.

The record of the roughly ten years of parliamentary politics
reveals the inability of the dominant parties to maintain internal
cohesiveness. The secession of the khatmiyyah faction from the old
NUP in 1956 has already been mentioned. The underlying reasons
for, and political effects of, this split will be described in greater
detail in Part II, as will the re-merger of these two factions into the
DUP in 1968. A similar treatment will be accorded to the intra-Umma
split from 1966 on into the Imam el-Hadi faction and the Sadiq faction
along with the ensuing consequences. What remains now is to consider
party effectiveness during elections, which is, of course, the most
crucial time for party performance. And it is in this issue area that
we can observe some of the Sudanese parties' most glaring weak-
nesses.

For one thing, there has been the rather haphazard way of fund-
raising, which showed very little organization at all, and depended
in large measure on voluntary contributions. These contributions
could come from various merchants, but also from foreign embassies,
depending on the timing of elections and foreign policy postures of the

---

[*] During Khartoum University Student Union elections along party
lines from 1966 to 1969, the highest score for Umma Youth was 6 percent, for NUP Youth 4 percent, and for PDP Youth 3 percent of the
total vote.[14] For more details, see Chapter 3.

rival parties. For example, it is no secret that the Egyptian government spent large sums of money on (and even made some personnel
available to) the NUP in 1953 and, to a lesser degree, the PDP in
1958. It has also been rumored strongly that the Umma party received
financial and technical support from Western nations in the 1960s. One
main reason for this sort of dependence has been the fiscal vulnerability of Sudanese parties in the absence of systematic dues collection.
A particularly drastic illustration was provided prior to the 1965
elections when the NUP president el-Azhari and his deputy Mubarak
Zarrouq decided to mortgage their houses in order to help defray the
party's campaign expenses.

A second weakness of Sudan's major parties has been their failure
to maintain active national organizations throughout the provinces
except at times of elections. This charge is less applicable to the
Umma party, which could after all rely on the ansar organization,
but hurt the NUP very much. A frequent complaint by Sudanese voters
was that they never saw party representatives except at election
times, when these "swarm out of Omdurman and descend upon"
provincial cities. But even that did not always happen. For example,
during the 1965 elections al-hai'ah al-'ammah of the NUP, an organization with "the sole function of election-machine" had no representatives of outlying provinces among its 234 members.[15] There
were virtually no registration drives by the NUP in the provinces
and very few organized rallies due to the party's weak financial
status.

A third weakness of the parties—one is tempted to call it an
indictment—has been revealed by their poor handling of the problem
of nominating candidates for territorial constituencies, with sometimes dramatic consequences. The only available data are from the
last two elections, but they illustrate our point very well: In the
case of 1965 the Umma party contested all 24 constituencies in Darfur
Province. It was represented by one candidate in only 8 of these and
in 6 by two; in 5 of the remaining districts there were three Umma
candidates, in 2 there were four, in 2 more six each, and in the last
one seven. One consequence of this disorder was that in constituency
no. 153 one NUP defeated six Umma men despite polling only 37 percent of the total votes. All told, there were 13 constituencies in
which the party that had obtained the largest percentage of votes
failed to win the assembly seat because of multiplicity of candidates.
The biggest loser was the NUP, which had to cede two constituencies
in Northern Province (no. 34 to an independent, no. 37 to an Umma),
one in rural Khartoum (no. 27 to the ICF), one in Darfur (no. 145 to
the Umma), and three in Blue Nile Province (nos. 81, 86, and 94 all
to the Umma). This Umma gain of five seats was more than offset
by a loss of six, namely two in Kordofan (no. 186 to the NUP, no. 188

TABLE 2.1

Number of Candidates by Party per Province, 1968

Province	DUP	Umma Sadiq	Umma Imam	Umma Total*	ICF	SANU	Southern Front	Socialists (combined)
Khartoum (13)†								
candidates	27	6	6	12	7	—	—	8
uncontested constituencies	—	7	8	4	6	13	13	5
Northern (17)								
candidates	44	9	4	17	4	—	—	3
uncontested constituencies	—	8	14	4	13	17	17	14
Blue Nile (45)								
candidates	73	42	48	95	4	—	—	10
uncontested constituencies	3	7	13	1	41	45	45	35
Darfur (24)								
candidates	20	41	38	82	2	—	—	1
uncontested constituencies	7	—	1	—	24	24	24	23
Kassala (23)								
candidates	38	13	9	24	4	—	—	7
uncontested constituencies	—	14	14	11	19	23	23	16
Kordofan (36)								
candidates	42	77	46	124	3	—	—	1
uncontested constituencies	—	—	4	—	33	36	36	35
Equatoria (20)								
candidates	18	17	7	30	2	3	14	1
uncontested constituencies	2	6	15	3	18	17	6	19
Upper Nile (18)								
candidates	21	13	6	29	—	18	12	1
uncontested constituencies	2	8	12	2	18	5	8	17
Bahr el-Ghazal (22)								
candidates	16	3	4	21	—	34	17	1
uncontested constituencies	8	20	18	10	22	1	6	21
Total (218)								
candidates	299	221	168	434	26	55	43	33
uncontested constituencies	22	70	99	35	192	181	178	185

*Umma total includes Sadiq, Imam wings plus "Umma general," which is not listed individually on this table.
†Parentheses indicate the total number of constituencies per province.
Source: Compiled by the author.

to an independent), three in Darfur (nos. 140, 147 and 153 to the NUP), and one in Blue Nile Province (no. 91 to the NUP). If we assume that each of these 13 constituencies had been carried by the party that actually obtained the largest vote total, then we may note the interesting result that the distribution of seats in the assembly would have remained almost the same, and that the geographic distribution would have been practically identical to the one in 1958. For example, the entire South and West of Kordofan would have been Umma territory except for the Nuba Mountains; in Darfur and Kordofan the NUP role would have been reduced to exactly that of 1958, and an exchange of constituencies in southern Blue Nile Province between Umma and NUP would have restored the 1958 pattern there, too.

Very similar patterns emerged for the 1968 elections; suffice it to present two of the most startling results: Constituency no. 59 in Blue Nile Province was won by the DUPs with only 27 percent of the vote against 72 percent of the two Umma factions, while constituency no. 49 in Northern Province was won by an Imam candidate with only 17 percent of the total vote against 65 percent of the DUP's. Incidentally, there were 44 DUP candidates in all, competing in the 17 electoral districts of Northern Province.

The most obvious reason for the phenomenon of multiplicity of candidates was the absence of primary elections as an instrument for determining a party's nominee. Upon inquiry, leaders of the two largest parties gave different reasons. Sayyed el-Azhari felt that prior to the 1965 elections "everybody expected a big NUP victory. Therefore, greedy individuals competed against each other as candidates, because they believed that anyone would win who was chosen by the NUP."[16] Umma officials explained that constituency committees did not function yet in 90 percent of the districts before the 1965 elections. Consequently, several men, each selected by a village committee, would apply to the province committee or to party headquarters for appointment as the party nominee in a particular constituency. However, in many instances the applicants were unknown to most members of either body, and it was decided that they should agree among themselves about the nomination. In the majority of cases agreement could not be reached, with the result that all or most applicants persisted in their candidacies.

At that time officials of both parties lamented this shortcoming and vowed to do better in the future. Alas, the evidence collected in Table 2.1 reveals an almost exact repeat performance in the 1968 elections. Undoubtedly, most DUPs again expected a big victory; in fact, in the case of the aforementioned constituency no. 49 several local clans in the rural Shendi area insisted on running their own tribal candidate in the expectation that any DUP would win there. Also, there is little doubt here that Umma constituency committees

again did not function well, but why not? We submit that the answer
to that question lies only partially in the lack of planning and inability
to enforce party discipline; an equally plausible factor is the charac-
teristically Sudanese tendency to assert personal independence at all
times from any individual other than a close relative, and especially
from orders of nonlocal administrators.

The Radical Parties

Although the Muslim Brotherhood and the Communist party of
the Sudan have been the deadliest of enemies during the past decade,
they also have shared several common characteristics. Both groups
began as clandestine organizations and were forced to continue that
way during their earlier years until after the 1964 Revolution. Both
groups have been strongly opposed by centrist governments as
"dangerous elements," and their leaders have received particularly
harsh treatment from the military regime of General Nimeiri. But
most important of all, both groups have appealed to essentially the
same strata of society, especially the younger educated, who have
become disillusioned with the repeated failures of traditional regimes
to solve pressing national problems. Their disillusionment centered
on both the goals and methods of traditional politicians, and culminated
in the conviction that these politicians will never be able to solve the
most pressing problems, because, for fundamental reasons, they and
their organizations were ill-equipped to deal with them. Thus, the
only alternative became a fundamental change in the approach to, and
the handling of, politics. At this point the two groups parted ways:
the Sudanese communists blamed all problems on "imperialism in
its various forms" and on the retention of "non-scientific methods;"
whereas the Muslim Brothers considered the prime cause of all evil
to be the intrusion of alien, that is, non-Islamic, concepts and practices into an Islamic society, all of which could be remedied only by
an eradication or "purification" of all alien innovations.

Organization

Because of the semiclandestine nature of both movements, the
information available so far has been spotty and often unconfirmed.
But we do know that the CPS first surfaced in the Sudan around 1946
under the disguise of various covers such as the "Sudanese Movement
for National Liberation," and the "Anti-Imperialist Front." It centered its original activities on the first recognizable industrial labor
group, the Sudan Railways workers, and also on some tenants in the
Gezira agricultural scheme.

The party was outlawed during the colonial and first postindependence regimes and was actively harassed by the Abboud junta.
The need to work underground plus the image of martyrdom among
young Sudanese urbanites actually combined to strengthen the party,
with the effect that it was the only well-organized political group at
the time of the 1964 Revolution. The organization itself followed the
pattern of other communist parties, emphasizing a tight network of
small cells. However, the major organizational achievement of the
CPS has been its ability to infiltrate executive committees of various
professional associations. This success was primarily due to the
communists' mastery of organizational techniques, which many had
acquired during periods of training in Eastern European countries.
Leadership formally resided in the Central Executive Committee,
but it has been assumed that most decisions were made by the party's
mastermind, the affable secretary-general Abdel-Kaliq Mahjoub.
After the latter's execution in July 1971, his position was reportedly
assumed by Muhammad Ibrahim Nugud. During periods of legality,
the party published its views in the Arabic-language Al-Midan (later
Al-Tali'ah) and the English-language Advance.

Meanwhile, the Muslim Brotherhood of the Sudan was founded at
Khartoum University in 1954/55 by some professors and students,
according to its leader, Hassan el-Turabi.[17] For the next nine years,
its social base continued to be purposely limited to students and
recent graduates "in order to retain the intellectual quality of the
movement."[18] After the October Revolution it was decided to start
some "kind of mass organization in order to participate in the upcoming elections." Because it was "undesirable to dilute the intellectual content of the movement by a large-scale absorption of
masses," the Islamic Charter Front (ICF) was formed. The Muslim
Brothers became the nucleus of this charter and determined its ideological direction, while "the masses were attracted by the Islamic
concepts." In the process the charter drew "many supporters from
enlightened groups in the NUP and among the younger Ummas." The
Muslim Brothers attempted to "draw people away from the sects
and to give them an alternative." They were convinced that the sects
"will be eroded by time and the spreading of education and democracy."

The Brotherhood has been tightly organized in individual cells
that conduct secret (that is, nonpublic) meetings in various locations
throughout the country. Its social and political views have been published in the ICF organ Al-Mithaq. Even though the former dean of
the Khartoum University Law School has been the most visible
leader as the Brotherhood president, the decision-making process in
the movement has been more collegial than in the traditional parties,
and usually includes the recognized intellectuals, who function as
party ideologues.

Appeal

   Predictably, the CPS attacked all other northern parties as reactionaries and rejected their policies as tools of Western imperialism,
notwithstanding a brief alliance with the PDP in spring 1965. It
advocated a Sudanized brand of communism supposedly not incompatible with Islam (as a gesture toward the many devout Muslims)[19]
along scientific socialist lines. This message fell on some receptive
ears among segments of workers and tenants in the Central Nile
region, and of students, teachers, and members of the new women's
organizations in the capital cities. During the height of its popularity
around 1970, the CPS had an estimated 6,000-8,000 members. The
party has succeeded in electing one member to parliament from a
territorial constituency in Khartoum Province, and a total of twelve
(including communist sympathizers) in the two elections for Graduates
constituencies.
   Its most volatile enemy has been the Muslim Brotherhood, which
categorically attacked all alien ideologies, and to whom communism
has been a special anathema. It advocated an Islamic constitution
and a return to the pure ways of old. The brotherhood was also
opposed to all forms of socialism because of their limitations on the
freedom of the individual. This opposition included denunciation of
Arab Socialism because it "was contrary to Islamic law." There
remains a suspicion, however, that the Brotherhood was motivated
to this stand by its enmity toward the Nasser regime, which had
oppressed Muslim brothers in Egypt.
   The ICF had a special appeal to university students. Dr. Hassan
interpreted this phenomenon as being caused by two main reasons:
"the example of good personal behavior, and the attractiveness of
the Charter's program." The former refers to the implementation
of the brotherhood code whereby "every member must practice Islam
on himself; in this way we try to improve society. Although we try
to improve the state itself, too, we concentrate our efforts on a
reform from within." The charter itself is very specific in describing
the steps that are necessary in order to bring about this reform from
within. Similarly, the charter outlines the policies that are necessary
to transform present society into an Islamic state. One reason why
many students are attracted to these programs is that the policies
and slogans are "not partisan, but national," and address themselves
to all problems of all Sudanese. "To us religion organizes one's
life. We cannot have a God who cares only for religion, but one who
cares for all aspects of life."
   With regard to interfaith relations, the charter claims that an
Islamic state does not threaten the interests of non-Muslims. "From
the beginning in Medina, Islam was a community of more than just

Muslims; there were Jews, Christians, and pagan Arabs as well.
Thus, an Islamic society need not consist of Muslims alone."
Dr. Hassan pointed out that he was among the first politicians to
propose a regional system of government for the Sudan after the
October Revolution. "After all, an Islamic state is one which does
not offend Muslims and does not offend non-Muslims. Southerners,
for example, should participate in politics not as Christians, but as
southerners. At present, the Muslims are offended by many practices
of the state, such as the condoning of prostitution, the public adver-
tisement of alcoholic drinks, and the practices of usury and gambling."
During the parliamentary elections of 1965 and 1968 the ICF received
its major electoral support from the Capital, Northern, and Eastern
provinces and nationwide slightly exceeded that of the radical left.

Performance

Given the very conservative nature of Sudanese society, both
radical movements have been rather effective during their relatively
brief history of working out in the open. Their movements had grown
during the 1960s, primarily because they focused on national issues
and capitalized on the younger generation's disillusionment with the
failure of traditional politics. Little is known about their recruitment
practices, except that they are aimed at secondary school and university levels.[20] Like other militant minority parties they have
shown greater internal cohesiveness than their larger rivals, and
their members have been more willing to contribute money and effort
to strengthen their organizations. It is also noteworthy that in 1968
the ICF in its 26 attempts, and the various leftist groups in their 33,
managed to avoid completely the multiple candidate problem that
had plagued them somewhat in 1965, albeit to a much lesser degree
than the major parties, as shown in Tables 2.1 and 2.2.

This is not to imply that all has gone well. The brotherhood
has undergone a small leadership crisis when some of its founding
members decided to withdraw after internal disputes in the mid-
1960s. Meanwhile, the CPS experienced an almost predictable split
into three wings: the orthodox Moscow oriented faction under Abdel-
Khaliq (until his execution in 1971), the Chinese oriented "revolutionary communist" faction, and a group professing "local,
Sudanized Marxism" without any ties or commitments to foreign
powers (identified with cabinet members Ahmed Suleiman and Farouq
Abu Issa). There can be no doubt that the CPS has included for some
time individuals who profess such theoretical priorities; what is not
so clear is the extent of the actual split within the movement, particularly in view of the many-sided attacks on communism from
within and without the Sudan. In this connection it should also not be

TABLE 2.2

Number of Candidates by Party per Province, 1965

Province	NUP	Umma	PDP	ICF	Communists*	Independents
Khartoum (13)†						
candidates	24	14	14	16	12	8
uncontested constituencies	—	2	1	—	3	—
Darfur (24)						
candidates	24	62	2	6	—	2
uncontested constituencies	4	—	22	18	24	—
Kassala (23)						
candidates	16	20	35	15	4	14
uncontested constituencies	8	10	—	9	19	—
Kordofan (36)						
candidates	60	70	14	18	5	19
uncontested constituencies	—	1	25	22	31	—
Blue Nile (45)						
candidates	71	77	35	22	28	6
uncontested constituencies	1	2	17	24	21	—
Northern (17)						
candidates	26	14	26	13	3	4
uncontested constituencies	—	4	1	4	14	—
Total (158)						
candidates	221	257	126	90	52	53
uncontested constituencies	13	19	66	77	112	—

*Category of Communists includes "sympathizers."

†Parentheses indicate the total number of constituencies per province.

Source: Compiled by the author.

overlooked that the CPS as well as the ICF have been financially
dependent on foreign contributors: the former from the usual sources
in communist countries and the latter from sympathetic regimes on
the Arabian peninsula.

The Regional Parties

A common theme among all regional parties from western, eastern, and southern Sudan is that they arose among the country's major
non-Arab peoples in response to perceived oppression, exploitation,
or neglect on the part of the "Arab-Nubian" dominated government
in Khartoum. Neither the Beja Congress from the Red Sea Hills
region, nor the Nuba Mountains Union from Southern Kordofan, nor
the Southern Liberal Bloc, constituted political parties in the classical
sense, but confederations of local groupings with limited objectives
and limited political activities. (The same argument holds basically
for the Southern Front and SANU, albeit to a lesser degree.)

Northern Movements

The first non-Arab political organization was the kutla as-suda
(Black Bloc), which was founded in 1938 by Dr. Adam Adham and
attracted followers primarily from educated Nuba, Fur, and fellata
living in the Khartoum area.[21] It was an association devoted to
furthering social and cultural interests of its members, not unlike
the Graduates' Congress during its earlier days. More significant
were the developments of 1954, when dissatisfaction among some
newly elected eastern and western parliamentarians over the policies
of the first Constituent Assembly led to the founding of the Nuba
Mountains General Union and the Beja Congress, headed by Dr. Belia.
Their initial strategy was to work within the established northern
parties, in the hope that bloc action would enable them to bargain for
regional interests on the party platforms. This strategy did not succeed, however, perhaps due to the inexperience of the bloc leaders
or to their lack of political clout. So by 1965, both groups decided
to contest elections as independent parties with specific proposals
that were written up in charters. For example, the Nuba Union constitution called for the unity of all Nuba, revival of the Nuba Mountain
Province as a separate administrative unit, abolition of the insulting
poll tax, a program of school construction for the western Sudan and
a policy of "Africanizing" Sudan rather than "Arabizing" it.[22] The
effective leadership of Philip Abbas among the Nuba and of Mohammad
Ahmed Awad and others among the Beja paid off in substantial election victories (see Chapter 7).

The Nuba proceeded to oppose the Mahjoub government's policies of military force in the southern Sudan and of pushing for an Islamic constitution. In January 1968 they formed a new bloc with SANU and Southern Front members of Parliament and submitted a list of 33 amendments to the proposed constitution calling, among others, for regional assemblies within a federal structure and for the removal of any allusions to Islam and Arabism.[23] Meanwhile, the 13 Beja parliamentarians moved into action in April 1969 when the three Congress members, one ICF, and nine delegates, who had been elected on the platform of the khatmiyyah based DUP, formed a parliamentary bloc and announced that they would henceforth support only those parties whose policies would bring improvements to their area.[24]

Yet despite their explicit platforms, cohesive organizations, and strong local support, both parliamentary groups were unable to accomplish their desired objectives. Although they could have benefited from superior leadership in parliamentary affairs (who couldn't?) their biggest drawback was that they were geographically limited in the number of potential assembly seats. The distribution of Umma-unionist members—in part due to khatmiyyah abstention—never permitted the regional groupings to acquire the necessary decisive roles in coalition schemes. The election returns of 1968 demonstrate that this message was not lost on local candidates or voters who continued to support their own men, although some had chosen to try out the alternative route of working within the more established parties (for details, see Chapter 7).

Southern Movements

The first southern political movement in recent history can be traced to 1951,[25] but did not take on concrete shape until 1953 with the founding of the Southern party. It won 9 out of the 22 assembly seats in the southern provinces, renamed itself the Liberal party in 1954 and remained the only formal southern party until the Abboud military regime outlawed all political activities in 1958.

After the junta was overthrown in October 1964, two new southern parties emerged on the political scene, and continued throughout the next five years as the major spokesmen for their region. One was the Southern Front, which drew heavily on southern civil servants and students in the Khartoum area. It was well connected to the Front of Professionals in the 1964 transitional regime and was thus able to land three ministerial positions in the first post-October cabinet and the southern member of the Supreme Council of State. The other was the Sudan African National Union (SANU), which grew out of an exile movement called SACDNU (Sudan African Closed Districts National Union) founded in 1962 by Father Saturnino,

Joseph Oduhu, and William Deng. In early 1965 SANU split into two factions, one headed by W. Deng and committed to working within the Sudan in the hope of thus affecting government policy, the other headed by Aggrey Jaden who returned into exile and attacked the alleged duplicity of both William Deng and the regime in Khartoum.

This exile faction had become convinced that a peaceful resolution of the southern conflict was unlikely and began to pursue a more militant policy vis-a-vis the Sudan government. Disagreement over tactics compounded by personality conflicts led to a further splintering of the group into an Azania Liberation Front (ALF) and a Sudan African Liberation Front (SALF); eventually they reunited in December 1965 as ALF with Oduho as president and Aggrey Jaden as vice-president.

The story of schisms within the exile movement continued as guerilla activities by the anya 'nya were stepped up inside the Sudan and the problems of military and political strategies mounted for an as yet disunited leadership. The Angudri Agreement of August 18, 1967 produced the South Sudan Provisional Government under Aggrey Jaden, in March 1969 the Balgobindi Conference in Yei District brought forth the Nile Provisional Government under General Tafeng, and it was not before the end of that year that the anya 'nya commander General Joseph Lagu brought the different rebel factions together in the South Sudan Liberation Movement.

We have listed these stations in the odyssey of the rebel forces as an illustration of the general problem that has afflicted southern politicians and their organizations during the past twenty years, namely an inability to unite, even in the face of the threatening powerful opponent. This inability has many root causes, but in this author's opinion results primarily from the persistence of tribalism in the South that apparently has prevented Dinka from trusting Shilluk or Bari or Nuer. An illustration of this point, also reflected by the admittedly inconclusive election data, is that SANU support has been particularly strong in Bahr el-Ghazal Province (main Dinka territory). The Southern Front leaders and their support stem mostly from Equatoria Province, as have most of the leading exile leaders, while the relatively conciliatory Buth Diu is a Nuer from Zeraf Valley.

There are other reasons for the general ineffectiveness of southern parties, which become clearer when we consider party performance in elections. Even if we grant the adverse security conditions and political instability in the South during the entire 1960s and before, and if we make further allowances for the lack of financial resources and poor communications networks, the fact remains that SANU and Southern Front won less than half of the assembly seats reserved for the southern provinces and managed to generate only 5.5 percent of the total vote during the 1968 elections. And these were the very two parties that had made continuous claims since 1964 about their great popularity back home as the true representatives of the southern people. This is not to imply that southerners prefer the northern parties even though those did outgain SANU and S.F. in mandates there. But it serves as an indictment for the organizational shortcomings of the latter two, if only in their failures to produce better registration drives and voting turnouts at a time when more than two-thirds of all seats were won with less than 2,000 total votes.[26] A further indication of inadequate organization has been the multiplicity of candidates, which bedeviled the southern parties almost as much as their northern rivals, as indicated in Table 2.1. And if the reader interjects accurately that many southerners had fled into the bush and therefore did not reside in their normal habitats, he must be reminded that the aggregate total of eligible northern voters then in the South was probably less than the number of wives of the combined southern chiefs.

One fatal flaw of all southern parties, which was just as present among the Beja and Nuba organizations, was that these movements were more characterized by their leaders' activism in Khartoum than by the presence of any ongoing organization; and no movement, regardless of how worthy its cause, can depend on its supporters' springing to life at election time if they have been ignored in the interim.

CONCLUSION

At the outset of this chapter we speculated about the effects of local identification on the establishment and growth of political organizations in the Sudan. We can conclude this study of political parties by examining the other side of this same coin, that is, the extent to which the parties have become national, or remained local, in orientation. One way of accomplishing this is by analyzing the geographic distribution of candidates per party, as depicted in Tables 2.1 and 2.2. This will enable us to obtain some better understanding of both the regional and nationwide efforts made by the various parties than a mere analysis of voting results would permit. (We are again confronted by the methodological problem created by the PDP "boycott" in 1965 and merger into DUP for 1968; but this should have little effect on the overall analysis.)

A comparison of the figures in Table 2.2 for the 1965 elections and Table 2.1 for the 1968 elections renders the following observations:

1. Khartoum was the most hotly contested province by all major parties, whereas Darfur was essentially fought over only by the Ummas and NUPs (DUPs).

2. The NUP-DUP had candidates in most constituencies (missing only 8 percent and 10 percent), followed closely by the Umma (missing only 12 percent and 16 percent).

3. The majority of all constituencies that were uncontested by the NUP in 1965 and the Umma in both elections were in Kassala Province, an obvious sign of deference to the (anticipated) strength of the PDP, which had entered candidates in all districts in 1965, and to the khatmiyyah/Beja strength in 1968. In fact, the three Umma factions were careful not to contest any Beja constituency in 1968.

4. Although Umma and PDP both base their support on regional and sectarian loyalties, the former attempted to become a "national" party whereas the latter did not.

5. The two southern parties contested only the three southern provinces in 1968, whereby the Southern Front spread its efforts more evenly than SANU, which was very Dinka-territory oriented.

6. The SANU strength in Bahr el-Ghazal Province seems to have been anticipated by the northern parties who had fewer candidates there percentagewise than in any other province.

7. The Islamic Charter Front concentrated its efforts on those regions that were known not to be areas of Umma strength. (This has led some observers to speculate about the relationship of the Umma and ICF presidents, who are brothers-in-law, and have at times shared the same house in Omdurman.)

8. The communists and other leftist groups contested one-third of all constituencies in 1965 and one-sixth in 1968, none in predominantly rural districts.

NOTES

1. The reader is referred to the rich literature on this subject in comparative politics, especially the writings of Samuel Huntington, David Apter, Myron Weiner, Gabriel Almond and Lucian Pye.

2. Among those that have been particularly useful to this author are C. G. and B. Z. Seligman, Pagan Tribes of the Nilotic Sudan (London: Routledge, 1932); E. E. Evans-Pritchard, The Divine Kingdom of the Shilluk of the Nilotic Sudan (Cambridge, Eng.: Cambridge University Press, 1948); and The Nuer (London: Oxford University Press, 1940); S. F. Nadel, The Nuba (London: Oxford University Press, 1947); Audrey Butt, The Nilotes of the Sudan and Buganda (London: International African Institute, 1952); P. T. W. Baxter

and Audrey Butt, The Azande, and Related Peoples of the Anglo-Egyptian Sudan and Belgian Congo (London: International African Institute, 1953); Francis M. Deng, Tradition and Modernization (New Haven: Yale University Press, 1971); Ian Cunnison, Baggara Arabs (London: Oxford University Press, 1966); Talal Asad, The Kababish Arabs (New York: Praeger Publishers, 1970). A very interesting account of life in a suburban village outside Khartoum is offered by Harold Barclay, Buurri Al Lamaab (Ithaca, N. Y.: Cornell University Press, 1964).

3. Asad, op. cit., p. 176.

4. For the most authoritative study of the Nuer, see Evans-Pritchard, The Nuer, op. cit.

5. Butt, op. cit., pp. 138-44.

6. F. M. Deng, op. cit.

7. For a better understanding of doctrinal matters, the reader is referred to J. Spencer Trimingham, Islam in the Sudan (London: Oxford University Press, 1949) and the various anthropolotical studies for the non-Muslim and marginally Muslim regions.

8. Ibid., chapters 5 and 6.

9. Ruth First, The Barrel of a Gun: Political Power in Africa and the Coup d'Etat (London: Penguin, 1971), pp. 266-67.

10. This information is based on a private talk with a high-ranking and extremely respectable Sudanese, who conferred with el-Azhari at the time in his role as leader of a Sudanese student organization. The source requested not to be identified.

11. First, op. cit., p. 138.

12. Speech by Ismail el-Azhari, March 17, 1965.

13. See also Trimingham, op. cit., p. 235.

14. See Salah el-Din el-Zein el-Tayeb, The Students' Movement in the Sudan 1940-70 (Khartoum: Khartoum University Press, 1971), pp. 17-18.

15. Statement by Director of NUP headquarters during an interview on June 8, 1966.

16. Interview with Ismail el-Azhari, July 4, 1966.

17. This statement stands in contrast to the assertion by Ishaq Musa Hussaini in The Moslem Brethren (Beirut: Khayat, 1956), pp. 82-83, that a "loose" branch of the Muslim Brotherhood was established in the Sudan in 1946 after a visit by some Egyptian members. According to other sources, the founder of the Brotherhood in the Sudan was Babikir Karrar. For a third interpretation that appears to be most plausible of all, see el-Tayeb, op. cit., p. 41. He reports that the Islamic Front was established in 1949, at which time it had no connections with the brotherhood in Egypt. In 1954 it split into two factions: the Islamic Group headed by Babikir Karrar and the Muslim Brotherhood, led by El-Rashid el-Tahir.

18. All quotations are based on a personal interview with
Dr. Hassan on July 2, 1966. Although I have spoken with other members of the brotherhood about their organization, the bulk of my
information is based on this interview.

19. According to an often repeated phrase by numerous Sudanese
communists. It has been reported that the flexible attitude of CPS
members toward Islam was symbolized by such things as having
prayer mats spread at party headquarters for the convenience of
pious members (see Haim Shaked, Esther Suery and Gabriel Warburg,
"The Communist Party in the Sudan, 1946-1971," in Michael Confino
and Shimon Shamir, eds., The U.S.S.R. and the Middle East [New
York: Wiley, 1973], p. 365).

20. El-Tayeb (op. cit., pp. 36-37) offers interesting reasons as
well as some historical data.

21. Philip Abbas Ghabashi, "The Growth of Black Political
Consciousness in Northern Sudan," Africa Today 20, no. 3 (Summer
1973): 32.

22. Ibid., p. 37.

23. Ibid., p. 40.

24. Morning News, April 23, 1969, quoted in O. Aguda, "Arabism
and Pan Arabism in Sudanese Politics," Journal of Modern African
Studies 2, no. 2: 187.

25. Oliver Albino, The Sudan: A Southern Viewpoint (London:
Oxford University Press, 1970), p. 31. For a summary of southern
political organizations, see Mohammad Omer Beshir, The Southern
Sudan: From Conflict to Peace (London: Barnes & Noble, 1973),
chapter 3.

26. The argument of government interference, as indeed
election data in general, by Oliver Albino, op. cit., just do not stand
up for any informed observer.

3

THE GROUP BASIS
OF POLITICS:
MODERNIZING ELEMENTS

It is first of all in the field of education that we look
for this creative up-surge—the true basis of our Revolution which will transform the social, economic and
political structure of our country and spread this liberating force through all walks of life. It is through education our nation will be reborn; it is through education
our people will learn the rights and obligations of
citizenship; and it is through education we shall produce
our intellectual and technical leaders and establish a
new relationship between nature and man and between
men themselves. . . .[1]

INTRODUCTION

A widespread view holds that so-called primitive or backward
societies are characterized by the pervasiveness of traditional values
espoused by their populations in almost all aspects of daily life, and
that such societies will modernize only if, and to the extent that,
education spreads. While such a view may have general validity, it
does not by itself help us to identify the interrelationships between
traditional and modernizing forces nor those aspects of a social
system for which educational growth can be dysfunctional. Furthermore, that view also implies a certain irrationality to traditional
behavior, whereas it seems just as plausible that, under certain conditions, adherence to traditional values may be a rational decision
even for educated individuals. Examples of this situation were
offered in the previous chapter, as in the case of educated civil
servants who found strength in continued ethnic associations because
of the heterogeneity of Sudanese society.

However, there can be little doubt that education per se constitutes the major variable that decreases the intensity of local, religious, and traditional-political ties as described in the previous chapter.
Concomitant with the breakdown of traditional ties and norms is the
search for new relationships; and in this sense education again plays
a major role by creating an awareness of group membership along
new and different lines, be they social, economic, or both. For
example, education is obviously the independent variable for the rise
of a (new) intelligentsia; it is also closely linked to the growth of
professional organizations, youth, and women's movements, and has
played a strong role in defining the human reservoir from which
civil servants and military officers have been drawn.

A second major force affecting backward societies has been
shown by anthropological and archaeological research to be economic
transformation of life-styles, such as from nomadic hunters to settled
cultivators, or from subsistence economies to cash crops and industrialization. In this case it is relatively easier for the observer to
measure economic impact, rates of change in selected areas, and
their varied payoffs, although economic change is usually accompanied
by social and psychological dislocations that are much more difficult
to quantify.

At this point we should clarify that normative prescriptions for
societal development are not among the objectives of this book, and
therefore the desirability of educational growth or certain economic
policies per se will not be assessed here. But we do want to assert
that these two variables individually and in interplay have contributed
to the emergence of relatively new groups in Sudanese society. These
are grounded in what we may call "modern" forms of associational
ties. ("Modern" is here not intended to connote "developed," but to
differentiate phenomena qualitatively from "traditional.") These
groups include the native intelligentsia, civil service, military
officers, the mercantile sector, trade unions, and other professional
associations. To the extent that the newly established single party
Sudanese Socialist Union draws its constituents from those groups,
it will also be included in the current chapter, rather than in the
previous one, which described the country's more traditional political
organizations.

The remainder of this chapter is devoted to brief surveys of the
roles, recruitment patterns, and interrelationships of these modern
groups amongst themselves and on politics in the Sudan in general.
In the concluding section we may speculate about the future potentials
of these groups, and about the direction of the ongoing struggle between these and the more traditional forces in Sudanese society.

THE INTELLIGENTSIA

From the Sudanese perspective the native intelligentsia would most probably be defined as including most of those who have graduated from secondary schools or higher. One should not conclude from this that exposure to certain levels of formal education turns Sudanese automatically into intellectuals by any means. Also, there are some genuine intellectuals in the country with little formal education, especially among poets and lyricists. Be that as it may, if one were to conduct a survey among Sudanese (both educated and illiterate), this author strongly suspects that the respondents would identify as intelligentsia those who have completed a certain level of formal education. Hence an analysis of the role of the intelligentsia should properly begin with an examination of Sudanese students as participants in the political process.

STUDENTS

For most of the Sudan's modern political history, students and recent graduates of institutes of higher education have been in the vanguard of various movements aiming to bring about political change.

In 1937 the Graduates' General Congress was founded as an association of Gordon Memorial College (later Khartoum University) graduates. Its original social and cultural functions were soon superseded by political activities and, in fact, the congress became the first overt native political organization in twentieth century Sudan[*] and served as the fountainhead for the independence movement and subsequent formation of political parties.

Soon thereafter, the congress developed an activist radical wing calling itself Ashiqqah—meaning "comrades" or "soul brothers" who had shared certain common experiences, especially in their school days. The Ashiqqah then became the backbone of the secularist National Unionist party (NUP), and its president, Ismail el-Azhari, the leader in the successful fight for independence.

---

[*] The White Flag League, founded by Ali Abdel-Latif in 1924, was more of an underground or semicovert society of a small number of Sudanese nationalists, who looked to tribal chiefs and religious notables for support. Its precursor had been the Union of Tribes' Society, founded by Ali in 1921.

More recently, some students have been in the forefront of opposition to the military regimes of Major Generals Abboud and Nimeiri, respectively. University students scheduled debates and seminars for discussing governmental policy on a variety of issues; others organized demonstrations with clear political overtones at times when antigovernment demonstrations were not permitted. While most of these activities included segments (albeit large ones) of the student bodies of Khartoum University, Cairo University—Khartoum Branch, and the Khartoum Technical Institute, some of the enthusiasm and organization spilled over to the Teacher's Training College in Omdurman and to several secondary schools.[*]

In each case the military regime has been careful not to overreact for fear of adding fuel to the students' fire. At the same time, the military has been conscious of the need to check such potentially dangerous sources of opposition. Army intervention on October 21, 1964, in open student discussions at Khartoum University led to some violent clashes and triggered the October Revolution that brought about the downfall of the Abboud regime. Ever since that time students have looked upon themselves as the vanguard of a progressivist, revolutionary movement and have been hailed as such by various leftist-leaning groups, including the Nimeiri junta at the outset. However, even that regime found it necessary in November 1969 and again in January 1970, at the height of its leftist-populist period, to counteract student rallies during which criticism of government policy was voiced. These events led to measures for bringing the university under tight control by the government. When students objected and raised the issue of academic freedom—which in this instance referred more to an expression of displeasure about the limitations on political freedom—the university vice chancellor was pressured into dismissing seventeen ringleaders and into issuing appeals to students for refraining from further antigovernment activities.

----

[*] Formal student organizations date back to about 1940 when the Higher Schools' Union was founded at Gordon Memorial College. (Incidentally, its first president in 1941 was Ahmed Kheir, subsequently foreign minister under Abboud, and the first vice-president, Mubarak Zarrouq, later a bulwark of the NUP and frequent cabinet member before his untimely death in 1965.) By 1947 secret groupings in secondary schools joined the College Union in a Sudanese Students' General Union. The former union changed its name to Khartoum University Students' Union after the formal establishment of that university in 1956 following independence.

Such stern action helped to cool off tempers, but not for very long. As government policies became more repressive, student reaction became more defiant. When matters threatened to get out of hand, President Nimeiri decided to intervene by personally appearing on the campus of Khartoum University and directly challenging student leaders to a confrontation (reliable reports indicate that this challenge included not only verbal confrontation); on several subsequent occasions the regime found itself unable to cope with the tension except by closing the campus down for extended periods of time.

Aside from these overt forms of political activism, the roles of students in political change can be observed through some of their explicit and implicit attitudes and orientations toward the social and political processes in their country. The following comments are not based on survey data but on a series of interviews and observations during a two-year period; because they do not result from in-depth research, they will be stated as broad generalizations.

As in most other countries, Sudanese students tend to associate with more radical views and organizations than the remainder of their fellow citizens. This situation is exemplified by voting results from two separate kinds of elections during the same year. The reader may recall that, in 1965, fifteen graduate constituencies had been set aside for educationally qualified voters. The overwhelming majority of the electorate was composed of university students and recent graduates. These men and women elected eight communists, two Muslim brothers, and five leftist "independents." By contrast, only three Muslim brothers and no communists were elected in the 158 territorial constituencies. In addition, this author personally observed in several polling stations the efforts of a considerable number of university students (both male and female) in voter registration, and voting "assistance" on election day, giving unmistakable instructions to their clients to vote for the extremist parties.

Shortly thereafter student council elections for the Khartoum University Students' Union (KUSU) in 1965, where candidates aligned themselves with existing political parties, yielded the following interesting results: 45 percent for the Extreme Left Alliance, 40 percent for the Extreme Right (Muslim Brotherhood), and only 15 percent for the traditional, moderate political parties that had obtained 94 percent of the popular vote in the recent parliamentary elections. During the next four years the electoral support for the traditional parties actually declined even further in KUSU elections.[2] The lesson here was fairly clear: Many young intellectuals felt frustrated about the unproductive and obstructionist tactics of old-line politicians in the face of mounting national problems. Moreover, there was virtually no one in the executive committees of the major

parties with whom students might have been able to identify; therefore, most of them became convinced that the prospects for making
their views felt by working within the system were dim indeed.

In private discussions over the years, this author has found
most students to be highly politicized even by European and Middle
Eastern standards, and verbally very committed toward certain
specific goals, yet frustrated about the apparent unlikelihood that
these goals could be achieved within the framework of the existing
social and political system in the country.

Politicization seemed to be unrelated to academic background;
the impression was that almost all male students took a much larger
interest in day-to-day politics than in their field of study. (Given the
nature of social customs, it was very difficult to speak with more than
a few female students, and any inferences about their views would
lack general validity. Female enrollments at Khartoum University
amount to about 10 percent of the total.) Students in the humanities
and social sciences seemed to be only slightly more sophisticated
in their analyses of these issues than students of professional
schools. In fact, almost all students who were observed reacted to
a sense of the inadequacy of, and/or irrelevancy in, the educational
system[3] and felt compelled to discuss their primary interests outside
the classroom in informal sessions. On the very few occasions when
such bull sessions were organized, the response and enthusiasm
were tremendous.

Student commitment to general progress seemed similar to
patterns found elsewhere in the Third World: Many students see
themselves as a vanguard for the people—the few fortunate ones who
had the opportunity of exposure to new and different ideas and institutions—and sense an obligation to challenge the various shortcomings of their societies. In a provocative article[4] Frank Pinner
has conceptualized two distinct functions in student behavior: trans-
gressive, that is, directed primarily against authority structures
(mainly found in disciplines requiring innovative research and independent thinking) and traditional, that is, socializing members into
roles as conventional citizens (mainly found in professional schools).
Our preliminary observations indicate that this distinction applies
only in a limited way to the Sudanese case. The majority of students
appeared to be rather ambiguous on those issues where ideological
commitment entailed personal involvement up to and including potential risks to their personal lives and careers.

While it is true that some students have been willing to pay for
their convictions with their freedom and a handful with their lives,
it is also true that many once-radical student leaders have been co-
opted rather quietly into the system upon or near graduation. One
very close acquaintance, who was known as a leader in the communist

student movement, confided that in his final year on campus he had to concentrate on obtaining a position with the Ministry of Local Government, not because it would afford a convenient base for attacking the system, but because of the various fringe benefits associated with the position. I might add that he justified this sort of behavior on the grounds that "everybody else is doing the same."

Similar attitudinal inconsistencies could be observed in other issue areas that potentially could affect the students' own future lives. They were in favor of liberating women, but not their wives; they admired the Egyptian life-style for its alleged progressivism, but did not recommend it to their own communities out of fear that the social price may be too high; northern students were very sympathetic toward their unfortunate brothers in the southern Sudan, but were not prepared to accept their southern colleagues as true equals in their own associations.

Many reasons account for these apparent inconsistencies, and they scan the spectrum from economic insecurity for the individual to the psychological insecurity of people who are caught up in the great revolution of social change that has been sweeping across Africa and the Middle East. Also, some aspects of student behavior may be explained as consequences of an inadequate educational and occupational system that has led most students to seek the "gentleman C" passing grade rather than a deeper search for knowledge in anticipation that personal contacts and not academic achievements would determine career opportunities after graduation.[5] This sort of situation breeds cynicism and frustration toward society at large and stimulates support for those groups within and outside the academic community that profess to expose and attack the existing hypocrisy.

Any conclusions about student activism must take account of the myriad causes, levels, and manifestations that only a comprehensive study grounded in an adequate methodological framework could reveal.[6] Given our self-imposed limitations, we may be left with little more than attempts at placing any conclusions within the comparative context of student activism elsewhere. From that perspective, Sudanese students were motivated into political action relatively less by academic institutional problems than were French or Germans in the late 1960s, less by international issues than were the Turks or Americans during that period, and more by domestic problems scanning the range from political and economic to social issues. Of course, we should not forget the psychological pressures of adolescence in general, and restrictive Sudanese social customs in particular.

Their activism rarely took the forms of petitions or other attempts to work within the system that are more common in

Northern European countries, nor the latent and covert frustrations experienced especially by their Egyptian colleagues, nor the small study groups popular in Eastern European universities, nor the forging of alliances with outside groups (workers, political parties) as practiced in some Latin American nations, but rather through the politicization of student unions and occasional mass demonstrations.

In terms of ideological commitment Sudanese students have been equally critical of British colonial policy, democratic politicians, military rulers, and so on, quite irrespective of their social background or future career goals. In contrast to most Lebanese and Egyptian students, the prospects of immediate cooptation into the system may have affected their style somewhat, but hardly the substance of their criticisms and, if at all, only near the very end of their academic careers, again a reflection of the considerable importance that the Sudanese attach to their rights of freedom of expression.

We can sum up these conclusions by noting that Sudanese students have at least considered themselves to be in the forefront of political change. While it seems true that these students have had somewhat exaggerated notions about the extent of their actual influence on politics—for example, by 1964 the Abboud regime was ripe to be overthrown with or without student help—it is nevertheless correct that some student groups have acted as catalysts for political action. In other instances future policies, including revolutionary ones, have been spawned in student discussion seminars, and we can expect that student opinions and activities will in all likelihood determine to a not inconsiderable degree the stability of the current and of future regimes in the Sudan.

PROFESSIONALS

Students who persist in their work eventually graduate into the various professions. The renowned Sudan scholar Peter M. Holt reported from an earlier experience as a long time member on a selection board of a secondary school, that he observed the following occupational choices (during the last decade of the colonial period). The best batch of secondary school graduates opted for the Kitchener School of Medicine, the next best went to the Law School, a few good eccentric types to the School of Agriculture (to be promoted to executive positions in agricultural schemes), the large mass to the School of Arts, who then became civil servants or teachers, and the "very bottom" group joined the Military College of the Armed Forces.[7] Although manpower requirements after independence effected some realignments in career opportunities—for example, various secondary

school teachers found themselves as attaches and counselors in the
diplomatic service just as six years earlier there had been a mass
exodus of teachers to the Gezira Board as block inspectors—the
basic pattern described by Holt has persisted on the undergraduate
level. The only significant change has taken place in the availability
of graduate programs at Sudanese universities and in the increasing
Sudanization of their academic staffs. To a lesser degree, the Military
College has attracted a few of the brighter students in recent years,
once the potential for upward mobility through a career in the armed
forces became clearer.

Strictly speaking, members of the native intelligentsia could be
found in all six of the above mentioned occupational groupings, and in
several other minor ones as well, but local opinion does not consider
the military or standard civil service sectors as possessing such
exalted status. It behooves us therefore to respect such wisdom and
to treat these groups separately below, and to reserve the remainder
of this section for a brief discussion of the political roles of edu-
cators, doctors, lawyers, and professionals in the mass media.

It would not be fair to blame (or praise) Sudanese professors
for the previously described politicization of their students. As a
group, Sudanese professors seem to be no more politically oriented
than their colleagues elsewhere and, if anything, more conservative,
simply by not being as overwhelmingly liberal as European and
American professors are by comparison. In fact, a good number
have prided themselves on being ''strictly neutral'' or ''completely
disinterested'' in politics. On the other hand, a distinctive feature
of a fair number of Sudanese professors is that those among them
who admit to an active interest in politics are not satisfied with the
more traditional roles of observers and critics—although these exist,
of course—but they display ambitions for direct participation through
high political offices or as active consultants to leading politicians,
or underground opposition leaders, as the case may be.

The image of the agitating egghead-philosopher who misleads
innocent youth, so well-developed in the minds of right wing conserv-
atives, applies more to some Egyptian faculty members at the
Khartoum Branch of Cairo University and to certain secondary school
teachers in the major cities, to the extent that it is at all applicable
in the Sudan. These ''propagandists'' have always constituted a
rather small percentage in their profession, even in the days of the
anticolonialist movements. In recent years, they have been credited
with disseminating leftist-socialist and conservative Muslim Brotherhood ideologies among students in urban areas and boarding schools,
with remarkable effectiveness at the secondary school level.

Lawyers and doctors occupy not only two of the most desirable
professions, as indicated in the career choices by students, but also

have had a disproportionately large influence in national politics, both
individually and through their associations. It is not unusual that
many lawyers have played prominent roles during the periods of
parliamentary democracy, because a background in law offers several
well-known advantages to ranking as well as aspiring politicians. The
rosters of political party executives are dotted with members of the
Sudan Bar Association, ranging from the late southern communist
Joseph Garang on the left to the northern ICF president Hassan el-
Turabi on the right.

In addition, the Sudanese courts have for many years maintained
a position of independence from the regime in power and were thus
able to affect political developments via the judicial process. The
courts proved their independence from government leaders time and
again. A clearcut example—and one not easily duplicated elsewhere
in Africa or the Middle East—was provided by the High Court verdict
to invalidate the government's decision in 1965, which had been backed
by an overwhelming assembly vote, to outlaw the Communist party
and to unseat its delegates in parliament.

Beyond that, the Sudan Bar Association has been an active and
vigorous association whose public positions have always been
respected by the body politic. In terms of sheer influence it probably
reached its zenith during the aftermath of the October 1964 Revolution
when it formed one of the pillars of the Front of Professional Organizations, which negotiated successfully the transition from military to
civilian rule.

One of its allies at that time was the Doctors' Association,
although it has never participated to the same extent in public affairs
as an organization. However, many of its members have been surprisingly active individually, so much in fact that many an observer
could not help but wonder about the intensity of political engagement,
which at times reached the point among some doctors of even closing
down clinics in order to pursue what seemed to be their first love.

Unlike their colleagues in most Western countries, Sudanese
doctors who can be described as politicized have tended to espouse
socialist principles; in actuality, some of the most active communists
in the Sudan belong to the medical profession. In this connection an
interesting hypothesis can be presented that may be worthy of further
study: although this writer lacks the statistical evidence, he has been
very much under the impression that most socialist-leaning doctors,
and those lawyers and other professionals who share this ideological
perspective, seem to have received their advanced training at
Egyptian universities.[8]

Speaking of Egypt, in recent years the engineering profession
has gained tremendously in stature there as well as in political
influence.[9] Despite the growing demand for engineering skills in the

Sudan, the leaders and rank-and-file of this profession have confined their public positions to technical matters. Theirs and similar other professional associations have refrained from overt or covert participation in political disputes, and their members, by and large, seemed to have adopted the same principle.

The only noteworthy exceptions to this rule have been journalists and members of the broadcasting services, whose daily routines require considerable attention to public affairs. The Sudan Broadcasting Service (Radio and Television) has always been government controlled, and its policies established by the Ministry of Information and Guidance. Local newspapers have experienced many ups and downs, not only in terms of their generally weak financial status, but also due to the fluctuations of government censorship, which ranged from strict control during periods of military rule to heights of press freedom during the middle and late 1960s. Because of their relatively small circulation, limited in part by the low level of literacy nationwide, Sudanese newspapers have not had the kind of propagandizing effects as those in Egypt, for example. The major journalists of the Arabic dailies are well known only in the three towns, and their impact on the shaping of public opinion, even during the heydays of democracy, has generally been quite small.

THE WOMEN'S MOVEMENT

It is difficult to think of another country in which women have had to combat as many obstacles toward social and legal equality of the sexes despite their many material contributions to the national welfare. In most parts of the Sudan women have carried not only the normal burden of raising generally large families, but also the physical burden of cultivating and harvesting crops, as well as the literal burden of carrying water overhead from wells to their dwelling places.

All along they were expected to defer to men in almost all areas, to the point of being excluded from their husbands' social life, to the concrete humiliation of having to use separate doors (along with the servants) to their separated quarters in the family compound. Other examples of social restrictions on Sudanese women have already been presented in Chapter 1 of this book; suffice it here to cite the anguish expressed so well by the feminist author Zeinab el-Fatih el-Badawi, which illustrates the frustrations of many Sudanese women:

When the women's movement started in 1947 we felt at that
time that the Sudan was the most disagreeable of all countries in which to be born a woman. Women in the mass
were isolated in the harem, absorbed in their engrossing
household duties, with no education, and with superstition
as a dominating power in their lives. Girls, backward and
uneducated, had to endure the inhuman operation of phar-
aonic circumcision, their right nostrils were pierced to
hold heavy wedding rings, their lips were tattooed, and
they had to go through the agony of the eventful forty days
of the marriage. Marriages were arranged between parents,
divorce and polygamy were practiced without any restrictions. The dominant status of the men was maintained
largely on the basis of the humiliation suffered by the
women.[10]

As had been the case with Sudanese men, the women's political
movement evolved from a cultural organization (the Educated Girls'
Association, founded in 1947 as a parallel to the Graduates' General
Congress of 1937), which in turn owed its existence to the growth of
girls' education in the country. This can be traced back to 1911,
when the father of girls' education, Sheikh Babikir Badri, opened the
first elementary school for girls in Rufa'a; other milestones were
the establishment of a Nurses' Training College in Omdurman (1925),
the opening of intermediate (1941) and secondary (1945) schools, and
the admission of three women students to the University of Khartoum
(1949).

Two years later the Sudanese Women's Union was established by
a relatively small number of educated women who were determined
to campaign for greater equality among the sexes. Their early
strategy was aimed at abrogating unfair legal treatment, especially
in divorce cases, but also in employment opportunities. The movement remained rather small and ineffective until it began to politicize
its demands by promising to support those political parties who
endorsed its major objectives. This opportunity arose in the post-
October days when the explicit militancy of some women's leaders
(in street demonstrations and work stoppage among nurses, for
example) earned them the respect of menfolk in the capital area,
and subsequently helped to win female suffrage. As it turned out,
the traditional center and conservative right wing parties ignored
the women's cause, and some of them actually tried to block their
voting rights; so it was not surprising that many educated young

women heeded their leader's[*] call and aligned themselves with the socialist and communist force of the left, who alone had promised to fight for women's rights and their integration into a modern society.

The data from the microstudy in Omdurman South (in the Appendix) reveal the impact of Sudanese women's organized efforts in one particular instance (during two elections in Omdurman) despite their not being taken very seriously at the outset by the male leadership. How and to what degree this newly found strength can be translated into continuing influence depends on many different factors, including the quality of future leadership and the responsiveness of the male establishment to this potential force. The regime of President Nimeiri has consistently made a point of recognizing the contributions of Sudanese women, and has included some of their leaders, such as Sitt Nafisah Ahmed el-Amin, in high government positions.

Just the same, the effectiveness of this, or any, feminist movement depends very much on the capabilities of its leaders in choosing their issues carefully as well as the necessary good judgment for refraining from actions that might alienate the powerful establishment and thereby become counterproductive. During the second parliamentary period the Women's Union opposed the conservative parties' plans for an Islamic Constitution, which effectively would have slowed feminist progress. This policy plus the enthusiastic support for the May 1969 Revolution earned initial appreciation from the Nimeiri regime, but the honeymoon was shortlived. In December 1970 President Nimeiri himself addressed the fourth women's conference at Khartoum University and admonished the union for its "politicized nature,"[11] and subsequently dissolved it along with the youth movement and Trade Union Federation in line with a general crackdown on leftists; the task of representing and organizing these groups was now given to the newly created Sudanese Socialist Union.

In retrospect it is interesting to note the changing tactics for permanent issues: In his volume on the life-styles of the Baggara Arabs,[12] Ian Cunnison reports a number of incidences of how in the old, traditional days women could influence men by spreading songs about them—heroic songs if they were brave, and mockery if they failed. And it appears that in the more modern times of the ballot box and the protest demonstration, Sudanese women continue to attract attention to their cause, at considerable risk to those men who might otherwise be disposed to ignore them.

---

[*]Sitt Fatima Ahmed Ibrahim, later elected to the Constituent Assembly by the graduates.

TRADE UNIONS

The labor movement in the Sudan exhibits several parallel features to the women's movement, especially in the areas of organizational growth and leadership orientation. Both movements evolved at nearly the same time and in a largely hostile environment, both opposed the conservative governments' policies during the first 15 years and formed pillars of support for the May 1969 Revolution, and in the end both ran afoul of the Nimeiri regime's efforts to broaden its popular base.

As had been the case with all political organizations in the Sudan, the first traces of the labor movement date back to the establishment of social and cultural clubs—the workers' clubs in Atbara (1934) and Khartoum (1935). The renowned Sudanese scholar Saad el-Din Fawzi attributed their importance to the fact that "they gave impetus to the emergence of industrial labour as a self-conscious class and provided much-needed centres for workers' activities."[13] The movement itself started in the summer of 1946 with two nearly simultaneous events: large numbers of Gezira tenants, of whom there were then 25,000 in all, went on strike over financial matters, and in the railroad hub Atbara a Workers' Affairs Association was founded, mostly by railroad workers. Further strikes ensued during the next two years, which contributed to the Sudan government's decision to promulgate a trade union ordinance in 1948. Within less than a year, workers' groups began to draft their organizational rules and to apply for registration. The first successful group was the Sudan Medical Association, which obtained registration on December 17, 1949;[14] during the next six years it was followed by more than 130 local and national unions, and by 1972 the official register listed 562 trade unions.[15]

Individual unions had originally been linked together in the so-called Workers' Congress (1949), which soon developed into the powerful Sudan Workers' Trade Union Federation (SWTUF) in 1950. For much of its official life span this federation has been able to play a more active role in, and leave a greater mark on, public affairs in its country than most of its counterparts in Africa and the Middle East. This phenomenon can be traced to at least two of its traits: the composition of leaders and membership on one hand, and the tactics employed in various confrontations with government or private management on the other. (In terms of sheer numbers, civil servants have constituted approximately three-fourths or more of the organized labor force.)

Regarding the latter, Saad el-Din Fawzi has identified as one of its most "significant characteristics the intense militancy of the movement, reflected in its excessive use of the strike weapon,"[16] resulting in the loss of 1,750,000 man-days between 1947 and 1952 alone.[17] Admittedly, in those preindependence years some strike issues had grown out of the psychology of the anticolonial struggle; but even after 1956 (except for periods of military rule) the damage caused by striking labor in the Sudan was extraordinarily large by Middle Eastern standards, and contributed to the decisions of the Abboud and Nimeiri juntas to interdict work stoppage. On the other hand, it must be acknowledged that union demands in the Sudan have frequently been met by employers, so much so that at least one observer has described labor legislation regarding pay, hours, paid vacations, and retirement benefits to compare favorably with that of Western Europe at that time.[18]

Most of the credit for the attainment of these benefits must go to the movement's leadership, which was made up primarily of full-time professionals who had been trained abroad in organization of labor, bargaining, and confrontation tactics. Because of their organizational skills on one hand and superior educational qualifications on the other, a sizable gap developed soon between these labor leaders and the masses of mostly illiterate workers. This high rate of illiteracy, coupled with worker satisfaction about SWTUF accomplishments, contributed to an atmosphere of apathy among most members toward union management, and thereby gave an "unduly large measure of power to a limited number of activists.[19] (Chalk up yet another score for Robert Michels!)[20]

All available evidence points to the fact that most, though not all, labor leaders at the executive level of the SWTUF were communists, despite the fact that extremely few of the rank-and-file subscribed to this ideological stance. As early as 1952-53 the Labour Department's Annual Report referred to SWTUF leaders as "self-avowed communists,"[21] and Saad ed-Din Fawzi in his comprehensive study of the labor movement was forced to conclude on their "virtual identity of views with those of the Communists" at home and abroad, also indicated by SWTUF's close alignment to communist-oriented labor groups on the international level,[22] and the Sudan Movement for National Liberation, an underground communist organization,[23] domestically. This pattern persisted for much of the following twenty years and received renewed publicity through the public hanging of SWTUF president Shafieh Ahmed el-Sheikh as part of President Nimeiri's proclaimed "Communist hunt-down" following the abortive July 1971 coup against his regime.

The phenomenon of noncommunist rank-and-file support for communist leaders in the workers' councils must be attributed to the fact that these leaders alone had campaigned for the welfare of Sudan's working classes, while the major political parties continued

to rely on sectarian or personalist loyalties. During earlier decades
these traditional loyalties outweighed new class consciousness, as
demonstrated by the parliamentary election results in 1953, 1958,
and to a lesser degree in 1965.* Throughout the first postindependence
decade the leftist leadership would regularly win electoral support
on labor-related issues in the industrial centers of Atbara, Khartoum
North, and the heartland of the Gezira Tenants Union in Blue Nile
Province, but rarely in local council or general assembly elections.
This pattern began to change noticeably in the middle and late 1960s,
when parliamentary election results in those areas clearly revealed
a lessening of traditional ties or a growing class consciousness
among workers or, in all likelihood, both.

THE MERCANTILE SECTOR

On the other end of the economic spectrum is the mercantile
sector, which has not yet emerged as significant in either the political,
financial, or social affairs of the Sudan. It would be beyond the scope
of this book to examine all the causes for this condition; suffice it to
point to the overwhelming share of traditional agriculture and pastoral
activities in the Sudanese economy (according to the last population
census more than 85 percent of the active population were engaged
in agriculture, forestry, and fishing)[25] and the fact that the largest
economic enterprises—agricultural plans like the Gezira, Geneid,
and many others, and Sudan Railways as the largest employer of
industrial labor—have always been government controlled.

Consequently, the private sector beyond the small shopkeeper
level has consisted primarily of a rather small number of local
merchants plus some import-export businessmen and the odd agricultural landlord. While a few of these have become wealthy, their
family assets can in no way measure up to those of rich Arabs or
Africans in neighboring countries. Whatever wealth has existed did
not suffice for a socially distinct upper class to emerge. I should
hasten to add that this latter phenomenon must be linked in some
degree to the generally egalitarian nature of Sudanese society which
frowns on conspicuous consumption, but also to the unavoidable

---

*In 1953 the Atbara workers voted in a solid bloc for the candi-
date backed by their sectarian leader, while the then executive
officer of the Sudan Railways Workers Union, one of the most prominent trade union leaders, got negligible support in his own headquarters in Atbara.[24]

fact that the environment offers little incentive or opportunity for a
life of luxury. As a result of their rather ascetic life-styles extending
even to consumption patterns for food, clothing, and entertainment
gadgets, the few wealthy Sudanese have never gained the sort of visi-
bility of Egyptian pashas, Ethiopian landlords, or Nigerian merchants,
for example.

This is not to imply that there are no rich persons in the Sudan,
or that they have no influence; but wealth has been perceived in a
relative vein, and its influence on other people remained primarily
local, especially in the vast rural areas of the North and South.

From the perspective of Sudanese politics, the mercantile sector
has been rather closely associated with the National Unionist party,
both as a source of financial backing as well as a means to gain
favorable access to import and export licenses. A perusal of key
positions in the Ministries of Commerce and Industries and Supplies
reveals them as strongholds of the NUP patronage system, at least
before the May 1969 Revolution. It is noteworthy that the Nimeiri
regime's intermittent policy of nationalizing Sudanese banking institutions and the few large private enterprises has turned into an
economic disaster; one reason, undoubtedly, was the new government's failure to appreciate the functionality of the allegedly corrupt
big merchant-NUP-Sudan Customs Department network for the
country's economic welfare.

THE CIVIL SERVICE

As in many other countries, the Sudan government, too, has been
the single largest employer; and the civil service has provided in
many ways the most direct form of contact for the ordinary person
with his government. Because of the central role assumed by the
state in the development plans of many Third World nations, the performance of the national bureaucracy becomes a major determinant
of progress, given the parameters that are imposed by the availability
of natural resources and the quality of political leadership.

It cannot be the objective of this book to examine the performance
of the Sudanese civil service, but an understanding of its role as an
element in the country's political life requires some sort of explanation for the apparent decline in the service's quality, because this
decline appears to be linked directly to certain policies of civilian
and military regimes.

It must be stated at the outset that the Sudanese civil service
enjoyed one of the finest reputations in the entire British Common-
wealth at the time of the country's independence, and has even been

compared favorably with the Indian civil service by some observers. Alas, with the passage of years a noticeable drop in performance became painfully obvious to even the most sympathetic Sudanophile. The fault did not lie with any one factor, as usual in such situations, and apologists could point to the normal drop in public service efficiency and educational standards after the departure of European colonial masters. However, the problem in the Sudan went much deeper, and by the 1970s there was widespread criticism from nearly all quarters.

A Nigerian political scientist at Khartoum University attributed the poor performance of civil servants chiefly to the unwillingness of their superiors to enforce discipline. He argued quite convincingly that their unwillingness results partly from local cultural traits, which urge that everyone should be on easy and accommodating terms with everyone else.[26] Family connections are also cited as promoting such behavior, since most of the country's public servants come from a relatively small area of the north, along the Nile.

But there are additional reasons for the bureaucracy's decline that have to do with political decisions of successive regimes. Probably the most harmful of these have been the series of purges of top-level bureaucrats following each newly proclaimed revolution in 1958, 1964, and 1969. These affected men of almost uniformly advanced training, great experience, and generally high standards of excellence, whose dismissals were usually based on nothing more than their "cooperation" with the previous regime.

A second factor has been a recruitment policy over the years that violated many principles of sound public administration. Not only was an individual appointment to a given position often more a function of ascriptive ties than achievement, as has happened in many other Third World countries, but overall recruitment policies resulted from political expediency rather than market demands. Examples are the mass hiring of thousands of school and university graduates prior to elections, also the across-the-board hikes of civil service salaries at times of political unrest—especially during military rule—in the face of inadequate financial resources. The outcome was overstaffing in just about all government offices with the now predictable result of output dropping to ever lower levels. It was an all too common sight for a visitor to find government employees either late for work, or departing early for some undefined "mission," or those who were actually at their crowded desks circulating the daily newspapers among themselves, while blue-covered files mounted before their eyes, only to rest undisturbed at great length under the ever present stone weights.

A third political factor for the decline in the bureaucracy's overall performance has been the enormous increase in the scope

of government activities. This particular point may be debatable
from a developmental perspective, but this author is inclined to
agree with Aguda's charge that state activities have been too extensive for the existing machinery to handle, while at the same time the
private sector has been actively, if unwittingly, discouraged.[27] This
has become particularly obvious after the large nationalization programs of private enterprises and banks by the Nimeiri regime. In
fact, both military juntas have been susceptible to the temptation of
ruling by decree; and because they perceived their military efficiency
to be superior to that of any civilian organization, the end result was
frequently a proliferation of programs and projects.

If administration under military rule suffered from having bitten
off more than it could chew, the problem during parliamentary periods
concerned more an apparent inability to select the proper tableware
for attacking the meal. At times it appeared that, regardless of the
issue at hand, civilian cabinet members could think of no alternative
but to appoint committees rather than, for example, to tackle the
matter with the available government machinery. The mushrooming
of committees is aptly described and decried in an article in the
daily El-Sahafa:

> In our country the Minsters believe that the people have
> no brains. The Minister of Communications announced
> that he will set up an investigation committee in the spe-
> cific criminal charges he made before the Assembly.
> What is the need for the committee while the Attorney
> General has a big office? . . . Then MP Abu Sineina
> announced that a Bor [a Dinka section] is beseiged by
> rebels. The Minister of Interior said he will set up a
> committee to investigate . . . a telephone call to the
> Armed Forces in Bor will reveal the truth or falsehood
> of the news. We are tired of these committees. We no
> longer believe in their usefulness or effectiveness. We
> believe that committees are set up usually for serious
> issues to hide them under the carpet.[28]

One consequence of this sort of pussyfooting has been a deterioration of civil service morale and ensuing lack of interest because
challenging tasks were not delegated to the local specialists. But
this was not the only reason for deterioration of morale. Toward the
end of the Abboud regime it had become increasingly apparent that
senior civil servants despaired of taking orders from frequently
ill-prepared and ill-advised military governors. When verbal requests
for a discussion of policy alternatives produced no satisfactory response, some senior officials simply withdrew into a pose of lethargy

and others began to sabotage junta schemes by slowing down the
bureaucratic machinery to all but a halt. The Nimeiri regime has
attempted to reorganize the civil service by realigning responsibilities at the cabinet level. (The twenty-seven ministries were organized
into six fundamental groups according to functional affinities.) But
unless it succeeds in reinstilling the long lost esprit de corps, the
structural change will accomplish little by itself.

THE MILITARY

Because the role of the army in Sudanese politics is a major
subject of Parts II and III of this book, we shall confine ourselves in
this section to a brief discussion of the military as an emerging
class.

It is probably correct to argue that members of the military
have developed a more distinct class consciousness at an earlier
time than any other of the groups discussed in this chapter. This
is particularly true of the officer ranks where the new sense of
identity, symbolized by the national uniform, has just about displaced
ethnic and sectarian allegiances, especially the latter. This is not
to imply that military officers have been ignorant of, or uninterested
in, the social backgrounds of their colleagues—far from it; yet such
knowledge takes more the form of awareness than perspective, and
differs sharply from the level of kinship/distrust felt by civilian
leaders in government and private enterprise.

The strong sense of group identity originates in part from a
sense of distinctness from the civilian sector that had been associated
with responsibility for most of the country's ills, but also in part
from a proud fighting tradition. This tradition goes back to a strong
warrior heritage among many ethnic communities (kept alive through
numerous folk songs and legends) on one hand, and to the distinguished
fighting record of Sudanese forces in World War II in North Africa,
and especially against the Italians along the Ethiopian border in
1940-41. The combination of traditional values and good field performance have made an attraction out of the military service: after
independence it was not uncommon that ten applicants vied for one
billet in the volunteer service.[29]

Noticeable Sudanese control over the development of their military sector dates to 1925 with the official designation of the Sudan
Defense Force, which eventually has been distributed throughout six
regional centers. In the early years most regional centers developed
their own politico-military identities, especially through strong
recruitment of particular ethnic groups, but this tendency was

reversed after independence in order to foster a greater sense of national awareness. (Undoubtedly, one contributing factor to this policy was the soul-searching following the outbreak of mutiny in the Equatoria Corps in 1955.)

Rising defense and internal security demands necessitated an enlargement of the military establishment over the years, and in 1972 a record 512 officers graduated from the Military Academy, as contrasted with about sixty during the 1950s.[30] It is thus not surprising that the previously rather high standards of training could not be maintained in all cases, but the rapid growth of the army, losses, and defections incurred in the southern operations, and purges or resignations following several coup attempts all had taken their tolls.[31]

Despite some allegations to the contrary, social background has not played a significant role either in officer recruitment or promotions, especially if we compare the Sudanese case with the recent examples of nearby Uganda (under General Idi Amin) or Syria (with the disproportionate influence of Alawites). This is not to deny that there has been a severe shortage of southern officers (and enlisted men) during at least the past twenty years, and that some northern tribes, particularly the Shaiqiyyah, have been very prominent in providing ranking officers during the first postcolonial decade. What must be kept in mind here is that admission to the military academy required successful graduation from secondary schools, and the geographic distribution of these schools in the Sudan has favored the inhabitants of the Nile region in the northern and central Sudan.

A quite different situation has obtained for enlisted men prior to the announcement of compulsory service in 1971. Local population pressures for inhabitants of economically poor regions made the military a desirable career especially for such as the Beja tribesmen of the eastern desertlands and Nuba hill dwellers from southern Kordofan; both have acquired excellent reputations as loyal and fearless soldiers, and have taken considerable pride in these accolades.

A particular strong point of enlisted soldiers has been their unquestioned loyalty to the national emblem and abstinence from involvement in partisan politics (except for the southern rebellion, which constituted a special politico-psychological problem for northern soldiers). A similarly apolitical orientation can be credited to most, though obviously not all, members of the officer ranks. This statement must strike many readers as paradoxical in the face of two successful military interventions in parliamentary democracy. What we intend to suggest here is that first, the coups d'etat were carried out by a small number of officers with no evidence of complicity by many colleagues. Second, even though most officers (not all) eventually agreed to support military rule in principle as a crisis measure, they did so because of their rather uniform contempt for civilian politicians; also, they had little choice but to go along with the new rulers. Third, and most important for our argument, the Sudanese officer corps (at least prior to 1969) has not had the sort of conspiratorial tradition of Syrian, Egyptian, or other Arab colonels who seem to delight in factional alignments and plotting the undermining of opposition groups.

Lest the wrong impression be created, it must be admitted that, once the military had gained formal control of the government, many officers retained a vested interest in securing some spoils of the system for themselves, while others were visibly proud to be associated with political decisions about their country's destiny.

There can be no doubt that foreign and domestic developments of recent years have affected the composition as well as the political attitudes of military officers. Involvement in anti-Israeli campaigns on the Suez Canal and in Equatoria Province,[32] exposure to Arab-socialist ideas during training programs in Egypt and at home, plus the effects of a more "Arabized" educational system than their elders had experienced, all combined to increase the politicization of junior officers. These factors were reinforced by the domestic upheavals of 1969-71, during which Ja'far Nimeiri's narrowly based regime progressively alienated first conservative and then left-wing support, and had to rely increasingly on the armed forces for political survival. The politicization of the military reached its zenith (in twentieth century Sudanese history) when the government decree of October 26, 1971, formally called on the armed forces to perform such nondefense missions as "active participation in national construction and development" and "protection of the revolution."[33]

As any successful or unsuccessful coup leader should know, politicization of the military can become a double-edged sword. As it stands now, the odds are virtually even that the very group that has been called on to protect the revolution may spawn the elements that eventually will overthrow it in turn.

THE SUDAN SOCIALIST UNION

The Sudan Socialist Union (SSU) held its inaugural meeting on January 2, 1972, at which President Nimeiri presented it with his regime's National Action Charter. That body's Constituent National Conference then discussed the Charter and approved it on January 10, thereby laying the foundations for the Union's proposed activities within the framework of the government's adopted policies.

These policy objectives were delineated in the six parts of the 54-page charter, addressing the issues of freedom, democracy, socialism; the economic, social, and cultural revolution; national unity; the people's struggle; foreign policy; and protection of the revolution.[34] However, despite its considerable length the National Action Charter contains little more than general principles about these broad issues; therefore, a Phased Program of Action was designed by the Preparatory Central Committee of the SSU and discussed during their November 11-14, 1972 meeting.[35] The following thirteen months allowed for further revisions and modifications before this program was submitted to the First National Congress of the SSR on January 21, 1974. It is as ambitious in substance as it is comprehensive in scope, and resembles in function a five-year development plan (without budgetary figures).

A careful reading of the charter reveals the heavy influence of Arab Socialist ideology as, indeed, the conception and organization of the SSU borrowed extensively—if not to say was directly copied from—the Egyptian Arab Socialist Union. The SSU has been designed as an umbrella organization for all progressive or nationalist groups, meaning the workers, cultivators, soldiers, intellectuals, and "national capitalists," in this order of identification in the second sentence of the charter preamble. Like its Egyptian counterpart, the union was to be ruled by a central committee (headed by President Nimeiri and then Secretary-General Ma'moun Awad Abu Zeid) and to vest its authority in a national conference in which the various component groups would all be represented, for example, the students' union, teachers' union, medical association, tenants' union, and so on. For this purpose all existing organizations, such as the SWTUF and the former Women's Union, were "encouraged" to dissolve themselves in order to be reorganized under the auspices of the SSU.

In his report to the First National Congress the secretary-general was able to point to considerable success in setting up the various component units of the SSU, which is hierarchical in structure. The smallest element is the basic unit (of which there were 6,381 by January 1974), followed by "branches" at "production sites" (1,892), divisions (325), areas (34), and province congresses (one per province). Their combined membership was announced as 2,247,000.[36] At the national level the SSU entails a national congress (which normally meets once every three years), a central committee, a political bureau, and the general secretariat.[37]

One of the main identified tasks of the SSU has been the development and strengthening of several popular organizations. The secretary-general's January 1974 report proudly claims that the Sudanese Youth Movement had 496,433 enlisted members, the Women's Union 507,000, that 7,545 Rural Development Committees represented

more than 2.1 million villagers, that there were now 78 separate
unions for tenants and peasants, and that the workers had been organized into 37 instead of the previous 650 trade unions.[38]

It is, of course, much too early to venture any conclusive assessment about the performance of this new single party, but some
peripheral observations invite a few comments.

At the outset the architects of the SSU have obviously been
inspired by the Arab Socialist Union (ASU) of Egypt, but seem to have
spent very little time analyzing the functional requisites for single
party effectiveness. Instead, one cannot avoid the impression that
Sudanese officials have once again been unduly mesmerized by the
glittering facade and clever publicity of an Egyptian phantom organization. But even if one were to assume that the ASU is alive and
well, of which it has ever been accused by knowledgeable foreign or
Egyptian observers, it still would not follow that an organizational
conception designed for the rather homogeneous Egyptian society
would function in the enormously heterogeneous Sudanese.

A recent look at SSU activities in early 1975 reveals a more
sober recognition by the new leadership of the task ahead in building
an organization to serve specifically Sudanese needs.[39] And perhaps
it is fair to suggest in retrospect that thoughtful Sudanese SSU pro-
tagonists never anticipated much similarity between their Union and
its Egyptian counterpart in any case. An illuminating anecdote gives
support to such a hypothesis. During General Nimeiri's initial discussion of his charter, a rural delegate in flowing jallabiyyah stood
up and interrupted his president with a "point of order." The point
of order turned out to be that the delegate desired the floor, and after
being informed by the president that this request was not a point of
order, he retorted that it was certainly a point of disorder that he
had to listen patiently while the president talked at great length; and
he insisted on being heard. The present Egyptian delegation of ASU
representatives and media personnel were aghast at such lack of
discipline, and expected terrible consequences for the undiplomatic
delegate. However, the incident was settled by nothing more than
gentle name-calling, and in a symbolic sort of way the Socialist
Union had been Sudanized.*

Thus far, the recruitment of more than two million members
into the various organizations units looks promising on the surface,
but does not, by itself, indicate more than a superficial commitment.
The real test of the organization will come in the future when it is

---

*It is also noteworthy that the strongly Egyptian-oriented Major
Ma'moun Awad Abu Zeid was soon pressured to resign as SSU
secretary-general, though in a totally unrelated context.

called upon to mobilize regime support from below, and to find a workable synthesis for the divergent objectives of Sudan's multifarious groups. Initial impressions so far have not been too encouraging. Not only did the organization take extraordinarily long to be set up and take (formal) roots, but the Peoples' Assembly elections of 1974 returned many old-time politicians to national office, an indication that much resocialization work is left for the proponents of the SSU before this body can become an effective link between people and government.

CONCLUSIONS

What lessons can be drawn from such developments, if any?

On one hand it seems clear that the effects of continuing educational growth, especially in rural areas, and of improved communications within the Sudan and to worlds beyond, will decrease the hold of traditional ties on the Sudanese masses and provide opportunities for a genuine reshaping of the country's social and political order.

But the mere presence of opportunities does not guarantee that these will also be exploited in intelligent fashion by the budding modernizers. For one thing, data from local and general elections as well as other forms of evidence demonstrate a steady decline of sectarian (but not necessarily tribal) allegiances in urban areas without an immediate forging of new ties to replace the older ones. For another, the ongoing struggle is not simply between old and new, traditional and modern. In fact, some of the country's most educated individuals have associated themselves politically with such conservative forces as the Muslim Brotherhood and Mahdist leaderships. Moreover, it must be recognized that the modern forces have been just as disunited as the traditional groups have been. Note, for example, the recurrent antagonisms between students and the military and the apparent apathy of most civil servants toward just about anything aside from job security and football scores. But we should not despair if the emerging picture contains more confusion than clarity, for the Sudanese have always managed to somehow absorb new challenges by adjusting their life-styles in their own fashion. One dominant impression for foreign visitors has been the indomitable resiliency of the ordinary Sudanese, for whom daily life may be fraught with all manner of hardships, but who will carry on with a cheerful disposition and deep faith in Providence.

If the visitor stays on for any length of time he cannot escape another pervasive impression, namely that in the capital area, virtually every Sudanese seems to know everybody else, and perhaps even be distantly related to whoever's name is mentioned. That, of course, is quite impossible; but the importance of marital relations to inter- and intragroup behavior should not be overlooked, nevertheless, for both practical and symbolic reasons. For example, with reference to the interrelationships of traditional and modernizing forces, we may note several intriguing marriages during recent years: SWTUF leader Shafieh Ahmed el-Sheikh to Women's Union president Fatima Ahmed Ibrahim, ICF president Hassan el-Turabi to Umma president Sadiq el-Mahdi's sister; also NUP president Ismail el-Azhari married his oldest daughter to a military colonel shortly before his death, the transitional government prime minister Sirr el-Khatim el-Khalifah is another brother-in-law to Sadiq el-Mahdi, and the formerly close Nimeiri associate, Major Abu el-Qasim Hashim, was a son-in-law of the "discredited" ex-premier Mohammad Ahmed Mahjoub, to list only a few.

If, indeed, such spectacular marriages have any demonstrable effects or other symbolic values at all—and we do not insist that they do—it may be that they represent a distinct Sudanese brand of managing tensions without necessarily overcoming them.

NOTES

1. Address by President Nimeiri on the occasion of the proclamation of the new educational ladder (no date given), reprinted by the Ministry of Education, Official Documents Services, May 1970.

2. Salah el-Din el-Zein el-Tayeb, The Students' Movement in the Sudan, 1940-70 (Khartoum: Khartoum University Press, 1971), pp. 17-18.

3. Which is also statistically indicated by the rather widespread dissatisfaction of students with the quality of their lecturers. Ibid., pp. 35-36.

4. Frank Pinner, "Tradition and Transgression, Western European Students in the Postwar World," Daedalus (Winter 1968), pp. 137-55, but especially pp. 142-47.

5. Another study by Clement Moore and Arlie Hochschild, "Student Unions in North African Politics," Daedalus (Winter 1968), p. 42, reveals that 61 percent of all Tunisian and only 39 percent of all Moroccan students consider competence to be a more essential ingredient than "pull" for getting jobs. I expect that the figure for Sudanese students would fall slightly below that of the Moroccans.

6. El-Tayeb, op. cit., presents a fairly comprehensive description of student activism, but does not explain the psychological

motivations of students in any detail, nor their reasons for aligning themselves with particular parties.

7. Interview with Peter M. Holt (London University) on October 10, 1966.

8. Note also the discussion in el-Tayeb, op. cit., pp. 40-41.

9. A very good study of Egyptian engineers is presented by Clement Henry Moore, "Professional Syndicates in Contemporary Egypt: The Demobilization of the New Middle Class," paper delivered at the annual meetings of the Middle East Studies Association at Milwaukee, Wisconsin, November 8-10, 1973.

10. Zeinab el-Fatih el-Badawi, The Development of the Sudanese Women Movement (published by the Ministry of Information and Social Affairs, Republic of the Sudan, no date given).

11. Carolyn Fluehr-Lobban, "Women, the Law and Socio-Political Change in the Sudan: Unveiling Myths about Arab Women," p. 5, unpublished paper presented at the annual MESA meeting at Milwaukee, Wisconsin, November 1973.

12. Ian Cunnison, Baggara Arabs (London: Oxford University Press, 1966), especially pp. 116-18.

13. Saad el-Din Fawzi, The Labour Movement in the Sudan 1946-55 (London: Oxford University Press, 1957), p. 34.

14. Ibid., p. 167.

15. Area Handbook for the Democratic Republic of the Sudan (Washington, D.C.: Government Printing Office, 1973), p. 226.

16. Fawzi, op. cit., p. 150.

17. Manfred Halpern, The Politics of Social Change in the Middle East and North Africa (Princeton: Princeton University Press, 1963), p. 327.

18. Helen Kitchen, "Trade Unions: Communist Stronghold," Africa Special Report 4, no. 1 (January 1959): 12.

19. Fawzi, op. cit., p. 99.

20. Robert Michels, Political Parties (New York: Free Press, 1962), especially Part VI.

21. Fawzi, op. cit., p. 118.

22. The WFTU rather than the ICFTU, ibid., p. 118.

23. Ibid., p. 119.

24. Ibid., p. 101.

25. See also Area Handbook, op. cit., section 3.

26. Oluwadare Aguda, "The State and the Economy in the Sudan: From A Political Scientist's Point-of-View," Journal of Developing Areas 40, no. 3 (April 1973): 443.

27. Ibid., pp. 431-48.

28. El-Sahafa, December 1, 1968, quoted in Aguda, op. cit., p. 442.

29. Area Handbook, op. cit., p. 301. A system of conscription was introduced fifteen years later to meet rising defense and internal security demands.

30. Area Handbook, op. cit., p. 299. The size of the total armed forces grew from 7,500 in 1956 to 20,000 in 1966 and approximately 50,000 in 1975.

31. Area Handbook, op. cit., p. 299.

32. Where some Israeli specialists supported the anya'nya rebellion against the Khartoum government, see Jerusalem Post Weekly, April 6, 1971, p. 7.

33. Area Handbook, op. cit., p. 303.

34. Al-Ittihad al-ishtiraki al-sudani, mithaq al-amal al-watani, January 2, 1972.

35. Democratic Republic of Sudan, Sudanese Socialist Union Preparatory Central Committee, Phased Programme of Action (January 2, 1974), p. 2.

36. Sudanese Socialist Union General Secretariat, Documents of the First National Congress: Report of the Secretary of the SSU (January 25, 1974), pp. 42-45.

37. Basic Rules of the Sudanese Socialist Union (February 2, 1974), Article 21 a-d.

38. Sudanese Socialist Union General Secretariat, op. cit., pp. 49-68. Additional mass organizations, for which no figures were listed, are the Cooperative Societies and the Fathers' Councils (for ''the supervision of education . . . and the instrument for creating coordination between the school and the home,'' p. 9).

39. Interview with the union's theoretician Ahmed Abdel-Halim on January 11, 1975, who also speculated that it will be at least another twelve years before the SSU will become a truly effective organization.

The Anglo-Egyptian condominium over the Sudan was terminated on January 1, 1956, the official date of the country's independence. Unlike the cases in the majority of Arab-African nations, this independence did not result from violent struggles of clandestine organizations or national liberation movements, but from the orderly process of parliamentary debate following equally orderly elections. Thus, the drama of Sudanese nationhood featured the ballot box at center stage at the time of inception, and subsequently during the first and third acts while the country was governed by parliamentary democracy. By contrast, the military rulers during the second and fourth acts decried the alleged futility, or perhaps more precisely the inappropriateness, of that form of government to local conditions. From this perspective alone it is clear that an analysis of politics in independent Sudan necessitates a close examination of the performance level of Sudanese-style democracy. There is, of course, another reason: Most standard dramas contain at least five acts, and close attention to the interplay of leading characters and dominant forces during the first four stages may enable us to anticipate subsequent developments.

Accordingly, the bulk of Part II will cover the ups and downs of parliamentary democracy and military rule since 1953, the year when Sudanese effectively began to control their own political destiny.

Yet before we proceed to examine the vicissitudes of recent Sudanese affairs, it seems appropriate to ask just why elections played such an important role in the inception of Sudanese nationhood. And furthermore, were the Sudanese actually ready for parliamentary elections, in view of existing conditions at that time (and even now)? These questions point to the need to examine the sorts of problems that arise when essentially Western institutions—liberal democracy and parliamentary elections—are introduced to, or imposed upon, a partly traditional and partly transitional society where the necessary social, economic, and political preconditions are mostly absent or only insufficiently present.

In the following chapter we shall try to deal with these issues and questions, and in the process provide some appreciation for the political and social atmosphere in the Sudan at that time.

131

4

A NEW EXPERIENCE:
STAGING ELECTIONS
IN A PRIMATIVE SETTING

> Where elections are taken seriously, the electoral routine
> is of central importance in politics, and compresses, as it
> were, the whole stream of politics into a narrow channel,
> in which it moves fast and with great intensity. . . No human
> observer can ever grasp the whole life of a political system
> in action, but more can be learned in a space of about three
> months during an election than in any other comparable
> period.[1]

The reader may recall that the Anglo-Egyptian Agreement of
February 12, 1953 called for the establishment of a neutral international commission that was to supervise general elections for a
Constituent Assembly. The elected representatives to this assembly
were then to deliberate the future constitutional status of the Sudan
by taking only one of two decisions, namely (1) that the Sudan shall be
linked with Egypt in some form, or (2) that the Sudan shall have complete independence.

Several reasons caused the Sudan government and the codominium
powers to decide on elections as the most practical method for resolving this issue. For one, the major participants in Sudanese public
affairs in the 1950s, the abovementioned authorities on the one side
and the various local political organizations on the other, could not
agree among themselves on either a specific settlement of the Sudan
question or on suitable approaches to a settlement. Since all parties
realized that the status quo could not be perpetuated for much longer,
they decided on elections as the only feasible method to overcome the
impasse. We may distinguish two main reasons for those disagreements:

(1) The "parental dispute" factor. Egypt desired to integrate
the Sudan into a political union under King Farouq, whereas Great

Britain opposed such an outcome. This issue was brought before the
U.N. Security Council, but could not be resolved there either. Subsequently, various proposals were suggested, such as popular referendum and decision by a specially selected council of leading Sudanese
citizens; either codominus was prepared to accept one of these alternatives, but they could not agree on the same one, out of fear that their
respective future interests in the Sudan might suffer.

(2) Sudanese factionalism. Given the absence of a unified popular
front among the Sudanese, and the existence of two large political
blocs each claiming to represent over 70 percent of the people, it was
quite impossible for any commission (international or Sudan government) to produce a political solution acceptable to a large enough
majority of Sudanese, so that political stability would be assured.
General elections provided the most practical way out of that dilemma.

Moreover, this decision was facilitated by the existence of such
conditions as the tradition of decision making in public matters by
some form of popular consent,* the fact that many Sudanese had acquired some voting experience during recent local council elections
in settled areas, the vogue factor, and the culture-transmission factor.
The "vogue factor" refers to the high prestige that liberal democracy
enjoyed as a political process in the early 1950s, and that was espoused by political leaders throughout the noncommunist world as the
ideal approach to political problems. Popular elections were considered to be an integral aspect of this approach. (Moreover, the
majority of the member countries in the United Nations, where the
Sudan question had taken up several sessions of the Security Council,
seemed to have been favorably disposed toward the holding of general
elections.)

The "culture-transmission" factor refers to the impact of
British culture and institutions on a good portion of Sudanese society.
Many Sudanese civil servants had been sent to the British Isles for
specialized training and had assimilated many British values, some
to the point of having become "more British than the British themselves." And it is easily observable to this day, that among the most
impressive aspects of British life for Sudanese is the functioning of
parliamentary democracy; and there are not a few Sudanese who long
for the return of the model of British democracy in operation. In addition, when Sudanese nationalists pleaded for self-determination in
the 1940s and early 1950s, they envisioned essentially a future status

---

*For elaboration, see Chapter 1. It may interest the reader that
almost all Sudanese questioned by this author about the extraordinarily
smooth performances of elections in their country felt that this phenomenon was attributable to the "native practice of democracy,"
discussed above.

like that of the British, meaning, among other things, a working democracy, and participation in public affairs by open elections.

The essential thrust of these introductory pages is to indicate the
existence of a favorable disposition on the part of Sudanese toward
decision making by popular consent. In fact, all four parliamentary
elections to date turned out to be remarkably fair and free from undue
outside influences and were unanimously praised as such by all parties
involved. (This is in stark contrast to information about elections in
a number of other African countries, such as Nigeria and Zaire
[formerly the Congo], which exhibited similar geographic and demographic heterogeneity as the Sudan. It also gives rise to the interesting
question of why elections in the Sudan went so much more smoothly
than they did in these other countries, a theme to which we shall return later on.)

Nevertheless, there were problems, as one would expect to arise
whenever general elections are to be conducted in an essentially backward and traditional setting. An examination of these problems can
tell us much about social and political conditions in the country and a
scrutiny of options and adopted solutions should help our understanding
of the appropriateness of elections and democracy as institutions in
the Sudanese political system.

In order to minimize definitional difficulties it seems fruitful to
accept as major problems those that were thus identified by officials
for the parliamentary elections of 1953, 1958, 1965 and 1968.[2] For the
purposes of this book, there is no need to consider administrative issues and difficulties. They can be divided into two groups: (1) Those
of an essentially technical nature that may, however, have limited impact on the political situation if they are not handled carefully, such
as supervising procedures for grievance cases, selection of neutral
symbols and colors for candidates, anticipation and handling of corrupt practices, acquisition of reliable data, the general problem of
communications, and the commission members' lack of familiarity
with local conditions; and (2) those that might appear as technical in
nature, but that may have considerable political consequences by affecting the outcome of the elections, such as staffing the Commission,
drafting the electoral rules, delimiting the territorial constituencies,
determining the eligibility of voters and candidates, educating the
general public about elections, selecting the proper methods for voting,
and finally the question of graduates' constituencies. In addition, there
were other matters that lie beyond the scope of our present concern
and shall be listed only, such as arranging transportation facilities,
financing the entire operation, securing storage space for equipment,
acquisition of buildings and supplies, and arranging visits to outlying
areas. These items will not be discussed here; however, the reader
is reminded that even such relatively simple matters (in advanced

countries) can constitute formidable difficulties in a developing nation and, more often than not, cause anger and frustration as well as serious delays in the progress of more important matters.

For this task we shall compare particular methods and alternatives, as well as their consequences for the electoral process and, in a larger sense, for Sudanese politics. Most of the discussion will center on conditions in 1953, but attention will be called to major amendments and changes in subsequent elections as necessary, at the risk that this inclusion may detract somewhat from our essentially chronological perspective.

The sequence of topics below is not according to any subjective order of importance, but rather follows a general progression from relatively more administrative issues (personnel, facilities and procedures) to relatively more politically controversial issues (eligibility and methods of voting, delimitation of constituencies, and so on).

We begin our survey of electoral problems with a glance at the members of the election commissions who, after all, stood to absorb the brunt of any criticism, or to earn praise for good performance.

THE COMMISSIONS AND THEIR STAFF

The composition of the 1953 Electoral Commission entailed some problems that the three subsequent commissions, fortunately, did not have to face: in 1953, the group's size was by necessity large with the result of some loss in efficiency; five of the members (the British, the Egyptian, and the three Sudanese representatives of NUP, Umma party, and the Southern region) were affiliated with groups that had considerable interests at stake in the outcome of elections, while the other two members (the Indian chairman and an American member) were unfamiliar with the Sudan, and, consequently, depended to some degree on the advice of the first five.

By contrast, the 1958, the 1965, and the 1968 commissions were made up of fewer individuals—three members instead of seven. Selection to the body was based not only on personal competence but also on "high moral standing and complete independence from any political organization."[3] The members, all Sudanese citizens, were appointed by the head of state (in December 1964, the Council of Ministers acted as such head) and as a group were responsible only to that body. This had the beneficial effect that the Commissions were independent of the governmental groups in power. Their members were able to proceed more efficiently with their tasks than their predecessors in 1953, who represented various interested parties and consequently found themselves frequently involved in hammering out compromises on almost

all important issues. One piece of evidence is that this author could
not discern any form of favoritism by members toward one party or
another during almost two years of very close association with the
1965 commission. Similarly, the political integrity of that commission
was never questioned in the press except once by the Communists after
their election defeat in May 1965 in a halfhearted gesture. (The communist diatribes were made for reasons of propaganda; individual
party leaders admitted privately the correctness of election results.)

   After independence, the northern members and the executive
secretary were senior civil servants with outstanding records as administrators; all had worked previously in various parts of the country and were, as a result, quite familiar with local conditions
throughout the Sudan. The southern members, Andrea Gori (in 1958)
and Monawwa Majok (appointed in 1966 and again in 1968) had less
background in administration and appeared to have played minor roles
willingly in deference to the greater experience of their northern colleagues; nevertheless, they took definite positions on any issue affecting the southern region, which, of course, was the reason for their
appointments in the first place.

   The general competence of the commissions was enhanced by a
certain degree of continuity. Both chairmen, Sayyed Hassan Ali Abdallah in 1958 and Muhammad Yussuf Mudawi in 1965, had worked
with the previous commissions and were able to put their experiences
to good advantage, the former as executive secretary in 1953 and the
latter as member in 1958. Munawwa Majok served on both commissions in the late 1960s. In addition, the 1958, 1965 and 1968 commissions enjoyed the very capable services of Abdel-Majid Awad el-Karim
as executive secretary.* The high reputation of the commissions'
members may be indicated, for example, by subsequent appointments
of two chairmen: Sayyed Hassan became permanent under-secretary
of the Ministry of the Interior, the most powerful and most prestigious
rank accessible to a career civil servant in the Sudan; while Justice
Muhammad Yussuf Mudawi—incidentally, an internationally recognized
authority on human rights—was appointed chairman of the Committee
to Investigate and Revise the Civil Service. Similar examples could
be given of the other members.

   These members confined their activities essentially to policy
formulation, while execution was vested in the hands of the Commissions' staff throughout the country. The proper functioning of the elec-

---

*On the other hand, the two northern members in 1968, el-Tayyib
Khalil (chairman) and Osman Ali el-Naw, had no previous experience
at commission headquarters.

tion machinery depended therefore to a large extent on the quality of those officials.

In retrospect the staff members, from province chief electoral officer to the assistant returning officer in a constituency, during all four elections deserved highest praise for their demonstrated dedication, competence, and impartiality. In fact, it is striking to observe the unanimity with which various writers on Sudanese elections* have lauded the performances of the election officers. This dedication resulted undoubtedly to some degree from training and professional pride in doing a job well; but perhaps even more important were two historical factors: The 1958 elections were the first after independence, and the first to be managed entirely by Sudanese; many citizens, and especially those in official capacities, considered elections to be a test of national maturity, and "initiation into nationhood." The 1965 elections followed on the heels of the overthrow of a military regime that had outlawed almost all democratic practices during its rule. What better way to substantiate the professed claims of thirst for democratic liberties than by a demonstration of how well an election machinery can function? It is to the great credit of the many election officers that in statements by the press and during interviews with various political leaders not one serious charge was made of partial behavior on the part of an officer. One explanation for this phenomenon was furnished by the chairman of the 1965 commission: "The Chief Electoral Officers are senior civil servants, assumed to be politically neutral and highly capable of carrying out their assignments. Their impartiality in choosing personnel for elections—registration—and returning-officers as well as assistants within their own provinces—is beyond suspicion. They are thought of as taking pride in their work and in the performance of their entire province. . . ."[4]

An example of such pride in good work during the 1953 elections is the well-documented case of Fath el-Rahman Beshir, who was an assistant to the district commissioner in El-Hosh (Blue Nile Province) at that time and was appointed as registration officer in that constituency. Fath el-Rahman worked long hours, sometimes around the clock, inspired by a keen sense of duty for providing his fellow citizens their first opportunity to earn political independence. At the same time, he felt an obligation to create and maintain an aura of confidence in the electoral process, if for no other reason than to prove that the Sudanese were worthy of the privilege of political participation.

—————

*Leo Silberman, Harold Gosnell, Basil Davidson, and the London Times correspondent.

On several occasions he was approached after hours by members of the local NUP committee past the deadline for registrations with requests to add lists of names to the registration roll. He experienced some personal anguish because of his close ties to the NUP (he was then a known sympathizer and became later a very influential member in that party). He tried to avoid clashes with party people by evading them as best he could under various pretenses. In the end he managed to adhere to his principles and ensured the impartiality of the elections. (The reader might be interested to note that the NUP candidate was defeated by one of the slightest of margins, 4,455 to 4,353.)

While it is impossible to ascertain how many other election officials were besieged by similar dilemmas as Fath el-Rahman Beshir, his conscientious behavior seems to have been characteristic of election officials in general. The author does not possess the necessary data to be able to draw any foolproof conclusions about the reasons for this kind of behavior; nevertheless, an educated guess would suggest that the reasons are essentially threefold: (a) outstanding training of Sudanese civil servants by British superiors of exceptional quality in the Sudan Service; (b) an aspect of Sudanese behavioral traits, which is admittedly a vague factor and difficult to document except by intuitive experience and objective observation; (c) the professional ethos that seemed to pervade the entire election corps and that can be illustrated by the account of a firsthand experience by an old Africa expert:

> . . . at Fashoda of the spear-bearing Shilluk, the Chief Electoral Officer of Upper Nile Province was explaining to a score of local schoolmasters and officials exactly how to conduct elections in an orderly and democratic manner among a people almost totally illiterate. A tired and conscientious Sudanese from Omdurman . . ., the Chief Electoral Officer has been wearing himself out with such explanations.
>
> He has gone into everything, into small things: 'Take your food and your bed and your cigarettes if you smoke . . . you can't leave your post and trek back into town once the job has begun. Above all, don't think of drinking . . .'
>
> And into big things: 'Be friendly with the voters. Don't force them. Don't ever take them into the polling room and let them drop their vote in front of you. That is absolutely wrong . . .'
>
> The demonstration lasts three scorching hours, down to a complete dress rehearsal.[5]

THE ROLE OF GOVERNMENT EMPLOYEES

One of the more delicate issues in free elections anywhere concerns the proper role of civil servants as participants in the campaigns. During the 1953 elections in the Sudan this issue became particularly sensitive, because it affected three nationalities of bureaucrats.

Article 36.1.c. of the Self-Government Statute provided, in effect, that any civil servant had to resign from his position before he could file his nomination papers as an election candidate.[6] This matter is rather clear and straightforward. Much more complicated was the fact that, by government order, civil servants had been forbidden to be members of political parties and/or to take part in politics in any way. While the first requirement is somewhat easier to police, it is almost impossible to control participation in politics in any way. The intent of this requirement was surely that a public servant should not use his official position for unduly influencing voters. He was reminded to that effect by instruction sheets from the Sudan government.

To what extent the different civil servants adhered to those instructions is rather difficult to determine, especially from historical perspective. Nevertheless, a brief sketch of the behavior of British, Egyptian, and Sudanese nationals in the Sudan government in 1953— admittedly based on generalizations—can aid our understanding of their respective group attitudes and political interests.[7]

There is little doubt that the vast majority of British civil servants in the Sudan were anti-NUP and, hence, tended to be sympathetic to the cause of the Umma party and the Socialist Republicans. (The Socialist Republican party was a minor party, led by rural notables, which contested only the 1953 elections.) There is considerable doubt, however, as to whether this sympathy did, in fact, induce Britishers to act in any way that by their own code of behavior would have to be classified as "incorrect." There might have been some potentially helpful hints to Umma candidates about campaign engineering, for example, but unlikely any concrete outright aid. Nonetheless, it would be a serious mistake to minimize the very real concern by Britishers for safeguarding their country's future interests in the Sudan, which hinged understandably on the disposition of the postcolonial regime toward the former mother country. This concern was reinforced by the considerable reservations of the British government toward the new revolutionary regime in Egypt. Evidence of British sympathies for the Umma party was subsequently provided by the unconcealed disappointment by British individuals, as well as such informed organs as the London Times, over the election defeat of that party at the hands of the NUP.

By contrast, the Egyptian civil servants in the Sudan government were clearly pro-NUP. Like the British, they made no efforts to hide their sentiments; yet, their different status and background prescribed for them a different role. They were not in the influential administrative positions that the British occupied, and that could (and might) have been used fairly easily as bases for manipulation. There is good reason to suspect that, had the Egyptians held similar positions of power, they might not have shown the kind of restraint and impartiality as the British did publicly. As it turned out, their channels of influence were mainly financial ones and adroit use of propaganda, especially in the urban areas of the North. They were aided in this respect by their background, and could pose as fellow-Arabs and Muslims who, after all, could "understand" the real needs of the Sudanese much better than the Inglizi (Sudanese for English) non-Muslim colonialists.

Charges against organized Egyptian interference in the 1953 elections were numerous and apparently correct in large measure. The extent of Egyptian activities just prior to the elections was so considerable as to move one Sudanese member of the Commission to file a separate "note of dissent" with the official report. Because much of the evidence in the government archives supports the charges contained in this note, some excerpts are presented for the reader's benefit:

(2) The result of the elections, to my mind, has shown without doubt that there was great interference which influenced the voters and consequently the results.
The following are some examples:
a) The Permanent Under-Secretary for Sudan Affairs, Sayed Dardiri Ahmed Ismail, accompanied by an Egyptian officer, Captain Mohammad Abu Nar, came to the Sudan in November last and distributed large sums as donations to Mosques and Schools in many parts of the Sudan. Both the time of their visit and the way they went about distributing these donations could have meant nothing other than propaganda to influence the elections, otherwise such payments would have been postponed until after the results.
b) The Egyptian Press, which is state-controlled, waged a ceaseless attack on the Umma Party and those who stand for independence of the Sudan.
c) The Egyptian State Broadcasting station directed all its efforts towards a continuous attack on the people favoring independence with a view to lowering the morale of their supporters.

d) A great number of Civil Servants and soldiers of Sudanese origin serving in Egypt were sent to the Sudan, on long
vacations with pay and other financial facilities to scatter in
the Sudanese towns and villages and to disseminate propaganda for the National Unionist Party. They were not voters
and some of them had not visited the Sudan for many years.
e) The enormous sums of money spent by the National Unionist Party during the election period were far beyond the
means of the party in question.
(3) I am of the opinion that in such cases the evidence required does not so much depend on proving individual or
specific instances as on the general trend of events and the
surrounding circumstances.
Khartoum, December 13, 1953. Abdel-Salam El-Khalifa
Abdullahi[8]

Not unexpectedly, these charges were vigorously denied at that
time by those involved; however, more than a decade later a good
number of influential NUP's confided to this author that the thrust of
the claims was essentially accurate.

As regards the Sudanese civil servants, we have already noted
previously that most of them seemed to consider the elections as a
test for their political maturity and, consequently, were very conscious
of the need to act properly. This resulted in rather guarded behavior,
which was further reinforced by the fact that all Sudanese officials
were subordinates to Britishers in one way or another.

More interesting than the role of the formal civil servants were
the activities of what might be called informal government officials,
namely the tribal leaders who performed various functions in the
native administration.

The 1953 commission's Report devoted a special section to the
"question of the participation of nazirs, omdas, sheikhs, and other
tribal leaders in the election campaign and in the election proper.[9]
From an operational point of view, this problem has been perhaps the
most vexing and insoluble one and simultaneously the one with the
potentially most wide-ranging political consequences. Since the Report
presented both a thorough analysis of the problem as well as the commission's response, the salient points will be quoted in full:

. . . One of the principal political parties undertook a campaign to induce the Commission to declare that since Government servants were disqualified by the Self-Government
Statute from membership of either House of Parliament and
had been forbidden by Government order to belong to a political party or take part in politics in any way, the tribal

chiefs should be similarly disqualified and debarred. It was
argued that even if they were not government servants within
the meaning of the Statute—a disputed point—they nevertheless played an important role in the administration of the
country, and many of them might be expected to attempt to
influence the outcome of the elections through the use of
their authority and position. These arguments were supported within the commission by two of its members, but
the majority of the members concluded that:

1. tribal chiefs were not "Government servants" and consequently could not be barred as such from standing as
   Parliamentary candidates, and logically should not be
   forbidden to canvass in their own behalf; moreover,
   Part III of the First Schedule of the Statute permitted
   both directly and by implication the candidature of
   tribal chiefs;
2. It should not be assumed that widespread abuse of the
   powers of the tribal chiefs was inevitable; and
3. The government should, however, be requested "to
   point out to the nazirs, etc., the impropriety of any of
   them mixing in election politics unless he himself is a
   candidate for election, and to warn them that appropriate measures will promptly be taken against anyone who
   uses the power of his office to influence the outcome of
   the elections.[10]

The government did comply with the commission's request and
instructed all district commissioners to call the seriousness of the
matter to the attention of the tribal leaders. This matter calls for
several observations.

First, although it is difficult to escape the feeling that the commission's response was anything more than a dressed up version of
doing nothing at all, it is just as difficult to envision a fair and workable alternative action in view of the limited powers of the commission. The chairman did, in fact, recommend to the Sudan government
that future commissions should be spared this problem by a policy
ruling on the part of the government itself. Second, the technical aspect of the problem is highly complex. On the one hand, the tribal
leaders were formally not bureaucrats; they were not required to
qualify for the position by competitive examination, nor could they
be promoted, nor did they receive anything but a nominal compensation from the government for their efforts. On the other hand, the
government did recognize them as legitimate rulers of their tribal
communities and granted them, in addition to the mentioned compen-

sation, various judicial and administrative powers. In other words, the authority of a native ruler had traditional and charismatic bases, and was complemented by government sanction. Third, it is not easy to define the limits of a native ruler's real power and even less easy to legislate against it. For example, in most tribes a young man could not marry a girl from outside his community without the nazir's approval.

The alleged use and abuse of this power is illustrated in the following sequence of letters to the electoral commission:

> One tribal Nazir, Mohammed el-Amin Tirik, who is Nazir
> Umum of the Hadendowa, has been able to remove 18 Omdas
> from their posts not because of errors made in the admin-
> istration of their omadias, but because they opposed the
> Nazir's will when he tried to impose a certain political
> point of view upon them . . . There is also the Nazir Yousif
> el-Agab, who was subjected to dismissal when he jointed
> (sic) the ranks of the opposition to the Sudan Government. He
> was reinstated in favour and honour when he declared his
> repentence and gave his full support to British policy in
> the Sudan. Then there is the recent and eloquent example
> of Sultan Jambo, who was chief and sultan of his tribe for
> 50 years, but when he supported the national point of view
> opposed by the British Administration in the Southern Su-
> dan, they used means, of which you are well aware, to dis-
> miss him and set up another who would follow the path
> desired by the British administration and direct the tribe
> to it.
>
> The most recent example is the case of the Wakil Nazir
> of the Hassaniyah tribe in Abu Guta, who used his police to
> call the people together and direct them in his political di-
> rection. After this, can you have any doubt or hesitance
> whatsoever regarding these Nazirs, Sheikhs, and Omdas?
> The ordinary individual, of whom the majority is made up,
> will not dare to oppose the will of the Nazir, Sheikh or Omda
> of his tribe because henceforth he would be exposed to op-
> pression, persecution, and hostility even as far as his liveli-
> hood is concerned . . .[11]

Among the abovementioned, the nazir of the Hadendowa (the same people Rudyard Kipling called Fuzzy-Wuzzies) was one of the most powerful men in the country; he won the election easily. By contrast, the Wakil nazir of the Hassaniyah was convicted on the charges and sentenced to three months imprisonment.[12]

The general problem was clearly a thorny one, and just solutions were hard to come by. Consider the hypothetical, but in actuality quite typical, case where a nazir informs (instructs?) members of this tribe to support his son as a candidate for Parliament. In a traditional tribal society most members do, in fact, expect to be guided in such matters by the leader's advice. Whether or not a chief should be allowed to involve himself actively in the campaigns—although he is an informal government official—seems to the author to be essentially a legalistic and perhaps academic problem; in reality, it is impossible to deny a tribal leader formally the exercise of those powers that he inherited by tradition. In this connection it is worth noting that even recent policy changes in local government have not succeeded in their aim of eliminating the influence of tribal leaders in various elections. (For details, see Chapters 3 and 8.)

DATA AND COMMUNICATIONS

One paramount difficulty throughout the preparations for elections in 1953 was the absence of reliable data and other documentary material on which the commission could base its various decisions. Necessary data include such items as maps, population surveys, information about seasonal movements of nomadic tribes, literacy figures, and other demographic information about age distribution and occupations. The relevance of this kind of material to the electoral process is this: According to the statute, the commission was to determine the eligibility of voters and candidates; it was to ensure that territorial constituencies included roughly equal numbers of inhabitants; it had to decide what particular type of voting method was appropriate for the inhabitants in each individual constituency, a decision that required knowledge of the social development of the peoples involved; it had to pass judgments on the feasibility of splitting up large nomadic units into parts and, in other instances, of combining sections of nomadic tribes with sedentary peoples in one constituency. Since elections were to be held simultaneously throughout the country, knowledge of climatic conditions in remote areas was necessary in order to make sure that every Sudanese was able to travel to the appointed locale, not only on the polling date, but for registration as well (which preceded polling by several months).

Some data were available, although only in crude and incomplete form, such as maps and metereological surveys. Since the first population census in the country did not take place until 1956, demographic data were not available in any systematic way, and information had to be gathered through personal inquiry and reliance on tax lists. Both of these sources were susceptible to charges of inaccuracy and of manipulation by interested bodies. Since the allocation of a tribal unit to a particular constituency depended on the assumed size of that unit, a miscalculation or a calculated error could easily lead to gerry-mandering and, hence, could directly influence the outcome of elections and with it the constitutional future of the country.

Unfortunately, the commission had few alternatives in the absence of a census. Questionnaires were mailed to all district commissioners (DCs) requesting them to provide the necessary information as accurately as possible. The DCs, in turn, had to rely on tax lists that were frequently anything but accurate. Since taxes are assessed to family units on a per capita basis, the sheikh in charge of a hamlet containing several family clans may be tempted to tinker with the list to reduce the tax assessment as much as possible. Several DCs gave vent to their suspicions in memoirs that such lists might include less than one half of the actual population. The reader may suspect that all lists were skewed in the same direction and that any inaccuracies might be relatively constant from district to district. That is not the case, however, since available information about sedentary peoples was more reliable—because more easily accessible—than about no-mads. In any case, the utility of tax lists was limited inasmuch as they covered tribal units, which did not necessarily coincide with the population of constituencies.

If a district commissioner corrected the figures and was found out, he stood a good chance of being accused by some party of interference in the electoral process. If he allowed an obviously incorrect figure to be passed on to the commission, he could be charged by another party of deliberately trying to mislead the commission. Most DCs were aware of the dilemma in which they found themselves and just tried to live with it.

The eventual solution was that the commission adopted a policy of making the Sudan government responsible for the provision of data—no matter how implausible they might be in some cases—and left it open to any dissatisfied party to seek redress in the courts. The assumption was that any statistics not contested could be considered reasonably accurate.

By 1958, and for all subsequent elections, the results of the first population census had become available; moreover the various commissions could draw on their predecessors' records, plus comments by interested parties about the accuracy of registration lists and thorough reports by their staff after elections. For example, the movements of most tribes within and across constituencies became fairly well known; likewise, the suitability of certain locations for polling stations, and the availability of such necessities as sufficient quantities of water for the voters and their herds could be ascertained with a reasonable chance of accuracy.

A very particular problem resulted from the considerable difficulties in communications between election officials and inhabitants of rural districts. This became crucial at three distinct stages: initially when the news about the fact of elections and its meaning was to be spread, at registration time, and finally on the polling date.

The reader can imagine the types of difficulties encountered: contacting wandering tribes whose whereabouts were not exactly known, or in the case of settled peoples, ranging far and wide over extremely difficult terrain to contact inhabitants of isolated hamlets containing, perhaps, no more than a few families. Given the considerable size of some constituencies and the sparse population density—the more so in physically large constituencies—the officer may be faced with going on a trek for several days to an outlying area only to find that the locals have hidden or disappeared upon receiving word that "somebody from the government was coming." Under such circumstances it is easy to see the temptation for an official to throw up his hands in despair and fail to contact some groups under his jurisdiction. If he was caught, however, he was open to charges of deliberately trying to deny the franchise to segments of the inhabitants in his area. Upon investigation many a tale was heard in 1953 about lorries and landrovers that broke down or got stuck in sand or mud, making it impossible for the official to reach his destination. On the whole, however, the officers made very great and conscientious efforts to contact all potential voters under sacrifices and hardships of sometimes extraordinary dimensions. The important principle of course, which also applies to almost every developing country, was that nomadic tribes and settlers in small distant communities should not be deprived of their franchise because of geographic difficulties in order to avoid overrepresentation of the settled urbanized population.

RULES, CORRUPTION, AND GRIEVANCES

One of the most desirable criteria of elections anywhere is fairness. Unfortunately, elections in many of the so-called developing nations are said to be characterized by excessive fraud and irregularities.[13] It would go beyond the scope of this book to inquire about the causes of fraud, and so on that seem peculiar to elections in developing nations. The importance of fairness is simply this: The

greater the number of known instances of fraud and other irregularities during elections, the less confidence the general public has in
the legitimacy of the regime and, hence, the greater the potential
source of instability. In short, it is highly desirable for more than
just moral reasons that irregularities are kept to an absolute minimum.

It was the task of the electoral commissions to anticipate possible
sources of such irregularities and to institute sufficient safeguards
against them without restricting freedom of participation. Since the
details of every step in the actual process of elections (that is, from
nominations to polling to vote counting) were known in advance, it was
fairly easy to identify those points in the procedure at which fraud
might be attempted: (1) forgery or fraudulent defacing of nomination
papers; (2) selling, defacing or unauthorized printing of ballot papers
or their equivalents; (3) tinkering with ballot boxes, such as stealing
them, putting unauthorized material into same, or unauthorized removal of ballots or their equivalents from boxes; (4) intentional false
counting of votes or inaccurate reporting of vote count; (5) illegal
financial activities such as bribery or excessive spending for campaign purposes; (6) illegal political activity, such as violation of neutrality by government employees, "harmful" propaganda, and the
"swearing" of prospective voters to support a certain candidate; (7)
impersonating others at the polls.

The first four items could be controlled almost completely by
the members and officers of the commissions, given attitudes of integrity and extreme care in the planning and execution of regulations.
Fortunately, such attitudes were prevalent in all four elections to the
extent that no complaints were lodged about the conduct of elections
regarding those four points.

The archives reveal that only one possible problem was anticipated in these areas, namely that some voters might not place their
ballot papers (or tokens) into the designated boxes, but rather smuggle
them out of the polling station and sell them for profit to interested
parties. This matter will be discussed below together with the issue
of proper voting methods. Suffice it to say that, where ballot papers
were used, the voter was required, after marking his ballot in secret
behind a screen, to deposit it into the box in full view of the presiding
officer and his assistants. This eliminated the chance of smuggling
the ballot out of the polling station.

The last three items on our list were much more difficult to control. Regarding bribery or excessive campaign spending, each candidate was allowed to expend a fixed number of pounds for campaign
purposes and was required to maintain bookkeeping accounts and to
present these if called to do so. The purpose of this regulation was

to minimize advantages based on financial status. Election officers throughout the country were asked to keep their ears and eyes open for such incidents, although they were not instructed to search actively for potential violators. Given the nature of social activities in the Sudan, where it is virtually impossible for any activity to remain secret in a community of any size, this provision was more effective than the outsider might suspect. In addition, all candidates and parties were informed of the Corrupt Practices Prevention ordinances of 1952 and 1957, respectively, and were encouraged to submit complaints against violators in the courts.

As it turned out, innumerable rumors circulated about illegal financing of election campaigns, ranging from unofficial charges against individuals to charges against parties and even a foreign government (Egypt). While the possibility of illegal traffic in money was very real, it was, nevertheless, almost impossible to prove in any given instance. The electoral commission adopted the quite normal policy of responding to charges of corrupt practices by requesting the claimants to furnish concrete evidence of a violation of the ordinance. Such evidence was produced in only a very few cases, and the courts disposed of the matters promptly.[14]

A different and rather difficult problem, which seems to occur in many countries where free elections are held, is the attempt by a voter to impersonate someone else at the polls. In order to obviate this possibility, the Sudanese commissions employed identifiers who in almost all cases were sheikhs of those villages or quarters where the voters from a particular polling station lived. To explain their function it may be well to illustrate the mechanics of voting.

A man enters the polling station and approaches the table with the ballot box. Around the table are seated the presiding officer and two official assistants. The man gives his name, which then is located in the registration list. The name is called out loud by the presiding officer so that one of the identifiers may confirm that this person is known to him and resides in the polling precinct. If none of the two or three sheikhs recognize him, he is asked where he lives and who his relatives are. If he can give satisfactory answers, he is allowed to proceed and is issued a ballot.

Because polling stations in sedentary areas comprise relatively small districts (rarely with more than three hundred registered voters), and because it is the sheikh's duty to know all people in his harah (village quarter or area), it is extremely rare that a man claiming to reside in the precinct is unknown to the sheikh. The chance of impersonation is more likely in urban areas where newcomers arrive constantly from the provinces in search of a livelihood; here it is possible that they may not be known to the sheikh. Also, the sheikh may be embarrassed to admit to not being familiar with some residents in his area and allow them to pass when he should have stopped them.

The chance of multiple voting is much greater in a country like Sudan if only because of the multiplicity of individuals who share the same name. "Family" names are most uncommon; a person's name consists of his given name followed by his father's and then his grandfather's given name. A very popular combination, for example is Ali Muhammad Osman. An indication of the degree of frequency is the fact that on one soccer team in Khartoum no less than three players had this name in common. Hence it is easy to see how an Ali Muhammad Osman may vote, using his correct name, yet not having registered.

An additional difficulty lay in the state most registration lists were in, particularly in view of the problem of arranging the names correctly in alphabetical order. It can be estimated that roughly three-fourths or more of all Sudanese names begin with one of three letters,[*] and it is exceedingly tedious to order names under such conditions, as anyone who has ever tried it can testify easily.[+]

Perhaps the most widespread, and certainly the most engaging, aspect of corrupt practices, especially in 1953, falls into the category of illegal political activity. The role of government employees has already been treated in the previous section. Here we wish to consider some aspects to campaign activities that may be judged to constitute "harmful propaganda."

The following two examples from the rural South and North, respectively, indicate the extremes to which election propaganda could be carried in regions with mostly illiterate and politically unsophisticated inhabitants. Fortunately, these examples were unrepresentative of general election behavior, yet they nevertheless illustrate how far out things could become. The first is based on a letter written to the electoral commission from NUP headquarters in Malakal, the capital of Upper Nile Province:

---

[*]Out of a total of twenty-eight; the three letters are alif, mim, and 'ayn, and examples of names beginning with one of these three are Ahmed, Ibrahim, Ismail, Ali, Osman, Omar, Muhammad, Mustafa, Mahmoud, Mahjoub.

[+]The author noted that in 1966 most literate Sudanese were not at all sure of the correct sequence of letters in the Arabic alphabet. A separate and somewhat amusing aspect of this same problem is that prisoners have been used on occasion to copy and perhaps edit registration lists.

I, Abdallah El Hag Muhammed Ali, President of the NUP
Province Committee at Malakal, wish to submit the following complaint under the Corrupt Practices Ordinance.

Sayyed Buth Diu addressed Nuer of Zeraf against our
candidate Bol Riak by saying:

1. If any voter casts his vote in favor of Bol Riak (he)
will undoubtedly be imprisoned for a term of seven years
or he will be hanged by the neck.

2. If Sayyed Buth Diu was not elected for Parliament,
Great Britain will declare war against the Sudan and
Egypt.

3. If Sayyed Buth Diu was not elected for Parliament he
will rejoin his government service and he will then revenge
(sic) from all who stood in his way.

4. Sayyed Buth Diu claims that he has powers to hang
Bol Riak or send him to jail.

All the informations (sic) took place under the very eyes
of sheikhs and councilors of Fagwir Rural Council Zeraf
Island who are ready to submit sufficient evidence.

With copies to various authorities

Signed . . .[15]

Buth Diu was the candidate of the Umma party and, according to
rumors, had received material aid and counsel from the British district commissioner. Neither these rumors nor the above charges
brought against him could be verified and, as a result, the case was
subsequently dismissed.

Several items about this letter are of interest and should be
clarified: first, in terms of content, this letter is not at all typical of
those found in the archives, but represents an extreme. Second, the
threats attributed to Buth Diu are ludicrous, of course—so much so,
that it might seem below the dignity of the commission at that time
or the reader right here to give the matter any second thought. But
at a minimum, they can give us interesting insights into the mentality
of the inhabitants of Zeraf Valley. The threats allegedly used by Buth
Diu referred to punishment by secular forces, imprisonment, foreign
intervention, threat of life, and so on, all matters that a Sudanese had
no control of whatsoever. If a man was to be imprisoned, this could
not be done except after trial by the British district commissioner.
Likewise, no one could be jailed without knowledge of the DC. So Buth
must have assumed (or at least pretended to assume) support by the
DC in his threats and, by implication, approval of the DC that voting
for Bol Riak constituted a sufficiently large crime to justify the
mentioned consequences. Unless Buth Diu was very close to the

district commissioner, he could never have gotten away with statements like these under the conditions of 1953.

But perhaps more interesting was the absence of the usual threats common in this part of Africa, namely threats that the spirits will punish the offender, that illness, plagues, and death will descend upon the voter and his family, and so on. As far as can be ascertained, it was more the rule than the exception that a candidate (almost always a prominent person in the tribe) would threaten the retribution of ancestors and other spirits toward anyone who dared oppose the "chosen one." (Any candidate who had any relationship whatsoever with a medicine man or a famous deceased warrior could claim that he was visited at night by the ghost of the deceased who "commanded" him to lead his people in elections as candidate.) Hence, Buth Diu's decision to use secular threats rather than spiritual ones is quite surprising and suggests that he must have occupied a fairly important government post. Third, lest anyone thinks that charges like the ones quoted in the letter are made only by despairing candidates with very little chance of success, it might interest the reader to know that Buth Diu was elected in the constituency by a four to one margin. He rose in parliament to become leader of a Southern faction and occupied a cabinet seat twice, the last time during the regime of Mohammed Ahmed Mahjoub in 1965.

Finally, in 1965 the author showed a copy of this letter to a school teacher (and active politician in the southern independence movement) from Upper Nile Province who knew both Buth Diu and Bol Riak. To the author's astonishment the letter produced neither a smile nor evidence of surprise on the part of the teacher, who felt that the charges in the letter were probably correct and who saw nothing unusual about them. Significantly, had this letter involved candidates in a northern constituency and had it been presented to an informed observer, his reaction would have been almost certainly an embarrassment about the implied low standard of politicking, accompanied by strenuous efforts to convince his listener that the charges must surely be vastly exaggerated and that anybody operating in such unworthy fashion should be condemned.

Just the same, notions about worthy or unworthy behavior are open to debate and local interpretation, especially when placed into the context of local value systems. The relativity of such values becomes clear when one considers the effects of religious attitudes (or sometimes superstitions) on public group behavior. In the northern Sudan, applications of religious pressures usually did not come out in the open, at least not in such a way that positive action would be taken by the authorities. An example of hidden pressures is contained in the following anecdote that was related to the author by an extremely close friend, who was then an executive officer in the NUP.

During the 1958 elections this NUP officer ran as his party's candidate in a rural area some distance north of Khartoum against a leading figure in the khatmiyyah sect, who was also very prominent in the People's Democratic party (PDP). The inhabitants of the constituency were about one-fourth village dwellers and three-fourths nomads. As it turned out, they split their votes almost exactly on this basis. The NUP candidate was a leading intellectual and well-known medical authority in the country; he was able to obtain the support of the educated (most villagers eligible to vote had received elementary schooling), while he lost almost all the votes of the nomadic sector. It appears, so the anecdote goes, that the sectarian opponent threatened the constituents to invoke his wrath upon all who did not support him. He claimed that on polling day he would transform himself in such a way as to be able to crouch inside the ballot box and would recognize every voter by his finger while the voter was dropping the token into the box. The educated constituents rejected this threat as ridiculous, whereas the great majority of nomads was not prepared to take their chances against the sheikh.

The purpose of inserting this anecdote is not to document an event that may or may not have taken place, but to illustrate the psychological conditions existing at that time in some areas. Were the story wholly unfounded and beyond the conceivable, my friend would have hardly thought of it in the first place (he related it in front of some other Sudanese). On the basis of his experience in the country and knowledge of the individuals involved, the author has no reason to doubt the reliability of the anecdote-teller.

On the one hand, it is significant that the khatmiyyah sheikh had to use threats in order to keep the nomads in line. This very fact suggests that the two voting blocs may not remain solid for any length of time. On the other hand, this anecdote illustrates the importance of sectarian loyalties, at least among uneducated voters. The degree of religious pressures on voting behavior throughout Muslim Sudan is evidenced by the results of the four general elections, which show that more than 95 percent of the constituencies in towns and cities were won by the NUP, whereas the Umma and PDP had to rely for support on rural areas. NUP support was strongest precisely where education had spread to the largest extent and where a fairly large percentage of civil servants lived. Conversely, the more backward an area, the stronger the influence of the two sectarian parties.

How did the electoral commissions respond to these and similar incidents? The members decided not to police campaign speeches because this could not be accomplished with the resources at hand. In the Sudan it has been customary for political rallies to be conducted in the evening under a format called "political night." Even if the commissions or any other body had opted for surveillance of such nights and for checking the candidates for reasonable accuracy in their campaign speeches, the really harmful propaganda that uses the form of a whisper campaign could not have been stopped anyway. Besides, the commission members felt that such policing was quite undesirable within the context of free elections. After all, the candidate should be judged by the voters at the polls, and not by election officers.

Of course, it was hoped that in such instances where the credibility gap became too wide, a reaction of common sense would rise to defeat the offending candidate. This placed the burden of judgment on the individual voter, and there were many—not all of them former colonial administrators—who thought that the local inhabitants were simply too uninformed and politically naive in order to make a sensible choice. There are two main rejoinders to such an argument: (a) A candidate is elected not because of any one particular quality, such as honesty or truthfulness, but as a general representative of a segment of the population whose members have delegated their legal authority to him for a limited time. The essential criterion here is not honesty or intelligence, although these are desirable, but a complex feeling that may perhaps be summarized by the term "trust." (b) If a man is voted into public office despite frequent and perhaps obvious deceptions of the voters, then this may be part of the price that the system exacts. There is no great profit in being moralistic about democratic elections. In no free election are candidates judged objectively on their actual accumulated merits; they are judged subjectively on their perceived merits. And although the idea might be distasteful, political savvy sometimes requires stretching the truth. The risk involved is clear and, usually once a man has been caught deceiving the public, his chances of election become minimal, especially in so-called primitive societies.

There is another point. It was not the task of the commissions to produce the ninety-two (in 1953) most qualified Sudanese legislators in the country—qualified in terms of education, political experience, or general wisdom—but to supervise the election process so that all ninety-two constituencies would be fairly represented. And if any objective is deemed particularly desirable in this process, it is that the elected representatives should be closely attuned to the political, social, economic, and spiritual needs of their constituents, regardless of how advanced or unsophisticated an observer might consider these needs to be.

Conversely, it was very clearly the task of the commissions to create channels for grievance cases. This was especially important for the right of appealing the decisions of registration officers regarding inclusion or exclusion of names on registration lists. The officers faced a rather difficult assignment because documentary evidence about a prospective voter's age and nationality was hard to come by, given the usual absence of birth certificates. As it turned out, election officials tried to use their personal judgment and informed all dissatisfied parties about grievance procedures. In view of the relative shortage of magistrates it was remarkable how many cases could be acted upon. The following figures from the 1958 elections are presented to the reader in order to indicate the magnitude of this problem: there were 16,000 appeals against inclusion, of which one-quarter were sustained, while applications for inclusion were submitted by 63,481, of which five-sixths were accepted.[16]

Much of the difficulty resulted from insufficient awareness or disorganization by individual Sudanese. In many districts hundreds and—in a few areas—thousands, appealed to the courts in anger after they discovered that their names were not included on the registration rolls (in almost all instances because they failed to register during the alloted period). Even though registration periods were extended, and magistrates worked around the clock to process as many cases as possible, inevitably there were some who forgot again or confused the deadline dates and were left out of the participation process. In general, these persons found it most difficult to understand the reasons for their exclusion, a matter that caused considerable consternation and disappointment at election time as the following fictitious, yet nonetheless all too typical, episode illustrates:

It was common for one Ahmed to travel over a considerable distance to the polls, stand patiently in a long line out in the scorching sun, only to discover when he finally arrived at the officer's desk that his name was not included in the list and that, therefore, he was not eligible to vote. "Why can't I vote?" "Because your name is not registered." "My name is not registered?" "Exactly." "So what?" "So you are not allowed to vote, because every voter has to be registered on this list, and anybody whose name is not on the list cannot vote." "By Allah, and by His Prophet Muhammad, who has ever heard of such a thing? I have come all the way from Umm Rahan and you say that I cannot vote!" "I am very sorry indeed; but these are the regulations." "Regulations! By the ears of the donkey! Who made up such regulations to disqualify me from voting? Am I not a resident of Umm Rahan, and are not all male residents of age of Umm Rahan eligible to vote? All the candidates said so, and if they all said so it must be correct!" "It is correct that all male residents of age from Umm Rahan are eligible to vote." "Then why are you refusing me? If you are a foreigner and don't know the people of Umm Rahan, then Sheikh Abdel-Rahman will vouch for me. He is a great sheikh, and may Allah give him long life. Give me this paper so that I may make my mark!" "I am sorry, but I can't." "But why can't you?" "Because, I told you before, the regulations." "You are a strange man, oh father (Abu) of regulations. Are you doubting the word of Sheikh Abdel-Rahman?" "No, I would never doubt his word." "Then you elevate your so-called regulations over the karamah* of Sheikh Abdel-Rahman!" "I am very sorry." "And I am sorry for you. May you eat these regulations and may the father of evil spirits fill your belly with regulations! Ma'a Salama." "Allah yisallamak." "Regulations! I have come all the way from Umm Rahan, and . . ."

VOTER ELIGIBILITY

One of the more interesting aspects of comparing the parliamentary elections emerges from a study of the eligibility requirements for voters. These requirements were specified by the Self-Government Statute for 1953, and by the Parliamentary Election Act for subsequent elections. For our present purpose it will suffice to focus on the voter qualifications for House territorial constituencies.†

Article 33.1 of the statute provided that a voter for a House territorial constituency in 1953 must be (a) Sudanese, (b) male, (c) not less than 21 years of age, (d) of sound mind, and (e) must have been ordinarily a resident in the constituency for a period of not less than six months before the closing of the electoral rolls.[17] Items (b) and (d) were implemented without difficulty; on the other hand, age, residence, and nationality could not be proven easily in many cases. With regard to age, for example, the previously mentioned lack of personal documents created the real possibility (with little practical remedy) that an enterprising individual could arrange to pad registration rolls with youngsters who supported his candidacy. The residency requirement was just as difficult to police without the availability of deeds for tracts of land. Nomads were even more affected than others by this because they could show in only a very few cases to have been— not to mention resided—inside a constituency for six straight months. In order that nomads not be disenfranchised completely, the 1953

---

*One of the highest social values, meaning nobility or honorableness in this case.

†The so-called Graduate Constituencies will be discussed in a subsequent section. An analysis of the Senate would not lend itself to a fruitful comparison, inasmuch as that camera was abolished during the military regime of General Abboud and later justifiably forgotten.

commission instructed its officers to be lenient in the application of
the residential rule.

The nationality requirement turned out to be the most controversial of all, even though one might have presumed otherwise, a priori.
In 1953 it affected three types of peoples—all quite numerous—two of
whom supported the Umma party and the third the NUP. The latter
group consisted of Egyptian-Sudanese, especially those who had
entered the Sudan during the condominium period, and who lived and
behaved in practically all matters like Egyptians rather than Sudanese.
(They would consider it an insult to be called "Sudanese;" their social
activities, like those of all other minority groups except the
Ethiopians—who in terms of numbers have been mostly prostitutes—
are conducted in closed circles, to which "normal" Sudanese have
virtually no access.) As indicated previously, their numbers were
swelled considerably by a virtual flood of relatives who just happened
to descend upon the Sudan near election time. As to the former, there
were the fellata on one hand, and marginal tribes living along the
Sudan's borders from Ethiopia to Chad on the other. The reader may
recall that, along all six of these border segments, members of any
one tribe could be found on both sides, and that they habitually mi-
grated back and forth for agricultural and political reasons. (An
example of the latter may be the arrival of the government tax collector.) Under these circumstances it would be quite easy for members of the Beni Amer, for example, to call on their brothers in
Ethiopia during election time.

The fellata constituted a different and unique problem. The term
fellata refers to all non-Sudanese westerners (originally to northern
Nigerians only) most of whom came to the Sudan on their pilgrimage
route to Mecca, and who supplemented their meager finances by
working odd jobs along the way. Their labor was in demand during
the harvest season and many decided on their return route to remain
in the more fertile and prosperous regions of the Sudan. Over the
years a large colony had assembled, now estimated at two million
members, many of whom settled on the banks of the Blue Nile south
of Sennar, and who have set up their own tribal hierarchy under a
Sultan. Some of these fellata have been in the Sudan for more than
three generations but are not considered to be strictly Sudanese by
the natives.

The question arising for the individual registration officer and
the election commission as well then was, just who is a Sudanese and
who is not? While the Sudanese Ordinance of 1948 provided some
answers, these were not very satisfactory on the whole. In essence,
everyone who could not provide reasonable proof that his male ancestors had lived in the Sudan since 1897 was not considered to be Suda-

nese. This was regardless of "how much a person wanted to be a
Sudanese!"

The commission could follow one of two basic approaches: It
could instruct its officers to accept all applicants except the most obviously unqualified ones (women, small children, Europeans, and so
on) and let any injured parties contest the individual decisions in
court, with the likely consequence of sizable roll-padding by Egyptian
visitors, border tribes, and fellata. (A number of pilgrims passing
through the country might have been persuaded to act as electors for
a small fee, posing as fellata, of course.) The alternative option was
the one eventually selected by the commission: to instruct the officers
to accept only those applicants who were qualified beyond the shadow
of a doubt, and let all others seek redress in the courts. This approach was legally justifiable and administratively simple. But due
to the inconveniences of mass scale appeals, the shortage of already
overburdened magistrates, and the sheer difficulty of proving the
birthplace of one's grandfather, this policy in the end prevented
large numbers of people from voting, who considered their home to
be in the Sudan and who wished to participate in the determination of
the country's future. Hence, the result was inconsistent with the
commission's general motto: "the largest possible franchise."

It is difficult to conceive why a policy could not have been followed of letting every person vote who was born in the Sudan, and
also to make some provisions for absentees, who could not be in their
original constituency at polling time. The actual decision seems especially injudicious if one considers the fact that for most Sudanese
participation was more important for psychological reasons than the
selection of representatives per se. Happily, several constructive
changes were introduced for subsequent elections. Although the residence requirement remained the same, a new Nationality Bill was
passed in 1957; also, the franchise was expanded for 1965 by lowering
the voting age to 18 years and by allowing women to vote for the first
time.

The reader may also recall that in 1953 many nomads had found
it difficult to vote because by polling-time they had moved considerable distances from their registration centers, and no provisions
could be made for them to cast their ballots elsewhere. Similarly,
civil servants and soldiers who were transferred before the polling
date also lost their opportunities to vote. This condition was remedied in 1958 when the commission instructed its polling officers to
"go out after" the nomads with mobile polling-units, of course only
if the tribal leaders had complied with the election staff's request to
notify them of the nomads' anticipated location at election time. This
procedure contained the potential risk that an unscrupulous returning

officer might choose among those nomadic groups that he "could find" and those that he could not. The chairman of the 1958 commission did not think, however, that this hypothetical situation occurred, or would occur in the future, since an officer who failed to contact a group of voters after having been informed of their whereabouts was liable to punishment through the courts if reported.[18]

The 1953 statute was the work of an international body that had to be mindful of its exposed public role, whereas the terms of references for the electoral commissions of 1958 and 1965 were defined by domestic politicians. Hence, the speculation may not be entirely unwarranted that the changes in age, sex, and nationality requirements were introduced primarily because the respective groups in power expected to benefit from them, and only secondarily, if at all, because the changes seemed more appropriate—in the sense of being fair and just—than the previous regulations.

The expansion of the electoral franchise to include women and the young was instigated by the United Front of Professional Organizations during the aftermath of the October 1964 Revolution. As we will try to show in subsequent chapters, the aim of this policy was to create a counterweight to the traditional parties in line with the goals of the "professionals" in the front.

Likewise, the new nationality requirement made a substantial difference in the eligibility of voters. The reader will recall that only those Sudanese were eligible to register in 1953 who could prove the residence of their ancestors in the Sudan from before December 13, 1897. This former ruling had excluded many residents of long standing, especially the fellata. Since the latter were all fervent ansar, they were considered to be a great potential course of electoral support by the Umma party members in the ruling coalition of 1957/58. Not surprisingly, the Sudanese Nationality Ordinance of 1948 was replaced by a new Sudanese Nationality Bill in 1957, which provided for citizenship by descent and by naturalization. Even though the substance of this bill seems perfectly justifiable and legitimate, its timing raised some eyebrows among neutral observers, because it was passed just shortly before the end of the registration period for the 1958 elections. Following its passage, a "flight of Umma cabinet ministers into the provinces" took place resulting in mass conferment of naturalization certificates on fellata and a number of other "Westerners."[19]

VOTING METHODS

Determination of appropriate voting methods was one of the most fascinating problems of the 1953 elections, and deliberations about alternative solutions necessitated a thorough evaluation of social and political conditions throughout the country. The great diversity of these conditions required that the eventual solutions be relative, that is, related to the particular needs and capabilities of the individual population units. It is easy to see that this commonsense approach interfered with the usual objective in general elections, namely uniform procedures, and thereby further complicated the task at hand.

There were four specific issues in 1953: (1) designating constituencies as either direct or indirect; (2) selecting the voting method for each district from among ballots, tokens, or acclamation; (3) determining appropriate means for identifying the various candidates by using colors, symbols, or both; (4) setting up a convenient schedule for polling sites and polling dates.

The task of the electoral commission was to develop impartial, comprehensive, and efficient procedures. This meant that in order to safeguard impartiality, no rules should be adopted that might favor one sector of the population (for example, the literates) over another. To maintain the freedom of elections, rules should be framed in such a way as to enable every voter to make his choice without fear of retribution. Ordinarily, this means secret voting. In order to achieve comprehensiveness, the adopted procedures had to take account of the various geographic and demographic patterns of the country, so that the nomads, for example, had the same opportunity to vote as the settled peoples. Another very important matter was comprehensibility, because polling procedures were totally unfamiliar to most Sudanese. Therefore considerable attention had to be paid to any existing traditional methods for choosing representatives in the country, and to the ways in which these could possibly be adapted to the needs at hand.

The Self-Government Statute provided that in at least 35 specified territorial constituencies (out of a total 92) elections should be direct, leaving it for the commission to add to this figure any of the otherwise indirect 57 constituencies, if local conditions seemed to warrant that.[20] In a direct constituency voting was to be conducted in a single stage by secret ballot, whereas in indirect constituencies voting was to take place in two stages: by a primary election of delegates to an electoral college and then a secondary election of the representative to the assembly.[21]

The relative merits and disadvantages of the two types were at that time perceived as follows: Direct elections minimize the

influence of local leaders by providing freedom from fear of retribution in the privacy of the polling booth. Thus fairness in terms of
equal opportunity for all candidates is more guaranteed than by the
rival method. For these reasons direct elections would tend to benefit
the NUP and harm the traditionalists, the Ummas and especially the
Socialist Republicans. An additional powerful argument, skillfully
employed by the advocates of direct elections, was that this method
raised local pride, whereas designation as indirect would—and did in
fact—result in hurt feelings.

The basic arguments in favor of indirect elections were well
stated by a Sudanese administrator in a nomadic area near Geneina,
as the following portions of his letter show:

1. Selection of delegates will be done after the customary majlis in which the issues involved will receive public
discussion.
2. Voting will be for local candidates.
3. This is the traditional way of dealing with political
affairs and commands the confidence of all concerned.
4. Opinions of those who represent distant voters not
present in the second stage will be heard with the knowledge that they are representative.[22]

At this point it may be fruitful to identify the various polling techniques under consideration and to compare their relative advantages
and disadvantages in the context of 1953.

Ballot

It appears reasonable to assume that under normal conditions
voting by secret ballot constitutes the most desirable polling method.
It accords the voter the optimum freedom of choice without fear of
retribution within the given range of alternatives. In the Sudan ballots
had been in use already for local elections in certain municipalities,
and it seemed justifiable to the commission that the experience gained
in those elections warranted retaining the method.

However, the utility of ballots was severely limited by the existing
low level of literacy variously estimated as between 2 and 5 percent
of the population. Experienced Sudan hands speculated that even the
substitution of colors or symbols for the candidates' names would
have resulted in much confusion, at least in the more primitive regions of the country, and probably would have led to considerable
spoiling of votes. The latter aspect was seen as the most pronounced

disadvantage of the ballot method, while its greatest advantage was
the elimination of possible cheating by voters.

Token

The second alternative was voting by tokens. Because this method
does not involve reading, tokens could be used in all those constituencies in which the commission deemed the level of literacy to fall
below a certain minimum standard. Determination of this level in
each case presented no problem. The real problem lay in selecting
the proper types of tokens so as to prevent duplications and forgery,
and in devising a method that would minimize confusion, such as
might result from the number of token-boxes in the polling room.

Under this voting method the voter was issued a token by the presiding officer and proceeded to enter the polling room where several
boxes were situated, one for each candidate, and he was expected to
drop his token into the box representing the candidate of his choice.
(In order not to jeopardize the voter's right to privacy, the election
staff had to remain outside the room.) Because the token method was
to be used in the more primitive regions of the country, not a few
local administrators (in point of fact, mostly British DCs) anticipated
that the bewildered voter—never having performed any such act
before—might not know what to do. He might drop the token into the
nearest box, or between boxes, or he might not understand which box
was to represent which candidate. In an effort to solve this problem,
quite a few enterprising officials submitted a series of proposals—
some very imaginative indeed—in order to facilitate the voter's task.
One method was finally adopted by most southern districts; there was
no uniformity in this matter. It shall be presented here because of
its originality and because, in a sense, it describes one aspect of the
level of social development in the southern Sudan rather eloquently:
A rectangularly shaped grass hut was constructed as a polling-station
in an unobstructed area, with an opening on one side for entering and
with an elephant-grass screen right behind the opening, thus shielding
the voter from an outsider's view. In the "room" the ballot-boxes
were lined up along the ground, each bearing the symbol of one candidate. Each box was connected to a long pole which passed through
the far wall of the hut and extended outside for another twenty feet
or so. At the end of this pole the candidate was seated and was thus
"tied" to his box inside. At eye-level a small horizontal slit was
left open in the wall through which the voter could see the candidates
sitting outside. He merely had to recognize his "choice," then to
follow the pole with his eyes through the wall onto the proper box.

In this way, it was felt, the voters should have no difficulty in connecting the proper box with their candidate.

The significance of this example is that it illustrates the need for extreme simplification of the voting procedures; the main reason being the total unfamiliarity of the electors with those procedures for parliamentary elections. However, this should not imply an inability to make an intelligent choice as such. Unfamiliarity with procedures incapacitated such peoples as southern Sudanese from effective voting only to a certain degree. They were quite capable of weighing pros and cons in choosing chiefs or deliberating on some local issues within the framework of their own rationality. This framework of rationality, while characterized by all the trappings of primitive or traditional society, did suffice to handle local (traditional) issues. It sometimes is only the introduction of alien concepts and procedures that confuses and incapacitates a traditional person. Often such confusion remains only temporary, until the alien concepts have been redefined within the framework of the old rationality or, as a result of such fundamental changes as the effects of education and experience, the old framework has been adapted to reconcile it with the new demands. It will be one of the conclusions of this book that Sudanese voters on the whole have succeeded in this process.

Acclamation

As the commission's Report indicated, there were several constituencies—five in the final assessment—in which the voters were deemed to be too unsophisticated to be able to use even the simplified token method. According to the statute, the only voting procedure left for accommodating these areas was acclamation. Since by definition all these constituencies fell into the category of indirect, acclamation was to be employed in the first stage, or primary election, only. The reader will recall that the purpose of the primary was for all qualified voters to choose an electoral college of specified size.

An example may be constituency no. 48, Southern Fung in Blue Nile Province (an enormous district, roughly 100 by 80 miles in area). This constituency was divided into 21 electoral divisions from which a total of 89 delegates were to be elected.* The system worked as follows: Any person who was qualified to vote was also qualified to

---

*According to the statute each division may be represented by from one to ten delegates, depending on the size of the population. The average was slightly over four.

be a candidate for delegate to the electoral college. On polling day all such persons wishing to be candidates were required to stand in something like a semicircle in an open area, and all voters present were asked to stand in single file behind the man whom they desired to be their delegate. The candidate with the smallest number of votes was eliminated, and his supporters were asked to redistribute themselves behind the remaining candidates. This process was repeated until the number of candidates left became equal to the number of delegates allotted to the electoral division.

This procedures was highly controversial among the various members of the commission, and unanimity on the number of constituencies using this method could not be achieved. The reasons were probably that acclamation excluded secrecy of voting, although this method was very comprehensible to the natives. This raises the major question as to whether or not in the absence of secrecy elections can be considered to be impartial and to guarantee the voter freedom from fear of retribution. This question is very difficult to answer. On one hand, the acclamation method increased the potential influence of local leaders tremendously; after all, who would be so foolish and oppose openly the candidate chosen by the sheikh or chieftain? On the other hand, one must take notice of the great amount of suspicion that primitive tribesmen would be expected to harbor against any procedures involving secrecy. Reports from the southern Sudan indicated that "local opinion holds that secrecy would be misunderstood and mistrusted,"[23] with the very real consequence of poor attendance at the polls.

Due to the complex implications of various voting methods, the 1953 commission was forced to decide on each case by majority vote. The final result was that the number of direct constituencies was increased from the original 35 to 68 of which in 30 cases the token method was used (including in all southern constituencies so designated) and in the remaining 38, ballot papers. Concurrently, the number of indirect constituencies was decreased from the original 57 to 24, of which in five acclamation was used; in the remaining nineteen, tokens were used in the first stage. For the second stage tokens were used for all 24 constituencies.

Identification of Candidates

A further task of the commission was to devise means for identifying the various candidates in an unmistakable fashion without at the same time prejudicing the voters in any way. Since the low level of literacy excluded the feasibility of printing the candidates' names on ballot papers in any constituency, the remaining alternatives were allocation of colors and/or symbols.

Once again, we are confronted by an apparently technical problem with all sorts of nontechnical consequences. The reasons are these: Whatever units of identification were chosen had to be sufficiently (a) distinctive from one another in order to avoid confusion, (b) numerous enough so that every candidate in each constituency could be allotted a different one, (c) easily recognizable and identifiable to the voter (this requisite excluded such items as airplanes, horses, or toilet bowls), (d) nonconnotative to the extent that this is possible.

Because there were up to eight candidates in direct constituencies, and a great many more at the first stage of indirect elections—the maximum number was eventually fixed at fifteen per electoral division—this meant that up to fifteen colors, symbols, or combinations thereof had to be selected.

An eloquent illustration of the difficulties involved here is contained in a letter by the then governor of Bahr El-Ghazal Province:

> . . . Colours themselves present a problem; some seem to find difficulty in distinguishing red from black, most find it difficult to distinguish green from blue. The Dinka range of colours is largely restricted to the hues of cows and Dinka would be apt to vote for the candidate (irrespective of who he is) presenting their favorite colour, usually red. A scheme has been thought of whereby candidates might be distinguished by the emblem of some animal—elephant, giraffe, crocodile, lion, etc. Unfortunately, Dinka tend to vote for their own totem-animal and those with no totem for their favorite species, probably giraffe; the crocodile candidate would get no votes.[24]

Letters from other areas, for example the Zande region in the South, suggested that voters would have difficulties distinguishing safely between more than black, white, and red: "For other colors there are not words in the local vernacular."[25]

The totem animal referred to above plays a very important role in the animistic orientations of most southern Sudanese. The southern member of the 1965 and 1968 Electoral Commissions, Munowwa Majok, explained the phenomenon to the author:

"At night a Southerner may dream about, say, a crocodile. The next morning he relates this experience to his friends: A crocodile visited me last night and said 'Wani, from now on you and I are brothers, and we must stand by each other's side.' Wani will consider the crocodile to be his relative."[26]

Interpretation of this anecdote is left to anthropologists and psy-
chiatrists. The reader should beware, however, of underestimating
the importance of such animism. British eyewitnesses gave several
accounts of incidents where armed southern guards refused to shoot
at certain animals and thus permitted injuries and deaths of humans
to happen, all because of animistic superstitions.

Suggestive connotations were not at all restricted to areas of
animism. During the course of the 1953 election campaign, many a
letter reached the commission's headquarters protesting against the
alleged abuse by a candidate of the symbols allotted to him and his
rival. A recurrent theme from the southern regions was that A, whose
symbol was an axe, would cut off the hands—the symbol of candidate
B—of all those who dared to vote for B. This threat carried connotations from the days of the slave raids in the southern Sudan, when
apparently the hands of many southerners were cut off by Arab
raiders.

In the more primitive areas of the North, Islamic allegations
were made by candidates who were allotted a tree as a symbol. As
may be expected, there were more harmless uses of symbols as
well: candidate with kerosene lamp, "I am the only light that shines
in this darkness;" candidate with native hut, "I give you shelter,"
and so on.

Against the background of these complex alternatives, the commission decided to resolve the problem by using a combination of
colors and symbols. Where ballot papers were used, the four colors
of red, black, yellow, and green in this order were selected. If the
number of candidates exceeded four, then symbols were printed below
the colors in the order of tree, elephant, hand, and so on.[27] In all
constituencies where tokens were used, symbols were allotted to the
candidates. They were assigned by drawing lots. In indirect constituencies, the candidates were given enlarged replicas of their symbols
with which to parade around in full view of the voters. The symbols
were also pasted on the ballot-boxes inside the polling stations in all
"token" constituencies.

In the author's opinion, the 1953 commission made the best of the
circumstances and deserves praise. It refused to be goaded by particular interests into an adoption of uniform practices throughout the
country, and recognized the need to adjust to heterogeneous conditions
with flexible standards without sacrificing principles. This fact is
undoubtedly one of the major reasons for the smooth performance
during all stages of elections. Also, the commission was aware of
the importance of experience—and the lack of it—in the election procedures in various parts of the Sudan, and it wisely adapted existing
methods for decision making in public affairs to suit the needs of

parliamentary elections. It is safe to assume that the opposite method—blind transplanting of foreign procedures intact into native settings—would have had much more unsatisfactory results as, indeed, has been proven in all too many instances throughout the world.

The three postindependence elections benefited from earlier experiences, and relatively little time was needed for deciding on the effectiveness of various polling procedures.

Article 9 of the Parliamentary Elections Act of 1957, stipulated that "the elections to both the House (sic) of Parliament shall be direct,"[28] thus eliminating acclamation and all other forms of indirect elections. Symbols were used exclusively for identifying the various candidates, and colors were dropped. Their assignment was accomplished by drawing lots out of a hat; there were no symbols allotted to political parties. As already mentioned elsewhere, the 1958 commission decided to employ mobile units on a large scale to facilitate voting for nomadic and seminomadic citizens. Another innovation, perhaps worth mentioning, was that special hours—or in some cases a second day—were set aside for women to vote since 1965. The purpose of this measure was to prevent that very traditionally oriented women would abstain from voting because of a reluctance to appear before large numbers of men at a public function.

DELIMITATION OF HOUSE CONSTITUENCIES

The Self-Government Statute had provided that there should be two kinds of House constituencies for the 1953 elections, the standard territorial variety, and a limited number of special ones for graduates. This latter category is rather unorthodox and deserves separate attention and explanation; we shall return to it at the end of this section.

The delimitation of territorial constituencies is almost anywhere a source of dispute, for the obvious reason that in a good many cases judicious manipulation of the boundaries may benefit political interest groups. This problem is accentuated in those areas where boundaries are to be drawn for the first time ever. Such was the case in the Sudan prior to the 1953 elections.

To be sure, the 1953 Electoral Commission was not empowered to amend the territorial delimitations of constituencies, which had been fixed by the Self-Government Statute. However, it did designate this issue as one of the six outstanding problems and recommended it to the Sudanese Parliament for early reevaluation. In actuality, the territorial boundaries were changed widely for the two subsequent elections of 1958 and 1965, and it is useful to understand the basic principles involved.

These principles are essentially twofold: constituencies should be roughly equal in the size of their populations, and they should exhibit some geographic continuity. A problem in implementing these guidelines arises because people do not tend to live on small islands or oases with nearly equal numbers of inhabitants. Therefore, it becomes a matter of staring at a map with accurate population distributions—an item usually distinguished by its absence in developing nations—and of deciding where to draw the first line. At this point the exercise takes on political overtones, since the lines can be drawn purposely in such a way as to benefit a particular party. Celebrated examples of this phenomenon exist in virtually all democracies and are denoted by the term gerrymandering.

Although a good number of complaints were lodged with the 1953 commission about alleged unfair alignments, the commission itself was prevented by statute from intervening in this issue. However, it did report that the House territorial constituencies varied greatly in the number of their inhabitants, estimating that those with the largest populations probably had four times as many people as those with the smallest.[29]

By contrast, the 1965 commission received very few complaints about constituency boundaries.[30] One reason may be that in 1965 a nonparty government had tried to solve a difficult problem as best it could, with little if any attempts at gaining unfair advantages from the delimitation of constituencies. However, such was not the case in 1958.

If one accepts the principle that constituencies should be roughly equal in size of population and that they should exhibit reasonable geographic continuity, then the possible kinds of manipulation may be identified as violations of either portion of this principle. Charges of such violations were raised by at least two observers of the 1958 elections, and were also insinuated by the attorney general of the Sudan. The latter was quoted by the 1958 commission as stating that:

> It is common knowledge that delimitation could be, if used
> unscrupulously, a very important factor in shaping the des-
> tiny of any election. The mere fact of placing this power
> in the hands of the government will give the opposition
> cause to denounce the delimitation as unfair. It is always
> wise to do justice but it is even wiser to show everybody
> that justice is in fact being done.[31]

Leo Silberman charged that "three constituencies were gerry-mandered (sic)—to no avail . . . for in each case they went to the

MAP 4.1

Gerrymandering I, 1958

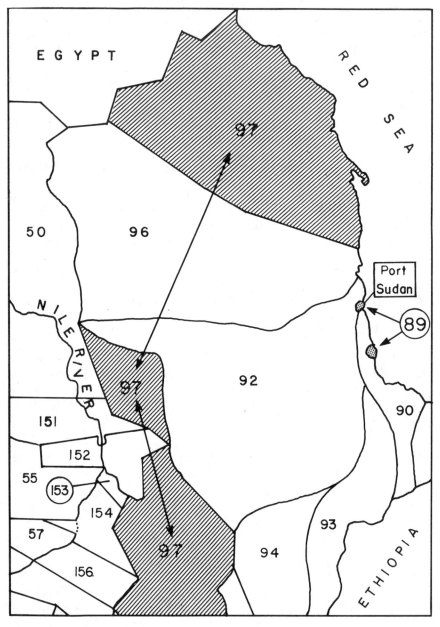

opposition. Yet no better testimony to the honesty of elections could be given than that in one of them, Khartoum North, the Minister of Interior was beaten, something unheard of in the Middle East."[32] Finally, P. M. Holt claimed that in 1958 ". . . more constituencies were formed in the central area of the Sudan, while the number of those in the north was diminished. The effect of this was to strengthen the voting power of the Umma Party as against the NUP."[33] Yet, an examination of the facts shows these allegations to be incorrect. While the number of constituencies increased sharply in Darfur, Kordofan, and Blue Nile provinces, these increases merely reflected necessary adjustments after the publication of the first population census. In fact, the provinces of NUP strength, Khartoum and Northern, averaged fewer inhabitants than the traditional Umma strongholds.[34]

A much sounder argument can be made that some gerrymandering took place within provinces. A study of Maps 4.1 and 4.2 suggests strongly that the ruling coalition in 1957-58 adjusted the boundaries of at least nine constituencies in disregard of the principle of geographic continuity in the hope of benefiting from the new arrangements. (See especially no. 97, Map 4.1 and nos. 117, 141 on Map 4.2.) And the election results seem to indicate that these efforts paid off in eight out of nine instances. Only no. 128 was lost to the NUP; apparently the chunk out of the Southern portion of no. 129 was not large enough (Map 4.2).

Meanwhile, the bases of the so-called graduates' constituencies were nonterritorial. The concept of graduates' constituencies may be unfamiliar to most readers, yet is by no means new, inasmuch as legislative bodies and electoral divisions during the earlier stages of representative government in Europe had been established according to distinct class or estates.[35]

The Self-Government Statute provided that three to five seats in the House of Representatives should be filled by victorious candidates in the Graduates' Constituencies.[36] Voters in these constituencies were to be graduates whose qualifications were essentially the same as those of the ordinary voter, except that there were no residence or sex (that is, being male) requirements; in addition, the voter had to have completed at least secondary school or its equivalent.[37]

No justifications for this franchise were spelled out in the statute, but a close reading of the archives suggests the following likely motives. Because of the very low levels of education and literacy in the country, some added weight should be given to Sudanese with higher education, albeit in a very limited way. Moreover, it was hoped that leading cabinet members could be drawn from among the victors in the Graduates' Constituencies. This line of reasoning rested on the premise that the most educated voters would elect the most capable

MAP 4.2

Gerrymandering II, 1958

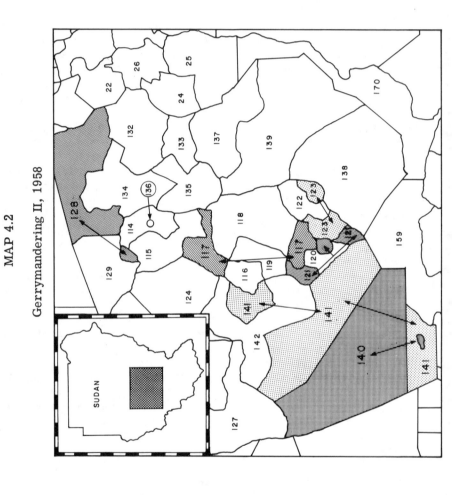

candidates, whereas in the predominantly rural territorial constituencies the winners would likely be tribal representatives whose major
and possibly only qualification was their tribal status. In this connection it is worth noting that members of the Cabinet had to be elected
to Parliament, according to the statute.[38]

The eventual decision was to reserve five constituencies for
graduates in 1953, and twelve years later to increase that number
threefold. By contrast, these special constituencies were abolished
for the 1958 and 1968 elections. We may speculate that the reasons
for these decisions can be traced in all cases to the prevailing political conditions.

The two logical justifications for abolishing Graduates' Constituencies in 1958 and 1968 were (1), that it was simply in the interests
of the ruling groups to do so, and (2), many people thought that the
idea of special constituencies was fundamentally irreconcilable with
democracy. The first argument is supported by the voting results.
In 1953 the graduates elected four NUPs plus one independent, who
turned out to be a member of the Anti-Imperialist Front. (A cover
organization for the then illegal Communist party of the Sudan.) Thus,
the ruling Umma party/PDP coalition could not realistically expect
to gain a single seat in the Graduates' Constituencies in 1958; elimination of that franchise was therefore one way to minimize the
strength of the NUP. The same basic argument applied ten years
later, with the minor modification that the NUP (DUP) now occupied
the role of establishmentarian coalition partner, with little effective
support among the bulk of eligible graduates, who three years earlier
had voted into power 13 candidates of extremist parties out of a total
of 15.

In 1965 Graduates' Constituencies were reintroduced after considerable agitation about the types and numbers of special constituencies. Finally, it was decided that there would be 15 Graduates'
Constituencies in addition to the 218 territorial ones. This decision
was made by the first transitional government, which was dominated
by the so-called Front of Professional Organizations, a group heavily
dependent on students, teachers, members of trade unions and other
professional groups. It mistrusted not only the overthrown military
rulers but also the traditional political parties, and espoused a more
radical political orientation than any previous ruling group since independence. It could reasonably expect to find support among the
graduates; the eventual results bear out the accuracy of this assumption.

CONCLUSIONS

The remarkable performance of the Sudanese in staging open and fair parliamentary elections has been acknowledged by many foreign and domestic observers, including the author of this volume. Several factors account for the overall success; yet a review of the particular issues would seem to indicate that the various commissions deserve special praise for their work.

The 1953 commission desired to maintain open channels of communication to its subordinates as well as to outsiders, and it made this policy publicly known. The results were threefold: (1) Internally the commission solicited not only information on substantive issues, but private opinions as well from the election staff in the provinces. For this purpose it scheduled regular meetings with the chief electoral officers in order to enable them to air their views, receive rulings on particularly complex issues, and provide the commission's members with data about local conditions and about the progress of preparations. (2) Each officially recognized political party was invited to appoint a permanent liaison officer who could meet with the commission on a regular basis. During such meetings individual requests—and complaints—of the parties were considered. At the same time, the liaison officers gained valuable insights into the functioning of the electoral machinery and had an opportunity to appreciate some of the difficulties involved in staging elections. (3) Private individuals felt encouraged to submit their views and suggestions to the commission which, unlike the British-dominated Sudan government, was not stigmatized as working for the interests of certain groups, but was generally respected as genuinely impartial. Newspaper editors joined the activities; in the end a number of quite useful—and many not very useful—comments emerged. The important point here is that the commission was not perceived as an aloof organization, but as a body to which access was possible; this heightened the sense of popular participation in an event that contributed to determining the country's destiny.

The commission's imaginative, innovative, and above all open approaches to its various problems was also instrumental in educating Sudanese public opinion about the electoral franchise in general, and about those requirements that were necessary to produce fair and effective elections in particular. All available evidence indicates that throughout 1953 the commission was able to command the respect and admiration of politicians and government officials alike. The foundation for this position was laid by the terms of the Self-Government Statute, which established the commission as an international body, independent from any government or political organization. It is to the credit of its members that they took advantage of this constitutional independence and established a series of precedents that legitimated the work of the subsequent commissions.

These successor bodies were able to adopt most of the established procedures, adding some points here or amending a directive there usually following informal consultation with all interested parties. The end-products of these deliberations took the form of a large number of pamphlets and instruction circulars that were mailed to all election officers. One cannot be but impressed with the thoroughness with which all relevant matters were covered in these instruction sheets. (The 1965 chairman explained somewhat apologetically that he was not about to take any chances with the imagination of his staff.) An example may be Directive No. 6 on Instructions to Polling Officers for Voting by Ballot Paper,[39] a hard-bound pamphlet of 14 printed pages, touching on all subjects from how to handle tensions near the polling station to the need to have, among other items, two pieces of red wax, one roll of twine, a roll of cord, and a match box ready for sealing the ballot box.[40]

NOTES

1. W. Mackenzie and K. Robinson, Five Elections in Africa, (London: Oxford University Press, 1960), p. 2.

2. Sources in addition to personal observation are the various reports of the electoral commissions of 1953, 1958, 1965, and 1968, articles written and public statements by the commission chairmen, and notes from the commissions' files ordered according to problems and issues. For more detail on data, and analysis of election commission performance, see this author's unpublished "Parliamentary Elections in the Sudan" (Ph.D. diss., Princeton University, 1967).

3. Criteria quoted by 1965 chairman of the electoral commission during an interview on March 1, 1965, from official documents from the office of head of state.

4. Interview with Justice Mudawi, March 1, 1965.

5. Basil Davidson, "Sudan's Orderly Elections," Manchester Guardian, February 25, 1958. This account referred to the 1958 elections but could apply equally to the preceding or subsequent elections, in this author's opinion.

6. Great Britain House of Commons Sessional Papers 1952-53, vol. 30, Command Paper 8904, The Self-Government Statute, p. 21.

7. The data are based on letters and accounts in the government archives as well as on passages in K. Henderson, Sudan Republic (New York: Frederick A. Praeger, 1965); Peter M. Holt, A Modern

History of the Sudan, (London: Weidenfeld and Nicholson, 1969); and
J. S. R. Duncan, The Sudan's Path to Independence (London: William
Blackwood and Sons, 1957).

8. Great Britain House of Commons Sessional Papers 1953-54,
vol. 33, command paper 9058, "Report of the Sudan Electoral Commission," Khartoum, October 13, 1953 (hereafter cited as Report),
pp. 19-20.

9. Report, pp. 8-9 and 24.

10. Ibid., p. 8.

11. Republic of Sudan, Ministry of Interior, Government Archives
on the Electoral Commission of 1953 (hereafter referred to as Archives), section on letters to the chairman of the Electoral Commission.

12. Report, p. 18.

13. See J. I. R. Scott, "Problems of West African Elections," in
What are the Problems of Parliamentary Government in West Africa?
(London: The Hansard Society for Parliamentary Government, 1958),
pp. 65-78. Also recent elections in South Asia and Latin America.

14. Report, pp. 17-18.

15. Archives, letter dated October 29, 1953.

16. Leo Silberman, "Democracy in the Sudan," Parliamentary
Affairs 12 (1959): 362.

17. Self-Government Statute, Part IV, Article 33.1.

18. Interview with Sayyed Hassan Ali Abdallah, May 18, 1965.

19. For evidence see Silberman, op. cit., p. 362, and an interview of this writer with a high member of the 1958 Election Commission who requested not to be quoted.

20. Self-Government Statute, First Schedule, Parts I and II, and
Part II A and B subsumed under Article 33.

21. Ibid., First Schedule, Part III, Articles 32.A.1 and B.2.i-v.

22. Archives, File EC1/A2.6 on Darfur Province.

23. Archives, letter to chairman of Electoral Commission.

24. Archives, letter from Owens to chairman of the Electoral
Commission, Wau, April 13, 1953.

25. Archives, section on technical problems.

26. Interview with Munowwa Majok, May, 1965.

27. Sukumar Sen, "The General Election in the Sudan," Foreign
Affairs Report 3 (India): 22.

28. Parliamentary Elections Act, Article 9.

29. Report, Appendix III, Article 4.b., pp. 22-23.

30. Private Interviews with the chairman of Electoral Commission, March, 1965, and subsequently. The situation remained basically unchanged for 1968.

31. Election Commission's Final Report, pp. 9-10, quoted by Leo Silberman, op. cit., p. 363.

32. Silberman, op. cit., p. 363.

33. Holt, op. cit., p. 179.

34. For specific figures and further details, see Peter Bechtold, "Parliamentary Elections in the Sudan" (Ph.D. diss., Princeton University, 1967) pp. 198-200.

35. Encyclopedia of the Social Sciences, vol. 4 (New York: Macmillan, 1931), p. 243. For example, in England, the nobility, the clergy, and the commons were represented in separate bodies.

36. Self-Government Statute, Art. 32.

37. Self-Government Statute, First Schedule, Part IV. For exact details see Article 33.2.

38. Self-Government Statute, Article 15.1.

39. Election Commission of the Sudan, Directive No. 6, 1965.

40. Ibid., pp. 12-13.

5

THE FIRST FIVE
YEARS, 1953-58

By 1953 two major constitutional issues faced the Sudan. One problem, which was to remain unsolved for almost 20 years, concerned the constitutional status of the southern Sudan (treated in greater detail in a later chapter). For most of the twentieth century, British colonial policy had treated this region as a distinctly separate entity with special administrative provisions known as the Southern Policy. In fact, speculation in official and unofficial circles linked the future of the southern Sudan with other East African Territories such as Uganda; and it was not until the Juba Conference of June, 1947, that these views were reversed and the administrative and political unity of North and South Sudan were affirmed as a matter of official policy.

With the issue of self-determination rapidly approaching, the sizable gap in economic, social, and political development between the two regions was recognized by the authorities, and the implied necessity to provide special treatment for the southern Sudan until that gap had been reduced significantly. Hence, the major domestic constitutional issue became the determination of the southern Sudan's relationship to the central government, and specifically the degree of regional autonomy under some sort of federal structure. Because of continuing differences among all policymakers before and after independence, this issue was not formally decided upon until 1972, and the Sudan has lived under a temporary constitution for more than 17 years.

Important as this matter has been, it was nevertheless overshadowed in 1953 along with all other domestic issues by the central constitutional question, namely whether the country should be linked with Egypt in some form or whether it should become independent. This issue was, in fact, the raison d'etre for general elections for the new Constituent Assembly, whose main task—according to statute—

was to decide on the future constitutional status of the Sudan, and which was given a three-year "transitional period" for accomplishing that task and for preparing the country and its people for its ensuing condition.

THE 1953 ELECTIONS

Five groups contested the 1953 elections: the Umma party, the National Unionist party (NUP), the Socialist Republican party (SRP), the Southern party, and various independents. Of these, the first two were the most important. Their origins and background have been described already in previous chapters, and it will suffice to restate their characteristics in capsule form.

The Umma party was a political organization drawing support almost exclusively from the ansar movement, the followers of the Mahdi. This following was, and continued to be, based essentially in the rural areas of central and western Sudan. Patron of the party was Sayyid Abdel-Rahman el-Mahdi, imam of the ansar and posthumous son of the famous Mahdi, while the party leadership rested with one of Abdel-Rahman's sons, Siddiq el-Mahdi. The party stood for complete independence of the Sudan and was popularly identified as pro-British. This image resulted probably from the rather close cooperation between the Sudan government and the Legislative Assembly—which had an almost exclusive Umma party membership— during the last four years plus before elections.

The chief rival was the NUP, which was headed by Sayyid Ismail el-Azhari, a former school teacher with a considerable backlog of political experience since the founding days of the Graduates' Congress. NUP following consisted in those days of two groups: (a) civil servants, businessmen and other educated members of professional trades residing in urban areas; (b) followers of the khatmiyyah sect who inhabit most of the northern and eastern regions of the Sudan, and whose spiritual patron had endorsed el-Azhari. The NUP denounced their Umma rivals as stooges of British colonialism and campaigned under the slogan of "unity of the Nile valley." In return for their pro-Egyptian policy they received considerable financial and other aid from Cairo, especially after the new revolutionary government came to power there under the formal leadership of a half-Sudanese, General Muhammad Naguib.

The Socialist Republican party was made up of a small group of conservative tribal chieftains whose support was entirely localized and consisted only of members of their immediate tribes. They advocated independence for the Sudan, but were opposed to Mahdi domination. Their opponents in the NUP and Umma labeled them as British stooges, who wanted to perpetuate British rule and influence in the Sudan. To what extent these charges were accurate is very difficult to determine. However, it seems clear that SRP members were mostly, if not all, ansar by religious affiliation and that they were discontented with the predominant influence of the Mahdi house in central and western Sudan. Almost immediately after elections the party collapsed and has not been resurrected since.

As a rule, "independents" were individuals who either desired genuinely to be free from identification with any party label or, more likely, were overlooked as candidates by the party of their choice, perhaps because the "price was not right," and decided, in a huff stirred by personal pride, to go it alone.

The Southern party was an association of some, but not all, southern politicians. Very little documented information has been available about this group, but it seems that the party comprised leaders of those southern tribes who could not be bought by northern parties. A report by the Sudan Political Service credited these leaders with enjoying the backing of the southern intelligentsia and the "great bulk of southerners."[1] As we shall see, the ordinary southerner tended to support his tribal leader regardless of party affiliation. The objectives of the party centered around the basic problem of safe-guarding the interests of southern Sudanese by fighting for regional autonomy or joining whatever coalition government could offer the most attractive possibilities in that direction.

Most southerners distrusted the northern politicians. There were a good many who feared being ruled by a northern majority after independence, and who wanted the British to remain in the southern Sudan. The behavior of northern politicians in the South, especially the mixture of condescending attitudes and outlandish enticements for voting support, did much to substantiate these suspicions.

In comparison to its rival, the Umma party was not very active there, perhaps because the Southern party leadership concurred with the Umma objective of complete independence for the Sudan. By contrast, the NUP was particularly zealous in wooing southern chieftains and, together with Egyptian officials, offered them sometimes fantastic promises, such as forty senior administrative posts following the British departure.[2] Another example is provided by the well-known and rather amusing anecdote about the "dancing major." This refers to the dispatch of the Egyptian special minister for the Sudan and close Nasser friend, Major Salah Salim, on a tour of southern provinces, during which nakedness and general backwardness took up much of the discussion. On at least one occasion the major tried to prove Egyptian historical and blood ties to the Dinka and, to strengthen his argument, partially disrobed as he participated in a tribal dance. (He attributed the difference in skin color to climatic effects.[3])

As may be expected, voting participation varied with the kinds of constituencies and the number of contesting candidates. It was lowest in the primaries of indirect constituencies and highest in the Senate elections.

In the House territorial constituencies, 282 candidates competed for 92 seats after withdrawals and rejection appeals had been completed. In ten cases candidates were returned unopposed, while, at the other extreme, as many as 8 competed in one constituency; the average lay around 3.

It may be of interest that a total of fifteen nominations were rejected, four because of illiteracy on the part of the candidates.[4] In this context it should be noted that the commission was informed after the elections that there was considerable difficulty in the South in finding suitable candidates more than 30 years old who could meet the literacy requirement.[5]

In 7 of the 24 indirect constituencies candidates were returned unopposed. In the remaining 17 participation varied from a low of 6 percent in the swamplands of Bor in Upper Nile to a high of 70 percent in Jur River South near Wau, the capital of Bahr el-Ghazal Province. The average lay at 26 percent, although this figure may prove less meaningful when considered closely. An examination of the situation at the individual polling stations within the 17 constituencies reveals that participation varied from zero to 98 percent of the registered voters. The commission's Report explains the relatively low overall average by suggesting that in many divisions only as many candidates presented themselves seriously as there were delegates to be chosen to the electoral colleges. Apparently, the voters had conferred informally beforehand and agreed on their chosen representatives so that there was no need for any large number to appear at the polling stations for formal voting.[6] (In fact, this interpretation became a powerful argument for discontinuing indirect elections subsequently.) Whenever there was a real contest, the voting turnout was considerably above average.

In the secondary stage of indirect elections participation was very high and only 35 of 1497 electors failed to attend.[7] The outcome in 7 of the 17 constituencies was extremely close, that is, the second place candidates obtained between 44 percent and 48.8 percent of the votes cast. This probably reflects deep divisions within the constituencies along tribal lines, since in most other cases the delegates— who surely conferred among themselves before polling—would have agreed on one or the other candidate with a bandwagon effect as a result. (This latter supposition is based on the author's several observations of club elections where the bandwagon effect was very strong.)

In 3 of the 68 direct constituencies candidates were returned unopposed. In the remaining 65 participation varied from the unusual low of 7 percent in the Shilluk swamplands of Upper Nile—the next lowest figure was 19 percent in a nomadic area of Darfur and there was only one more in the twenties—to a high of 77 percent in Zande East in Equatoria. The national average was 54 percent, with the turnout in the capital being just under 50 percent.

In the Graduates' Constituency 1,849 persons voted out of 2,247 registered voters, which amounted to 82 percent.[8]

The distribution of seats in the Constituent Assembly by parties was as follows:

TABLE 5.1

Distribution of Seats After 1953 Elections

Party	House of Representatives	Senate		
NUP	50	21 elected + 10 nominated = 31		
Umma	23	4 elected + 4 nominated = 8		
SRP	3	1 elected + 0 nominated = 1		
Southern party	9	3 elected + 3 nominated = 6		
Independents (including southerners)	12	1 elected + 3 nominated = 4		
Total	97	30	20	50

Source: Compiled by the author.

The Senate nominations were made by the governor-general in accordance with Article 31 of the Self-Government Statute. The striking majority of NUP seats won in the Senate reflects the fact that Senate electors represented to a great extent the same social groups on whose support the NUP was, and continued to be, based: local council members (that is, mostly civil servants), schoolmasters, teachers, and some graduates.

A close look at the House elections supports this relationship. In the Graduates' Constituency the NUP gained 4 seats while the fifth one was won by an independent (who was in actuality a member of the outlawed communist movement). Geographic voting patterns may be inferred from the following table on party gains in the House Territorial Constituencies, broken down by provinces:

TABLE 5.2

Distribution of Seats by Party per Province, 1953

Province	NUP	Umma	SRP	Southern Party	Independents	Total
Blue Nile	6	10	2	—	—	18
Darfur	2	6	1	—	2	11
Kordofan	11	6	—	—	—	17
Bahr El Ghazal	1	—	—	2	4	7
Equatoria	—	—	—	5	2	7
Upper Nile	4	—	—	2	2	8
Kassala	6	1	—	—	1	8
Khartoum	9	—	—	—	—	9
Northern	7	—	—	—	—	7
Total	46	23	3	9	11	92

Source: Compiled by the author.

Of special interest are the following observations: (1) the NUP sweep in Khartoum and Northern provinces in which almost all voters are settled in riverain towns. The results in Kassala—6 out of 8— reinforce this pattern, although the overriding influence of the khat-miyyah sect (which had endorsed the NUP) must not be overlooked. (2) Umma support came almost exclusively—22 out of 23 seats won— from the three central-western provinces, historical strongholds of Mahdism. (3) The three SRP seats were won in traditional Umma territory, a fact that supports the original contention, namely that the Socialist Republican party constituted an alliance of local chieftains who were dissatisfied with certain aspects of the Mahdi family's centralistic policies in Omdurman. (4) Independents won all but one of their seats in areas inhabited by Southerners (or non-Arab Africans in portions of Darfur), a fact that reflects the inability of the founders of the Southern Party to accommodate Southerners across tribal lines.

Reaction to the voting results was understandably mixed. The National Unionists attributed their triumph to "the peoples' endorse-ment of our farsighted plans and our common determination to liberate our beloved country from the shackles of colonialism." The British were noticeably caught off guard since they had expected an Umma victory. Their reaction was "unconcealed disappointment in the elec-tion results,"[9] caused no doubt by a kind of shock about what seemed like ungratefulness on the part of the Sudanese. After all, the Sudan had always occupied a special place in the hearts of the British; some of their very best officers had spent long years in the Sudan Service in great dedication and under extreme hardship. Their emotional commitment found expression in the London Times, which called the Egyptian efforts prior to the elections "reprehensible interference into Sudanese affairs . . . in which every effort is being made to con-fuse the issue. . . ."[10] After the results were known, the tone shifted to cynicism about the "childishness of Sudanese politics" (because some independents had decided to cast their lot with the NUP once they had observed the trend of events).[11]

The Umma leaders were terribly disappointed, of course, and put the blame for their fiasco on foreign interference rather than their own organizational shortcomings. Sayyed Siddiq el-Mahdi, the president of the Umma party, announced that "Umma did not recog-nize the validity of the elections, which had been influenced by Egyp-tian money and propaganda, and would take steps to make their position clear to the Sudanese and to world opinion. . . ."[12] The force of this statement is somewhat tempered when contrasted with the commission's assertion that the voting results found a remarkably popular acceptance.[13]

In retrospect, the NUP support at the polls exceeded by far the expectations of the British and the Umma party leadership for two reasons: the traditionalists (for example, Ummas) underestimated the degree of secularization that had taken place in the Sudan, and the British underestimated the appeal of nationalistic movements.

To be sure, the Umma party patron, Sir Abdel-Rahman el-Mahdi, had himself been fairly active in the independence movement. Yet there were several reasons why he and his party did not reap as much credit for its success as the NUP's did: (1) Because of the visible all-pervasive presence of Britishers, independence for the average Sudanese was to be obtained from the United Kingdom and not from Egypt; this is precisely what NUP slogans called for. (2) The original "struggle for self-determination" began in the Graduates' Congress, an organization soon dominated by Ismail el-Azhari, the subsequent leader of the NUP, and from this perspective, the heirs of the graduates were more deserving of credit for independence. (3) Many Sudanese who were not strongly attached to either the mahdiyyah or khatmiyyah sects per se became alienated from the former group following the militant fanaticism exhibited by ansar youth organizations in the western region prior to elections. (4) During the four-year life span of the Legislative Assembly the Umma party shared the burden of government with the British, although not in equal proportions. It was a period of much labor unrest, demonstrations, and economic hardship; hence the Umma party was much more exposed to criticisms of various sorts than the rival parties, who had boycotted the Legislative Assembly.

Meanwhile, the great majority of the British in the Sudan did not perceive the considerable and widespread appeal of nationalism, because they simply refused to perceive the Sudanese as anything but very backward and needing Britain's paternalistic protection. The average district commissioner was unshaken in his belief that traditionalism exerted, and would continue to exert for a long time, a tight grip on local life-styles and aspirations. What the British failed to recognize, of course, were fundamental distinctions in the various forms and expressions that traditionalism may take. As colonial administrators they were very aware of the cultural and socioeconomic gaps between themselves and the rest of the Sudanese; yet they could not comprehend how many Sudanese were already considering themselves to be rather modern and advanced—compared, of course, to other Sudanese.

This form of colonialist perception—which, incidentally, persisted among the vast majority of British employees even many years after independence—can be constantly reinforced by observing the private behavior of Sudanese elite members. To cite just one example of many possible ones: A highly educated (Oxford) senior civil servant and leading figure in United Nations missions, who has been personally well-known to this writer, habitually eats the same food as his servant does, although he could easily afford the, to him, familiar Western food; he changes after work from his black custom-tailored suit into the native jallabiyyah at home, walks barefooted, disdains luxury furniture well within his means, and so on.

In conclusion, the NUP landslide victory may be attributed to all of these factors: a platform attractive to Sudanese at this particular juncture in time, a superior organization based on superior talent in terms of education both at the top and in the medium ranges of the party structure, solid financial backing and good coaching in application of the resources, an opponent who overestimated his own strength and underestimated the size of the task, and a clean image in the independence movement.

PARLIAMENTARY DEMOCRACY: THE FIRST FIVE YEARS

With an absolute majority for the NUP in both Houses, the road seemed to be clear for its leader, Ismail el-Azhari, to enjoy the fruits of victory and to entrench himself as the main force in directing the future course of his nation. And indeed, Prime Minister el-Azhari proudly presented the first All-Sudanese Council of Ministers on January 19, 1954, consisting of 9 Northerners and 3 Southerners.

Alas, trouble appeared as quickly on the political scene as a swarm of house flies over a dish of mulkhiyyah.* In little over two years the el-Azhari regime was to stagger under three major crises.

First, the opening of the Constituent Assembly had to be postponed when the arrival of one of the foreign dignitaries, President Naguib of "sister" Egypt, was met at the airport by a mob of perhaps 40,000 ansar, who had been called in by the Mahdi leadership to demonstrate the "people's desire for independence" and, coincidentally, Umma party misgivings about Egyptian interference on the NUP side.[14]

To what extent these street demonstrations and riots influenced el-Azhari to reevaluate his Nile valley unity policy is difficult to determine. There are strong indications that this policy had been aimed primarily at getting the British out of the country with the aid of Egyptian allies, and did not in actuality constitute el-Azhari's visions of the Sudan's destiny. Some reliable Sudanese sources went even further in claiming to this author that el-Azhari had privately assured them during an overseas meeting prior to the 1953 elections that the NUP slogan was merely an expedient to attract Egyptian political,

---

*Mulkhiyyah is a popular meal in the Nile valley.

financial, and propaganda support, but that he never intended to opt
for anything less than total independence.[15] Be that as it may, once
the Constituent Assembly had been elected, an all-Sudanese cabinet
had taken office, and the period of British rule was clearly drawing
to an end, a strong reliance on Egypt became less a necessity and
more a potential liability (especially after the half-Sudanese President
Naguib was replaced in Cairo by the less predictable Nasser). When
the motion for total Sudanese independence was finally proposed to the
Constituent Assembly, Ismail el-Azhari rose and, in a dramatic gesture, urged his NUP followers for unanimous approval of a motion
that only months earlier had been the Umma party slogan. The immediate result of this act was to propel Sayyed Ismail into a heroic
role at home, but this also earned him the lasting distrust and opposition of the Nasser regime in Egypt.

The second blow to the el-Azhari government occurred in August
1955, when a mutiny broke out among southern troops in the Equatoria
Corps of the Sudan Defense Force. The mutiny was merely the first
climax of a deepseated crisis that had been brewing for a long time
and that centered around the animosities between northern and southern Sudanese. Some of the origins and dimensions of this conflict
have already been alluded to earlier; suffice it here to point to the
widespread fears among southern leaders that the imminent independence of the country would herald northern subjugation of, and discrimination against, the less developed and relatively defenseless
Southerners.

To many southern minds, an example of such biased treatment
was provided by the work of the Sudanization Committee, which had
been appointed on February 20, 1954. Its task was to consider which
posts in the civil service would be given to Sudanese. Even though
southerners, along with all other groups, were sufficiently cognizant
of the shortage of qualified personnel from their region, they were
nevertheless shocked to learn that in the final allocation 796 out of
800 positions went to Northerners.

It is always difficult to speculate about the direct causes of spon-
taneous violence. It may very well be that the mutiny was originally
aimed at little more than a graphic demonstration of southern grievances to an imperious and preoccupied North, yet it resulted in rioting
and heavy loss of life for northern civilians in the South; even more
southern citizens were killed during the subsequent retributions by
government forces. As such, the mutiny initiated a bloody civil war
between northern and southern Sudanese that was to last almost 17
years, at tremendous cost to all concerned.

For the el-Azhari regime the mutiny constituted a temporary
setback in prestige, but was soon pushed into the background by pre-
occupation among northern politicians with imminent independence,

and also by a phenomenon that was to characterize all parliamentary regimes, namely inter- and intraparty squabbles.

As previously described, the ruling NUP drew its support from two groups: secularized urbanites and followers of Sayyed Ali el-Mirghani. The leader to the khatmiyyah sect had decided to support the NUP partly because of the latter's pro-Egyptian policy, which corresponded to the traditional position of the khatmiyyah, and partly as a counterweight measure to the political influence of the Mahdi family. Thus the NUP appealed to two distinct sections of the populations that had very little in common from a social, religious, or economic point of view. They were held together by their pro-Egyptian policy before the 1953 elections and the mutual desires of their two leaders to limit the political influence and personal ambitions of Sir Abdel-Rahman el-Mahdi

The first of these common bonds disappeared as soon as el-Azhari let on his inclination to opt for Sudanese independence, thus reversing his election slogans and antagonizing his pro-Egyptian followers (not to mention the Egyptians themselves). The second became more tenuous when the khatmiyyah faction within the NUP reacted to this policy by attempting to undermine el-Azhari's position within the party. The first cracks appeared in December 1954, when three prominent khatmiyyah ministers under the leadership of Mirghani Hamza bolted from the cabinet and the NUP, and formed the short-lived Republican Independence party. To compound matters, the time seemed opportune for some of el-Azhari's old personal enemies from the Graduates' Congress days to attack his leadership. During the ensuing power struggle, el-Azhari was able to retain his position only by purging the party executive council of personal rivals and other pro-khatmiyyah leaders. After many intrigues and political maneuvers, the pro-Egyptian wing finally broke off from the old NUP in June 1956 and formed a new party, the People's Democratic party, under the sponsorship of Sayyed Ali-el-Mirghani. El-Azhari continued as president of the NUP, which now adopted an increasingly secular and middle class outlook and policy.

At this point it may be worthwhile to clarify the meaning of secularism in the Sudanese context. Secular ideas do not involve a rejection of the Koran and of Islamic principles, nor does secular behavior manifest itself in a refusal to perform the normal obligations of a Muslim. Sudanese who do not perform their prayers regularly, or who drink alcoholic beverages, and so on, could be found among supporters of the NUP, PDP, and Umma party alike. In fact, the only group which has been set apart by the strict adherence of its members to Islamic codes of behavior has been the Muslim Brotherhood. The distinction between NUPs on the one hand, and followers of the khatmiyyah and mahdiyyah on the other, rested in the rejection by the former of personal allegiance to the sectarian leaders. For example, Ismail el-Azhari was known to be a very pious and devout man; yet he had been popularly acclaimed as the leader of the secular forces in the Sudan. His political associates and mass followers came from the most educated strata of Sudanese society. As a group, these people have attempted to reconcile their religious beliefs and practices with the social and economic demands of mid-twentieth century life. What has set them apart from the fervent supporters of the sectarian movements have not been religious dogma or even ritual, but the fact that the latter follow unquestioningly the edicts of their sectarian leaders.

The important lesson to be drawn from the developments within the old NUP is one that has consistently characterized the conduct of domestic politics within the Sudan. There have been always two factors at work: sectarian loyalties (or aversions) and personal rivalries. Even though the careful observer may be tempted to conclude that both appear to have been present at all times, a more correct interpretation would be that personal rivalries supercede ideological considerations in importance. The prime motto of Sudanese politicians has been pragmatism and a keen sense of distrust for anyone outside their small, closely-knit ethnic groups. Ideological pronouncements merely serve as instruments for winning the temporary support of certain sectors of the population. In a country like Sudan, where no one faction commands absolute majority support, this sort of behavior necessarily leads to unstable coalition politics, a pattern that characterized the three years from late 1955 until the military coup d'etat of 1958.

It began when the Umma opposition, Mirghani Hamza defectors, and other dissidents combined to deal el-Azhari a parliamentary defeat in a vote of no confidence on November 10, 1955. Although the prime minister recovered a few days later and was reinstated by a bare majority of two votes, the signs of his vulnerability had become unmistakable. These indications plus opposition desire to be associated with independence combined to produce a historic meeting between Sir Abdel-Rahman el-Mahdi and Sayyed Ali el-Mirghani, the two patrons of the mahdiyyah and khatmiyyah sects, respectively. The immediate impact of this meeting on December 6, 1955 was to pressure el-Azhari into broadening the base of his coalition; in the longer term it laid the groundwork for the ouster of the NUP from power seven months later.

These machinations were temporarily interrupted by the independence celebrations on January 1, 1956, when the flags of Egypt and Great Britain were lowered for the last time from the staffs at the White Palace on the Blue Nile. Ismail el-Azhari must have enjoyed his proudest moment when the Sudanese tricolor was raised.

But time and political intrigues march on. Less than a month after the PDP secession from the NUP, el-Azhari lost a vote of confidence by a resounding two-to-one margin on July 4, and at once tendered his resignation. He was replaced as prime minister by an ex-soldier, Abdallah Khalil (Umma), who headed an Umma-PDP coalition government for the next two and one-third years.

This coalition was strictly a marriage of convenience of two partners with opposite foreign and domestic political interests save one: to exclude their NUP rivals from office. In that latter goal they succeeded, and even managed to perpetuate themselves at least temporarily by extending the life of the Constituent Assembly until summer 1957, when a new Parliamentary Election Act was adopted. This act called for general elections in early 1958, thus providing Sudanese voters with the first real opportunity of a clear choice among rivaling factions and policies.

THE 1958 ELECTIONS

The contestants for seats in the new parliament were the Umma party, PDP, NUP, Anti-Imperialist Front, and the Southern Liberals. The front was a cover organization for the then illegal Communist party of the Sudan. Its membership was small and concentrated its efforts on students, trade unionists, women (although they still could not vote in territorial constituencies), and members of the intelligentsia. Gosnell reports that they advocated "industrial development for the Sudan, a larger percentage for the tenants on the Gezira cotton lands, a living wage for Sudanese workers, the emancipation of women and greater recognition for the intellectuals."[16]

Primarily because of deepseated tribal cleavages, the southern politicians have never been able to achieve a similar degree of organization and cooperation among themselves as the Northern parties. In 1953 there was a Southern party, but the majority of southern constituencies were won by independents. In the interval between the two elections regional antagonisms mounted and climaxed in the bloody clashes of August 1955. Bitter experiences gained during the Sudanization episode convinced the southern politicians of the need to pool their resources; for by now their only hope for future peace and prosperity lay in negotiations with the Northerners for some form of regional autonomy. Toward that end they formed a loose bloc, the Southern Liberal party, and campaigned on a platform of seeking constitutional guarantees for the federal status of the southern Sudan. However, it should be pointed out that the majority of Southern politicians did not join this bloc out of a real sense of urgency to unite; rather, they could not afford domestically to appear opposed or luke-warm to the Liberal party's slogan of "federalism for the South."

The three remaining parties all favored some form of socialism, positive neutralism, and rapid economic development. In addition, all candidates promised to work for better health and educational stand-ards, and improvements in the communications network. In a newly independent country it is to be expected that all politicians espouse such objectives; the policy differences between parties are likely to be found not in substantive issues, but in the attitudes of individual leaders toward approaches to these problems. The PDP tended to be somewhat pro-Egypt and the Umma pro-West, with the NUP condemn-ing both of these tilts. All parties held out economic benefits to the voters, with the NUP probably presenting the most practicable pro-gram; but such nuances held little meaning for the electorate at large. What did influence many voters, however, was an electoral alliance that the Umma and PDP had entered into.

As previously stated, their coalition was a marriage of conveni-ence, primarily designed to bring down the NUP leader and to exclude him from power for the time being, and only secondarily an alliance of conservative interests against the secular modernizing NUP, as some writers on the subject[17] have suggested.* Nevertheless, this new alignment made a considerable impression on the Sudanese masses and helped to crystallize the two opposing fronts: For the devout members of both sects it was the signal to oppose the dangerous new secularism of the Unionists, as the sectarian leaders had put it; for the urban educated it was further proof of the need to combat the restraining influences of the traditionalist religious leaders. The ef-fective outcome of the alliance was an agreement between Umma party and PDP not to oppose each other in any constituency, but to pool their efforts for a defeat of the NUP.

Registration of voters began in September 1957, and was com-pleted by mid-November. After the courts had disposed of all appeals and objections, the revised registration rolls were published on

---

*Admittedly, both sectarian leaders were aware of various fac-tors that eroded the loyalties of some of their followers and sent them into the NUP camp by default, as it were. Nevertheless, the antago-nism between leaders and followers of both sects was considerably stronger than the cleavage between sectarian and secular forces. As subsequent events showed, Umma and PDP politicians were incapable of cooperating for any length of time, precisely because of this deep-seated antagonism and mutual suspicion, which both sides have har-bored for one another for almost a century.

January 21, 1958.[18] They contained the names of 1,582,909 male Sudanese, or about 77 percent of the total number of qualified voters for
the House of Representatives.[19] This meant that the average number
of registered voters per constituency was roughly 9,100; in reality,
the figures for constituencies in settled areas were much higher and
for those with nomadic inhabitants correspondingly lower.

On election day 658 candidates presented themselves to the electorate competing for the 173 seats in the House, and 146 contested the
30 elective Senate seats. The NUP entered candidates in more constituencies than any other party, because the Southern Liberals, PDPs,
and Ummas all concentrated on certain regions. In contrast to 1953,
no candidates won unopposed.

Polling took place during a ten-day period between February 27,
and March 8, 1958, in order to enable election officials to travel to
outlying areas in physically large constituencies. Voting participation
was appreciably higher than had been the case in 1953; this time about
70 percent of the registrants in the North turned out, in many urban
areas as many as 95 percent.[20] There were no disturbances on polling
day and it is to the credit of the organization and performance of the
electoral commission that no serious complaints were lodged against
it.[21] Eyewitness reporters were overwhelmed by the orderliness of
the voters at the polling stations and by their evident dedication to pass
this "test of nation-building."[22]

Table 5.3 shows the distribution of seats in Parliament after the
February elections:

TABLE 5.3

Distribution of Seats After 1958 Elections

Party	House of Representatives	Senate
Umma	63	14
NUP	44	5
PDP	26	4
Southern Liberal bloc	40	7
Total	173	30

Source: Compiled by the author.

Noteworthy are the sizable parliamentary gains of the Umma
party and the Southern Liberals; and these must be explained. The
Southern Liberals represented by no means an effective organization,
but merely a name behind which virtually all southern politicians
campaigned. Victory in 40 southern constituencies therefore did not

signify regional cohesiveness; in fact, there was less than met the eye.
As soon as elections were over, in some instances as soon as vote
counting had been completed, various southerners left the bloc and
joined either the northern coalition or the NUP in opposition, depending
on the attractiveness of the respective offers and on the alignments of
fellow southerners. The result was that the Liberal bloc lost much of
its voting strength and, in effect, saw its members support either el-
Azhari or Abdallah Khalil in the vote for prime minister. Some southerners, especially in Upper Nile Province, had received campaign
assistance from northern parties and joined the parliamentary delegations of these parties immediately after elections.

The spectacular rise in Umma party fortunes in the Senate may
be attributed simply to the revision of the eligibility requirements,
enabling all male Sudanese over 30 years of age to vote. This helped
to overcome the built-in advantage that the NUP had formerly enjoyed
when Senate electors had educational prerequisites. Umma party performance in the House of Representatives can be observed by examining the regional distribution of seats as depicted in Map 5.1. As
already indicated, results from the three southern provinces do not
portray an accurate picture, because those areas shown as won by
Ummas or NUPs were in most cases not actually won by party members, but by southerners who decided to support either of these parties
rather than the rump Liberal bloc.

An examination of the six northern provinces easily reveals the
regional character of Umma party and PDP strengths. The former
virtually dominated the western areas and found much support in the
southern Gezira, while the latter prevailed throughout the northern
and eastern sections of the country. (Apparent exceptions to this rule
can be explained in most cases. For example, constituencies no. 93
and no. 94 in Kassala Province are inhabited mainly by tenants in the
Gash River Agricultural Scheme, an enterprise virtually ruled over
by the powerful nazir of the Hadendowa, Muhammad el-Amin Tirik
who, as the reader may recall, cast his lot already in the 1953 elections with the Umma party. The reason for Umma support in this area
is historical and can be traced back to the days of Osman Digna, one
of the celebrated emirs of the Mahdi, who hailed from that region in
Eastern Sudan. The victory of the Umma party in constituencies 145
and 146 of Northern Province may be explained by the strong ansar
movement in the areas of Old and New Dongola, which these constituencies comprise and where the Mahdi was born.) NUP victories, on
the other hand, were confined mostly to urban areas, such as El-
Fasher, the capital of Darfur, Port Sudan in Kassala, and the four
largest towns in Kordofan: El-Obeid, Dilling, Kadugli, and Rashad.
The rest of these three provinces voted overwhelmingly for the coalition. This pattern of urban NUP support was maintained in Khartoum

MAP 5.1

Pictoral View of 1958 Election Results

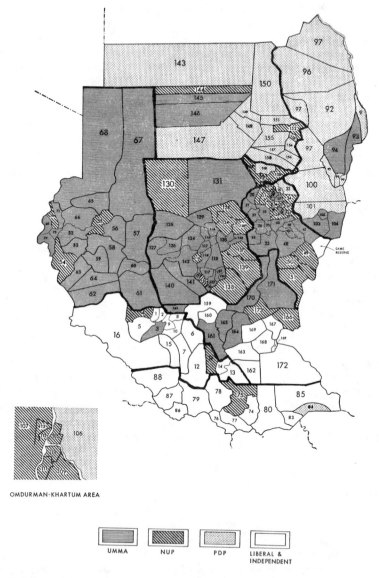

OMDURMAN-KHARTUM AREA

UMMA NUP PDP LIBERAL & INDEPENDENT

Source: The Middle East Journal 12, no. 4 (Autumn 1958), frontispiece. Reprinted by permission of The Middle East Journal.

Province, where only the PDP was able to garner one rural constituency, and to a slightly lesser degree in Blue Nile, where assembly seats were distributed more evenly among the two major parties than in any other province. Here we notice that Umma strength was concentrated in the Southern Gezira and centered around Kosti on the Nile, where the Mahdi movement originated and continues to be strongest. (The Mahdi started his movement from Aba Island, just north of Kosti.) The NUP, on the other hand, won all constituencies in the irrigated portion of the Gezira with the exception of the three gerrymandered districts 27, 28, and 29. Constituency no. 38 near the southern border of NUP strength was also won by the Umma party, although it was surrounded by NUP territory. The reason is that the inhabitants of this district, who are mostly ansar by religion, could hardly afford not to vote for the most influential local citizen in the area, the nephew of the imam of the ansar. The two PDP victories (in constituencies no. 32 and no. 33) took place in areas that fall only administratively within Blue Nile Province; its inhabitants were mostly nomadic and belonged, like their cousins in neighboring Kassala Province, to the khatmiyyah-oriented Shukriyyah tribe.

A comparison of voting trends between the 1953 and 1958 elections is handicapped by the unequal increase of constituencies per province since 1953. The data in Table 5.3 and on Map 5.1 alone therefore do not reflect the real shifts in seats gained by the various parties. This shortcoming can be remedied by comparing the numbers of seats won with the total number of seats in each of the six northern provinces for both elections. Because the PDP did not come into existence until well after the 1953 elections, it will be necessary to combine its parliamentary seats in 1958 with those of the NUP; this method will allow us to compare the relative strengths of the Umma party and NUP/PDP (the old NUP in 1953) over both elections.* The results appear on Table 5.4, whereby the first figure in each entry represents the number of seats won per province and the second the total number of constituencies in that same province. For example, the entry in the Umma party column for the 1958 elections in Northern Province reads 2/16; this means that the Umma party obtained two of the sixteen seats

---

*Admittedly, such an approach is methodologically not completely sound, because Umma party and PDP had agreed not to oppose one another in the 1958 elections. However, it is the only possible manner in which shifts in voting behavior can be studied effectively. In any case, given the strong position of the PDP in North and East, it is unlikely that the Umma party would have won any more seats in "open" competition in 1958 than it did.

TABLE 5.4

Distribution of Seats by Party per Province, 1958

Province	Year	NUP	PDP	NUP/PDP	Umma
Northern	1953			7/7	-/7
	1958	2/16	12/16	14/16	2/16
Kassala	1953			6/8	1/8
	1958	1/16	10/16	11/16	5/16
Khartoum	1953	8/9		9/9	-/9
	1958		1/9	9/9	-/9
Blue Nile	1953			6/18	10/18
	1958	16/35	2/35	18/35	17/35
Darfur	1953			2/11	6/11
	1958	3/22	—	3/22	19/22
Kordofan	1953			11/17	6/17
	1958	10/29	—	10/29	19/29

Source: Compiled by the author.

of that province. The first two columns refer to the 1958 elections
only, while the third and fourth cover both polls.

Table 5.4 reveals that there were no shifts at all in Khartoum
and virtually none in Northern Province. In Kassala and Blue Nile
Provinces we notice respectable shifts in seats gained; in the former
the Umma position improved especially in the newly settled areas
near Gedaref, while in the latter the NUP increased its share from
one-third to just over one-half. This may be accounted for by the
considerable social and economic benefits that inhabitants of the irrigated Gezira region received during the NUP regime and that were
not maintained at the same pace during the rule of the new coalition.
In allocating economic and social services, the Umma party always
seemed to be preoccupied with the western region, a matter that the
Gezira tenants apparently remembered.

The most noticeable shifts took place in the two western provinces
of Darfur and Kordofan. Whereas the NUP almost maintained its proportion of seats in Darfur, the Umma party picked up all the rest, including those that had gone to independents in 1953. In Kordofan the
NUP lost heavily at the expense of the Umma party. This, as well as
the Darfur situation, can be explained essentially by two factors: (a)
gerrymandering, which has been discussed already in the previous
chapter, where it was shown that eight of nine gerrymandered constituencies in the West were won by the Umma, and (b) the conferring of
naturalization on a great number of fellata just prior to elections, all
of whom were fervent ansar and, perhaps, the most militant supporters
of the Umma party.

That gerrymandering played a considerable role in the outcome
of the 1958 elections is further suggested—but not proven—by the fact
that the NUP obtained the largest number of total votes on a nationwide basis, although it won only one-half of the number of seats of the
coalition partners. There were other reasons responsible for the defeat of the NUP: (a) the great advantage of Ummas and PDPs in being
able to pool their resources and thereby limit their campaign expenses; (b) the apparent absence of outside financial support for the
NUP in contrast to 1953; in fact, if any foreign aid was given at all,
the recipients were more likely the Umma party (from Western
sources) and the PDP (from Egypt) in addition to the Anti-Imperialist
Front, which almost certainly has received aid from Communist
countries; (c) overconfidence on the part of the NUPs, which resulted
from the very successful 1953 elections, thereby causing a false sense
of security among leading NUP figures. Just days before the 1958
elections Ismail el-Azhari was quoted as expecting NUP victories in
between 115 and 123 constituencies.[23] The miscalculation of NUP
strategists was based mainly on their misinterpretation of the 1953

results: they read them as an endorsement of NUP policy and leadership and as a rejection of conservative sectarianism, when in reality
the NUP victory probably resulted more from a popular rejection of
British support for the Ummas and Socialist Republicans than from
approval of NUP accomplishments.

COLLAPSE OF DEMOCRATIC ORDER

Even though the coalition partners achieved a sizable election
triumph, their regime was not to enjoy political stability much beyond
the victory celebrations. It was undermined—some would argue, it
undermined itself—by the four ever-present issues of party factionalism, foreign affairs, an unstable economy, and the lingering problem of the southern Sudan.

The latter conflict was temporarily subdued on the surface, but
continued to smolder below, as fear and mistrust had now been reinforced by memories of actual bloodshed. While it may be difficult to
pinpoint analytically the specific effects of this conflict on domestic
politics in 1958, it is rather easy to link its general impact to dimin-
ishing economic resources, deepening factionalist politics, and to a
dwindling sense of national identity for both northerners and southerners.

Although factionalist behavior has always dominated modern Sudanese politics, it achieved a pinnacle of commotion, counterproduc-
tivity, and public ridicule after the 1958 elections. We have already
noted the curious alliance of Umma party and PDP, forged primarily
to exclude el-Azhari and his NUP from power. It was curious because
in the domestic realm there could be no greater mistrust and personal,
social, and political incompatibility than that found between followers
of the khatmiyyah and mahdiyyah sects. And so, when several public
figures proposed to reward an aging and ailing Abdel-Rahman el-
Mahdi with the titular position of president as a gesture for his long
fight for independence, the Mirghanis reacted with apprehension and
immediately perceived an Umma-Western scheme to institute a Mahdi
monarchy. Their already lukewarm support for their majority partner
cooled even further to the level of repeated administrative noncoop-
eration and then to the point of public disagreement with coalition
policies. Not unnaturally, this led the Umma leadership to approach
the potentially less disagreeable NUPs to join into a grand coalition
and, with the encouragement of their patron, to pursue this strategy
throughout autumn 1958. The negotiations received a severe jolt,
however, when in October strong rumors circulated in Khartoum
about a PDP-NUP reconciliation following a well-publicized meeting

in Cairo between their respective leaders in the presence of Gamal Abdel-Nasser.

Nasser was then at the zenith of his influence throughout the Arab world as the president of the new United Arab Republic and the hero of uncounted millions, especially following domestic upheavals in Iraq, Lebanon, and Jordan.

The political crises in those countries had increased the apprehension of Western powers to other trouble spots in the entire Middle East and alerted them to possible Nasserist takeovers in various countries, including Sudan. Such apprehensions were fueled by official Egyptian territorial claims in 1958 on the Halaib area in the extreme northeast of Sudan. According to many local observers, the Sudanese responded to this threat by "standing unified as one and ready to meet the Egyptian challenge physically, if necessary." Consequently, those powers and the Umma party, who had always enjoyed rather close ties, decided to intensify and deepen their relationship for a mutual protection of interests. But as the Umma leadership leaned more to the West than ever and accepted massive U.S. aid under the implied auspices of the Eisenhower Doctrine, the PDP tilted further and further to the left in its support of Egyptian policy on the Suez crisis, the Soviet-inspired arms deals, and the "revolutionary, anti-imperialist" wave surging across the Arab World. In short, the irreconcilable positions of the coalition partners became too obvious to ignore for even the proverbial man in the street of the capital.

The capriciousness of party politics in 1958 was distasteful enough for the ordinary Sudanese. But when it became compounded by economic reversals, the atmosphere changed from distasteful to unbearable. Foreign exchange reserves had dwindled from £62 million to £8 million,[24] and the balance of trade continued in a negative spiral with no relief in sight following a poor cotton crop harvest. Import restrictions on important consumer items added to the open grumbling; and soon public demonstrations ensued. The lack of systematic management and public order was patently clear and could not even be ignored by the well-disciplined military.

What was also clear was that during the first two and one-half years after independence, all three major political parties had taken turns as coalition partners in the government without making any appreciable progress in the public affairs of the country. The high hopes of the independence days had given way to growing disenchantment with the unproductive bickerings among the various politicians. By November 1958, several factors combined to produce a heightened sense of national crisis: economic setbacks coupled with a sharp decline in foreign exchange reserves, a series of costly strikes in the nascent industries and social service sectors, constant floor-crossings by opportunistic parliamentarians in the weak coalition government, the same government's inability to make any progress in controlling or extinguishing the continued rebellion in the southern region, and everpresent rumors regarding subversion by, or possible invasion from, Egyptian quarters.

The confluence of these pressures convinced practically every politically conscious Sudanese that the existing liberal procedures and regulations might simply have been too much to handle for relatively inexperienced and bickering politicians. Hence, few rose to defend the parliamentary democracy that had lasted for almost five years when Major General Ibrahim Abboud reluctantly acquiesced to the private pleas of his old schoolmate, Prime Minister Abdallah Khalil, that he assume power until such time that "the mess could be straightened out, stable economic and political conditions would come about, and the army would return to its barracks."[25] Thus ended Sudan's first experiment in parliamentary democracy.

NOTES

1. K. Henderson, Sudan Republic (New York: Frederick A. Praeger, 1965), p. 172 n.

2. Ibid., and Oliver Albino, The Sudan: A Southern Viewpoint (London: Oxford University Press, 1970), p. 33.

3. Albino, op. cit., p. 33.

4. Great Britain House of Commons Sessional Papers 1953-54, vol. 33, command paper 9058, "Report of the Sudan Electoral Commission," Khartoum, October 13, 1953 (hereafter cited as Report), p. 13.

5. Ibid., Appendix III, Art. 4.c.

6. Ibid., p. 16.

7. Figures computed from data in Report, Statistical Supplement.

8. Report, p. 18

9. Mekki Shibeika, The Independent Sudan, (New York: Robert Spellers & Sons, 1959), p. 490.

10. London Times, November 6, 1953.

11. London Times, December 1, 1953.

12. Press conference, in part reprinted by London Times, December 1, 1953.

13. Report, p. 17.

14. For a detailed and colorful account, see Ruth First, The Barrel of a Gun: Political Power in Africa and the Coup d'Etat (London: Penguin, 1971), p. 136.

15. Private interviews with high government officials close to the NUP, who must remain anonymous.

16. H. F. Gosnell, "The 1958 Elections in the Sudan," Middle East Journal 12 (Autumn 1958): 416.

17. Especially Silberman and Gosnell, op. cit.

18. Silberman, op. cit., p. 362.

19. Ibid., p. 362; figures on registration for Senate elections were not available.

20. Silberman, op. cit., p. 365.

21. Silberman, op. cit., p. 365, and Gosnell, op. cit., p. 409.

22. Silberman, pp. 361-2 and Basil Davidson, "Sudan's Orderly Elections," Manchester Guardian, February 1958.

23. New York Times, February 28, 1958, p. 7.

24. First, op. cit., p. 141.

25. Statement broadcast by Ibrahim Abboud, November 17, 1958.

6

MILITARY INTERLUDE:
THE REGIME OF
IBRAHIM ABBOUD, 1958-64

THE NOVEMBER 17 REVOLUTION

The radio broadcast by Brigadier General Ibrahim Abboud on November 17, 1958, left no doubt about the new ruler's perceptions: the country was facing a national crisis of such serious proportions that only army intervention could avert a total disaster. Rarely could one find sober political observers in more agreement concerning the first half of this assertion; in fact, popular relief about the (at least temporary) end of parliamentary government was nearly unanimous. But whether or not the military possessed any particular expertise in solving the crises at hand was a matter of (private) debate. If there was any consensus at all, it was that no one could possibly create more havoc in all areas of public affairs than the previous regimes had, and one might as well give the men in uniform a turn to show what they could accomplish. After all, what other alternatives were there?

A contributing factor to this sort of acquiescence was the examples of successful military coups d'etat in Egypt (involving a half-Sudanese, no less), Iraq (July 1958), and Pakistan (several Sudanese officers had developed strong professional contacts with Pakistani counterparts in the Ayub Khan regime). Although by late 1958 the Egyptian Revolution of 1952 was still the only successful military takeover in the postcolonial era in Africa, it nevertheless made a very strong impression on many northern Sudanese for whom Egypt specifically, and the Muslim Middle East in general, have always been the windows to the world.

For the purpose of this chapter it is unnecessary to recount the details of the army's seizure of power.[1] Instead we shall focus on

the performance of the new rulers, by concentrating on the major issues of economic and political stability, the ways in which the junta
attempted to resolve these issues, and its relationship to existing political groups. The format will be a general survey rather than in-
depth description, in line with our overall goal of tracing major trends
and policy shifts of the various Sudanese regimes.

Even if we accept the premise that the Egyptian example of military takeover in a time of national distress was vivid in the minds of
many Sudanese by November 1958, we must emphasize a salient distinction between the two cases: namely, that the military junta in
Egypt had planned for some time to overthrow the incumbent regime,
whereas the Sudanese military had not and was not prepared for the
event. There is considerable circumstantial evidence, but no proof
as yet, that Prime Minister Abdallah Khalil invited his longtime friend
Ibrahim Abboud to assume temporary control of government until the
political and economic crises had abated.[2] Abdallah Khalil understood
military thinking about civilian politics, as he himself had spent 32
years in the army. Further evidence for the "handing over" hypothesis is given by his apparent expectation that he would be included in
the new regime's Council of Ministers, along with el-Azhari and other
politicians.[3] It came as a great shock to him when instead he was
(briefly) imprisoned by the Abboud junta, and subsequently learned
that all top government posts were allocated to military officers.[4] Yet
the lack of preparedness very much characterized the nature of military rule in the country during the next six years and, indeed, the
"overthrow" of the junta in October 1964 as well.

During these six years the country was governed by a Supreme
Council of the Armed Forces under the presidency of Major-General
Ibrahim Abboud. As the name implies, this Council was the official
supreme authority in the country, and its membership varied in size
from an original high of 13 to the eventual low of 8. It was complemented by the Council of Ministers as the only other policy-making
institution.

The Abboud cabinet was characterized by unusual stability of
membership and by the prominent role of military figures as heads
of key ministries. These assertions are borne out by a careful analysis of the initial appointments in both bodies in November 1958 and
the three subsequent changes in 1959, 1960 and 1963. Of the 16 total
portfolios, 8 remained unchanged during all four cabinets, and another
4 were merely reshuffled among various ministers. This represented
the highest degree of stability of all post-1953 regimes until this day.
The portfolios of Prime Minister and Defense (both held by Abboud),
Interior, Local Government, Information and Labor, Commerce, Industry and Supplies, were all retained by senior military officers,
who were simultaneously members of the Supreme Council. In

addition, the two cabinet posts of assistant commander (Hassan Beshir Nasr) and secretary to the Supreme Council of the Armed Forces (Maqboul el-Amin) remained in military hands, as could be expected. The only prestige ministerial appointment left for a civilian was the Ministry of Foreign Affairs, in which the lawyer Ahmed Kheir was trying to project a nonmilitary image to foreign diplomats and to the outside world.

Despite the formal separation of powers, actual policy making was practically restricted to inner circles of the Supreme Council. Economically, this body performed with considerable efficiency; politically, increasing ineffectiveness marked its tenure. The new economic policies, for example, resulted in domestic stability (following the bans on public strikes, demonstrations and political organizations), in a twelvefold increase of foreign exchange reserves in less than two years, and in an encouragement to foreign aid donors and private investors to participate in the planned economic growth. That the new regime had acquired an excellent credit rating was demonstrated by a loan of $15.5 million in June 1969 from the International Bank for Reconstruction and Development (IBRD, or World Bank) to complete the long-planned Managil Extension to the Gezira Agricultural Scheme.[5]

Much of the economic success was due to a more realistic cotton marketing policy[6] than had been in effect (the former coalition government had insisted on adhering to fixed prices for cotton despite the decline in world demand), and also to an improvement of internal communications facilities, especially in rail and air transportation. In addition, many of the new projects—for example, land distribution, housing developments, and crop diversification—produced profitable short-term returns.

Many Sudanese experienced a previously unmatched standard of living, yet they became increasingly dissatisfied with the military regime. Why? Two basic reasons stand out. First, the economic success quite understandably led the planners to bigger and more costly projects. Initially, a five-year and then a ten-year plan with an estimated outlay of over 500 million pounds sterling were devised. Many mistakes were made in the process, some of which were attributable to the limited experience of the planners in such magnitudes, and others to creeping corruption and military pork-barreling. More and more informed Sudanese started to wonder about the financial sources for such projects as the new dams at Roseires and Khashm el-Girba. (The first was partially financed by World Bank, U.S., and West German construction loans; the second was designed to provide irrigated land for the resettled Nubians who had been displaced by the rising waters of Lake Nasser.) Rumors of an imminent economic collapse began to spread.

Second, growing civilian distrust of the military regime swept the country. This distrust manifested itself by popular refusal to give credit to the military for the recently accomplished economic progress, and was (incidentally) one explanation for the acceptance of these rumors.

The growing gap between the regime and the population can be explained partially by noting how the military leaders became more and more accustomed to the prerogatives of power, less tolerant of counseling civilian influences, and less appreciative of the precarious foundation on which popular acceptance of military rule had been based.

When the military took office on November 17, 1958, it had the tacit approval of leaders of the major political factions, in particular the two sectarian patriarchs, Sayyid Abd el-Rahman el-Mahdi and Sayyid Ali el-Mirghani. Moreover, each faction demanded some kind of assurance that its interests would be represented directly by some military members in the Supreme Council of State. In fact, the initial legitimacy of the military regime was based precisely upon the junta's acceptance of this demand. An example of one such set of parallel civilian military contacts is provided by the powerful Brigadier Ahmed Abd al-Wahhab, who was generally recognized as a link to the Umma party, and Brigadier Mohammad Ahmed Irwa, who was known for his ties to the khatmiyyah sect.

As time went on, however, two developments occurred that upset this unwritten agreement: One, internal strife within the military led to the expulsion of some members (most notably, Brigadier Abd al-Wahhab) and the general reshuffling of the Supreme Council in a manner not entirely acceptable to the civilian politicians. Also, intramilitary dissension was manifested by three attempted coups in March, May, and November of 1959, all within one year of the advent of the Abboud regime. The first two involved Brigadiers Abd el-Rahim Shannan and Mohieddin Abdallah, the respective commanders of the northern and eastern regions, who had been disgruntled over their being left out of the Supreme Council of the Armed Forces. The abortive November 9 coup was launched at the infantry school in Omdurman. Five ringleaders were arrested, tried, sentenced to death and publicly hanged as an example to deter others. And although Supreme Council strongmen like Brigadier Hassan Beshir Nasr moved to purge the officer corps of dissident elements, the facade of internal solidarity within the armed forces began to crack and would never again be restored.

Two, with the passage of time, the junta became less and less responsive to the political interests of its civilian associates as well as the factional interests in the country, and eventually began to ignore them. Henceforth, outcries for a return to civilian rule were heard with growing frequency and intensity. Evidence for these efforts was

provided by a series of private contacts and written memoranda, signed
by the former presidents of the two largest political parties calling on
General Abboud to effect the "promised return to full parliamentary
government."[7]

The military reaction to these developments was predictable.
Having failed to create a political organization or movement through
which it could mobilize popular support for its policies and having
seen its informal civilian support progressively withdrawn, the junta
adopted increasingly repressive measures in order to silence the opposition. As mentioned previously, political parties and trade union
activities had been outlawed in November 1958, and the press was
heavily censored. Therefore, one of the few remaining forums for
dissent was the university campus. As soon as students and professors became too vocal in their misgivings about government policy,
the junta decreed the University of Khartoum Act in February 1961 to
bring the university directly under government control; in November
1963 it was incorporated under the Ministry of Education. These acts
only increased the isolation of the regime from the population, however, and drove the opposition underground where it became more
difficult to control. Before long, the mounting conflict led to the arrest
of twelve prominent politicians, including the leaders of the NUP,
Umma and Communist parties in July 1961.[*] It should be noted here
that the Communist party of the Sudan had become a focal point for
political dissidents, and soon the major target of the Abboud junta's
crackdown on civilian opponents.

Illegal demonstrations, distribution of antigovernmental leaflets,
increasingly vicious whisper campaigns, and an "infiltration" of the
junior officer ranks by sympathizers of civilian rule followed. The
last activity became so successful that most junior officers refused
to support the junta during the October 1964 uprisings. Indeed, in
those months it became fashionable and exciting for students and young
would-be intellectuals to distribute Communist party leaflets, despite
their personal aversions to Marxism, if only to experience the satisfaction of participating in the sole available form of political protest.

The role played by the civil service was also important. Many
senior officials had become disenchanted with the junta's policy of
placing the provincial bureaucracies under inexperienced military
governors whose decisions tended to be arbitrary. They responded
by practicing increasingly passive resistance to the military regime,

---

[*]They were eventually released in January 1962, but this common
experience left a marked impression on many leaders and contributed
to a more cooperative political stance during the next few years.

by failing to carry out executive orders or by slowing down the bureaucratic machinery to all but a halt.

Perhaps the negative attitudes of civil servants and other educated Sudanese could have been avoided, had the government provided them with more meaningful opportunities for political participation. Even though the regime did attempt to generate popular support through a system of local councils, this effort proved to be ineffective in substance and expectation. The system of councils was apparently modeled after Pakistan's "Basic Democracy," and was adapted to Sudanese conditions by Chief Justice Muhammad Abu Rannat, who headed a commission charged to "consider the best ways for the citizens to take part in the government of the country."[8] Eighty-four Local Councils were inaugurated on July 1, 1961, with two-thirds of their members elected directly or indirectly, depending on the "maturity" of the particular electorate. These Local Councils were designed as the base for a pyramidal structure in which a Central Council was to form the apex. By mid-1962 the formal framework had been erected for a new legislature (key steps were the Provincial Administration Act of 1960 and the Central Council of 1962) and local government elections could be held in early 1963.

There is every indication that the Abboud regime intended sincerely to permit some measure of democracy, but was unsure in defining appropriate parameters and in handling the demands of various interest groups. The result was that the former party leaders discreetly called on their supporters to boycott elections; nevertheless, a number of distinguished names appeared on the council roster.[9] When this body did assemble, from November 1963 (and throughout its second session in 1964), it was received with mixed sentiments by the public. On one hand its members were reputed to be junta collaborationists, or opportunists attracted mainly by impressive salaries and other fringe benefits, but lacking ethical legitimacy in the eyes of the urban intelligentsia. On the other hand verbal charges by some council members about alleged inadequate press freedom, and incoherent southern policy, and especially inefficiency and corruption in the administration received surprising coverage in press reports and thus contributed in no small part to the arousal of public opinion.[10] This logical inconsistency was perhaps an indication of the increasing refusal by members of the informed public to give any credit to the military rulers, regardless of the merits of their record.

Yet the record of the Abboud regime reflected a number of positive achievements, especially in the economic realm, as already described earlier. In addition, the junta deserved credit for winning a more favorable Nile Waters Agreement (1959) from Egypt than any previous government, and also for an unspectacular but steady and comparatively successful foreign policy toward its other neighbors as well as Europe and the United States (for details, see Chapter 10). But when a regime falls from public favor, the causes are generally found not only in controversial policies, but also in its inability to project a popular (and dynamic) image. Both of these factors were to haunt the Abboud regime.

The growing isolation of the military rulers has already been alluded to earlier. This was compounded by the fact that, with the passage of time, the junta lost much of its broadbased image and many Sudanese felt that the country was, in effect, run by four men: President Abboud, military strongman Hassan Beshir Nasr, Justice Abu Rannat, and Foreign Minister Ahmed Kheir, while the others merely executed those policies decided on by the big four. Complicating matters further was the fact that all four were Shaiqi by origin and adhered to the khatmiyyah sect, thereby further alienating the ansar and, to a lesser degree, Ismail el-Azhari, whose NUP had been hurt considerably by the secession of the khatmiyyah faction in 1956. Another piece of circumstantial evidence of the regime's khatmiyyah orientation was suggested by the fact that the interment of twelve politicians in Juba (1961-62) included leaders of all parties except the PDP.[11]

In addition, the regime suffered from a sort of generation gap. President Abboud, commissioned in 1918, was perceived as a kindly father figure, who could not and would not harm anyone. His position was thought to derive primarily from the fact that he happened to be the armed forces commander-in-chief in the autumn of 1958, but not due to ambitions for power nor political savvy. His presidential style appeared to be that of a reluctant guardian who had been appointed to look after inexperienced youth. By contrast, the other members of the Supreme Council were much younger (all had been commissioned between 1937 and 1942) and seemed to pursue personal as well as political interests. They were the ones who were popularly blamed for the junta's various wrongdoings, especially alleged corruption and immorality. It is significant that Ibrahim Abboud's generally well-meaning paternalistic image continued long after the termination of military rule in October 1964, and that many critics of his regime were convinced of his ignorance about the "shocking" behavior by his lieutenants.

The Abboud regime was thus poorly equipped to handle the various political issues confronting it. In addition to the aforementioned problems, further challenges emerged in the form of two essentially regional matters that had national repercussions due to the governments' less than skillful handling and that in the end contributed heavily to the erosion of the junta's domestic support. One was the problem of resettling those Nubians of the Wadi Halfa region who had been displaced by the rising water table resulting from the construc-

tion of the Aswan High Dam. The other, similarly inherited, problem
was the continuing rebellion of some southerners against perceived
northern domination. Both problems were admittedly difficult and
could potentially have become the undoing of any regime. Yet it was
the unimaginative and heavy-handed manner with which the Abboud
government tried to tackle them that produced an unexpected level of
protest, and culminated in violent demonstrations and near insurrection in Wadi Halfa in 1960, and in an unprecedented degree of bloodshed, loss of life and home in the southern provinces.

Lest the impression arise that these critical comments are intended to minimize the scope of the problems, the author wishes to
state emphatically his empathy for the Abboud regime's difficult task
in coping with highly complex and emotionally explosive issues. There
is also no denying that the government tried sincerely to solve these
problems as best as it knew how. If there is an indictment, it must be
directed at the incompetence of those top-level officials who, by training and experience, were obviously incapable of successfully performing tasks of such magnitudes. Evidence that both issues could have
been resolved more congenially was provided by the superior management of Egyptians who similarly had to relocate thousands of Nubians
in one case, and in another instance, the successful approach by President Nimeiri's government to the Southern Problem. The downfall of
the Abboud regime in both crises was probably due to the regime's
overall method of operation: its impressive successes in economic
matters had apparently misled the rulers into applying the same
economic output-oriented strategies to essentially noneconomic and
nonmilitary tasks that would have required more political sensitivity
to the anxieties of ethnic minorities.

THE PROBLEM OF THE SOUTH

The junta's approach to the southern question deserves some
special attention here, if only because it exacerbated hostile feelings
between the regions probably more than any other government had in
the twentieth century. This is not to argue necessarily that this military regime was particularly sinister or cruel—some southerners
might wish to argue so, but the point remains definitely debatable.
Rather, the confluence of the evolutions of Sudanese politics on one
hand, and the Southern Problem on the other, led the Abboud regime
to try a particular set of policies that in the end had the effect of coalescing hitherto disunited local factions into a relatively common
front, and also in a later stage resulted in a large scale civil war.
The point here is that historical antagonisms, including the specter

of the recent 1955 riots, the general problems associated with nation building in the first decade of independence, the futility of parliamentary rule within the Sudan, and the sometimes compatible, sometimes clashing, forces of ethnic and nationalistic ferment sweeping across Africa, all combined to impress a set of policies on the Abboud government, which must have seemed well-conceived to these men from their own perspective, but proved to be totally dysfunctional.

Mistakes included goals as well as methods. The latter aspect was well described by Mohammed Omer Beshir when he observed that earlier "the existence of a parliamentary system . . . had acted as a restraint on those in the North who advocated the use of force to suppress those who called for federation or separation in the South. . . . Now the advocates of compulsion and integration of the North and South by force of arms had the upper hand."[12] Beshir also noted correctly that the military regime was quite consistent in suppressing opposition in the South in the same manner as it had done in the North.[13]

The objectives of the junta were quite simple: to foster national integration and unity. This was to be accomplished primarily through assimilation of cultures by pushing a policy of Arabization and Islamization in the southern provinces. To outsiders, this policy must—and did—appear highly chauvinistic and insensitive to the southerners' native life-styles. And although a liberal-minded observer will likely agree with such an assessment, fairness demands that this issue is placed into its proper historical and cultural context by examining the premises of northern thinking. For one thing, Islam and the Arabic language had, in fact, been the catalytic agents in creating a reasonably integrated—though not homogeneous—culture out of a multitude of ethnic tribes in the North; the thought that this same formula might also be applicable to the South was therefore not that strange, albeit rather unsophisticated. For another, in 1954 an international commission on secondary education, with no northern or southern Sudanese members, had recommended that Arabic replace English and that all mission and private schools be taken over by the government.[14] The Abboud regime merely took this advice at face value and proceded to implement it, just as it would any other program. One secondary and six intermediate Islamic institutes were established in the South, mosques were constructed in numerous locations, and "military governors and administrators devoted much of their time and energies to spreading Arabic and Islam and to suppressing the opposition."[15]

All private schools throughout the country had been nationalized and integrated into the public school system soon after independence. But whereas private schools continued to exist in the capital area of the North, the opening of new missionary schools in the South was

forbidden. In view of the fact that virtually all educated southerners
had been products of missionary schools, they were particularly receptive to the protests of missionaries against these discriminatory
policies. Soon the Christian clergy/southern intelligentsia alliance
was seen in Khartoum as evidence that the missionaries were guilty
of divisive tactics and had to be confined in their activities.

Meanwhile, the southern leaders saw Arabization and Islamization,
as well as specific practices such as shifting the weekly day of rest
from Sunday to Friday, not from the theoretical perspective of nation
building, but as further evidence of the historical continuation of
southern domination by northern "Arabs." Not surprisingly in this
atmosphere, the two fronts became polarized, and previous neglect
and aloofness were now replaced by direct confrontation.

This outside observer is forced to conclude that both parties
overreacted to a bad situation, primarily due to their common lack of
mutual understanding. The government promulgated the Missionary
Societies Act of 1962 and eventually announced on February 27, 1964,
the immediate expulsion of all foreign Christian missionaries from
the southern provinces. This affected 272 Roman Catholic Verona
Fathers and 28 Protestants;[16] the virtual absence of indigenous clergy
left the southern church in an almost total disarray for years to come.
Although the foreign missionaries' apprehension about mounting government restrictions during the late 1950s and early 1960s was very
understandable, there is also evidence that some of them had actually
contributed to the polarization of attitudes by derogatory comments
about "those ruthless Mohammedans who are not to be trusted."
These and similar statements touched raw nerves among southerners,
whose practice of oral tradition had kept gruesome memories of leg-
endary (northern) slave raids alive anyhow.

Regarding other policy areas one cannot but agree with the analysis of Robert Collins, a leading scholar of the southern Sudan, who
noted that "the military government . . . had noticeably failed to gild
the bitter pill of Arabization and Islamization with economic development. When the British left the Sudan in 1956 there were numerous
schemes for developing the Southern Sudan. Like education, however,
most of these projects had been postponed or abandoned in favor of
economic undertakings in the North."[17] Sugar schemes, paper factories, fish canning and meat packing plants are among ready examples of projects that were originally planned for the southern
region, but were eventually located in the North, frequently under
less favorable (economic) conditions. In fact, development of the
South was simply neglected; although this statement could be made
about the poor regions of the extreme eastern and western Sudan as
well, it was small consolation to the already otherwise harried
southerners.

A similarly bleak situation persisted in the realm of public administration. Southerners had already felt discriminated against by
the results of the Sudanization campaign. Moreover, civil service
recruitment and appointment practices have long been a bone of southern contentions. One cannot improve on Robert Collins' description
of this issue when he wrote:

> All the principal administrative posts, Governors, Deputy-
> Governors, and District Commissioners in the Southern
> Sudan, were held by Northern officials, while those South-
> erners occupying more junior positions were transferred
> to the North where their influence was negligible. The army
> and police were predominately staffed by Northern Suda-
> nese. Provincial Councils were introduced to provide
> ostensibly a medium for discussion and debate, but the
> Southern members were nominated by the governor while
> the Executive Councils were completely controlled by
> Northern administrators and residents.[18]

All these practices, well-intentioned or not, eventually combined
to produce violent political and military actions among southerners.
It began with student demonstrations and strikes in Rumbek and Juba
secondary schools, later in 1962 spread to other public schools in the
South, and culminated temporarily in the establishment of a southern
political resistance movement (SACDNU, later SANU) in exile under
William Deng, Joseph Oduhu, and Father Saturnino Lahure. As already
described in Chapter 2, the effectiveness of this movement was severely limited by internal splits among its leadership. One byproduct,
however, was the convening of an embryonic guerilla army by Joseph
Oduhu in September 1963,[19] which was then officially named Anya-
Nya and planned a series of coordinated attacks in first Equatoria,
Upper Nile, and then Bahr el-Ghazal Provinces. Meanwhile, the exodus
of ordinary southern citizens into neighboring countries swelled from
a trickle in 1955 to tens of thousands.

The military government responded to these various developments by reimposing the old Closed Districts Ordinance that severely
limited travel to and from the South, by negotiating extradition treaties
with Uganda and Ethiopia in 1964 in order to stem the flood of refugees
there, and by stepping up its military campaign against the Anya-Nya
outlaws. These internal policies were supplemented by diplomatic
efforts abroad to counter the growing image of "persecution of
Christians" by depicting imperialists and missionaries as the real
source of the problem, and southern politicians in exile as stooges
and agents of foreign powers.[20] In this perception the Khartoum

government was undoubtedly influenced by the dual role of the leading
rebel figure, Father Saturnino, as well as open sympathy for the
southern cause in Roman Catholic countries of Western Europe.

In the end, none of these policies proved very effective, and the
junta was indirectly admitting as much by the establishment of a commission of enquiry in September 1964 to investigate conditions in the
South and suggest possible remedies. This action was stimulated in
part by recognition of the need to find some solutions to a severe national crisis and source of major economic drain, but also in part by
the growing restlessness in northern political circles over the various
previously described difficulties that had continued to accumulate over
the years.

By the autumn of 1964 the military leadership had earned the animosity of students and teachers, politicians and civil servants, journalists, doctors, lawyers, trade union leaders, and even junior
members within the armed forces. In the end, the continued ferocity
of the rebellion in the southern provinces merely provided the spark
that lit the fire of the October Revolution of 1964.

THE OCTOBER 1964 REVOLUTION

In terms of strict chronology, the 1964 Revolution can be traced
to mid-October when a student meeting at the University of Khartoum
took up the "problem of the South," and outspoken attacks on government policy ensued. The same regime, which earlier that year had
reluctantly granted permission for public discussion groups in order
to improve its image, now reversed itself and banned future meetings
of the discussion circles. On the evening of October 21, students met
on campus for the explicit purpose of defying that ban. The government took up the challenge, and the subsequent confrontation had all
the trademarks of student-police battles throughout the remainder of
the 1960s: an initial recital over the loudspeakers warning students
of the illegality of their actions, the hurling of tear gas grenades, the
chasing of the offenders into their hostel-sanctuaries, culminating in
isolated physical encounters in which the baton-wielding police inevitably came out the better. Only this time the ending had an unfamiliar twist, when errant shots struck a few students and one,
Ahmed Qurashi, died of his wounds that same night. And although the
government later presented a long list of plausible explanations for
this unfortunate and undesired outcome, (for example, the police commissioner was sick at home, the minister of the interior out of town, and
some orders may have been bungled by inexperienced deputies), it

could not be absolved of its responsibilities for the tragic death by any of the excuses, because in the smalltown atmosphere of Khartoum nearly everyone who needed to know about the developments was in a position to be informed in sufficient time to act or respond.

The response came with a vengeance. Hundreds of students had congregated at the hospital and, on the following day, formed the backbone of a funeral procession that eventually attracted perhaps as many as 30,000 marchers, led by university professors in formal gowns and chanting ominous slogans. During the next two days one could hear scattered rifle-shots and smell the fumes of overturned and burnt official cars in the northern portion of Khartoum.

Another large procession formed on Saturday and achieved great symbolic success when the local police sanctioned the march after some High Court judges so instructed them by invoking their "superior authority." By now more and more people realized that the power of the Supreme Council was disintegrating visibly. During the next two days feverish negotiations took place between council members and leaders of the popular movements. These leaders would later constitute themselves into the Front of Professional Organizations (see Chapter 7). Meanwhile, a general strike was called to bring down the military regime, rumors circulated in the capital of imminent intra-army coups, trucks and trainloads of strike sympathizers began to arrive from provincial towns, and some residents in the capital barricaded railroad and river bridges by deflating the tires of taxis, private cars, and even some trucks that were donated for that purpose by their owners.

Brigadier Hassan Beshir Nasr made one last attempt to save the military regime by proposing stern measures for cracking down on the demonstrators. Some junior officers interpreted his proposals (possibly correctly) as designed to substitute himself for President Abboud, and weighed several options to counter this threat, including the direct seizure of power by themselves. In this atmosphere of tension and confusion further violence was averted through the astute intercession of several medium rank officers stationed in the Khartoum area, whose personal ties gained them close access to the Supreme Council members on one side, and impeccable personal and professional reputations drew the respect and admiration of more politicized junior officers on the other. They impressed on both military factions the precariousness of their own individual positions, and in the end persuaded all sides, including the new Front of Professional Organizations, to accept a compromise solution in the form of a peaceful transition to civilian rule.

Accordingly, on the evening of Monday, October 26, President Abboud in a radio address announced the dissolution of the Supreme

Council and the cabinet, and agreed to remain as head of state until
a new transitional government could be formed. As it turned out, he
was to abdicate completely only a few days later.

The October 26 speech was greeted by unrestrained euphoria.
Men were literally dancing in the streets; women gave off the shrill
joy-noise usually reserved for weddings and celebrations over a new-
born son. Continuously honking taxis and buses carried passengers
gratis to huge gatherings in public squares, and those who could find
no other forms of transportation literally raced there on foot—some
men even carried their wives on their backs, a completely incongruous
picture for the usually reserved Sudanese.

Perhaps one ought not to overrate the significance of this emotional release, particularly in view of subsequent developments; but
the question does seem appropriate: Just why were these people so
happy to see the end of military rule?

Surely not because of economic pressures, for the slight drop in
foreign exchange reserves affected very few people at that time, and
whatever inconvenience resulted was definitely outweighed by the considerable rise in the standard of living since 1958. Similarly, it is
difficult to conceive serious popular misgivings based on ideological
grounds (except for the few supporters of radical movements): After
all, the junta pursued social and political programs that reflected
rather closely the essentially conservative nature of Sudanese society.
Aversion to military rule per se may have motivated some Sudanese,
but many of the demonstrators against the Abboud regime in late October were the very same (groups of) people who openly welcomed the
Nimeiri coup in May 1969. The real answer may very well lie in a
character trait of ordinary Sudanese who have traditionally attached
great importance to various freedoms of expression, and who chafed
under the increasingly repressive policies of the military. By the end
of October 1964, popular sentiment was directed not so much against
President Abboud—the most visible symbol of the regime—as against
his tough-minded and humorless lieutenants, whose ideas of public
information seemed to be a steady release of congratulatory telegrams
to themselves.

NOTES

1. For such details see Ruth First, The Barrel of a Gun: Political Power in Africa and the Coup d'Etat (London: Penguin Press,
1971), pp. 229-32.

2. However, in a recent publication M. O. Beshir describes Umma party complicity in the military takeover in some detail. See Mohammed Omer Beshir, Revolution and Nationalism in the Sudan (New York: Barnes & Noble, 1974), p. 207.

3. First, op. cit., p. 230.

4. First, op. cit., p. 230.

5. Peter M. Holt, A Modern History of the Sudan (London: Weidenfeld and Nicholson, 1961), p. 192.

6. K. Henderson attributed this to an adjustment of prices, which resulted in a quadrupling of sales, Sudan Republic (New York: Frederick A. Praeger, 1965), p. 133.

7. First, op. cit., p. 244. For details of this and similar communications, see First, pp. 243-44.

8. Ibid., p. 241, for further details see also Henderson, op. cit., pp. 139-45.

9. Henderson, op. cit., p. 144.

10. Henderson, op. cit., p. 144.

11. Mohammed Ahmed Mahgoub, Democracy on Trial: Reflections on Arab and African Politics (London: Andre Deutsch, Ltd., 1974), p. 186.

12. Mohammed Omer Beshir, The Southern Sudan: Background to Conflict (London: C. Hurst, 1968), p. 80.

13. Ibid., p. 81.

14. Robert O. Collins, The Southern Sudan in Historical Perspective (Tel Aviv: Shiloah Center, 1975), p. 75.

15. Beshir, op. cit., p. 81.

16. Beshir, op, cit., p. 82.

17. Collins, op, cit., p. 77.

18. Collins, op. cit., p. 75.

19. Collins, op. cit., p. 79.

20. Beshir, op. cit., p. 86.

THE TRANSITIONAL PERIOD

On November 1, 1964, Ibrahim Abboud was sworn in as president of the Sudan, and a prominent educator, Sirr el-Khatim el-Khalifah, as the new prime minister. The first transitional cabinet, as it was to become known, was dominated by a new coalition of leftists who represented a neophyte political group, the National Front of Professional Oragnizations. This body had been instrumental in pressing for the resignation of the junta, which was completed on November 16, when President Abboud announced his retirement and transferred the powers of head of state to the transitional cabinet.* The front was to contribute significantly to the political evolution during this crucial period of Sudanese history, and thus deserves some scrutiny.

The front had been proclaimed on October 25, 1964, and consisted initially of Sudanese faculty members of Khartoum University and Khartoum Technical institute, the respective student unions, and Sudanese judges and lawyers. Almost immediately, they were joined by representatives of workers, peasants, and other professional associations.

Up until that time, most Sudanese lawyers, doctors, engineers, teachers, and so on had maintained politically independent positions,

---

*The ex-prime minister, M. A. Mahgoub, described the transfer thusly: ". . . we got rid of Abboud, prepared a statement for him which he read." According to Mahgoub, Abboud's last requests were a common photo, a pension, and permission for his son to continue his stay in the United Kingdom, all of which were granted.[1]

215

not so much due to personal aloofness from public affairs as to their alienation from the petty bickering and unprincipled floor-crossings among traditional parliamentarians. Yet the leaders of these associations tilted noticeably leftward in their public statements despite their officially independent status. This posture may have resulted in part from a natural tendency to oppose the perceived reactionary military policies, but it could also be attributed to the clever infiltration by Communists into executive positions of the major associations. The reader should recall that all political parties had been officially outlawed during the six years of military rule, yet the Communists had continued to function, albeit underground, while all the others actually disintegrated as organizations. Thus, when the Abboud regime fell in October 1964, none of the traditional political parties were ready to step into the newly-created vacuum; only the Communists were prepared to act. They had realized that their best strategy was to align themselves with independent groups opposed to the former junta and its policies. Through considerable organizational talents, acquired in part during intensive cadre training in Eastern Europe, they were able to gain access to, and frequently control of, professional associations despite their own small numbers.

One example is provided by the Gezira Tenants Association, which was led for many years by Sheikh el-Amin Mohammed el-Amin, a Communist who was able to get more concessions from the government for the tenants than any other person. After the October Revolution Sheikh el-Amin declared his association's solidarity with all other professional organizations in the front, and wound up as a minister in the first transitional cabinet. All this despite the fact that there were very few genuine Communists among the tenants in the Gezira—possibly less than 5 percent of the voting population as subsequent elections indicated. There is strong evidence that the tenants' loyalty to Sheikh el-Amin was cultivated over the years on the merits of his accomplishments as a bargainer and representative of their economic interests, and was not influenced by his political-ideological affiliation. A parallel case is presented by the Trade Union Federation and its leader el-Shafieh Ahmed el-Sheikh.

These examples should not be misconstrued to connote a belittling of the noteworthy role that the Communist party of the Sudan has played over the years as major campaigner for various social and economic reforms. In fact, the CPS has been the most persistent proponent of the interests of workers and tenants, whereas the other Sudanese parties generally ignored those interest groups.

One consequence of the successful infiltration by leftists of professional organizations was that the Executive Board of the front, which consisted of 15 members, was dominated by 11 Communists and pro-Communists, the latter having preferred different identificational labels. The Front executive blamed all wrongs on reactionary groups and imperialist designs (meaning the traditional parties and the Western powers, respectively) and held out as a remedy the solidarity of all progressive forces in the country. This talk appealed especially to the workers (who have been chronically underpaid), the students, teachers, and other recent graduates of secondary schools and universities. The latter thought of themselves as the real heroes of the October Revolution, since it was they who were initially involved in antimilitary activities. The slogan called out to these young people, "You are the guardians [san'iyin] of the glorious October Revolution," fell on receptive ears.

All along the leftist leadership realized that its numerical base was still small in comparison to that of the traditional parties. One possible remedy was to enlist the support of the Sudanese Women's Organization and, hopefully, through it the majority of all Sudanese women. Accordingly, the "heroic role of Sudanese women in the October Revolution" was played up by the regime. (The educated women and those organized in professional unions, that is, nurses, typists, and so on, had displayed their disapproval of the military regime in October by marching in demonstrations just like virtually everybody else.) The United Front actively encouraged the leader of the women's organization, Fatima Ahmed Ibrahim, to call for a liberation of Sudanese women from backward customs and traditional personal restrictions, and pledged its support for these demands. Not surprisingly, the front gained the sympathies of many Sudanese women in the capital, especially among the younger educated.

As this very brief and incomplete survey shows, the Front had reasons to expect political support, including favorable returns at the polls, from both the women and the younger groups among the population. They were able to pass a motion in the Council of Ministers enlarging the franchise to include all Sudanese over 18 years of age. The three traditional parties, Umma, NUP, and, at the start, the PDP as well, obliged in this strategy by vigorously opposing the motion. As we shall see subsequently, this opposition was not lost on the newly enfranchised.

Consistent with its strategy of appealing to new or modern forces, the Front also proposed special constituencies for workers, tenants, intellectuals, and finally tried to resurrect the old Graduates' Constituencies. The ensuing developments illustrate dramatically the state of political turmoil of those days; and the eventual solution turned into a bitter lesson for the defeated, not to be forgotten for the remainder of the decade.

The scenario unfolded like this: With the passage of weeks, the traditional parties became reorganized ever-so-slowly and began to demand a larger share of power, meaning greater representation in a cabinet, on the strength of their claims to have the support of more than 90 percent of the Sudanese people, a not unreasonable figure at the time. The front responded by embarking on even more leftist policies, perhaps in the hope of attracting new supporters. The more radical the actions and pronouncements of the front became, the more vociferous were the demands of the old politicians to change the composition of the cabinet. There was talk of, and even genuine concern over, "saving the country from Communism." The traditional parties publicly called for holding general elections at the earliest possible opportunity so that the new cabinet would "represent the true wishes of the Sudanese people."

The front countered these demands by adopting two approaches: at first it rejected the call for elections as impractical while the state of emergency persisted in the southern provinces. At this point the Umma party, NUP, and Muslim Brotherhood joined into an alliance of forces demanding immediate elections in all parts of the Sudan where the state of emergency did not exist, that is, in the six northern provinces. The PDP broke ranks in a calculated risk and joined the front in resisting elections. One encounters various explanations for this decision by the PDP leadership. A most likely motive may have been a certain bitterness among members of the PDP-executive toward the Umma and NUP, stemming from earlier experiences when the PDP had been a junior member in two ruling coalitions: as a wing of the old NUP before 1956, and with the Umma party just before and after the 1958 elections. Those PDPs probably speculated that, given the regional and sectarian support of the party, there was virtually no chance of ever obtaining the number of seats that the NUP and Umma could expect to win. Hence, they decided to gamble on a complete reorganization of political forces in the Sudan in the process of which, they hoped, the Umma and NUP would disintegrate. Undoubtedly egged on by their Egyptian mentors, they cast their lot in an alliance with the Communists and some professional organizations, including the Trade Union Federation, as a "progressive front" to oppose the "reactionaries."*

The new turn of events caused the conservative alliance to press even harder for elections and to support these efforts with a show of force. Responding to the call of the Umma president, Sayyid el-Sadiq el-Mahdi, tens of thousands of ansar poured into the capital from the western and central provinces, roaming the streets at night, and

---

*Another interesting sidelight is the observation that Muddathir Abd al-Rahim made in a different context, namely that the majority of Sudanese Communists and left-wingers have a khatmiyyah background.[2]

chanting mahdiyyah war songs. Although there were relatively few incidents, the Front decided not to risk an open clash of supporters and agreed to hold elections in early spring.

After the tensions had subsided somewhat, the front employed a second strategy by proposing elections in which constituencies were to be based not on territorial, but on professional grounds. The population would be represented by three groups: workers, tenants, and intellectuals (mutathaqqifin), all given equal numbers of deputies. References were made to the progressive forces in the United Arab Republic where representation of professional classes had "proved itself" in the Arab Socialist Union.

It took the conservative groups about two days to realize that such an arrangement would, in effect, perpetuate the status quo and, incidentally, do away with their political organizations. The ansar were called back into Khartoum, demonstrations ensued, and the Front of Professionals—which by then had lost the active support of many, if not most of its rank-and-file members—virtually collapsed.* A compromise solution was worked out whereby elections would be held in March or April in the six northern provinces and in the Graduates' Constituencies, which were revived for that purpose. On February 24, 1965, a new cabinet was formed with a slight majority representation of the Umma party, NUP, and Muslim Brotherhood alliance. This majority was effectively increased by the refusal of the PDP to occupy the three positions that were allocated to it in the new 15-member cabinet. The front for all practical purposes had collapsed.

The provision for graduates' constituencies was received without any public opposition at the time. The conservative parties were glad over having averted a larger evil and did not seem to mind the concession; moreover, the NUP expected to garner most of the fifteen seats. The radical elements welcomed these special constituencies as an expected source of political support. These feelings were to change considerably after the election results had been announced, as we shall see subsequently.

---

*Members of the Engineers' Association, for example, who had joined the front after the October Revolution in an effort to combine forces with other independents and as a means of demonstrating their disapproval of traditional party activities, became weary of radical statements and policies of Front executives, who obviously acted more and more in the interests of their (the Communist) party.

THE 1965 ELECTIONS

The 1965 parliamentary elections differed from the two preceding ones in several fundamental aspects: 1) the Sudanese voted for only a unicameral legislature, with the Senate no longer in existence; 2) the franchise had been enlarged to include younger age groups (the minimum age being 18 rather than 21 years) and women for the first time ever; 3) because of the unstable situation in the southern provinces, the elections were limited to only the northern region of the Sudan;* 4) for the first time the very holding of elections was disputed by some major political organizations with the subsequent result that one large party decided to "boycott and resist the illegal elections;" 5) for the first time the Sudanese voters were not choosing between essentially the respective organizations of three dominant personalities—a secular and two sectarian leaders—with rather similar party platforms, but between traditional and radical movements that offered opposing approaches to national problems, and that were both determined to eliminate the other's political organizations if victorious.

A proper understanding of the effects of these differences on the outcome of elections requires a brief survey of the contesting parties and of their positions on some of the major issues prior to the 1965 elections.

Contestants

An official publication of the Electoral Commission lists 12 political parties as contestants in the 1965 elections. They were: The National Unionist party (NUP), the Umma party, the Communist party, the Islamic Charter Front (ICF), the Peoples Democratic party (PDP), the Islamic Front, the Trade Union Association, the Socialist Democratic Congress, the Revolutionary Communist party, the National

---

*Deputies from 21 southern constituencies were returned unopposed and, after a highly controversial verdict by the Supreme Court, joined the Constituent Assembly as members. All this despite the fact that southerners did not participate in any elections, and that the Council of Ministers had postponed officially the holding of elections in the South. The 21 took their cases to court and obtained a favorable judgment on the ground that they had complied with all rules concerning nominations.

Loyalty party (in Arabic, <u>Al-Ikhlās Al-Watani</u>), the "Socialist Groups" (in Arabic <u>Al-Tajamm'u Al-Ishtirāki</u>; a better translation might be "Socialist Throng or Bloc."), and the Beja Congress.[3]

For our purposes we will be concerned only with six groups, the first five on the list plus the various independents. The remaining seven (plus three organizations that for unknown reasons were left off the list, namely the National Reform party, the Islamic Socialist party, and the Tenants' Union) were either cover organizations for one of the other five, or were local groupings with no impact at all on the national scene:

1) The Islamic Front ran only three candidates, all in the capital. This writer was unable to discover any differences in political orientation or public pronouncements between these and members of the Islamic Charter Front, an umbrella organization for a series of Islamic parties, but heavily dominated by the Muslim Brotherhood.

2) The candidates competing behind the party labels of the Trade Union Association and the Tenants' Union did not represent these two bodies in the conventional sense; rather they were members of the respective radical left wings, who used the labels in the hope of attracting widespread support among members of these associations. Prior to general elections, the Communist or Communist-leaning leadership of these bodies had lost showdown elections within the unions to more moderate elements. Now they decided to run for the Constituent Assembly anyhow, but wished to avoid the Communist label for fear of losing marginal supporters. It is significant that in the two constituencies where candidates ran under the Trade Union Association name—in the industrial areas of Khartoum and the railroad hub Atbara, respectively—the Communist party had entered no candidates. The same situation prevailed in the twenty constituencies of Blue Nile Province and the one in Kordofan where the Tenants' Union candidates were unopposed by official candidates of the Communist party. The Communists, by contrast, had four candidates in Blue Nile Province, all in large towns. This suggests that their sympathizers in the Tenants' Union selected their particular party label because they feared, and rightly so, that the term "Communists" carried distinct negative overtones in the conservative countryside.

3) The Socialist Democratic Congress and the Socialist "Groups" or Bloc entered only one and three candidates, respectively, who were widely known to be Communist sympathizers—especially Abdein Ismail of the former, who exposed his political leanings as minister of local government in the first transitional government after the October Revolution—but who preferred to campaign under a different label.

4) The Revolutionary Communist party—actually the "Communists of the Revolutionary Command"—constituted the Peking-oriented

faction among Sudanese Communists. It entered only two candidates in elections—in the industrial areas of Khartoum North and Wad Medani—and received minimal support at the polls. For statistical purposes the election gains of this faction will be subsumed under the heading of Communist party. I must point out, however, that in both constituencies the revolutionary Communists ran candidates in direct opposition to the orthodox or Moscow-oriented Communists.

5) The National Loyalty party and the National Reform party were represented by only one candidate each in adjoining districts of rural Khartoum Province. It appears that both candidates decided to found their own party after they failed to obtain the nomination from the NUP.

6) The Islamic Socialist party—which has been described by some as the party of four individuals, all active in the Executive Committee—for all intents and purposes should be a member unit of the Islamic Charter Front. After its maverick secretary general, Babikir Karrar, fell out with the charter leadership, he decided to boycott elections, but apparently failed to notify his supporters in one Blue Nile constituency in time, with the result that his candidate out-polled the PDP representative (whose party was also boycotting elections).

For all practical purposes the Beja Congress and the Nuba Mountains Federation should be treated as independents. (The latter revived its organization for the 1965 elections, even though all candidates were formally listed as independents.) As already explained in Chapter 2, both groups came into existence because their founders expected to use them as leverage for procuring economic and social services for their regions by voting in blocs in a constituent assembly in which no single party could be expected to obtain an absolute majority of seats. They represented the great bulk of non-Arabs indigenous to the North; as such the degree of their identification with the main unifying element in the northern Sudan—assimilated Arabized culture—was less than that of practically all other northern tribes. Moreover, the Beja and Nuba inhabit the most underprivileged economic areas of the North, and have been considered to be among the socially most backward of all Sudanese tribes, both in the North and in the South. (The Beja are a predominantly nomadic people of Hamitic origin who inhabit the area in and around the Red Sea Hills between the borders of Ethiopia and Egypt. Their three largest tribes are the Bisharin, the Amarar, and the Hadendowwa (popularly known as Fuzzy-Wuzzies). The Nuba are a sedentary tribal grouping of disputed origin who inhabit the hill regions of southern Kordofan.)

The two remaining types of independents were either individuals who experienced a genuine desire to be completely disassociated from the established political parties and organizations, or persons, usually local sheikhs, who were unable to obtain the official nomination of their party (in most cases the NUP) and therefore decided to stand as independents.

In this connection it should be noted that all candidates in the Graduates' Constituencies were officially listed as independents. The Electoral Commission decided that the nature of these special constituencies made the designation of party affiliation undesirable. Nevertheless, it was common knowledge that the communists and the Islamic Charter Front both had entered slates of ten officially approved candidates; the communists added five names of persons who were "supported by the party."[*]

In various sections of previous chapters the roles of the traditional parties have already been described. For the present purpose of introducing the official contestants for the 1965 elections it will suffice to restate briefly that both Umma party and PDP based their support on sectarian loyalties, and that the NUP was the major secular party deriving its support from merchants, civil servants, and other members of the middle class primarily in urban areas. Meanwhile, the Islamic Charter Front and the Communist party of the Sudan entered elections officially for the first time. Both appealed to essentially similar groups in Sudanese society, namely those politically conscious citizens who had become disillusioned with the repeated failures of traditional politicians in handling old and new problems by traditional methods. The ICF was the more untried of the two contestants and could be certain only of the electoral support of the Muslim Brotherhood core. The more experienced Communists had solidified their traditional influence among portions of workers and peasants in the Central Nile region and extended their appeal to students, teachers, and the active members of the new women's organizations.

Issues

The main public issues prior to the 1965 elections concerned the pros and cons of the different approaches that were advocated by various parties toward solving the three basic outstanding problems

---

[*]Quoted from handbills that were posted to billboards and affixed to trees throughout the capital prior to voting in the Graduates' Constituencies. These handbills also gave names and portraits of the endorsed candidates.

facing the country: the southern question, the state of the economy, and the nature of "post-October" Sudanese society.

The first involved the realization that in view of the rapidly deteriorating situation in the South something constructive would have to be done soon in order to keep the nation from disintegrating as a unit. The state of emergency throughout the South persisted, and attacks on government positions by the rebel Anya-Nya movement mounted in scope and success. However, what really brought home the seriousness of the situation was the outbreak of racial rioting in Khartoum on December 6, 1964, during the course of which at least hundreds, and probably thousands, were killed. It would take too much space to trace the causes and origins of this violence here; the main point to be made for our present purposes is that for most politically aware northern Sudanese the intensity of racial dissonance in the country at large, and the urgency for immediate action, was graphically demonstrated for the first time.

The second problem involved realization that foreign exchange reserves were rapidly dwindling due to overambitious long-term projects by the military rulers. As a result, imports of vital consumer goods (the Sudan must import almost all industrial materials, also most medical supplies, and certain types of foodstuffs, in addition to the usual luxury items) had to be curtailed in a manner directly felt in the marketplace. Furthermore, unemployment in the urban areas was rising because of the inability of the industrial and commercial sectors to absorb the constantly swelling urban populations. Unlike most developing nations, the Sudan had not experienced visible unemployment in the rural areas; in fact, some agricultural schemes suffered from seasonal labor shortages. However, in the cities a steady influx of rural people plus increased life expectancy due to superior medical care combined to double the population in a decade. Pressure on the government to respond to this problem became particularly strong since the publication of a United Nations study in August 1964, in which the Sudan was categorized as one of the very few underpopulated countries in the world in relation to its economic potential.[4]

The economic difficulties were compounded by the government's failure to sell most of the 1964-65 cotton crop by April 1965, and by an almost endless series of strikes, spurred on by the Federation of Trade Union Associations and condoned by the transitional governments, which seemed to be torn between wishing to establish some order in the chaotic situation and hoping that continued disorder would create the necessary atmosphere for a truly revolutionary upheaval. This indecision on the part of the government reflected the split of alliances within the Council of Ministers; the front members were hoping for more chaos—somewhat illogically—while the traditionalists became alarmed to the point of pressing for immediate elections. (The leftists gambled on a public showdown in February 1965 by calling for a general strike; yet their call was heeded only by an insignificant number of workers in Atbara and Khartoum North, and constituted a visible setback to their policy.)

The third problem concerned the aforementioned struggle over political and social priorities for the country. It posited traditional forces, who desired to reestablish the status quo ante the military regime and who promised the usual gradual steps of economic and social development, against the radical, leftist elements demanding a thorough overhaul of political and social conditions based on the elimination of conservative and sectarian organizations. This struggle was manifested in the purges of a considerable number of senior civil servants throughout the bureaucracy under the instigation and official order of front ministers, and the criminal trials of former members of the military junta. These trials were preceded by massive propaganda, accusing the ex-junta members (except for the pensioned-off Abboud) of a long list of criminal offenses. When the prosecutor was unable to provide substantial evidence for most of the charges, the former "show trials" received second billing to local third division football scores. It became quite clear that the leftist leadership aimed at destroying both the quality of the civil service leadership by removing top men from their positions (on the grounds of collaboration with the previous regime) and the esprit de corps within the bureaucracy by threatening the job security of large segments of this body by intimating strongly that promotion may become a function of ideological commitment rather than achievement or personal contacts. There was serious talk of forming a revolutionary vanguard— consisting of workers, peasants, and intellectuals—for the task of rebuilding Sudanese society along "scientific lines." This revolutionary vanguard had taken credit for bringing down the military regime and warned the "Sudanese masses to watch out for the reactionaries who were bent on stealing the gains of the October revolution." Such pronouncements were well received by a surprising number of Sudanese in the towns and in portions of the Gezira. Although virtually everyone knew that the slogans were advocated foremost by Communists, and although relatively few Sudanese cared to be associated with the Communists, there were, nevertheless, many persons with genuine social and economic grievances. They despaired at the inability of traditional politicians to ameliorate their conditions and therefore became quite sympathetic to any group or organization that identified with their problems, and that furthermore promised a fresh scientific approach towards solving them.

How did the five major political parties respond publicly to the issues at hand?

Regarding the question of social and political priorities, the NUP advocated gradual secularization, the Umma party was most conservative (since it had the most to conserve), while the PDP changed from an initially conservative stance in early winter to an adoption of socialist slogans following its political alliance with the Communist party in late winter. The effective consequence of this alliance was that PDP leadership groups polarized into a leftist faction, which verbally adopted Castroite attitudes but acted more in a pro-Nasser fashion, and a conservative faction emphasizing khatmiyyah ties. The Muslim brothers and Communists both desired a thorough reordering of Sudanese society, the former along militant Islamic and the latter along Marxist lines. Although the Communists went to great lengths in asserting that socialism was not at all incompatible with Islam— incidentally, a proposition to which all other parties publicly agreed— the Ummas, NUPs, and especially the Muslim Brotherhood denounced the communists as godless agents of a foreign power.

Except for the standard and well-known Communist formula, none of the major parties offered any new plans for reviving the economy. The Umma party favored an increase in economic aid from the West, while the CPS advocated exclusive trade ties with the Socialist countries. All five parties talked about some form of socialism, from the African to the Arab to the scientific variety, yet all took extreme care not to commit themselves to any detailed program. It was obvious that the term "socialism" was espoused because it was in vogue, not because it offered any concrete visions for solving economic problems.

All parties avoided carefully the growing problem of unemployment in the towns. There was much talk about Sudanization of the posts held by foreign specialists, but realistic politicians, especially in the NUP and Umma party, prevented such talk from amounting to anything more than expedient rhetoric. Shortly before elections the NUP ministers managed to push a decree through the cabinet whereby the government was to absorb several hundred high school graduates in the civil service, against the recommendations of the foreign economic advisors. This measure, along with an Umma-sponsored decree for raising the salaries of almost all bureaucrats, was clearly designed to placate a sizable portion of voters.

The issue that was probably the most important in the minds of the electorate was the handling of strikes by the transitional government. Soon after the Front of Professional Organizations had come to power, it announced to all sectors of Sudanese society its resolve to improve the general living conditions and invited all aggrieved parties to present their claims to the front with the promise of "speedy and positive action" on all justified complaints. The response to this invitation was overwhelming. Practically every organized group in society petitioned to the government for higher wages

and better social services. Although many of these petitions were
probably justified—but not necessarily to the extent of the financial
demands—the government was predictably unable to respond favorably,
except in a very few cases. The aggrieved parties were told that their
requests were receiving careful study by various committees. As
time passed and the discrepancy between continued front promises
and actual delivery became more and more evident, the petitioning
groups, one by one, went on strike.

The front did not know how to handle this situation—it certainly
did not want to emulate the junta's policy of outlawing strikes—with
the consequence that during almost every week in the early spring of
1965 one group or another opted for work stoppage. In many instances
necessary social services were disrupted, such as when hospital
nurses and telephone employees walked off their jobs. (This author
could not escape the strong suspicion that the latter tried to reinforce
their bargaining position by crossing some wires in the central telephone switch station, because one could dial the same local number
ten times in succession and be connected to ten different parties,
some in distant provinces.) The chief victim of this situation was the
general public, which became increasingly restless in view of the
near-chaotic conditions and which identified the leftists in government
as the real villains. The clamor for elections grew in the hope that
a strong government could deal with the crisis. The Communists and
PDPs, however, opposed the holding of elections. Their explanation
for this position was that the situation in the South still prevented
elections at that time.

The Southern Problem, as the reader will recall, was showing
signs of getting out of control, especially after the racial clashes of
December 6, 1964. In an effort to find a peaceful solution, the government invited all Sudanese political parties (and some foreign observers) to a "round-table conference on the problem of the southern
Sudan" in Khartoum during the period of March 16-25, 1965. All
Sudanese parties did, in fact, take advantage of the opportunity to
publicize their views at this conference before a captive audience of
African and overseas observers. The focus of this chapter does not
permit an elaborate analysis of the proceedings;[5] suffice it here to
state that unfortunately, though understandably, the northern parties
used the forum of the conference primarily for presenting their respective positions with an eye on the upcoming elections. This statement should not be taken to insinuate that the official party views
were insincere; however, no observer could avoid the impression
that the parties failed to address themselves to any realistic analysis
of, or solutions to, the problem at hand. Such strategy called for
popular policies, not difficult choices, and thereby contributed to the
basic failure of the round table conference. Not only were the northern

parties unable to agree on a common ideological approach to the southern question, but they actively used this issue as a political football in the arena of partisan politics.

As previously noted, the PDP and the Communist party had entered into an "alliance of progressive forces" against the conservative front of Umma party, NUP, and Muslim Brotherhood. When the latter trio pressed for the staging of general elections, the former refused to go along on the grounds that elections in the South were impossible at that time, and that elections in the North only would lead to a separation of the southern provinces from the rest of the country. Although these statements were given wide currency in the Sudan, it is this writer's opinion that they were made only for strategic reasons, and quite unrelated to the problem in the South. This hypothesis is based on the following observations:

In the first transitional cabinet the leftists, through the Front of Professional Organizations, enjoyed a ruling majority that was totally disproportionate to the numerical support of the various political groups in the country. Quite naturally, the leftists did their utmost to remain in power. Even though their influence had been curtailed in the newly-formed cabinet after February 24 it was, nevertheless, still disproportionate to their voting strength in the country: the PDP was allocated the same number of portfolios as the NUP and Umma party, while the Communists were offered one cabinet post—a matter of considerable importance to a minority party and something that it could not hope to retain after elections.

Initially, both PDP and CPS refused to join the cabinet and clung to the argument that general elections must be preceded by a solution of the Southern Problem, an arrangement that promised to continue the status quo for a long time. The leader of the PDP, Ali Abdel-Rahman, called the holding of elections "high treason" and announced that his party would "boycott and resist them."[6] The Communists asserted that the "reactionaries were planning to rob the people of their Revolution" by intriguing to hold elections.[7] After the conservative alliance managed to force through a decree in the Council of Ministers to hold elections in April, their opponents filed suits declaring elections at first unconstitutional and then the Council of Ministers—of which they were members—as illegally constituted. After both suits were dismissed by the High Court, the Communists made an about-face and decided to participate in elections after all, whereas the PDP leadership confirmed its earlier decision to "boycott and resist" the elections. However, this final decision met considerable opposition within the ruling circles of the PDP; in any case, it had come too late in order for the party's candidates to withdraw their nominations without forfeiting the deposits. In the end all PDP candidates obtained some votes, despite the fact that most of them—although not all—had informed their electorate of the party's decision to boycott elections.

On the eve of polling day the one issue that stood out most clearly in the minds of voters—in those areas where issues rather than personalities determined voting behavior—was the desire to end the confusion of the last few months, the charges and countercharges by officials, the chaotic strike situation, and the stream of conflicting statements in radio and press, by ascertaining once and for all who had the right to speak for "the people" (a recurrent phrase invoked by all major parties at the time).

Voting Analysis

Registration for voting in the 1965 elections was limited to the period of January 15-March 12, 1965; about two million signed up for the 158 territorial and almost 20,000 for the graduates' constituencies. The geographic distribution of registrants and voters for both categories is depicted in Tables 7.1 and 7.2. It is noteworthy that over one half of both the qualified and the actual graduate electorate resided in Khartoum Province, a fact that supports the Umma exminister's argument that the institution of graduates' constituencies strongly favored certain regions over others. For the territorial constituencies registration figures varied from a low of 3347 in a nomadic district in Darfur (constituency no. 148; Dar Masalit North-East) to a high of 25,473 in Wad Medani Township (capital of Blue Nile Province); however, such figures below ten and above twenty thousand were rare, and most clustered around the national average of twelve thousand. The voting turnout at domestic polling centers for graduates and for territorial constituencies in general fell somewhat below expectations. This was probably because a sizable proportion of PDP members heeded the appeal by the party leadership to boycott elections; this interpretation is supported by the noticeable drop in voting participation in Kassala Province, the traditional area of PDP strength.

The relatively high voting turnout in Blue Nile Province reflected the fact that this province—and especially the Gezira area—has traditionally been the most closely contested of all. The reader may recall that the inhabitants of the western region have been known to be strongly pro-ansar, those of the northern and eastern regions just as strongly pro-khatmiyyah, and the capital province has been dominated by the NUP in all elections. This leaves only the Blue Nile Province among those in the North and here competition for loyalty and votes has been fairly equally divided between Umma and NUP.

TABLE 7.1

Registration and Voting in Graduates' Constituencies, 1965

Province/Zone	Registered	Qualified	Voters	Voting Turnout in percent
Khartoum	11,203	9,871	6,735	68.2
Northern	969	925	698	75.5
Blue Nile	2,269	1,871	1,403	75
Kordofan	744	608	436	71.7
Darfur	357	319	227	71.2
Kassala	604	554	378	68.2
Red Sea Hills	429	392	302	77
Upper Nile	132	105	74	70.5
Bahr el-Ghazal	47	39	23	59
Equatoria	116	105	62	59
Total domestic	16,870	14,789	10,338	70
London	337	323	283	87.6
Moscow	414	402	365	90.8
Washington	202	186	168	90.3
Prague-Bulgaria	382	308	288	93.5
Cairo	845	837	689	82.3
Bonn	160	120	77	64.2
Lebanon-Baghdad	106	103	98	95.1
Paris	87	83	62	74.7
Saudia	262	237	199	84
Lagos-Somalia	—	—	—	—
Tanzania-Leopoldville	24	18	17	94.4
Nairobi-Addis Ababa	—	—	—	—
Asmara	—	—	—	—
Total foreign	2,819	2,617	2,246	86
Grand Total	19,689	17,406*	12,584	72

*The main reason why almost 2,300 applications were rejected was—according to the chief registration officer—that many applicants were confused about the details of voter qualifications. Apparently, they thought that a four year attendance of secondary schools sufficed to meet the requirements when, in fact the rule called for successful completion of the comprehensive final examinations at the end of the fourth year at secondary school.

Source: Compiled by the author.

TABLE 7.2

Registration and Voting in Territorial Constituencies, 1965

Province	Registered Voters	Approximate Average per Constituency	Actual Voters	Voting Turnout in percent
Khartoum	214,363	16,500	120,135	56.0
Blue Nile	696,393	15,500	454,351	66.4
Kordofan	437,969	12,000	240,718	56.2
Northern	175,400	10,300	99,342	56.6
Kassala	225,840	9,800	97,842	43.3
Darfur	209,915	8,750	113,841	54.2
Total	1,959,880	12,404	1,126,229	58.1

Note: The registration totals include the figures for constituencies no. 92 (in Blue Nile Province) and 185 (in Kordofan), where no voting took place because the candidates were unopposed. The figures for voting turnout are based on the results from 156 constituencies only, that is, minus nos. 92 and 185.

Source: Compiled by the author.

231

One index of the intensity of this competition—and the reason for the high voting participation—is the substantial ratio of closely contested to one-sided election races: 26:18 in Blue Nile Province as compared with 12:23 in Kordofan, for example. It is significant in this connection that almost all of the 26 closely contested constituencies in Blue Nile Province were located in the Gezira scheme proper, whereas most of the one-sided election races took place in nomadic and seminomadic areas.[*]

In all, 12,584 graduates voted for 87 candidates in the 15 graduates' constituencies, while 1,126,228 persons voted for 733 candidates competing in the 158 territorial constituencies. After all election returns were announced, the seats in the new Constituent Assembly were divided among the parties as follows:

TABLE 7.3

Distribution of Seats After 1965 Elections

Party	Territorial Constituencies	Graduates' Constituencies	Total
Umma	76	—	76
NUP	52	2	54
ICF	3	2	5
PDP[*]	3	—	3
Communists	—	8	8
Communist "sympathizers"	—	3	3
Independents[*] (including Beja Congress)	24 (10 Beja)	—	24
Total	158	15	173

[*]Two additional candidates won under the PDP label, but requested, after election results were announced, to be considered as independent and of the Beja Congress, respectively; they are included among the independents in Table 7.3.

Source: Compiled by the author.

A quick glance at Table 7.3 reveals the striking fact that the two by far most successful parties in the territorial constituencies, as well as the independents for that matter, failed conspicuously in the

---

[*]The settled areas around Kosti are in-between cases; they do not belong to the Gezira scheme, but are inhabited mainly by tenants and sharecroppers who work in the Mahdi estates. The overwhelming majorities obtained there by Umma party candidates were entirely expected.

Graduates' Constituencies. Whereas the moderately oriented parties obtained 98 percent of the seats in the former, they were able to win only two of fifteen (both NUP) in the latter. This curious result becomes even more intriguing when we realize that the two victorious NUP candidates belonged to the extreme radical (left) wing of that party, and that one of these, former-Minister Saleh Mahmoud Ismail, had been publicly reprimanded by Ismail el-Azhari for "irresponsible statements which did not reflect NUP policy" just prior to elections.

Graduates' Constituencies

Any analysis of such extraordinary results in the graduates' constituencies requires an appreciation of the changing social background of the electorate and their degree of organization. In the 1953 elections graduates had been essentially established members of an emerging middle class in the Sudan, including middle- and upper-level civil servants, teachers, lawyers, doctors, engineers, and a few merchants. Their political attitudes could be described as primarily favoring secular and liberal domestic policies in addition to firm opposition to British rule in the country. By 1965 this group still existed, but it had become a minority among the voters in the graduates' constituencies. The majority was made up of young men and women under 25 years of age (unfortunately, no detailed figures are available about their personal characteristics However, a sampling of the opinions of election officers suggests that about one half seemed to be 21 years of age and younger, at least in Khartoum Province where more than 50 percent of all graduates voted). Most of them were either unemployed or dissatisfied with the type of occupation that their secondary school certificates enabled them to obtain. As a rule they were frustrated by the inability of native institutions to accomplish rapid social and political change in the country, about which their expectations had been raised in school and by such organs as the "Voice of the Arabs" radio. Their disillusionment with the performance of traditional political organizations in a series of successive governments turned them increasingly toward extremist organizations that espoused radical solutions for these complex problems. A telling example is presented by the Khartoum University student body elections, where left-wing groups obtained 45 percent and the Muslim Brotherhood movement 40 percent of the vote as compared with 15 percent for supporters of three traditional parties. We may grant that these results reflect, to a certain degree, the normal proclivity of young people for radical ideas that promise sweeping changes, positions that tend to become more moderate with the passage of years; nevertheless, it became

very clear to this writer in the course of many interviews and informal talks that the younger educated generation in the Sudan considered
the traditional leadership to be out of step with its aspirations and
problems, an assessment that was probably quite correct. Moreover,
it should not come as a surprise that these young people were unfa-
vorably disposed toward the older parties, which had objected to the
lowering of the voting age and to the enfranchisement of women.

There could be little doubt about the degree of organization of
these voters. As already mentioned, the Communists and Muslim
brothers had both urged their supporters to vote for complete slates
of ten candidates; in addition, the Communists endorsed five other
"sympathizers" who preferred not to be associated with the Communist lable. The Umma party had virtually neglected the graduates'
constituency since it did not expect to gain more than two seats, if
any. The NUP, on the other hand, anticipated to win between 12 and
15 seats on the basis of the 1953 election results.[8] When the extent
of the communist campaign efforts became clear, the NUP belatedly
made a weak attempt to present a list of ten rather obscure names
in the NUP newspaper.

Any observer in the vote counting center realized soon that candidates who were not endorsed on any list had very little chance for
success because of the apparently prevalent pattern of bloc voting.
For example, whenever a particular ballot paper contained in the top
row the name of a Communist candidate, the probability was over 95
percent that the remaining names were those of Communists and their
sympathizers, too. Similarly, a ballot listing a Muslim brother in the
top spot could be counted on not to include the name of a Communist.

The relative success of the Communists, as compared with the
Islamic Charter Front, stems from two facts: The Communists had
a proportionately larger following among men qualifying as "graduates," and the Muslim brothers could not expect any support from
female graduates, because of the brothers' explicit opposition to any
change in the restricted role of women in Sudanese society. One chief
reason for the poor showing of the NUP, in addition to the factors
already listed, was the party's failure to present any attractive candidates. Several NUP friends told this author privately that they had
only two or three men from their party worthy of support and would
have to give their remaining votes to "outsiders." They, and the independent voters, tended to select candidates on the basis of popularity, a not uncommon motivation in such circumstances. Of course,
this situation benefitted nationally known personalities regardless of
their political affiliation. In this context it may be interesting to
present the six top vote getters in order: Hassan el-Turabi, the
leader of the Muslim Brotherhood and former dean of the Khartoum
University Law School; Saleh Mahmoud Ismail, the controversial

ex-NUP minister (see above), who was endorsed by the Communists;
Fatima Ahmed Ibrahim, the president of the Sudan Women's Association, who evidently obtained the support of both the Communists' and
the women's blocs; Hassan el-Tâher Zarrouq, the editor of Al-Midan,
the Communists daily newspaper; Mahjoub Mohammed Saleh, the editor
of the Al-Ayyam daily newspaper, running under the Socialist-Demo-
cratic label; and Joseph Garang, the editor of Advance, the English-
language organ of the Communist party. They were followed by eight
lesser known candidates, seven of whom were Communists. The final
seat was won by Mohammed Yussuf, the cofounder of the Islamic
Charter Front. The impact of bloc voting can be seen in the fact that
some rather obscure Communists were able to defeat such nationally
known figures—and very capable men, indeed—as Beshir Mohammed
Sa'id, associate editor of Al-Ayyam and managing director of the
English-language daily, The Morning News, who lost out just barely,
Hamza Mirghani Hamza, well-known minister in the pre-Abboud
cabinet, several retired army generals and some members of very
prominent business families.

Territorial Constituencies

Because of the proportionately small number of electoral seats,
the results of voting in the graduates' constituencies held primarily
prestige value for the competing parties. The bulk of campaign efforts and intensity of competition were concentrated on the territorial
constituencies. As shown by the data in Table 7.3, the Umma party
gained almost one-half of these and the NUP one-third. A more accurate appraisal of the relative strengths of the various parties is
rendered by an examination of the geographic distribution of assembly
seats (Map 7.1) compared with the percentages of votes polled by each
party per province (Table 7.4).

A glance at Map 7.1 reveals few surprises. As expected, Umma
strength lay essentially in the western and central regions, while the
NUP controlled the urban, settled areas along the Blue Nile and the
joint Nile. Results for the PDP in the 1965 elections cannot be analyzed meaningfully, because the party's decision to boycott elections
distorted the voting patterns in traditional centers of khatmiyyah
strength. Nevertheless, we may note that the seats won by the PDP
are located in the northern and eastern parts of the country. It is
significant that neither Umma party nor NUP profited measurably
from the boycott, since most constituencies in khatmiyyah areas
were won by independents or members of the Beja Congress. The
other concentration of seats for independents is near the bottom
center of Map 7.1 in Kordofan, where candidates of the Nuba Mountain Federation of Independents won out in seven constituencies.

MAP 7.1

Pictoral View of 1965 Election Results
(six northern provinces)

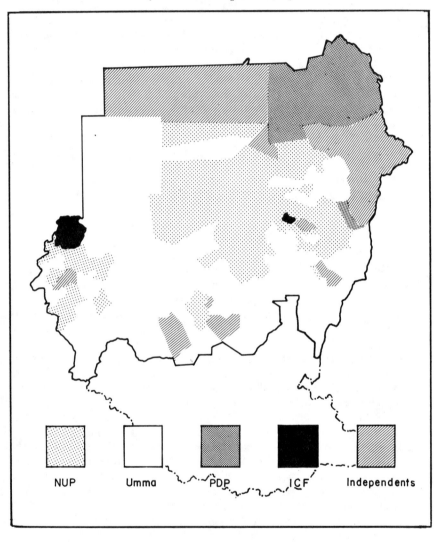

NUP   Umma   PDP   ICF   Independents

TABLE 7.4

Percentages of Votes Obtained by Parties per Province, 1965

Province	NUP	Umma	ICF	PDP	Communist	Independent	Others
Northern	57.3 (10)*	18.8 (4)	6.5	5.1 (1)	—	6.5 (2)	3.2 Trade Union .4 Social Bloc
Darfur	23.9 (6)	66.5 (16)	2.7 (1)	.7	—	3.2 (1)	
Kassala	23.6 (2)	30.1 (7)	10.7 (1)	5.6 (2)	.8	4.0 (1)	22.1 Beja Congress (10)
Blue Nile	31.7 (14)	52.1 (29)	3.6	.9	.4	1.3 (2)	6.5 Tenants' Union .9 Socialist Group
Kordofan	33.1 (9)	53.2 (19)	2.8	.5	.2	8.6 (8)	.04 Tenants' Union
Khartoum	49.7 (11)	16.9 (1)	11.6a (1)	.2	11.1	2.1	3.0 Trade Union 2.9 Socialist Democratic Congress .1 Others
Total	34.7	45.3	5.1	1.5	1.5b	3.9b	5.9b

*Parentheses indicate the numbers of seats won.

aIslamic Front total added to Islamic Charter Front

bdifferent, and perhaps more meaningful, combinations yield these results:
  1. Beja Congress plus Independents = 5.9 percent
  2. Socialist Bloc plus Socialist Democratic Congress plus Communist party = 1.9 percent
  3. Trade Unions plus Tenants' Union = 3.3 percent
  4. those listed in 2, plus those listed in 3-5.2 percent

cthe percentage figures are based on all votes cast, invalid ballots (about 3 percent) account for the remaining totals.

Source: Compiled by the author.

A comparison of Map 7.1 with Map 5.1 on the 1958 elections results indicates a remarkable continuity in the geographic distribution
of seats, as long as one compensates for the withdrawal of the PDP
in 1965. For example, the findings in Darfur, Khartoum, western
Kordofan, and the "Umma belt" extending from the White Nile through
the southern Gezira into southern Kassala are virtually congruent.*
If we combine the Beja seats with those of the PDP in 1965, then the
pattern in Kassala Province and in eastern Kordofan exhibits close
similarity to the one in 1958, especially if we make allowances for
gerrymandering in the earlier elections. In fact, the only noticeable
change in 1965 is the decline of NUP seats in the northern Gezira,
although the NUP retained control of the large settled towns along the
Blue Nile

Further analysis of voting results yields the following observations about party gains and losses: the PDP could not expect to fare
better than it did after its declaration of boycotting elections. Leaders
of the Islamic Charter Front were disappointed in the results; evidently they had underestimated the task of campaign organization. In
view of their limited financial resources and their total inexperience
in preparing for participation in nationwide elections, their electoral
gains were quite satisfactory. The Communists and their affiliated
groups did surprisingly well in the cities, compared with popular estimates by both Sudanese moderates and foreign observers of the appeal
of communism in the country.

Just the same, the Communists, too, were initially disappointed
with the outcome at the polls, since they had expected to carry at
least six constituencies in the capital alone.[9] Needless to say, such
expectations were quite unwarranted and rested upon an incorrect

------

*The reader is cautioned against two potentially misleading as-
pects of this kind of pictorial representation: 1. The different sizes
of various constituencies may give a distorted impression of party
strength; for example, the center of Map 7.1 depicts a large contigu-
ous area of NUP seats, over one-half of which actually consists of a
mere three constituencies inhabited by the (traditionally pro-NUP)
Kababish nomads. By contrast, the small triangle at the bottom center
represents seven Nuba independents. 2. The map reveals only the
number and location of seats won by various parties—which is its
purpose, of course—but does not indicate the actual voting strength
of the respective parties. The first difficulty presents no real problem as long as the observer is aware of the variations in the size of
constituencies. The second one can be overcome through the study
of the percentages of votes obtained by the parties in the six provinces.

interpretation of popular support of the transitional government just after the overthrow of the military regime. What Communist leaders apparently failed to realize was the genuine popular wave of disapproval of the leftist-instigated series of strikes prior to elections. One basic weakness of the Communist leadership throughout this period has been the gap between its ability to stimulate popular demands, and its inability to provide leadership in making strikes or similar measures produce the desired objective.

The very considerable success of independent candidates can be laid to their skill in exploiting the poor organization of the Umma party and the NUP in peripheral areas and to the appeal of regional groupings that promised to pursue the local interests of non-Arab peoples in the Nuba Mountains, the Red Sea Hills (the Beja) and in Darfur (the Fur), and that were victorious there by very large margins in 7, 10, and 1 constituencies, respectively.

As expected, the Umma party and the NUP were the two most successful parties, and collected about five-sixths of all electoral mandates between themselves. The former again dominated the western and central rural regions, and the NUP the urban areas along the main rivers and the larger provincial towns elsewhere. A comparison of the ratios of parliamentary seats gained by these two parties in the six northern provinces in both the 1958 and 1965 elections indicates a remarkable consistency: 62:40 in 1958 and 76:52 in 1965, both in favor of the Umma party. However, neither the Umma nor the NUP leadership quite expected the old pattern to persist. The former was pleasantly surprised by their relatively strong showing in the North, in Blue Nile Province, and in the adjoining sector of southern Kassala. The latter had openly anticipated an absolute majority of assembly seats because of a presumed decline in sectarian loyalties during the interval of military rule, and because it expected the Umma party to flounder under a lack of leadership following the death of the posthumous son of the Mahdi, Sir Abdel-Rahman, in 1959. As it turned out, the Umma party possessed the superior election machinery of the two, the more dynamic leadership and, apparently, larger financial resources publicly rumored to have stemmed from the Western world. The NUP suffered from a lack of party unity and discipline (see Chapter 2), and there is every indication that it was also guilty of overconfidence. (The president, Ismail el-Azhari, confided in a private interview that he had expected his party to obtain at least 90 to 100 seats after the PDP announced its decision to withdraw from the competition.)

A NEW GAME OF MUSICAL CHAIRS

When the new Constituent Assembly was convened on June 10, 1965, the NUP and Umma party agreed to share power in a grand coalition that seemed to guarantee long-term stability on paper. The coalition controlled at least three-fourths of all assembly seats, and there was genuine fear among the minority parties that the majority would force through constitutional amendments to its own advantage and thereby change the basic power configuration for the foreseeable future. Such fears proved to be totally unjustified. Not only did the coalition partners miss golden opportunities to foil their opponents, they actually proceeded to undermine each other so extensively as to render the government incapable of acting on any major issue. In the long run, the inter- and intraparty blood-letting proved so disastrous as to cause the eventual collapse of parliamentary democracy altogether.

What makes these developments even more astonishing is the fact that civilian politicians had apparently failed completely to draw appropriate lessons from the recent past. Such lessons would have taught them, at a minimum, the need for constructive cooperation if the alternative of military intervention was to be avoided. Also, another lesson would have required recognition of the emergence of new political forces in the country that represented the aspirations of a substantial proportion of the younger generation, and that could not be dismissed by mere appeals to traditional symbols of loyalty.

A point of utmost importance here is that civilian politicians were given a golden opportunity to create a viable system after October 1964. For many reasons, the previous military junta had fallen into such disrepute that even senior officers who privately had little confidence in the effectiveness of parliamentary government nevertheless agreed throughout 1965 and 1966 that a return to military rule was "unthinkable." As it turned out, the opportunity was abysmally wasted, and by May 1969, if not before, the return of army rule was warmly welcomed by almost all politically conscious Sudanese.

What went wrong, and why? These questions are sufficiently important to our understanding of Sudanese politics to warrant a close look at the four-year period from May 1965 to May 1969.

Our analysis must begin by examining the two governmental seats of power, the Supreme Council of State and the Council of Ministers. The former had been designated as the formal seat of authority in the country within days after General Abboud's resignation as president. In order to enlist a broad spectrum of support during that unstable period it was decided that the Supreme Council should be constituted by five members, each representing a different faction, and that its chairmanship should rotate among the members. Accordingly, five individuals were appointed on December 3, 1964, and sworn into office.*

At first, this arrangement seemed to function very well. Even though the Supreme Council was formally vested with ultimate constitutional authority, the diffusion of power among five persons of limited political experience achieved the desired purpose of minimizing the risk of renewed centralization of power, and practically left the body with an essentially ceremonial function. Real political power resided in the Council of Ministers and in the position of the prime minister.

Unfortunately, such good sense did not prevail for very long. The reader should recall that Ismail el-Azhari had aligned his NUP with the Umma party around the turn of the year, apparently with the idea that the Umma leadership had the wherewithal to force the issue of holding elections immediately, if necessary through street battles. After this tactic had succeeded, el-Azhari began to champion the new Umma party president, Sayyid el-Sadiq el-Mahdi, as the future prime minister, in exchange for being assured the office of president of the republic.

Once the smashing electoral triumph of the coalition partners had been accomplished, the plan could be implemented, albeit with two minor modifications. One was the temporary postponement of Sadiq's accession to power until after he had completed his thirtieth year of age, and the second was a (also temporary?) concession to retain the Supreme Council as a five member body. Toward that end, council chairman pro tem Ibrahim Yusuf Suleiman was prevailed upon to resign his seat on May 31, 1965, and Ismail el-Azhari was subsequently sworn in, not merely as his replacement in that body but as the permanent chairman of the council. In effect, el-Azhari became head of state for the next four years.

Pleased though he was, the old independence fighter soon indicated his dissatisfaction with a purely ceremonial role and moved to enhance the political scope of his office. This led predictably to a series of conflicts, and was illustrated in the somewhat amusing dispute between the president and the prime minister, M. A. Mahjoub, on October 20, 1965 over the right to represent the Sudan at an African summit conference in Accra. While some outside observers attributed such wrangling to the understandable desire for an official vacation abroad—the journey to Accra was routed via Paris—the direct

----

*They were all respected senior Sudanese: Drs. Abdel-Halim Mohammed (Umma party), Tijani el-Mahi (NUP), and Mubarak Sheddad, also Ibrahim Yusuf Suleiman, a former senior civil servant. A southern member was to be added as soon as possible.

participants took the matter rather seriously. After the prime minister asserted himself in his perhaps most forceful decision while in office, first three and then all six NUP cabinet ministers submitted their resignations under obvious pressure from the Republican Palace. This incident was symbolic for the importance of personal jealousies and party rivalries even among coalition partners. Beyond that, it signified that the Supreme Council had now become politicized, that its real authority was no longer diffused but had been centralized into el-Azhari's hands, and that the latter could be counted on to involve himself directly in future political affairs.

As previously mentioned, the counterweight to presidential influence was located in the prime minister's position and in the cabinet. And it was here, in this observer's opinion, that the battle for democracy in the Sudan was lost in the final analysis. A strong prime minister with effective control over his own cabinet not only could have warded off interference from the Supreme Council, but also could have implemented constructive programs for economic, social and political progress, thereby further enhancing his own political support base.

Unfortunately, that was not to be. The initial appointment to the premiership fell upon Mohammed Ahmed Mahjoub, a man of considerable skill in foreign diplomacy but greatly lacking in personal leadership and decisiveness. Although his selection was initially viewed as a temporary measure by both Ismail el-Azhari and Sadiq el-Mahdi, the new prime minister developed a liking for the aura of his new position. Mahjoub was widely known as vain, thrived on flattery, and seemed unable to accept criticism either objectively or stoically. He took great pride in his own intellectual prowess, and described himself publicly as his country's foremost poet on at least one occasion known to this author.[10] He soon moved to combat any strategies aimed at his removal. Yet calls for just that mounted near the end of 1965 and during most of the ensuing half year. They were generated not only by Sadiq's partisan supporters, but primarily resulted from popular misgivings about the government's frequently ill-conceived and mostly indecivise policies in the political and economic realms and regarding continued unrest in the Southern provinces.

We shall return to an analysis of governmental performance in the economic sphere, and regarding the Southern Problem, in a concluding chapter. Suffice it here to summarize that during 1965 government revenue and foreign exchange reserves declined rapidly while unemployment in the urban areas rose sharply, and that meanwhile the insurrection by Anya Nya rebels in the South reached such serious

proportions that government troops controlled little more than the
three provincial capitals of Malakal, Wau, and Juba.*

Perhaps the most damning indictment of the Mahjoub regime lay
in its relative neglect of these two national problems in favor of persistent involvement in political maneuverings in Khartoum and Omdurman. For one thing, there was the rather inept handling of protests
by minority parties. Thus, the acting secretary of the PDP was arrested on July 2, 1965, along with 18 associates, following their
protest over the arrest of their party leader six days earlier. The
leader, Sheikh Ali Abdel-Rahman, may very well have been guilty as
charged. (He was indicted for inciting riots at a polling station in the
Khashm el-Girba area at election time, during which 14 persons were
killed, the only black mark of an otherwise very fair election procedure.) But the handling of that incident portrayed a government defen-
sive and unsure of itself.

The same could be said after it had enacted a law on December 9,
1965, banning the Communist party of the Sudan, confiscating its property, and ousting its eleven representatives from the Constituent
Assembly. The anti-Communist move can be traced in part to the
astonishing electoral success of the party secretary-general in a by-
election in Omdurman during November 1965 (see Appendix), which
frightened the conservative alliance into concrete efforts to limit the
CPS activities. The immediate cause was an incident at a semipublic
meeting in Omdurman, where a young man—later officially identified
as a card-carrying CPS member—defamed Islam in general, and the
Prophet's family in particular. Aroused masses demonstrated spon-
taneously before the parliament building demanding the outlawing of
the Communist party. The CPS leader, Abdel-Khaliq Mahjoub, subsequently challenged this law as unconstitutional in the Sudanese
courts which, after lengthy delays, overruled parliament in a decision
on December 22, 1966; yet the Supreme Council of State, under el-
Azhari's guidance and with the concurrence of the Umma party leadership, reaffirmed the ban on the party on April 16, 1967. Small wonder
that the rhetoric about preserving the newly won democratic freedoms
had acquired a hollow ring in the ears of astute Sudanese.

But the most damaging blow to political stability was delivered
by the party chieftains' wrangling over ministerial appointments and
overall leadership. At the time of the April 1965 elections the two
coalition partners had agreed to share equally twelve cabinet posts

---

*During a visit to the southern provinces in January 1966 this
writer observed that government soldiers were camped on both sides
of the airport landing strip in Wau, and along the roads from airport
to city in Wau and Juba in order to secure these strategic areas.

under an Umma premier (the remaining three seats were allocated to southerners). Quite understandably, the Umma party executives insisted on control over such prestigious portfolios as Defense, Foreign Affairs, Interior, Local Government, and Information and Labor, as compensation for their numerical concessions to a minority partner. Yet a glance at cabinet shifts during that four-year period reveals several interesting facts: a gradual shift of influential portfolios into NUP hands, the remarkable retention by a handful of prominent NUPs of their cabinet seats, albeit with sometimes changing portfolios, and the equally remarkable absence of any continuity by Umma ministers. All of this, plus the above-mentioned wrangling, can be appreciated more clearly through an understanding of intra-Umma party divisions and their exploitation by el-Azhari.

It has already been stated on several occasions that the Umma party has been the political organization of the ansar sectarian movement. During the 1940s and 1950s its leadership had been unified in the person of its patron, Sayyid Abdel-Rahman el-Mahdi. After the latter's death and that of his son, Siddiq, the leadership became divided along functional lines. The bright young Oxford-educated Sadiq el-Mahdi assumed the political helm as president of the Umma party, while his uncle, Imam el-Hadi, retained the religious title of spiritual head of the ansar. Even though both leaders operated initially from the same base of supporters, their professional roles understandably led to somewhat different policy priorities and, eventually, somewhat different perspectives. The imam was naturally more conservative in outlook and had his most loyal supporters in the most conservative rural areas. By contrast, his nephew championed more progressive ideas and commenced to rebuild the Umma party from a sectarian movement, in which ansar would follow their leader blindly into any policies, to a political organization pursuing specified political, economic, and social objectives. Through this latter innovation, but primarily because of Sadiq's personal qualities, the party began to attract some younger intellectuals who otherwise would have resented a traditional sectarian affiliation.

The potential division between the supporters of Sayyid el-Sadiq and Imam el-Hadi did not surface until the former had turned 30 years of age, had won a by-election in Blue Nile Province, and had taken his seat in the assembly. Soon thereafter, open criticism of Prime Minister Mahjoub's performance reached a crescendo on June 27, 1966, when a censure motion accusing his government of "failure and corruption" was narrowly defeated. In a public speech the prime minister denied allegations of an economic crisis and claimed that "rebellion in the South has been completely crushed." Such assertions caused hysterical laughter "even in the nearby zoo," in the words of an old Sudanese political observer. A few days later the

Umma Party Parliamentary Group (a sort of caucus) decided by an overwhelming majority to withdraw their support from the government over the angry objections of the Imam. When Mahjoub refused to resign, a vote of no confidence was called for on July 25, which won by a 126-30 margin (15 abstentions). Two days later Sadiq was elected as the new prime minister while Imam el-Hadi denounced the attitude of the Umma members of parliament and declared the coalition with the NUP as void. Sadiq retorted quite correctly that the NUP coalition partner was the Umma party and not the ansar movement. And so the battle was joined.

In the opinion of many astute Sudanese and foreign observers, Sadiq el-Mahdi set up the first effective political machinery since the country won its independence. He staffed his cabinet appointments and top ministerial positions with competent young men like Omar Nur el-Dayem and began to tackle national problems with broad and comprehensive programs. These policies won him general admiration and increasing political support in non-Umma areas, even among southern politicians.[*] Alas, they also aroused the personal jealousies of his uncle, the imam, and also of Ismail el-Azhari, who became increasingly fearful of Sadiq's growing reputation and presumed ambition for exclusive national leadership under a rumored switch to a presidential system (U.S. style). So, the two traditional leaders joined forces. The imam pressured Sadiq to alter his policies. The latter refused on principle, but was forced to grant some concessions in order to retain the necessary backing of the ansar. On December 6, 1966, he replaced Omar Nur el-Dayem and Mohammed Hilu Musa as cabinet ministers with Mohammed Khogali and Ahmed el-Mahdi, respectively, both staunch supporters of the imam. Seriously weakened, Sadiq nevertheless pressed on with his programs, but not for long. In late spring 1967 el-Azhari decided to withdraw NUP support from the government; Sadiq lost a vote of confidence in the Constituent Assembly on May 15 by a relatively narrow margin, was forced to resign, and joined his Umma wing to the parliamentary opposition of a few Muslim brothers and a few independents. The former premier, M. A. Mahjoub, was hoisted back into his old position and presided over a shaky coalition of NUPs, PDPs, three southern groupings, and the imam wing of the Umma party.

With slightly less than one half of the Umma party in a coalition government and the other half in opposition, and with the PDP in a stage of parliamentary limbo, confusion and derision reached such a

---

[*]By-elections throughout the three southern provinces took place in March 1967 to fill the 36 vacant seats; the two most successful parties were Umma with 14 and the SANU with 10 seats.

point that grumblings about the desirability of a military takeover could be discerned more and more. At this stage, el-Azhari persuaded the other factional leaders to schedule new parliamentary elections for early 1968. Fearful that the Umma party might once again obtain a relative majority of assembly seats, el-Azhari managed to forge a merger of his NUP with the PDP into a Democratic Unionist party (DUP) on December 12, 1967. Bitterness among Umma factions remained so strong, however, that the party could not be united even in the face of the new DUP merger, and thus both factions contested the upcoming elections separately.

But bitterness was not confined to the former majority party. Many NUPs were openly embarassed by their leader's opportunistic manipulations; others resented the rapprochement with the PDP and privately pledged their support to Sadiq el-Mahdi. Similarly, regional movements in the South, West, and East were unable to achieve their earlier degree of unification and organization. And finally, the leftist forces were severely handicapped by the official ban on the Communist party, and at election time were splintered into nine different factions. In all, the official report of the 1968 Electoral Commission listed 28 political entries.

This proliferation of contesting groups was symbolic for the state of political turmoil in the country. The atmosphere of uncertainty was heightened by constitutional challenges over the official term of the Constituent Assembly, which led to a near brawl among representatives and culminated in the assembly's dissolution by the State Supreme Council. By election time in mid-April it seemed that nearly every active politician was angry at somebody and that the electorate was thoroughly bewildered by the ongoing intrigues. The prime issue, therefore, was a quest for security and stability.

THE 1968 ELECTIONS

Between January 13 and February 28, 1968, over 3 million Sudanese registered for the upcoming elections, two-fifths of them women. The absolute figures for both men and women were all-time highs in the history of Sudanese elections; however, this did not necessarily indicate greater political interest per se, but rather reflected in part general population growth and, in part, the availability of a well-functioning election machinery dating back to 1965. The geographic distribution of registrants and voters is depicted in Table 7.5 which also reveals the effects of the state of public security on both aspects: registration in the three southern provinces was lowest, particularly in Equatoria (average 12,500) and helped to bring down the national

TABLE 7.5

Registration and Voting in 1968 Elections

Province	Registrants		Voters			Percentage of voters to Registrants
	Total	Approximate Average	Total	Invalid	Valid	
Equatoria	50,191	2,500	22,383	196	22,193	42
Khartoum	273,254	21,000	193,938	4,541	189,397	71
Northern	239,092	14,000	183,281	3,382	179,899	77
Blue Nile	842,006	18,700	612,542	17,670	594,872	73
Upper Nile	204,375	11,350	58,994	105	58,889	29
Bahr el-Ghazal	296,728	13,500	106,865	403	106,462	36
Darfur	359,896	15,000	213,240	6,209	207,031	59
Kassala	252,138	11,000	164,899	3,255	161,644	65
Kordofan	533,438	15,000	306,763	7,378	299,385	58
Total	3,051,118	14,000	1,862,911	43,139	1,819,772	61

Note: The official report of the 1968 Electoral Commission breaks down these figures by sex; unfortunately the commission's overall voting statistics are misleading and partially inaccurate because in certain areas separate tallies by sex were not kept. We do know, however, that 1,882,113 men and 1,169,005 women were officially registered, and that in 22 of the 218 constituencies female registration figures exceeded male ones. Some of the totals are inaccurate and have been corrected here.

Source: Republic of the Sudan General Elections Commission, Final Report of the 1968 General Elections (Khartoum: Government Printing Press, 1969) (in Arabic), Appendix "ba, 3."

TABLE 7.6

Official Election Results, 1968

Party	Votes	Percent	Number of Candidates	Number of Constituencies Contested	Seats Won
DUP	742,236	40.80	299	196	101
Umma-Sadiq	384,986	21.15	221	148	36*
Umma-Imam	329,952	18.13	168	119	30*
Independents	70,047	3.85	72	59	9
SANU	60,493	3.32	55	37	15
ICF	44,552	2.45	26	26	3
Umma	43,288	2.38	45	33	6*
Southern Front	39,822	2.19	43	40	10
Socialist Front	21,814	1.20	5	5	—
Socialists	19,690	1.08	12	12	—
Beja Congress	15,382	0.85	11	10	3
NUP	10,159	0.56	3	3	—
Not identified	8,264	0.45	2	2	1
Tenants Union	6,661	0.37	8	8	—
Workers Force	5,204	0.28	1	1	1
Nuba Mountain Federation	3,171	0.17	2	2	1
Nile	2,704	0.15	5	5	2
Free	1,844	0.10	7	7	1
Islamic	1,772	0.096	1	1	—
Western Sudan Union	1,695	0.093	3	3	—
Communists	1,652	0.091	2	2	—
Democratic South	1,535	0.084	3	3	—
Unity	1,478	0.081	4	4	—
Workers Federation	668	0.037	1	1	—
Peace	387	0.021	4	4	—
Socialist Democrats	220	0.012	1	1	—
NUP-Sadiq wing	63	0.003	1	1	—
Congress of New Forces	33	0.002	1	1	—
Total	1,819,772	100	1,006	—	218

*In some constituencies there were entries under Umma party, in addition to the Sadiq and Imam wings. The combined total for the Umma party was 72 seats.

Source: Republic of the Sudan General Elections Commission, Final Report of the 1968 General Elections (Khartoum: Government Printing Press, 1969) (in Arabic), Appendix "wāw, 8."

average to roughly 14,000 per constituency. (This time there were only 218 territorial constituencies; the graduates' constituencies had been abolished.) Also, the percentage of registrants to actual voters was again lowest in the southern provinces, clearly a function of the hazardous conditions there.

Polling commenced on April 18 and was again staggered for several days. After all votes had been counted, the results were announced at the beginning of May. Table 7.6 gives the official election results.

Even a cursory glance at Table 7.1 calls immediate attention to the disastrous effects of Umma factionalism. Not only were the parliamentary mandates nearly evenly divided between opposing wings, thereby effectively negating each other, but a close study of individual constituencies demonstrates that the party unnecessarily lost many seats to its DUP rival—10 in the two western provinces alone, in which the combined Umma total exceeded the DUP vote. Particularly shocking to many was the parliamentary ouster of ex-premier Sadiq by a strong imam supporter, Muhammad Daud el-Khalifah (a distant relative of the famed Khalifah Abdullahi). Sadiq had been simply too busy

TABLE 7.7

Distribution of Seats after 1968 Elections

Party	Number of Seats
DUP	101
Umma (Sadiq)	36
Umma (Imam)	30
Umma	6
Islamic Charter Front	3
SANU	15
Southern Front	10
Beja Congress	3
Nuba Mountains Federation	2
Nile	1
Independents	9
Workers Force	1
Unidentified*	1
Total	218

Note: *The winner of constituency no. 31 (Omdurman South) was listed by the commission as having "no identified affiliation;" in reality he was the secretary-general of the Sudan Communist party.

Source: Compiled by the author.

with parliamentary maneuvering and had to pay the price for virtually ignoring his home constituency. Nevertheless, he remained Umma party president and was determined to carry on with his mission. (Incidentally, his prominent relatives, Hassan el-Turabi and Ahmed el-Mahdi, similarly lost their seats, the latter to the prime minister, M. A. Mahjoub.)

Another noteworthy result was the relative ineffectiveness of regional interest parties in South, West and East, and the failure of leftist and rightist movements to broaden their appeal. This and other observations can be made more clearly if we examine the geographic distribution of assembly seats compared with the percentages of votes polled by the major contestants in each province (Table 7.8).

A voting analysis of the southern Sudan must be prefaced by the caveat that irregular and uneven security conditions produced a very distorted outcome; it was much skewed in favor of Northern parties whose main supporters were located in southern cities, where security was relatively adequate and participation of settled peoples was predictably highest.

The biggest beneficiary of this situation was the DUP, whose traditional support among northern merchants and civil servants helped it to obtain 15 seats even though it was outpolled by the Umma factions and southern parties in all three provinces. Some victories fell into the category of ''cheap,'' as in constituency no. 107 where a total of 235 DUP votes sufficed to gain the mandate. A similar case was provided by constituency no. 104 (also Upper Nile) which went to the Umma party with 400 votes only.

Particularly surprising to many observers was the poor showing of the southern parties, particularly the Southern Front and SANU (Sudan African National Union), who had long claimed in Khartoum to enjoy the ''complete'' backing of southern Sudanese. In actuality, they were able to carry only Bahr el-Ghazal Province, where they also obtained over two-thirds of their nationwide totals. Only in that southwestern province did the distribution of seats correspond roughly to the popular vote. By contrast, in Equatoria the Southern Front could gain only 3 of the province's 20 mandates for the Umma party and the DUP with a combined 58 percent of all votes.

Whereas it is quite hazardous to draw many inferences from these voting results in the South, such is not the case concerning the northern Sudan, where both registration figures and voter turnout reached very satisfactory levels. These were highest in the two most densely populated provinces of Blue Nile and Khartoum, where also the most closely contested races took place.

A glance at Table 7.8 reveals overwhelming victories of the DUP in Northern, Kassala, and Khartoum Provinces, the traditional

TABLE 7.8

Election Results By Party Per Province, 1968

Province	DUP Num-ber	Per-cent	Umma-Sadiq Num-ber	Per-cent	Umma-Imam Num-ber	Per-cent	Umma Num-ber	Per-cent	Independents Num-ber	Per-cent	ICF Num-ber	Per-cent	Socialists plus Socialist Front Num-ber	Per-cent	Southern Front Num-ber	Per-cent	SANU Num-ber	Per-cent	Others Num-ber	Per-cent	Total
Khartoum	99,837 (11)*	53	17,806	9	8,338	4.4	—	—	5,004	3	18,566 (1)	10	35,947 (1)	19	—	—	—	—	3,899	2	189,397
Northern	127,839 (13)	71	12,426 (1)	7	3,852 (1)	2	3,676	2	17,791 (1)	10	5,394	3	5,812 (1)	3.3	—	—	—	—	3,109	1.7	179,899
Blue Nile	246,349 (27)	41	127,719 (5)	21	159,089 (9)	27	15,634 (1)	2.6	21,862 (2)	4	10,459 (1)	1.8	8,938	1.5	—	—	—	—	4,822	0.8	594,872
Darfur	49,139 (4)	24	85,702 (13)	41	63,752 (7)	31	3,987	2	—	—	1,864	1	216	0.1	—	—	—	—	2,371	1	207,031
Kassala	87,079 (15)	54	14,890 (1)	9	18,590 (3)	11	4,056	2.5	19,675 (4)	12	6,100	4	11,254	7	—	—	—	—	—	—	161,644
Kordofan	103,000 (16)	34	107,195 (6)	36	69,611 (9)	23	1,035	0.3	15,586 (5)	5	1,684	0.6	1,187	0.4	—	—	—	—	87	0.05	299,385
Equatoria	4,490 (6)	20	5,406 (6)	25	420 (1)	2	2,485 (3)	11	965	4	485 (1)	2	—	—	6,654 (3)	30	458	2	830	3.7	22,193
Upper Nile	12,393 (6)	21	13,331 (4)	23	3,837	6.5	1,852 (1)	3	4,304	7	—	—	—	—	10,213 (2)	17	11,115 (4)	19	1,844	3	58,889
Bahr el-Ghazal	12,110 (3)	11	511	0.5	2,463	2.3	10,563 (1)	10	3,413 (1)	3	—	—	—	—	22,955 (5)	22	48,920 (11)	46	5,527 (1)	5	106,462
Total	742,236		384,986		329,952		43,288		70,047		44,552		63,354		39,822		60,493		22,489	1.2	1,819,772

*Parentheses indicate the number of seats gained.
Source: Republic of Sudan General Elections Commission, The Final Report of the 18 April 1968 General Elections.

strongholds of the PDP and NUP. The Umma showing was similarly impressive in Darfur, but suffered badly in Kordofan and Blue Nile, where it could obtain only two-fifths of all mandates despite enjoying clear-cut margins in the popular vote. The Islamic Charter Front on the extreme right and the various Communist and Socialist groupings on the left could manage good showings only in the capital province, although the latter were able to win one seat with a minority vote in the railroad hub of Atbara and also obtained one-third of the vote in the port city of Port Sudan. In the country's three other large towns of Wad Medani, El-Obeid, and Kassala they received 8 percent of the popular vote in each. The Beja Congress declined in importance, but put up a stiff fight in four losing causes in addition to its three victories. The same can be said for its western counterpart, the Nuba Mountains Federation, which won only two seats outright, but provided all three winning candidates listed as independents in Kordofan.

In view of the events leading up to the 1968 elections, probably the single most interesting questions were: Just how significant for the victory was the December 1967 merger of NUP and PDP? What were the effects of intra-Umma divisions on the overall election outcome?

A close examination of all 218 constituencies individually showed a remarkable continuity of party support going back to the 1965 and 1958 elections, especially in the six northern provinces. Seen in this light, the merger meant essentially a pooling of the respective regional strengths of the NUP and the PDP; it is doubtful that the combining of votes within individual constituencies accounted for more than 5 percent of all seats gained. If anything, an examination of the popular vote indicates a relative decline in DUP strength compared with the 1953 elections when both factions were united under the auspices of the old NUP: In 1968 the combined totals of the three Umma segments barely exceeded that of the DUP, although the party fell considerably short in its acquisitions of mandates.

These observations receive added meaning when we compare the electoral performances of the five major contestants in 1968 with those of 1965. The comparison is limited to the six northern provinces, because elections in the South in 1967 and 1968 took place under such unusual circumstances as to make any inference of questionable value.*

---

*We are, of course, obliged to alert the reader to some methodological difficulties inherent in the comparisons of Table 7.5: In 1965 the PDP had boycotted the elections, hence its support figures are misleading; nevertheless, a comparison of popular votes by the two major contestants over the years should suffer little. Also, some socialist groups may object to being placed into one category with others

The figures in Table 7.9 enable us to notice several interesting facts: 1) Despite all the feverish activity in the capital during the intervening three years, the voting results in Khartoum Province remained virtually identical. In fact, both the one Umma loss and one Communist victory came about by absolute minorities and could easily have been reversed. 2) In the western provinces of Darfur and Kordofan there was similarly little change, although the Umma party increased its popular support slightly, but lost out in parliamentary seats in Kordofan, as previously explained. 3) In the traditional khatmiyyah strongholds of northeastern Sudan the NUP clearly benefited from added PDP support; even though the Umma party, ICF, and Beja Congress basically maintained their absolute followings, their relative share of the popular vote declined due to the active participation of khatmiyyah adherents in 1968. 4) The same could be said for Blue Nile Province, which includes areas of khatmiyyah strength in its eastern portion, thus accounting for the increase in DUP totals; however, the dramatic Umma party loss of half its mandate here resulted almost directly from the intraparty fratricide, to the direct benefit of the DUP.

We conclude this analysis of the 1968 elections with some speculations about the effects of the DUP merger and intra-Umma divisions by hypothesizing different circumstances—being fully aware of the pitfalls inherent in such speculations.

The most difficult projections are those concerning the strength and appeal of an independent PDP organization which had been effectively inactive for almost 10 years. But it appears likely that the PDP would have gained about 25 seats in the 6 northern provinces, leaving the NUP with more than 70, not quite enough to form a working majority with the imam faction of the Umma party, its previous partner. On the other hand a unified Umma party could have bested even a merged DUP, when we consider that in the 4 central provinces alone it could have added a net of 16 mandates where its combined vote exceeded that of the DUP. We recognize that a majority of party votes does not guarantee electoral victory due to the frequent multiplicity of candidates (see Chapter 2). In either hypothetical situation, the distribution of assembly seats would have required the formation of coalition governments, and there is no reason to suppose that political stability would have been any greater than it turned out to be, although it is difficult to imagine how it could be any less, as we shall see in this final section.

---

under that label and with the Communists; however, it seems fruitful to compare the trends of the extreme left along with the extreme right over the years.

TABLE 7.9

Comparison of 1965 and 1968 Election Results By Party Per Province
(in percent)

Province	NUP	PDP	Umma	ICF	Independents	Leftists*
Northern (17)+						
1965	57.3 (10)	5.1 (1)	18.8 (4)	6.5	6.5 (2)	3.6
1968	71 (13)		11	3	10 (1)	3.5 (1)
Darfur (24)						
1965	23.9 (6)	0.7	66.5 (16)	2.7 (1)	3.2 (1)	
1968	24 (4)		74 (20)	1		0.1
Kassala (23)						
1965	23.6 (2)	5.6 (2)	30.1 (7)	10.7 (1)	26.1 (11)	0.8
1968	54 (15)		22.5 (4)	4	12 (4)	7
Blue Nile (45)						
1965	31.7 (14)	19	52.1 (29)	3.6	1.3 (2)	7.8
1968	41 (27)		50.6 (15)	1.8 (1)	4 (2)	0.4
Kordofan (36)						
1965	33.1 (9)	15	53.2 (19)	2.8	8.6 (8)	0.2
1968	34 (16)		59 (15)	1	5 (5)	0.4
Khartoum (13)						
1965	49.7 (11)	12	16.9 (1)	11.6 (1)	2.1	17
1968	53 (11)		13.4	10 (1)	3	19 (1)

*Leftists include both wings of the Sudan Communist party and the various socialist organizations.
+Parentheses indicate the number of assembly seats.
<u>Source:</u> Compiled by the author.

COLLAPSE OF THE DEMOCRATIC ORDER

When the Constituent Assembly held its first meeting on May 27, 1968, a new coalition government had been forged by the DUP and the imam wing of the Umma party. Its first deed was to reelect Ismail el-Azhari as president of the Supreme Council of State along with one other DUP and two Umma supporters of the imam, as well as one southerner.* This act marked a departure from the previous policy of broad representation within the Supreme Council to a new elevation of partisanship. More important, though, was the composition of the new cabinet, which now included a mixture of five former NUPs and four former PDPs on the DUP side, two Southern Front leaders and five members of the Imam wing of the Umma party, including the new, and old, prime minister, M. A. Mahjoub. The latter's already suspect effectiveness was not at all helped by the fact that he represented a minority faction (of the total Umma party) in a minority coalition (vis-a-vis the DUP).

Once again, the ruling alliance had formal control over the vast majority of assembly delegates; nonetheless, political stability failed to ensue for fairly obvious reasons. Specifically, the DUP merger had moved the khatmiyyah faction into the position of closest ally to el-Azhari's central leadership, a position formerly held by the traditional wing of the Umma party. This development caused Imam el-Hadi to reconsider the merits of intra- versus interparty feuding, with the result that he and Sadiq eventually agreed to reconcile their differences publicly and to reunify their respective factions. However, the process of actual unification took inordinately long, despite the fact that Khartoum newspapers had carried announcements to that effect as early as autumn 1968. The public could read about almost daily meetings of various officials of party X with one another and with delegates of rival parties; party rhetoric consistently emphasized assurances of mutual support for prospective partners as well as reassurances of lasting loyalties to old allies.

In reality, the six or seven months prior to the May 1969 coup were filled with intrigues and counter-intrigues, fence-mending and other behind-the-scenes machinations on the part of virtually all leading political figures in the country.[11] Near the end of this period one could observe the rather bizarre spectacle of el-Azhari contacting his erstwhile avowed enemies, the Communist party and the Sudan

---

*They were Khidir Hamad (DUP), Daoud el-Khalifah (Umma—the father of Muhammad D. el-Khalifah), Fadl el-Bushra (Umma) and Jervis Yak (southerner).

African National Union (SANU), to inquire about the possibility of
forming coalitions.[12] Rumors and speculations abounded wildly, and
the political atmosphere appeared to grow more hectic by the hour.
One day el-Azhari would announce complete abstention from interfer-
ing into intra-Umma politics, the next day he would publicly hint of his
party's probable opposition to the likely Umma candidate for prime
minister.

The most disastrous aspect of this party infighting was the virtually total neglect of major national problems. There seemed to be
simply not enough time to worry about dwindling foreign exchange reserves, rising unemployment, the shortage of certain essential consumer goods, and the continuing rebellion in the South. (An indication
of this may be found in newspaper reports that were completely dominated by party politics and largely failed to report about the cited
major issues.) It was not long before the troubles of the countryside
had reached the capital itself. Given the legacy of political activism
at Khartoum University, its campus had often been a barometer for
detecting political tension at large. In early November violent clashes
took place at its campus and soon thereafter at the Khartoum branch
of Cairo University, during which scores of students were injured,
mostly Communists and Muslim brothers. The government's weak
response was to close down the university indefinitely. To make
matters even worse, two weeks later the prime minister suffered a
stroke and was flown abroad for urgent treatment, not to return until
three months later.

More and more concerned Sudanese began to speak of a national
crisis and to search for drastic remedies. One such possible remedy
was temporary strongman rule by the fairly well proven Sayyid el-
Sadiq. Another was the everpresent possibility of, as some had felt
all along, sorely needed intervention by a military group. We may
now speculate that, in the final analysis, both of these considerations
are likely to have loomed large in the minds of the ringleaders of the
May 25 Revolution. The civilian elements among them were known
leftists[13] who bore a strong resemblance to the group originally in
power during the early stages of the transitional regime following the
October 21, 1964 Revolution. On the one hand they had everything to
fear from a strong, unified Umma party, led by the staunchly anti-
leftist Sayyid el-Sadiq; on the other hand they perceived the need for
military backing for themselves. They found this backing in a group
of relatively obscure officers led by Colonel Ja'far el-Nimeiri, a
career soldier with a record of having led previous unsuccessful
coups.

But there was one more opportunity to avert military intervention.
On April 11, 1969, the two factions of the Umma party officially announced after months of negotiations that their internal rift had been

bridged and the party was now unified. Within days they obtained the support of the two southern parties, various independents, and even some disaffected DUPs, for the purpose of toppling the Mahjoub regime. On April 24, the prime minister submitted his resignation to the cabinet, explaining in part that "government business suffers from the contradictory actions of the coalition parties and their political maneuvers," but agreed to stay in office until a new coalition could be formed. On May 7, the Umma party and DUP headquarters issued a communique announcing their agreement on principle policies, including the bases for the much needed and long delayed new constitution.

As so often happens at historic moments, timing became a crucial element. The major parties had wasted enormous amounts of time jockeying for positions of individual advantage in their reconciliation meetings while national crises kept mounting. Meanwhile, a group of "free officers" and their civilian allies had decided on overthrowing the government. Undoubtedly, the rapprochement of Umma party leaders hastened their decision to strike before Sadiq el-Mahdi could resume political power in Khartoum. What happened next precisely has never been officially disclosed, and several conflicting versions have circulated about the occurrences of those days. Some observers have pointed ominously to certain highly unusual events, such as Prime Minister Mahjoub's permission for parachute exercises and for the arming of soldiers in the Khartoum area just prior to the takeover, at a time when most senior military officers were out of the country. Mahjoub himself rejected such implications forcefully, and instead shifted much of the blame on inadequate security investigations.[14]

Such speculations may be intriguing, but in the final analysis remain conjectural. What does matter is that governmental performance and the political behavior of parliamentarians during most of the previous four years had produced a spectacle of factional politics at its worst, and in the end it was not at all surprising that the majority of politically aware Sudanese welcomed the coup d'etat of May 29, 1969 with a collective sigh of relief.

NOTES

1. Mohammed Ahmed Mahgoub, Democracy on Trial: Reflections on Arab and African Politics (London: Andre Deutsch, Ltd., 1974), p. 192.

2. Muddathir Abdel-Rahim, Imperialism and Nationalism in the Sudan (Oxford: Clarendon Press, 1969), pp. 133-34.

3. Electoral Commission of the Sudan, A List of Political Parties Contesting the 1965 Elections in the Sudan (Khartoum, 1965).

4. United Nations, Population Growth and Manpower in the Sudan, 1964.

5. The interested reader is referred to an article by G. Shepard Jr., "National Integration and the Southern Sudan," Journal of Modern African Studies 4, no. 2 (1966): 193-212, which deals with the proceedings of that conference; Dunstan Wai, ed., The Southern Sudan and the Problem of National Integration (London: Frank Cass, 1973), Appendices IV, V; and M. O. Beshir, The Southern Sudan; From Conflict to Peace, (London: Barnes & Noble, 1975), Chapter 1 for the most comprehensive treatment.

6. The Morning News, April 9, 1965.

7. Advance, February 14, 1965; and numerous times in Al-Midan.

8. These statements are all based on interviews with party officials prior to elections.

9. This estimate was made by several leading Communists during a private interview just prior to the vote count.

10. Apparent support for this interpretation, plus further insights into Mahjoub's personality, can be gained from reading his recently published book, Democracy on Trial: Reflections on Arab and African Politics, op. cit.

11. For details, see accounts in the independent daily newspapers El-Ra'y El-Amm, El-Ayyam, and El-Sahafa from August 1968 to May 1969.

12. El-Sahafa, April 14, 17, 20, and May 3, 1969 editions.

13. A very interesting and detailed account of their identity, meetings, and strategy is rendered in Mahgoub, op. cit., p. 232-33.

14. Mahgoub, op. cit., pp. 224-25. He also reported May 23, 1969 as the date of the party agreement instead of May 7.

8

RENEWED INTERVENTION BY THE MILITARY: THE REGIME OF JA'FAR NIMEIRI

THE MAY 1969 REVOLUTION

A successful coup d'etat requires organization, skill, proper timing, and a substantial measure of good luck. A prime example for this generalization is provided by the political career of Colonel Ja'far Mohammed Nimeiri, who had been involved in several abortive coup attempts before he finally succeeded on May 25, 1969.[1] On that day, he and the small inner circle of "free officers" took advantage of the absence abroad of at least a dozen of the army's senior commanders[2] and the general air of listlessness that envelops Khartoum at this time of annual record-breaking temperatures; the result was a smooth and bloodless takeover.

The first public act after the coup was the formation of the Revolutionary Command Council (RCC), consisting of the then 39-year old Nimeiri, one lieutenant colonel, seven majors, and the retired former chief justice of the High Court, Babikir Awadallah. The latter became both prime and foreign minister of the first post-coup cabinet, which was heavily dominated by Communists and those other "socialist" forces that had been prominent in the first transitional government after the October 1964 Revolution.

In order to minimize the dangers of a counter-coup from within the military, the RCC retired most senior officers, especially those

---

Portions of this chapter were previously published in an article by this author, "Military Rule in the Sudan: The First Five Years of Ja'far Numayri," Middle East Journal 29, no. 1 (Winter 1975): 16-32.

associated with the Abboud junta or anyone suspected of sympathies toward the traditional parties. Lawrence Fellows of the New York Times reported on June 4, 1969, that about 300 officers and men had been either dismissed, arrested, or sent home; only one general officer, a brigadier, remained in the army.[3] Cynics, however, claimed that "everyone with a higher rank was pensioned off to create room at the top"; President Nimeiri actually moved to fill the new vacuum by promoting all nine RCC members in rank, but the other eight publicly declined.[4]

The new regime faced three major challenges of which the first two were inherited from the defunct parliamentary regime: 1) continued rebellion in the southern provinces; 2) a badly tottering economy with rapidly dwindling foreign exchange reserves; and 3) the expected political opposition from those groups whom the military had replaced. It is most interesting that in less than three years in power President Nimeiri reversed his policies on all three issue areas dramatically. These reversals are worth examining, particularly in the context of the ruler's changing perceptions of and motivations toward public policy.

While Ja'far Nimeiri had acquired considerable experience in coup-making, he had none in governing, and few specific goals at the outset. During his first two years in power his policies were characterized by vague ideological preconceptions that he labeled as conforming to "Arab socialism." Subsequently, and particularly after the July 19, 1971, coup attempt against him, he became considerably more pragmatic.

This latter development can be explained by an analysis of unfolding events in 1970-71. By contrast, it is much more difficult to pinpoint the sources of the earlier ideological posture, in part because events are simply too recent in order to furnish sufficient information and insights. In part also, there are two equally persuasive interpretations for Nimeiri's early posture. The first of these credits Nimeiri with having developed his own ideological perspective from a combination of factors. Most prominent among these were his admiration for the Egyptian leader Gamal Abdel-Nasser and his particular brand of Arab socialism on one hand, and on the other his bitter experiences with the Abboud military government as well as the subsequent parliamentary regime, both of which Nimeiri considered to be hopelessly reactionary and from whose hands he had suffered after having been involved in unsuccessful attempts to overthrow them. This interpretation further holds that Nimeiri became convinced of the bankruptcy of all the traditional political parties and saw his only allies in those "true nationalists" in the post-October 1964 United Front of Professionals, which was briefly in charge during the early phases of the then transitional regime.

The second interpretation is far less generous. It considers Nimeiri to have been—and, perhaps, still to be—a relatively unsophisticated, if genuinely sincere and patriotic officer. According to this version Nimeiri did not forge political support in a coalition of leftist nationalists. Rather, these nationalists used him and his presumed military power base in order to overthrow, and subsequently crush, the conservative political organizations in the northern Sudan.* Still according to this second interpretation, Nimeiri was duped into embracing an ideological position and specific policies that had been contrived by outsiders, and it was not until about a year and a half later that he began to recognize these manipulations.

There is, of course, a third and quite plausible interpretation, namely that Nimeiri and his free officers genuinely subscribed to the stated ideological positions, yet needed political allies among civilian groups that, in turn, were looking for military support among perhaps unsuspecting, yet nevertheless relatively agreeable officers. From this latter perspective it is hardly relevant who used whom; subsequent events revealed the point where initial bedfellows parted company.

But let us return to the three issue areas. Almost immediately after May 25, 1969, the new regime outlawed all existing political parties, confiscated their properties, and arrested virtually all political leaders save those who managed to escape abroad. President Nimeiri announced the arrest of 64 politicians, and Premier Babikir Awadallah said that some would be tried for corruption, and some for having bent the Sudan's interim constitution to keep eight Communists from taking their seats in Parliament, thus "thwarting the electorate."[6] The only group receiving lenient treatment was the Communist party, which managed to place in cabinet posts half a dozen members plus several others who, though officially neutral, in effect leaned heavily toward the party and found positions in both the cabinet and the Revolutionary Council. Prominent leftist CPS "sympathizers" in the Council of Ministers included Khalafallah Babikir and Abdel-Karim

---

*An intriguing insider's story has been revealed through the ex-Prime Minister Mohammed Ahmed Mahjoub. According to this, on the surface quite believable, account, a broad leftist front was constituted in December 1968, composed of the Communist party, the Trade Union Federation, the Socialist Democratic Front, and the Arab Nationalist movement. Its political leadership included Babikir Awadallah, Abdein Ismail, and Abdel-Khaliq Mahjoub. This committee drafted a charter, which Babikir Awadallah subsequently used as an original platform of the May Revolution. He had allegedly encountered disagreements with his civilian colleagues in late April/early May 1969, and then decided to contact the free officers' movement.[5]

Mirghani of the post-October 1964 transitional cabinet, and Amin el-Shibli and Mekkawi Mustafa of the Socialist Democratic Front.

One of the first public acts of the new rulers was to recognize East Germany and, three weeks later, the Provisional Revolutionary Government (Vietcong) of South Vietnam. In the domestic sphere, the forced retirement of ten civil and four shari'ah judges as part of judicial reorganization,[7] and the liquidation of the system of native administration for much of the northern Sudan were similarly effected within one month. These measures, coupled with the arrests of Sadiq and Ahmed el-Mahdi, were clear signals of the May Revolution's leftist orientation and demonstrated intention to attack the bases of traditional groupings.

The new government's major opposition could therefore be expected to lie with the conservative forces from the old party system. Ismail el-Azhari by 1969 no longer posed the threat that he did earlier to the Abboud regime, in part because the glamor of the independence struggle was no longer fresh in the public mind, but also because his role in coalition forging (DUP) and undermining (Umma) had so tarnished his image even among younger NUPs that his own political support base in the urban Sudan had shrunk to a size probably no greater than the socialist supporters of the May Revolution.

This left the old Umma party as the chief threat to the new regime. President Nimeiri soon recognized that his major opposition would come from the masses of ansar with their paramilitary organizations in central and western Sudan. (In addition, there was the potential appeal by mahdists to the great numbers of army regulars whose sectarian affiliation was ansari.) The feeling of animosity between these two forces was mutual and was returned in kind by the ansar leader, Imam el-Hadi el-Mahdi. (The Minister of Interior, Major Farouq Osman Hamdallah revealed on November 25, 1969, that Imam Hadi had "sealed off Aba Island to any strangers, including government officials.")[8] Their clash came early, and with encouragement from his two most powerful allies, the civilian Premier Babikir Awadallah and Major Khalid Hassan Abbas, both strongly pro-Egyptian and anti-Mahdi, Nimeiri succeeded in severely damaging the ansar organization and eliminating its leader, while their landholdings were confiscated. The initial confrontation occurred during the last days of March 1970 in street clashes in Wad Nubawi on the outskirts of Omdurman. After considerable loss of life on both sides, Nimeiri was pursuaded by junior RCC members, particularly Major Abu el-Qasim Mohammed Ibrahim, to take the fight directly to the opposition stronghold on Aba Island, the birthplace of the Mahdist movement in the nineteenth century, where the Imam el-Hadi had now taken refuge. The ensuing battle took on the proportions of a small war (including strafings by the Sudan Air Force); in the end Aba was taken and the imam was killed during the struggle. (There have been conflicting versions about the details of place and circumstances of his death. His erstwhile political ally, M. A. Mahjoub, charged President Nimeiri with ordering the bombardment of Aba on March 27 by rocket-firing MIG fighters, and implied the use of foreign pilots in the absence of trained Sudanese.)[9] Other organizations were similarly controlled, albeit not as harshly.

For similar reasons the senior ranks of the civil service, police, and judiciary were purged of all officials who were associated with the old regime through appointment tactics, "reactionary" programs, or simple corruption, or were suspected of ideological opposition to the newly conceived socialist policies.

All banks and foreign properties were nationalized in May and June of 1970 and the assets of large landowners and most businessmen—especially those previously associated with the conservative parties—were expropriated.[10] Existing economic plans were scrapped and replaced by new ones based on "scientific and socialist principles." Foreign economic and military aid came from Communist countries more than ever before, while the small diplomatic and commercial presence of Western states was further reduced.

These developments, along with prospects of Revolutionary Council orders decreeing a new National Charter, to be followed by establishment of a Socialist Union, were so closely patterned after the Egyptian model that one could practically refer to copying. This close association with Egyptian politics—and via Egypt, with the new revolutionary regime in Libya that had instituted almost identical reforms—found its counterpart in the area of foreign affairs. It resulted in a militant espousal of the Arab cause in general, and led through the Tripoli Charter Agreement of December 27, 1969, to the so-called Tri-Partite Arrangement on coordination of foreign policy with Egypt and Libya. The fact that Arabism was anathema to the non-Arab southern population was ignored.

Hence, it was not surprising that southern political leaders mistrusted the new military rulers in Khartoum, despite assurances of new attempts at reconciliation of the North-South conflict. President Nimeiri demonstrated the sincerity of his efforts to bring about a solution by publicly promising regional autonomy within a unified Sudan and by appointing a prominent southerner (the Communist lawyer Joseph Garang) to the newly created Ministry of Southern Affairs in June, 1969. Yet when initial efforts at a diplomatic solution failed to gain the confidence of southern rebel leaders—who, after all, had had negative experiences with a previous military regime—Nimeiri lost his patience with the rebels and shifted from a political to a military approach. Not surprisingly, the results were disastrous as, indeed, they had been in the economic realm as well.

Fortunately for the Sudan, most of the policies discussed above were reversed within a relatively short time span, albeit not without considerable struggle and sacrifice. The process was incremental and cumulative, as the new president acquired more experience and eventually began to draw lessons from earlier failures. Yet these lessons were not immediately effective. During much of 1970 and early 1971 President Nimeiri responded to mounting criticism with stubborn rigidity and made himself increasingly aloof to the point of issuing decrees without consulting relevant cabinet members. In fact, it may be accurate to describe Nimeiri's popular support as having reached an absolute nadir in early July 1971 and to suggest the apparent paradox that he regained it only after his regime was temporarily overthrown during the three-day July coup. But this suggestion requires some systematic explanation.

As indicated earlier, Nimeiri in 1969-70 found himself caught between two cross-pressures. First, he felt compelled to assert his militant Arabism, especially in view of the restrained attitudes on this issue shown by the previous regime; simultaneously he must have been conscious that excessive involvement in Arab affairs would invite an immediate backlash in the southern provinces and among pro-Mahdi northern Sudanese. Second, Nimeiri's early political support came from a leftist coalition that was opposed not only by the conservative traditional power blocs in the Sudan, but also by Colonel Qaddafi of Libya and King Faisal of Saudi Arabia. In fact, the latter was rumored to have secretly begun to finance anti-Nimeiri plots by conservative elements, while the former was reported to have stipulated that Sudan's partnership in the proposed Federation of Arab Republics hinged on the removal of Communist elements from official positions.

Thus, the role of the Communists had become an issue in Sudan's foreign relations with her neighbors at about the same time that it posed the first intra-RCC dispute. Prime Minister Babikir Awadallah was publicly reprimanded by President Nimeiri following an October 1969 speech in East Berlin (rebroadcast on Radio Omdurman with the aid of a Communist sympathizer), in which he called the Sudanese Communists the "vanguard" of the May Revolution, without which "the latter could not manage."[11] And although it was open knowledge that the Communists had received special favors from the May government through the skillful intercessions of the former chief justice, President Nimeiri was keen to maintain a public image of equal treatment for all political parties. Babikir was pressured to resign the premiership, but remained in the cabinet as foreign minister and minister of Justice.

In those days Nimeiri was understandably preoccupied with the safeguarding of his regime from conservative challengers. For that reason he may have accepted Communist backing temporarily as the

lesser of two evils, even though he personally did not sympathize with
Marxist ideology. Also, he resented and resisted the interference of
neighboring Arab leaders into his choice of cabinet members, until he
learned to his dismay that some of these cabinet members had openly
(and others secretly) opposed many of his policies. As argued elsewhere, Communist leaders opposed the Tripoli Charter openly as inconsistent with Sudan's national interests, and privately for fear of
suffering the fate of their Egyptian colleagues at the hands of the anticipated invasion of the Egyptian secret police in a federation.[12] When
some of them publicly questioned his leadership abilities and challenged his right to commit the Sudan at the November 8, 1970 Cairo
Conference to an Arab federation without consulting his council members, Nimeiri retaliated against the Communists. On November 16 he
dismissed Lieutenant Colonel Babikir el-Nur Osman, and Majors
Farouq Osman Hamdallah and Hashim el-Atta from the RCC and their
cabinet posts, and castigated Communist opposition to the Arab federation as the work of "selfish and unpatriotic agents of alien interests."[13] He also purged 13 junior officers from the army as
suspected communists. These actions provoked some student demonstrations at Khartoum University and distribution of leaflets by a
self-styled Sudanese free officers group who denounced the president.[14] Nimeiri responded by placing the CPS leader Abdel-Khaliq
Mahjoub under house arrest and by issuing a stern warning to university students.

However, the communists were determined to strike back, by encouraging and organizing further demonstrations at Khartoum University, and by attacking the Nimeiri regime through newspaper articles
from Beirut (al-Kifah). At this point the president decided on the same
kind of all-out confrontation that he had previously waged against the
ansar. On February 12, 1971, he took the issue to the Sudanese people
by calling on them to "crush the Communist Party,"[15] which he accused of "the most dreadful types of sabotage." Because in one form
or another the CPS had been an important force during the first two
years of the Nimeiri regime, it is worth listing here in excerpt form
the seven categories of crimes with which they were charged by the
president:

> Firstly—They consider any person outside their alleged
> party's orbit as incapable of shouldering any responsibility
> and as a mean reactionary.
> Secondly—To assume power they are ready to trample
> down all the moral values of our people. . . .
> Thirdly—They oppose any noble aim, no matter what it was
> as long as it is not of their initiative. . . They have opposed
> the educational system. . . the Tripoli Charter. . . .

Fourthly—They are practicing sabotage in the production
units. . . creating an atmosphere of chaos to impede production; publishing secret leaflets; propagating destructive ru-
mours and injurious lies. . . .
Fifthly—They are idolizing individuals and I wonder why
they deprive the reactionaries from something they deem
it lawful for themselves?
Sixthly—At this critical stage of our people's struggle
against colonialism, their treason reached the extent of
printing false and poisoning leaflets and throwing them in
front of foreign embassies so that these embassies may
transmit the leaflets' contents to their countries. They are
sending reports and hostile leaflets to some embassies and
governments abroad claiming that the situation in the Sudan
is unstable and that all agreements with it should be frozen.
Seventhly—They falsely attack the Armed Forces as a distinguished class.[16]

To show that he meant business, the president set an immediate example for attacking CPS strongholds by dissolving some farmers' and
students' unions that allegedly included large numbers of Communists.[17] Thus the reversal of relations had been completed in less
than two years.

As Ja'far Nimeiri stepped up his campaign against the Communist
party, two developments occurred that he certainly had not anticipated
when coming to power in May 1969. First, the Kremlin leaned on
Egypt's President Sadat to use his presumed influence for pressuring
Nimeiri toward abandoning his "Communist hunt." Second, Nimeiri
found his political support so dangerously eroded that he was compelled to engage in some fence-mending activities with conservative
sectors of the former civilian regimes, who in turn applauded and encouraged the curbing of Communist activities.

During the next several months the various rival political factions continued to channel their activities, and frequently conflicting
interests, toward the existing political leadership. In essence, the
Communists plotted the subsequent July coup against Nimeiri, while
the Muslim brothers engaged in similar activities with Saudi support.
The traditionally pro-Egyptian factions, for example, Vice-President
Babikir Awadallah and Defense Minister Khalid Hassan Abbas, espoused essentially Egyptian interests as usual, while the more conservative ex-Umma party faction reasserted their wariness over
Egyptian designs on Sudan. Meanwhile, the southern Sudanese leaders
were extremely unambiguous in their stand that any official (northern)
Sudanese involvement in Arab affairs would be further proof to
Southern rebels of the government's anti-South position. Nimeiri's

immediate response was to reject all these groups as insufficiently nationalist and try a go-it-alone policy.

But no man can govern a country for very long without some base of political support, and the politics of all-out alienation soon caught up with the leader. Subversive activities mounted, and President Nimeiri's own security investigators claimed to have detected nine plots against him during a six-month period in 1970 alone.[18] It was small wonder that the regime became increasingly jittery.

A good example for this situation was provided during and after the funeral of Ismail el-Azhari's brother in Omdurman, which attracted a huge crowd despite the fact that he had been a rather ordinary person. This outpouring of sympathy left a deep impression on el-Azhari himself, who was still suffering from shock over his imprisonment in Kobar, the confiscation of his house, and the public statements on radio about his alleged corruption. The combination of personal loss, public slander, and poor health took its toll: Sayyid Ismail suffered a heart attack and died soon thereafter in a hospital. According to usually very reliable sources, the regime tried to minimize the news, but it "spread like fire; people were pouring onto the streets, dashing in-and-out around tanks and armored cars. Even airplanes were circling overhead the cemetery; the regime was as scared as everybody else."[19] Within a few weeks, a military court had sentenced more than twenty persons to terms of imprisonment for "shouting anti-government slogans" during the funeral of Ismail el-Azhari.[20] In the absence of a Lou Harris poll on presidential popularity, the Sudanese townspeople were signaling their disenchantment with their rulers.

THE JULY 1971 PUTSCH

But disenchantment alone does not remove a military junta, although it can smooth any transition in the case of a takeover. Whether or not the Communist leadership banked on popular discontent in its strategy for July 1971 is difficult to assess. It is clear, however, that this leadership had decided to strike back against the president's announced hunt as far back as November 1970, and had planned on a putsch at least since February 1971.[21]

Perhaps it was indicative of President Nimeiri's insulation from political opinion centers that he expected no retribution from the left. In May he ordered the dissolution of the trade union, youth, and women's movements, whose leaderships had been infiltrated by Communists, and decreed that these groups would be reorganized under the auspices of the newly to be created Sudan Socialist Union.

Communists continued to be rounded up, and, on July 18, Nimeiri boasted of his successful control over the CPS in connection with his announcement of "another shipment to Zalingei (prison)."

On the very next day Major Hashim el-Atta led a successful coup d'etat against the government by following almost exactly the script used by his antagonist two years earlier. As it turned out, the putsch was rather shortlived and its leaders became the eventual victims.

It is of course always difficult to speculate what might have happened under different circumstances. But generally reliable information suggests that the popular reaction on July 19 was not particularly unfavorable, and most Sudanese seemed willing to reserve judgment until more was known about the identity and policies of the insurgents. Certainly Ja'far Nimeiri had acquired enough enemies during his first two years in office among all civilian factions, and now he was being challenged from within his only remaining base of power. It appeared as if there would be no popular uprising to save his junta, until the new rulers committed a literally fatal mistake. They permitted a demonstration through the streets of the capital whose marchers carried red flags, as they praised the "dawn of a new age" under the insurgent leadership. Hashim el-Atta's address over Radio Omdurman did the rest, when he spoke of "an industrial and agricultural revolution which would pursue a non-capital path for development,"[22] and gave similar hints of the coup leaders' orientation. Thus the identification of the putsch with the Communist movement became clear in the public mind. Immediately the enormous anti-Marxist sentiment within the Sudan and in neighboring countries sprang to life and eventually rescued Nimeiri's regime, which otherwise almost certainly would have been doomed.

In the foreign press much credit has been given to Presidents Sadat's and Qaddafi's intervention on behalf of Nimeiri: the former had sounded a warning over the "Voice of the Arabs" radio network that he "stood with" his prospective confederation partner, while the latter ordered Libyan Air Force jets on July 22 to force down a BOAC airliner carrying two rebel leaders (who were subsequently handed over to Nimeiri for trial and execution). While it is true that the Egyptian government eventually permitted the Sudan Defense Minister Khalid Hassan Abbas—who had been abroad on July 19—to lead a Sudanese contingent from the Suez front to Khartoum, the fact is that the physical liberation of the Nimeiri group from the People's Palace was made possible by the movement of the Northern Defense Corps from Shendi toward Khartoum, hours after the Libyan capture of putschists' announced leader. It is noteworthy that the Khartoum-based July 19 leader, Major Hashim el-Atta, called on the people to "protect the real revolution against outside interventionists" as soon as the column from Shendi began to head for Khartoum, and that only relatively few diehards accepted his call to defend the new regime.

During the ensuing confusion Ja'far Nimeiri managed to escape his guards at the presidential office, and soon rallied some local forces against Hashim el-Atta. Within a day the loyalists had rounded up the major insurgents and then embarked on perhaps the most extensive Communist hunt-down in Middle Eastern experience. In less than a week, more than a dozen putschist officers had been tried, sentenced to death, and executed by firing squads, and such civilian leaders as CPS secretary-general Abdel-Khaliq Mahjoub, the SWTUF president Shafieh Ahmed el-Sheikh, and the southern lawyer and ex-minister Joseph Garang were hanged.

Several aspects of this July 19-22 episode are worth commenting on. For one thing, the hasty trials and prompt executions shocked large segments of the Sudanese public, not so much because of any lingering sympathies for the Communist leaders, but because there had been a tradition of bloodless coups in the Sudan, and violence for political causes (except in the case of the southern rebellion) had always been considered to be bad manners. Several explanations can be offered for this deviant behavior: Ja'far Nimeiri's expressed personal anguish over the treatment of loyal soldiers at the hands of the putschists, the "demonstration effect" of court martials and executions in a similar coup attempt in Morocco only two weeks earlier, and the strong revulsion that most Sudanese have experienced vis-a-vis Communists, and that might cause them to overreact in a manner unlikely under different circumstances.

Second, the true strength of the Communist movement was exposed for the first time. Until then, the CPS had always operated behind some cover organization or in an alliance with other leftists, and their sympathizers—especially the young in the Three Towns—had consistently overestimated their own strength by equating overt antipathy toward other civilian or military groups with actual commitment to the Marxist cause. Undoubtedly, there have also been many who were attracted to the CPS by its apparent superior caliber of leadership, organization, and dedication. But when the chips were down on July 22, 1971, not many were willing to risk their lives or their freedom; perhaps more significantly, the rather overwhelming distaste among the vast majority of Sudanese for anything "Communist" came to the fore openly. The sudden and soaring popularity of Ja'far Nimeiri from this date onward is in no small measure due to his uncompromising response to the Communists, as well as to the logically rather curious notion that, in psychological terms, Nimeiri had become the "savior" from the "Communist menace."

A third noteworthy outgrowth of the July 1971 events was the dramatic deterioration of Sudan's relations with East European countries. East Germany and Bulgaria* were accused of complicity in the plotting of the putsch, and Soviet military advisors could rightly be charged with indirect intervention on Hashim el-Atta's behalf: First when they silently witnessed the military preparations at the Shagara barracks, and also when they later attempted to stall the Nimeiri rescue mission from Wadi Saidna Base. After returning to full control, the president accused the USSR openly of intervention and threatened to sever diplomatic relations. Although the latter never did occur, the experience of those days must have helped to prepare the ground for subsequent rapprochements with Western nations.

Finally, in an interesting reflection on the proverbial Sudanese pride, very little credit was given to outside help in restoring Nimeiri to power. In general conversations one could not escape the impression that many Sudanese searched consciously for reasons to downplay Egyptian help in airlifting Sudanese troops to Wadi Saidna. That the Libyan president's unusual act of commandeering an international passenger liner helped to break the back of the putschist organization could not be denied. On this score one could encounter a certain degree of national embarrassment, in the sense that Sudanese clearly disliked the notion of being indebted to a "small" country like Libya, whose people and governments had never rated highly in the general esteem of the Sudanese public.

A SWING TO THE RIGHT

Of course, the July events forced Ja'far Nimeiri to reassess his policies completely. His major conclusions were that his and the Sudan's future lay with an emphasis on domestic rather than foreign priorities, and that any institutional changes would have to be fitted to Sudan's peculiar conditions rather than conform to any particular ideology. This turnabout from previous postures was remarkable, if we recall that Ja'far Nimeiri had initially associated himself with Presidents Nasser and Qaddafi in their tri-partite scheme in 1969 primarily because of the anticipated increase in his own political legitimacy, at a time when his personal leadership was frequently challenged and his regime was precipitously narrow-based. After

---

*Abdel-Khaliq Mahjoub had escaped from a prison camp on June 30, 1971, and was allegedly hiding out in the Bulgarian embassy, from where the government charged that he masterminded the conspiracy.

July 1971, his crackdown on Communists, diffidence toward Sadat's intercessions (and symbolically toward Arab affairs), and his concentration on solving the southern conflict substantially enhanced his political support at home, which now interestingly enough rested considerably on opposition to membership in any Arab federation.

After the security forces had completed their roundup of more than 3000 persons[23] in connection with the July putsch, Nimeiri moved to consolidate his position by purging his government of known or suspected enemies, and by simultaneously seeking a new and broader base for his own support. His first act was to dismiss five ministers on August 3: the known Communists Farouq Abu Issa and Muawiyya Ibrahim, Sid Ahmed el-Jak and Murtada Ahmed Ibrahim who had both been nominated in Hashim el-Atta's proposed cabinet, plus Yahyah Munawwar. At the same time a reorganization of Sudan's trade unions was proclaimed for the express purpose of minimizing existing and future Communist influence in leadership positions by altering the selection process for executives.

The purging of leftists was accompanied by a new program providing for more popular participation in government, at least on paper. Thus, a referendum for voting on the presidency was announced, to be held in early September, and a temporary constitution was promulgated by the RCC on August 13, calling for the creation of a Peoples' Assembly, which was to be charged with drafting a permanent constitution.

The referendum was duly carried out, and on October 10 Radio Omdurman announced that 98.6 percent of the electorate had voted "yes" to President Nimeiri,* who was formally installed in his office for a six-year term on October 12. During the next two days the government machinery was reorganized into six functional categories of ministries, and a new cabinet was announced to reflect the administrative and political changes. To further consolidate control, a decree on October 26 proclaimed SSU ownership of the Sudanese press,[24] 5 trade union leaders were expelled on December 18 "in line with instructions to eliminate subversive elements,"[25] and a 15-member political bureau for the SSU was formed in early January 1972.

Elections for the Constituent Peoples' Assembly were scheduled for September 22–October 4, 1972, when more than 2000 candidates presented themselves to the electorate.[26] Even though this body was given the sole task of drafting and debating a permanent constitution

---

*The electors had two choices: They could vote yes by placing their ballots into a box bearing Ja'far Nimeiri's picture, or no by placing them into an unmarked box. The official results were: 3,839,374 yes, and 56,314 no votes.

the actual work of writing this document was handled by a few insiders, most notably Dr. Ja'far Mohammed Ali Bakhit, the junta's resident intellectual. (Besides his official function as minister of Local Government, Ja'far occupied strategic posts in the SSU, Peoples' Assembly, Sahafa newspaper, and Khartoum University.) There is every indication that the assembly amounted to little more than a rubber stamp for policies decided higher up; nevertheless, even cynics had to concede that, genuine popular participation or not, the Sudan had at last gotten a permanent constitution on May 8, 1973, nearly twenty years after the first freely elected Constituent Assembly had set down to consider the various options.

What made the drafting of such a constitution possible in the first place was the removal of the largest single obstacle to this goal to date, namely the regional conflict between North and South. In an act of great statesmanship Ja'far Nimeiri overcame the legacies of all previous administrations plus, in a sense, his own personal background, and forged an accommodation with the southern anya'nya rebels, which culminated in the Addis Ababa Agreement of March 1972. (It was later revealed that the draft constitution for this settlement had been prepared and accepted by the RCC already in September 1971 and circulated among southern intellectuals in the Khartoum area for amendments and approval. The timing therefore substantiates the earlier hypothesis concerning the rulers' reassessment of priorities after the July putsch. The peace settlement was actually finalized between the respective negotiators in Addis on February 27, 1972, but could not be ratified by official representatives until March 27 for technical reasons. Its accomplishment has been celebrated annually on March 3, proclaimed as National Unity Day.) The Agreement provided for substantial autonomy for the southern region, including establishment of a Southern Assembly at Juba, and amnesty for and absorption of rebel soldiers into the Sudan's armed forces. The General Amnesty Act became effective on March 3, 1972, and seventeen days later the state of emergency was officially lifted after more than 16 years. A High Executive Council for the Southern Region was formed under the chairmanship of Vice-President Abel Alier who, during National Unity Day celebrations one year later, was able to cite considerable progress for the area.[27] The composition of the Southern Defense Corps was completely reconstituted, and now contained 6,000 northern and 6,000 southern troops. In a significant gesture of reconciliation, the former anya'nya commander Joseph Lagu was made a brigadier general.

This act risked the potential wrath of Arab nationalists and Islamic fundamentalists at home,* and required a disassociation from involvement in Arab affairs abroad. As time passed, most northern Sudanese came to recognize the wisdom of this policy; theirs and the southern population's great admiration for Nimeiri raised his stature to something akin to a Sudanese Lincoln. With the implementation of the Addis Agreement, autonomy changed from a southern vision to reality: a 60-member Regional Assembly was elected in November 1973+ and officially opened on December 15 by President Nimeiri in Juba; and the Bor Dinka Abel Alier was sworn in as the official head of the southern regional government.

In the economic realm private capital was encouraged to participate in a variety of new projects, and foreign aid was again sought from all quarters to finance new schemes, such as the ambitious agricultural development at Rahad. Toward that end, the Development and Promotion of Industrial Investment Act of 1972 offered special incentives to the Sudanese private sector, and on 23 August, 1972, the president approved a law to encourage foreign investment (incidentally, less than a month after the reestablishment of diplomatic relations with Washington). On January 22, 1973, a presidential decree rescinded previous orders by which a number of private enterprises had been expropriated.[28]

By early 1975, newspaper headlines and radio broadcasts left the inescapable impression that "development" had become not only the magic slogan, but actually the top priority of the government. The main emphasis was now on exploitation of the country's considerable potential in agriculture and animal husbandry, but any reasonable economic project was officially endorsed, regardless of the identity of the entrepreneur or the source of his funds. In areas of scarce resources much improvisation has been in evidence, as exemplified by the massive Anti-Thirst Campaign designed to increase water supply, especially in the well-populated Western provinces.

Relations with Arab neighbors no longer followed ideological predilections but were based on pragmatic assessments of Sudan's national interests in a changing world. That is to say, although

---

*In a speech on July 22, 1972, President Nimeiri confirmed that an antiregime plot of civilian and military dissidents had been discovered, who apparently objected primarily to the, in their eyes, overly lenient and generous government posture vis-a-vis the southerners.

+Voting took place from November 14-28, and of the 60 assembly members, 30 were to be elected in territorial, and 27 more in provincial, constituencies.

General Nimeiri continued to show special sympathies for other military regimes (on several occasions he enthusiastically welcomed successful military coup leaders from diverse regions of Africa and Asia into the brotherhood of presidents in uniform), particularly those embracing Arab socialism like the FAR states Egypt, Libya, and Syria, he was no longer beholden to the Nasserist rejection of moderate and conservative political systems. In fact, when his government opted to postpone membership in the FAR until some unspecified future date and almost simultaneously reestablished diplomatic ties with Washington, Nimeiri balanced the cooling off of relations with Egypt and Libya through rapprochements with the monarchical rulers of Saudi Arabia and the Gulf sheikhdoms. This shift in orientation became especially clear after the ex-Defense Minister Khalid Hassan Abbas resigned his positions in the cabinet and SSU on February 13 and the ex-Premier and ex-Foreign Minister Babikir Awadallah and the ex-SSU Secretary-General Ma'moun Awad Abu Zayd followed suit in May 1972. They had all been known for their strongly pro-Egyptian ties, and their departure coincided with the rising influence of Foreign Minister Mansour Khalid, who favored a more neutral position in global and intra-Arab affairs.

In the domestic political realm steps were undertaken to reestablish contacts with progressive leaders of traditional parties. This should not be misinterpreted as an attempt to resurrect old ghosts—the Socialist Union is intended to function as an exclusionary single party—but merely to capture an aura of peace and accommodation. And it is in that spirit that the ex-Umma party president Sadiq el-Mahdi was returned from Egypt to Sudan, at first to remain under house arrest, but was finally released in December 1972 (incidentally, less than one month after the release of the Muslim Brotherhood chief, Dr. Hassan el-Turabi). Similarly, his uncle Ahmed el-Mahdi and the erstwhile prime minister Mahjoub were permitted to return in 1974 after nearly five years in exile. Although Sadiq and other prominent former politicians have been detained from time to time after periods of local unrest, the junta for its part has consciously avoided the earlier atmosphere of confrontation and bitterness. In fact, there have been widespread rumors that Nimeiri offered Sadiq a formal position in his government, but that the latter refused by insisting on the "illegality" of the military regime. In any case, the government showed its good will by desequestrating the properties of Sadiq and Ahmed el-Mahdi on May 21, 1974.[29]

Ja'far Nimeiri's new posture of pragmatism is undoubtedly one main reason for his dramatic rise in popularity, because it corresponds to the general Sudanese distaste for fanaticism in all public matters except football and religion. And the longer the president has been in office, the more his actions have reflected growth through experience, and a genuine self-confidence in his ability to know and do what is best for his country. This theme has been reflected in many speeches from 1972 on, and is well depicted in the following excerpts from an address to the SSU Constituent Congress in January, 1974:

> The May Revolution personifies the best in us. . . it is a call to go back to the roots of our cultural heritage. We are destined by the force of things to resist all that which has been left behind by history. Only then could we propel the innate and positive energies in our national character to work to build a new Sudan.
> While colonial cultural oppression may have tried to isolate us from our cultural and spiritual heritage by belittling it, the May Revolution has now voiced a call to go back to our origins, to rediscover ourselves, to lay aside cynical doubts and to muster enough self-confidence and moral courage to persevere in the national effort.
> . . . We do not espouse pre-ordained dogmas to guide us in political action. We are not the disciples of any pundit of political theory. We are resolved to build our country inspired by its heritage, national conscience, objective prevalent conditions and national characteristics, making use of our own experiences and our independent thinking. . . We will not copy. We will be very discriminating. . . .[30]

Another chief source for Ja'far Nimeiri's recent popularity has been his obvious sincerity and his dedication to work as hard as possible for the welfare of his country. It is to his great credit that he has spared no effort to learn at first hand of his people's concerns by traveling extensively throughout all regions of the country—unlike his predecessors—and by meeting the greatest possible number of Sudanese face-to-face without permitting himself to be shielded from unpleasant encounters through layers of intermediaries. In fact, if it were necessary to attach one single label to this most recent Sudanese president, it would have to be that he has been truly a "man of the people" in every sense of this term.

Some observers may have been cynical about his intentions when Ja'far Nimeiri first "went to the people" only weeks after the July 1971 putsch, in order to be confirmed as president by popular referendum. But with the passage of months it became clear that the junta leader intended to maintain close contact with the ordinary Sudanese, not only in the accessible cities and towns, but in the rural provinces as well. At the time of heightened anti-Communist fervor in 1971-72, the president's office in the People's Palace announced every Thursday the village or town in which Ja'far Nimeiri would perform his Friday prayers. (It was intriguing to observe how many "secularized" Sudanese in Khartoum were publicly signaling their "conservative" sentiments by wearing the native jallabiyyah in their offices instead of the usual western suit, and by attending prayer services on Fridays in unaccustomed numbers.) In a different atmosphere three years later, the president appeared to have embarked on a whirlwind travelling campaign, touring from province to province, and opening a new factory here and dedicating yet another development project there. These journeys have had the added purpose for the ruler to learn firsthand about particular local problems and, as he often does in rather populist fashion, to offer personal, immediate, and concrete solutions. From roughly the turn of 1973-74 on, this policy has been supplemented by a monthly radio program through which President Nimeiri maintains what is officially referred to as a "dialogue with the Sudanese people," but is more accurately a sort of monthly report of the state of the nation.

These efforts at maintaining open channels of communications informally were to be complemented by the new Peoples' Assembly, whose 250 members were to be 90 percent elected.* It is, of course, too early to make judgments about the political effectiveness of that body; nevertheless, a few initial observations can be made.

A careful perusal of the membership list reveals very few known quantities among those elected in the urban territorial constituencies, some familiar names from rural areas, and many prominent appointees. Whereas the first development was entirely to be expected in the light of recent history, the second one must have been sorely disappointing to the leadership in Khartoum. After all, the May Revolution had consciously set out to destroy the bases of traditional groupings, yet the assembly elections returned members whose names have traditionally been associated with the elite among conservative native administrators, such as Abu Sin, Ali el-Tom, Zubeir Hamad el-Malik twice each (see "The Politics of Localism," Chapter 2) from the northern region, and even more familiar names from the South. In another vein, the appointment of so many prominent leaders in the Nimeiri government (especially the SSU elite) raises the question, if

---

*The exact breakdown for the May 1974 Peoples' Assembly is: 125 territorial constituencies (100 North and 25 South—this discrepancy is due to southern representation in the 60-member Regional Assembly), 30 representatives of administrative units in local government (3 per province), 30 for popular organizations (the village development committees, youth and women's unions each had one delegate per province), and 40 representatives of 27 specified professions. The remaining 25 members were to be appointed by the president.

their appointments reflected uncertainty of electoral success and therefore an attempt to avoid the risk of possible embarrassment to the "democratic" regime.

It is even more premature to judge the performance of the assembly. Reports indicate that there has been much lively debate, in true Sudanese fashion, but that the delegates fell in line meekly behind government policy when the first critical situation arose (during the sharp increases in sugar prices in late Fall 1974). Anyone familiar with Sudanese conditions cannot expect such a role to last very long; the guess here is that the assembly will either assert itself progressively vis-a-vis the executive branch, or disappear altogether, perhaps dragging the regime along. This observer does not believe that Ja'far Nimeiri desires a docile assembly in the Egyptian mold, but appreciates honest discussion and disagreement over policies; most recent events (early 1975) actually indicate a willingness to accept constructive criticism, all within limits, of course. (The Peoples' Assembly debated the propriety of apparent conflicts of interest on the part of the finance minister; this incident eventually culminated in a major cabinet reshuffle on January 25, 1975.)

The accounts of the last several pages should not be construed to suggest that all has been well, thanks to this new openness and pragmatism. There has been enough politically inspired labor and student unrest that the government felt it necessary to close down Khartoum University for considerable periods (including much of 1974 and 1975).[*] The chronic economic problems have remained and continue to require ever greater resources in order to finance desperately needed rehabilitation programs in the South.

Even though the return of Southern refugees has been virtually completed, the region itself is not free from political unrest, as the Juba riots over the proposed Jonglei Canal project,[+] the short-lived

---

[*] Student unrest on February 8, 1974, led to a closing of Khartoum University until the beginning of the new academic year in August. During September 1973 many public schools were closed and a state of emergency was declared for two weeks, following demonstrations against the government and strike threats from six major trade unions. The most recent incident followed the abortive coup attempt by Lieutenant Colonel Hassan Hussein Osman on September 5, 1975, after which some supporters were discovered on campus and the university was shut down until January 1976.

[+] Student riots took place in Juba between October 14 and 16, 1974, during which at least two persons were killed and more than 200 were arrested. The riots were touched off by local opposition to the Egyptian-Sudanese project to save water by "straightening out" the course of the White Nile north of Jonglei.

Akobo mutiny of March 2, 1975,* and other, more general dissatisfaction with the performance of the regional government indicate.
There have also been more direct challenges to the Nimeiri regime,
such as the abortive January 1973 coup of twelve army officers led by
Brigadier Abdel-Rahim Shannan, whose history suggests an apparent
addiction to plotting against military juntas. More ominous were continuing antiregime conspiracies throughout 1975, such as the two
communist and "leftists" plots revealed by Nimeiri himself during
his April 14 address to the nation,[32] and in an interview with the Kuwait daily Al-Qabas in June,[33] respectively. Even closer to the mark
came the shortlived (106 minutes!) coup by Lieutenant Colonel Hassan
Hussein Osman on September 5, who seized the broadcast station in
Omdurman early in the morning and from there charged the Nimeiri
regime with suppression of freedom (press, university), the establishment of a police state, and corruption.[34] In this connection one cannot
help but note that the Nimeiri regime has already eclipsed all Sudanese
records for governmental longevity on one hand, and for enduring—and
surviving—a staggering number of coup attempts on the other, as
paradoxical as this may seem.

Moreover, in a series of public speeches throughout 1974, and
again in September 1975, President Nimeiri revealed Libya as the
new refuge for, and occasional coconspirator with, regime opponents.
The difficulties with the Libyan government began after the Sudanese
indicated their reluctance to join the Arab federation, escalated when
the Khartoum regime blocked Libyan aircraft from using Sudanese
airspace for delivering arms to Uganda's President Idi Amin in September 1972, and came to a head when the Libyan regime mounted a
press campaign in summer 1974 and gave aid and comfort to anti-
Nimeiri Sudanese elements.

Additional indications that Nimeiri's hands may not be very firmly
on the wheel are given by major cabinet shakeups in Juba and Khartoum. While the very close relationship between the president and his
deputy Abel Alier has been a source of mutual support, it entails the
simultaneous danger that local dissatisfaction could easily turn into a
political liability through the close identification of both men's achievements and shortcomings with those of their respective allies. This
may be the reason why Nimeiri approved on July 24, 1975 Abel Alier's

---

*On that date some southern troups killed their southern com-
mander and 12 other soldiers, mostly northerners. After a lengthy
investigation Vice-President Abel Alier announced on July 30, 1975
that 8 soldiers involved in the incident had been executed, 2 were given
life imprisonment, 39 received prison terms ranging from 1-15 years,
while 13 soldiers were acquitted.[31]

decision to replace five well-known Southerners in his regional cabinet, Joseph Oduhu, Ezbon Mondiri, Toby Maduot, Michael Tawil and Mosel Chol,[35] after persistent popular grumblings about alleged inefficiency and favoritism in the Southern regional government. A similar shockwave could be felt in Khartoum in late January after President Nimeiri announced cabinet changes affecting practically every well-known minister, Dr. Ja'far Ali M. Bakhit, Dr. Mansour Khalid, Omar el-Haj Musa, Ibrahim Moneim Mansour, through removal or effective demotion (officially, reassignment to lesser posts). Because these individuals had been viewed as virtual pillars of the central administration and its policies, the outside observer could not help but wonder if these civilian ministers had erred by doing their jobs too well and thereby acquiring more independence and prestige than suited the power holders in the inner military circle.

Such speculation may, of course, be quite erroneous; but even if it were correct, who is to say that the adroit juggling of portfolios is a sign of political weakness rather than strength? The future will provide the answers, to be sure; but if the past can serve as a guide, one must recall that politically aware Sudanese have usually viewed intraregime power plays and cabinet reshuffles rather dimly.

The encouraging aspect of this apparently bleak picture has been the junta's ability to isolate its opponents in such a way that they no longer form a cohesive force with identifiable group support in the Sudan, but rather a motley band of individuals whose only common characteristic has been opposition to Ja'far Nimeiri. During several public addresses the president singled out Philipp Abbas (Nuba Mountain), Sherif Hussein el-Hindi (ex-NUP), Omar Nur el-Dayem (ex-Umma party), Babikir Karrar (ex-Islamic Socialist Front)—and less frequently, Izz el-Din Ali Amer (CPS)—who reportedly have formed the so-called National Opposition Front. But if past history is any guide to future developments, it would suggest that the viability of the Nimeiri regime depends much more on governmental performance in critical areas at home than on discontent of regime opponents outside the country.

In the final analysis the degree of political stability of this or any other Sudanese government depends primarily on its effective performance in critical areas. We shall try to examine this issue in the remaining part of this book.

NOTES

1. Ruth First, The Barrel of a Gun: Political Power in Africa and the Coup d'Etat (London: Penguin, 1971), p. 274, lists Nimeiri's previous political activities as well as a detailed description of the takeover on May 25.

2. Ibid., reports the absence of 14 commanders.

3. New York Times, June 8, 1969, p. 24.

4. First, op. cit., p. 276.

5. Mohammed Ahmed Mahgoub, Democracy on Trial: Reflections on Arab and African Politics (London: Andre Deutsch, Ltd., 1974), pp. 232–33.

6. New York Times, June 8, 1969.

7. Arab Report and Record, 1969, p. 263.

8. Ibid.

9. Mahgoub, op. cit., p. 237.

10. For details, see Arab Report and Record, 1970, pp. 273, 300, 332.

11. New York Times, October 28, 1970 (Cairo dateline).

12. Peter Bechtold, "New Attempts at Arab Cooperation: The Federation of Arab Republics, 1971-?" Middle East Journal 27, no. 2 (Spring 1973): 160.

13. During a major speech in Khartoum Stadium on November 16, 1970.

14. Washington Post, November 30, 1970.

15. Text of President Nimeiri's "Address to the Nation, February 12, 1971," (Omdurman: Guidance Printing Press, 1971), p. 14. According to other reports, the CPS simply went underground, and continued to maintain an active organization by having its members meet under the guise of "bridge parties."

16. Ibid., pp. 7-10. For reasons of space, only the essential phrases of the seven individual charges have been reproduced.

17. Arab Report and Record, 1971, p. 116.

18. Area Handbook for the Democratic Republic of the Sudan (Washington, D.C.: Government Printing Office, 1973), p. 310.

19. This account was offered by several reliable sources who requested to remain anonymous.

20. Al-Ra'y al-Amm, October 31, 1969.

21. According to a statement by Lieutenant Colonel Babikir el-Nur Osman in London on July 21. (Article by Peter Harvey in the Manchester Guardian, July 21, 1971.) See also Al-Akhbar (Beirut), March 2, 1971.

22. Radio Omdurman, July 20, 1971, as quoted in The USSR and the Middle East, eds. Michael Confino and Shimon Shamir (New York: Wiley, 1973), p. 360.

23. On December 1, 1971, the government announced that 3,179 persons had been detained after the abortive coup (Arab Report and Record, 1971, p. 631).

24. Ibid., p. 560.

25. Ibid., p. 656.

26. Arab Report and Record, 1972, p. 459.

27. Arab Report and Record, 1973, p. 111.

28. According to the Arab Report and Record, 1972, p. 383, the government announced its consideration to return small businesses to the private sector as early as August 10, 1972.

29. Arab Report and Record, 1974, p. 202.

30. Broadcast by Radio Omdurman, reproduced in Foreign Broadcast Information Service, January 26, 1974.

31. Arab Report and Record, 1975, p. 422.

32. Ibid., p. 228.

33. Ibid., p. 370.

34. Statement broadcast over Radio Omdurman on September 5, 1975, reproduced in Foreign Broadcast Information Service, September 5, 1975.

35. For further details, see Arab Report and Record, 1975, pp. 421-22.

PART

III

PATTERNS AND
CONCLUSIONS

The main purpose of Part III is to compare the relative effectiveness of civilian and military rule in the Sudan, to be able to draw more meaningful conclusions about the nature of the political process and the efficacy of political systems there. Most Sudanese politicians and ordinary citizens, as well as local and foreign observers, will agree that the key issues facing all Sudanese governments have been political stability and national integration foremost, with the major prerequisites of general economic and social progress as well as a sound, balanced foreign policy secondly. Accordingly, we shall compare governmental performances in the political, economic, social service, and foreign policy sectors during the past two decades, paying heed not only to overall results in these various categories, but to methods and perceptions of the rulers as well.

Most of these topics have already been discussed in relatively chronological sequence in the previous four chapters—albeit in varying degrees of detail and depth. It makes sense, therefore, to treat each category separately for analytical purposes in order to facilitate comparisons, in full recognition, of course, that policy decisions on various issues are frequently interrelated. Organizational considerations call for a separate treatment of foreign relations, in part because the preceding four chapters concentrated heavily on domestic issues, and in part due to the subject matter itself. (During the past generation the Sudan fortunately did not have to face any real external threats to its sovereignty, and foreign relations therefore concerned essentially such issues as political ties, diplomatic affairs, and foreign trade.) For those reasons the two substantive chapters of this concluding part have been divided into analyses of governmental performances in the domestic and foreign policy realms, respectively.

One final comment: Any comparison of different regimes over time is difficult by any standards and may be inherently unfair, particularly because changing conditions alter both the priority of problems and the available tools for resolution. Nevertheless, a study of the different rulers and political systems of independent Sudan would be incomplete without at least some attempts at comparison, no matter how general the conclusions.

9

THE TESTS OF
GOVERNMENTAL PERFORMANCE:
DOMESTIC ISSUES

By definition, each event is unique, and the environment that helps to shape this event is constantly changing. In order to facilitate the dual task of comparing the performances of governments operating under varying circumstances, and of examining sufficiently important issues, it is necessary to focus on relatively broad topics at a rather general level of analysis. The main body of this chapter therefore deals with broad comparisons of the four sets of Sudanese governments since 1953 concerning regime legitimacy and basic political effectiveness, contributions to economic and social development, and the handling of the North-South conflict. The even more general question about the suitability of both parliamentary democracy and military rule for Sudanese conditions will be analyzed in the concluding section.

POLITICAL EFFECTIVENESS

Political effectiveness is closely related to both legitimacy and stability of the regime in question; without legitimacy, there can be no stability, and without stability, no regime can effect any program. However, this statement should not be misconstrued to connote a sequential relationship in which "legitimacy" acts always as an independent variable. In actuality, both phenomena will influence each other; for example, the effectiveness of a regime tends to increase its legitimacy in the eyes of the public also.

As we apply these rather abstract concepts to the Sudanese case, we are immediately reminded of one of the main themes of the preceding chapters, that is, the proverbial instability of Sudanese governments. Therefore let us compare some key components of political effectiveness as well as regime legitimacy in the hope of deriving possible further insights into the chronic condition of political instability in the Sudan.

In order to avoid confusion and/or the need for lengthy clarifications of the various meanings of legitimacy, we shall limit this concept to two aspects: the "legality" of a government, which tends to be particularly important in the early stages of coming to power, and the extent of popular acceptance, something of relatively greater significance as time goes on. Legitimacy of military rule versus parliamentary democracy will be discussed in the concluding section of this chapter; our present comments will refer only to the specific Sudanese governments since 1953.

If we consider the legality aspect first, it is clear that the two parliamentary governments of 1953 and 1965 (and to an only slightly lesser degree the transitional government of 1964) were completely legitimate, unlike the two military regimes. This observation goes beyond the rather simple constitutional interpretation of legality to include the almost universal recognition by the Sudanese public of the legitimacy of liberal democracy. Not only was this latter form so specified in the temporary constitution, but it corresponded to the previously alluded to proclivity among the Sudanese for decision making by majlis and the widely cherished custom of free expression about any and all social and political matters. By contrast, both military juntas were initially regarded as illegal in the sense that they usurped control of the state, yet not equally so. For one thing, the Abboud regime came about more through a sort of concurrence with, than conspiracy against, the civilian predecessors. For another, by 1958 the idea of a military takeover had acquired the status of a possible model for modernization through Sudan's foremost cultural reference (Egypt), whereas after October 1964 military rule was rejected as undesirable and "totally unfitting for Sudanese conditions." (The Sudanese were proud to point to their difference with Egyptians in this matter, in the sense that the Sudanese would never tolerate a military dictatorship for as long as their northern neighbors.)

Yet with the passage of time the initial legitimacy of the two parliamentary regimes was eroded by their woeful performances, whereas support for the military juntas actually increased intermittently whenever their record in office so warranted it. It is interesting that these relative increases moved in opposite directions: popular acceptance of the Abboud junta decreased steadily as time went by, whereas the legitimacy of the May regime was lowest of all four during its early years (as indicated by the widespread opposition in civilian and military circles) and rose only after Ja'far Nimeiri embarked on his highly personalized "Sudan-first" and people-oriented campaign after mid 1971.

Political effectiveness can depend on a myriad of factors. Here we shall limit ourselves to some general comments about a few indicators, such as substantive programs, decision-making styles, representativeness of the regime, cabinet stability, availability of channels of political communication, and domestic tranquility (except for the Southern Problem, which will be treated separately below).

A general shortcoming of all Sudanese regimes except, to some extent, the May government, has been their lack of specific policies. This manifested itself in the by now familiar pattern of identical proclamations by new rulers of dedication to "progress," "democracy," and "solidarity with Arab and African causes." Initially, the concrete applications of these general principles invariably turned out to be almost complete reversals of whatever their predecessors had done, but after the dust had settled, they drifted slowly back into earlier patterns. Even former premier M. A. Mahjoub admitted to the absence of overall planning when he wrote that the "basic cause of trouble was that the parties found themselves without any particular aim. . . They had no defined programs to deal with economic or social development. . ."[1] The same basic charge can be laid to the first military regime, which was unprepared for its new role of governing, but improvised rapidly. The second military regime, however, began with apparently well-defined concepts for establishing a socialist state, only to have to retract many of its earlier policies before two years had elapsed.

As regards decision-making styles, the military rulers proved to be much more efficient than the parliamentarians, as could be expected, but also more rash and inexperienced. Whereas some officer-politicians were prone to impulsive actions if the submitted evidence seemed convincing on the surface, their civilian colleagues often gave the impression of deliberately paralyzing their own governments by endless bickering and/or persistent referral of urgent problems to unwieldy committees. Even the most sympathetic Sudan observer could not escape the dominant impression that during the past two decades wise, decisive, and effective leadership has been one of the most needed yet conspicuously unavailable commodities. It appeared that decisive leaders either lacked political bases and/or experience, or that experienced politicians lacked decisiveness or wisdom. This may appear to be a harsh statement, but countries like Sudan with enormous social and economic problems as well as a most heterogeneous society are in desperate need of strong leadership during the critical stages of nation building and simply cannot afford to be governed by men of any standard but the highest.

One consequence of such societal heterogeneity is that it heightens the importance of governmental responsiveness. In the absence of a strong, charismatic leader who can hold the body politic together through centralized control in the hope of speeding national integration, the alternative requirement is to respond to the diversity of groupings through some system of proportional representation or outright decentralization. Because the Southern Problem will be analyzed separately below, the present comments will be confined to the extent to which the various governments were able to remain representative of the major political groupings in society at large. On this count the two parliamentary regimes scored predictably higher than their military colleagues, especially if we recall that the NUP, Umma party, and the PDP all participated in some form in coalition governments during both periods of civilian rule. However, this apparent plaudit is somewhat diminished by the failure of the party leaderships to include genuine representatives of non-"Arab" minorities from South, East and West in prominent positions. The army rulers, by definition, represented a different class; but if we examine the composition of their ruling councils, we may note that the Abboud junta began with an originally relatively broad base in terms of political orientations, which shrank over the years, whereas the May Revolution began most narrow-based of all and has ever since attempted to widen its appeal.

Sometimes the Council of Ministers can serve the same function of providing some form of proportional representation. In fact, an examination of all post-1953 cabinets yields the distinct impression that cabinet portfolios have been frequently used to "balance the ticket." However, such balance did not reflect the society at large or even the various factions within the political groupings, but rather the political allies of leading personalities in coalition governments. One consequence of this pattern has been that up until now there has not been one single, truly representative cabinet incorporating all points of view. (The second transitional cabinet in February 1965 came close, but was handicapped by the refusal of CPS and PDP ministers to occupy the seats allotted to their parties.) On the contrary, Umma ministers were either all followers of Sadiq el-Mahdi or of Imam el-Hadi, NUPs/DUPs were all beholden to Ismail el-Azhari or to Ali el-Mirghani and so on, except for a brief period after the 1968 elections.

A close examination of cabinet appointments over the years reveals some other interesting patterns. For example, there is the remarkable continuity during the Abboud period, when only a total of 17 different men served. This figure compares to 34 cabinet officers during the first parliamentary government, 63 during the second, and 83 during the first five and two-thirds years after the May Revolution. Even if we make allowances for the notable increase in portfolios from the mid-1960s on, and especially most recently, we are still struck by the fact that the Abboud regime held by far the lowest

appointment rates per ministry and per year.* This meant that Abboud's three cabinet changes entailed more a reshuffling of portfolios
than a wholesale exchange of ministers, whereas the inflationary
figures from the two parliamentary periods reflect several complete
changes of coalitions (in 1956, 1965, 1966, 1967 and 1968). The extraordinary instability of the Nimeiri cabinets results only in small part
from the need to add southern representatives and northern specialists
to a restructured government, but primarily from the series of political upheavals, the uncertainty of temporary alliances and, apparently,
some poor personnel choices as well.

As we shall argue again later, a key requirement for political
stability is to provide for some channels of communication between
ruler and ruled, not only for interest articulation and aggregation, but
also to permit participation from below as well as responsiveness to
popular demands from above. On this score, neither the parliamentarians nor the military rulers have performed particularly well so
far. The former permitted freedom of speech and association (except
for "subversive elements"), but never created effective channels for
dialogue with the ordinary Sudanese. Although individual politicians,
like most of their countrymen including military officers, have been
personable and accessible, their many social contacts amounted to
little more than "talk." But kalaam, and especially kalaam faadi
(Arabic for "talk" and "empty talk," respectively, a favorite local
description for much of the ongoing conversation and argumentation),
could not lead to genuine "interest aggregation," because major political decisions remained the prerogative of a few selected individuals.
Everyone else was viewed as not sophisticated enough to participate
meaningfully, and was therefore expected to follow the edicts of his
leader.

This sort of elitist perception prevailed among military rulers as
well, except that it emanated from a general disdain for the supposedly
inherent ineptitude and/or corruption of civilian politicians. A prevalent feeling among junta leaders and other officers has been that one
could not, or should not, trust anybody outside the military establishment with the more important affairs of state. One manifestation of
this attitude was, of course, the outlawing of all private political organizations by the military regimes and the relatively severe press
censorship. The Abboud government was never able to solve this
problem, and its only attempt to broaden participation was Abu

---

*Appointments per ministry were 2.0 compared to 4.6 for Nimeiri
and 4.9 for the second parliamentary regime. Appointments per year
were 5.3 for Abboud, 14 for Nimeiri, and almost 20 for the 1964-69
period.

Rannat's scheme of local councils, which never matured to the desired level. The Nimeiri regime has been trying to remedy this situation through the establishment of the mass-based Socialist Union, which has already been discussed in earlier chapters. The initial effectiveness of the SSU suffered undoubtedly from two handicaps: one, Sudanese are neither used to nor do they like political organizations imposed on them from above; and two, the immediate repression of potential opponents of the May Revolution left behind an air of cautiousness and timidity that is not likely to change very quickly unless the current leadership indicates a greater willingness to accept divergent views and public criticism. Meanwhile, the most effective "interest-aggregator" of all may very well have been President Nimeiri himself, as a result of his frequent visits to all parts of the country and his demonstrated accessibility and genuine interest in the concerns of his fellow citizens.

The final item on our list of indicators of political effectiveness is domestic tranquility, although its utility as a measure of regime performance tends to be evidenced more clearly in its opposite, domestic unrest. Here we note that for much of the past twenty-five years, attempted coups, riots, and demonstrations have been part of the political scene. Some of these disturbances can be attributed to the relatively open nature of Sudanese society, in comparison with the much more controlled Egyptian one, for example, which has appeared to many Sudanese as an at least mild form of police state.

A closer examination of these incidents reveals that domestic unrest has been highest during the Nimeiri regime, which has outlasted nearly a dozen known coup attempts so far by opponents ranging from conservative to radical elements to so-called "racialists" (regional insurgent groups) from within and without the military. Similarly, the traditional hotbed of antigovernment demonstrations, Khartoum University, experienced more disruptions of classroom activities and of its administrative structure after May 1969 than ever before. In a comparison of domestic unrest per length of rule, the transitional government of 1964-65 would rank second, to be followed by the Abboud regime (similarly plagued by coup attempts and student demonstrations, but fewer and spread out over time) and the first parliamentary government (which encountered labor unrest and public strikes through much of the 1950s). Only the second parliamentary regime was able to enjoy relative tranquility, if one does not place too much weight on the anti-Communist demonstrations of November 1965 and the abortive military coup attempt of December 1966.

This brief survey of selected indicators of political effectiveness reveals a rather uneven, and not particularly favorable, record for the various Sudanese rulers. These patterns remain unchanged when we examine one of the key political problems since before independence, namely, resolution of the North-South conflict, although we are happy to be able to report at last a happy ending.

THE PROBLEM OF THE SOUTH

The enormity of the so-called "problem of the southern Sudan" cannot possibly be dealt with adequately in a book of this kind. Fortunately recent years have witnessed a steady flow of increasingly superior analyses of this topic;[2] thus we are able to confine ourselves here to brief comparisons of the performances of the several post-independence regimes in tackling this very complex issue.

An even cursory study of events during the past two decades yields two equally dominant and obvious conclusions: first, the two military regimes had a much greater impact on this problem than the several civilian ones; second, whereas the Southern policy of the Abboud junta proved counterproductive and did much to escalate the conflict, the approach of the Nimeiri regime not only stands out brightly as the only successful one, but is likely to enter into history as the major accomplishment of the May Revolution.

It makes sense to examine at first the relevant perceptions of the various governments. Here we must be impressed by the consistent inability of Khartoum politicians prior to 1969 to recognize accurately southern feelings of social injustice resulting from genuine fears of personal discrimination, and political and economic neglect. While lip service was paid to the idea of national unity under a system of equality, blame for existing and growing disharmony was most notably placed on such outsiders as colonialists, missionaries, and the ever-present "imperialists." Although it is true that these latter forces may have contributed to part of the recognizable differences between northerners and southerners, the governments in Khartoum seemed to insist on maintaining foremost a posture of "it is not our fault," instead of accepting ethnic, linguistic, and religious differences as a point of departure for constructive policies.

For that reason, too, all pre-1969 policies emphasized cultural assimilation as the correct solution, undoubtedly spurred on by historical experiences in the northern region. Whether such intentions were good or evil can easily be debated at great length, but without much profit. What matters is that a policy of cultural assimilation always tends to be fueled by the value system of the majority (the North). Thus, each increase in pressure from the North only heightened the sense of psychological and physical insecurity among southerners and finally resulted in parallel increases of direct resistance.

Generalizations are always unfair to some people, yet they can help us point out significant group differences. One way of characterizing northern attitudes and behavior toward southerners during the first 15 years after the 1953 elections is to recall the pervasive haughtiness among northerners toward their southern fellow citizens. This applied equally to relations among members of the intelligentsia, traditional elites, and common folk. Attitudes of northern cultural superiority were easily observable in employment practicies, educational institutions, and areas of social contact like the marketplace, cultural events, or even the football field. Whether technically justified or not, such behavior left deep psychological scars on sensitive southerners on one side and formed the basis for misguided policies from Khartoum on the other.

During the parliamentary periods such policies were characterized by unreasonable promises for, and/or outright attempts to buy, political support from southern chieftains by the various party lead leaders—and concomitant disdain for the younger educated "troublemakers." Such behavior sprang undoubtedly from the quite correct perception that southern tribal chieftains represented the real base of political control in the region, and that their support for a given party would automatically deliver the remainder of the tribe to that party. It is ironic that such (good political) tactics should have been used by northern politicians in the South, when these same politicians had decried similar British dealings with traditional elements, and disregard for the budding northern intelligentsia, as "colonialist" and "imperialist" practices only a few years earlier. In all fairness it must be added that during his shortlived interlude as prime minister, Sadiq el-Mahdi had developed a more comprehensive and analytical approach to solving the Southern Problem.[3]

The policies of the Abboud junta have already been described at some length in Chapter 6. They can be summarized as steadily increasing pressure for cultural assimilation, backed by military force as soon as local resistance emerged. So it was left to the leaders of the May Revolution, and their intellectual and political forerunners in the post-October 1964 transitional government, to recognize the bankruptcy of earlier policies and to try a genuinely different approach. Only two weeks after coming to power, President Nimeiri issued his famous June Declaration in which he committed his government to the resolution of the North-South conflict as a top priority. Perhaps the most important element of his approach lay in the acceptance of a new and different premise for analyzing and eventually resolving the problem. Because of its contextual importance it is worth quoting the key paragraph:

. . . The revolutionary Government is confident and competent enough to face existing realities. It recognizes the historical and cultural differences between the North and South
and firmly believes that the unity of our country must be
built upon these objective realities. The Southern people
have the right to develop their respective cultures and traditions within a united Socialist Sudan. . .[4]

These words were backed up by an extension of amnesty laws,
plans for economic, social, and cultural development of the South, the
appointment of a southerner to the newly created Ministry of Southern
Affairs, and the training of numerous southerners in preparation for
administrative duties. The rest of the story is familiar by now, and
culminated with the granting of regional autonomy to the South. It is
a measure of the accomplishment of Ja'far Nimeiri that the only internal criticism and opposition since 1972 has come from conservative
northern circles, and that he has probably been even more popular
among southerners than his Bor Dinka vice-president Abel Alier.

ECONOMIC PERFORMANCE

We have already suggested in Chapter 1 that economic performance is a key determinant of governmental stability, if only because
of the primacy of economic concerns in the overall development of
newly independent countries like Sudan. It is easy to assert such a
basic premise—incidentally, one shared by all Sudanese politicians
according to their public utterances. Yet it is much more difficult to
compare the economic effectiveness of the several regimes short of
embarking on a detailed analysis of the Sudanese economy, something
clearly beyond the scope of this book. Our objective here is rather
modest: to gain some sort of comparative perspective by analyzing
a few of the standard economic indicators for which reasonably reliable data have been available. Seen in this light, any conclusions must
remain tentative and await more systematic analysis by competent
scholars.
  At the very outset we can note that all Sudanese governments
operated under very similar limitations set by the virtual absence of
mineral resources in the country, and therefore did not have direct
access to the kinds of capital funds for economic development that
have been at the disposal of their neighbors on the Arabian peninsula,
for example. The central questions therefore become: How well have
the several governments husbanded their (fixed) existing assets? In
what ways have they attempted to develop additional resources?

A glance at some standard economic indicators reveals relatively
little difference; that is to say, there is neither a dramatic reversal
of fortunes over time, nor the sort of spectacular imbalance between
production and consumption that one can witness in a good many emerging nations. For example, both gross domestic product and per capita
income have risen steadily since 1953, but not spectacularly. If one
controls for inflation, the interesting result emerges that the only
slight downturn occurred in 1957-59 and 1963-65. After the necessary
adjustment for time lags in accounting are made, these periods can be
recognized as corresponding exactly to the final years of the first
parliamentary and first military regimes, respectively. The consumer
price index has similarly risen steadily; the only two notable developments there have been the spectacular rise from 1969 on and the earlier disparity between consumer and wholesale prices from 1953 to
late 1958. The foreign trade statistics show a slight deficit throughout
the past twenty years, but it is remarkable how close the value of imports was kept to that of the exports, if we consider the overriding
need for Sudan to import machine goods and other manufactured items
in the absence of a native industrial establishment. In fact, the only
time when imports exceeded exports by more than 20 million Sudanese
pounds was during the last three years of the Abboud junta's reign.

Thus, the general picture portrayed by these indicators suggests
both remarkable consistency and fiscal responsibility on the part of
all Sudanese governments with very minor and brief exceptions. Yet
from another perspective, the relative consistency in economic indicators over the years can signify economic stagnation, a condition
that comes into clearer focus when we turn our attention to the record
concerning initiation of new projects.

The observer cannot escape a sense of almost extraordinary pas-
sivity, notwithstanding a few isolated projects here and there. The
overall impression is that the Sudanese much prefer the marketplace
to the economic planner's institute, a behavior trait that seems to
apply to governments and private citizens alike. For example, the
Northern merchant is visible in the local suq (marketplace) throughout
the country and obviously capable and contented in this role; rarely,
if ever, does he venture out to invest any profits in someone else's
schemes. (Southerners so far have been conspicuously absent from
any "modern" economic activities.) Similarly, successive Sudanese
governments seem to have viewed the economic realm from the perspective of a "holding operation," contented to maintain the projects
initiated by the colonial administration or foreign businessmen. This
does not mean, of course, that Sudanese are, or have been, uninterested in profit or economic growth—quite to the contrary. But their
interest has generally taken only the form of asking outsiders to draw
up development schemes, or simply waiting for an international body,

such as the IBRD or a U.N. agency, to survey local conditions and tell
the Sudanese government what ought to be done. The implied criticism
of this posture addresses itself to the apparent lack of local initiative,
creative designs, or both.

In practice, this meant that the parliamentary regimes, like many
liberal democracies elsewhere, have used the economic realm primarily for political spoils. Thus, one could observe import and trade
licenses going to urban politicians and pump schemes to rural sectarian chieftains. Such practices would not be objectionable per se had
they been integrated into a larger plan for overall development, but
this was almost never the case. During periods of military rule the
existing central planning offices became somewhat more adventurous,
but only by Sudanese standards. This may have been due, in part, to
the fact that it was no longer necessary to placate nonmilitary sectors
with economic favors.

The foregoing is not intended to belittle such projects as the
Khartoum-Wad Medani Road, or the giant Roseires Dam and Khashm
el-Girba Development by the Abboud junta, nor its demonstrated ability to line up bilateral and multilateral aid donors from abroad. There
have been a number of other noteworthy industrial projects, but none
of these reached the scale that was either necessary for development
or possible given local resources.

The rather disastrous early record of the May Revolution has
already been described in Chapter 8, and it can only he hoped that it
will be compensated for by the ambitious new development programs
that are currently underway. As belated as some of these reorienta-
tions have been, it is nevertheless to the credit of the current government that in 1974 it decided to place top priority on further exploitation
of the greatly underused agricultural potential of the Sudan,[5] and that
it has similarly recognized that the totally inadequate transportation
system constituted one of the greatest bottlenecks to progress. Accordingly, the Development Budget for 1974/75 reserved 32.5 percent
of its total allocations to this sector, and specific plans have been
drawn up and are already partly implemented for increasing and up-
grading the road, rail, and river navigation networks. Such pragmatic
policies have fortunately met with a favorable international response,
and for the first time since independence one can say that there is a
large flow of foreign capital available for investment in the Sudan.
The only danger at present is that the economic planners in their enthusiasm may commit themselves to too many long-term projects
without visible short-term returns and that the required down payments on joint ventures and loan installments will devour the rest of
the already inadequate foreign exchange reserves. For example, in
March 1975 Sudan was forced to purchase $18 million in Special

Drawing Rights from the International Monetary Fund in order to al-
leviate balance of payments problems resulting from export shortfalls
in 1974.[6]

As already pointed out in Chapter 1, Sudanese society has generally been very egalitarian, and this characteristic extends to the
economic sphere as well. Consequently, feudal landlord-tenant relationships or great inequality of income as could be found in prerevolu-
tionary Egypt and Ethiopia next door have not constituted any problem
for Sudanese governments. The main form of inequality that has
existed was more an outgrowth of local life-styles in impoverished
rural areas. Once again, it has been to the credit of President Nimeiri
that he, unlike his predecessors, has consciously concerned himself
with the lot of the subsistence dwellers in the provinces and has at
least shown the necessary goodwill to correct these conditions. But
because of the immensity of the country and the nearly complete absence of a modern infrastructure, any improvement here will come
about only very slowly. For this reason self-help projects have been
emphasized, and these have been coupled with the provision of other
social services, which is also the final topic of our comparative survey.

SOCIAL PROGRESS

It is necessary to realize that Sudanese have traditionally perceived progress not so much in pecuniary terms, but in slightly vaguer
notions about the quality of life. This perception, incidentally, may be
one reason why the so-called Protestant work ethic has conspicuously
failed to gain momentum in the Sudan, and conversely explains the very
great importance that has generally been attached to the provision of
social services. Journalists, politicians, or local administrators on
tour of the provinces have consistently reported the chief concerns of
rural Sudanese as the need for more educational and health facilities,
plus more adequate water supply for man and beast.

Happily it can be acknowledged that all Sudanese governments
have responded to the overwhelming thirst for more schools, teachers,
and educational materials as best they could, in view of the scarce
financial resources available. Educational statistics since 1950 show
a steady and sizable rise for every year at all levels, including a constantly growing share of females in the public schools and university
enrollments. Given the extraordinarily low literacy rates at the time
of independence, much ground still remains to be covered; however,
the record of all Sudanese governments, as well as the overall quality
of education, has been quite good by African and Middle Eastern
standards. The only real deficiency lies in geographic distribution,

whereby the southern provinces foremost, and the western region
second, have not received their share of educational facilities as yet.
In the former case the fault lies primarily with the side-effects of
civil strife, and in the latter case all governments are equally to blame
for their benign neglect of peripheral areas.

An even greater disparity can be seen in the distribution of health
care facilities, be they hospitals, beds, dispensaries, or local health
centers. A particularly drastic, though not surprising, statistic shows
that in 1973 there were more doctors in Khartoum (464) than in the
rest of the country combined.[7] Also, there were only 4 health centers
in the 3 Southern provinces in 1971 out of a total of 109; two years
later this figure had improved only slightly to 10 centers out of 139
nationwide.

The relative shortage of clean water in many rural areas has been
recognized at least since the 1960s, but the drilling of wells in semidesert areas, and allocation of diesel pump schemes along the Niles,
have been handled haphazardly much of the time. The above reference
to shortage was described as relative, because in absolute terms there
is no shortage of water in the Sudan, only maldistribution. This author
once calculated that if it were either necessary or desirable the entire
population of the Sudan could be settled on the banks of the Blue, White,
and joint Niles, plus the Sobat and Bahr el-Ghazal rivers, and the resultant population density would be only one-sixth of that of Egypt.

For the record, several additional items deserve to be mentioned.
The parliamentarians have been reasonably responsive to local demands for better social services, but these services have been allocated primarily to areas of party strongholds along the Niles in the
North and in the Gezira. The first military junta ventured into new
housing projects in urban areas, and marginal improvements in sani-
tation and electrification. The post-October transitional government
was instrumental in helping Sudanese women to gain greater participation in public life, whereas the Nimeiri regime gave further emphasis to technical education, women's role in society, and especially
greater attention to the social needs of the formerly neglected rural
masses.

It is obvious that much still remains to be done; the immensity
of the country on one hand and the shortage of funds for crash programs on the other, have tempted many administrators simply to
throw up their hands in despair. The best prospects for remedying
this situation in the short run may well lie with the SSU-sponsored
village development committees, if their theoretically well-designed
plans can be implemented through adult education and self-help programs.

CONCLUSIONS

The foregoing survey of governmental performance in four domestic issue areas leaves us, quite predictably, with rather mixed results. A summary in capsule form might read somewhat like this: In the paramount political realm none of the several regimes were able to create the necessary preconditions for stable and effective rule; in the economic sector the two military juntas have been more enterprising than their civilian predecessors, but also more prone to mistakes; and in the areas of social development and regional integration, the current government under President Nimeiri has been most successful by far since it focused its attention on the everyday problems of the simple, ordinary Sudanese.

The implicit reordering of priorities, plus the demonstrated willingness to implement development programs in line with those new priorities, has yielded a dramatic increase in the popular support for the remaining leaders of the May Revolution who, interestingly enough, had to overcome the broadest spectrum of opposition during their first two years in power, and had operated from the narrowest base of legitimacy of all Sudanese regimes. This observation about the positive correlation between governmental performance and regime legitimacy brings us back to an earlier theoretical question concerning the general legitimacy of parliamentary and military rule within the context of Sudanese politics. Even though the analysis of foreign policy performance is yet to come, it seems appropriate to speculate about these theoretical relationships at this point, because Sudanese foreign policy on the whole has tended to be an outer manifestation of the interplay of the more dominant internal factors.

For a start, all available evidence seems to indicate that the vast majority of Sudanese have no theoretical preference for a particular political system. They will demand governmental responsiveness and individual liberties, but apparently could envision a "practical democracy" even under an authoritarian ruler—or vice versa—depending on the style of the leaders. From this perspective it behooves us to examine the relative efficacy of these two prevalent forms of government under Sudanese conditions.

Parliamentary Democracy

Many factors have contributed to the demise of parliamentary democracy in the Sudan. Most apparent was the widely felt disillusion-

ment with traditional parties and politicians, one might say, the Sudanese variety of "old politics." Although a nucleus of Sudanese with
latent yearnings for a "New Politics" has been in existence for some
time, most of these were followers of the extreme right- and left-wing
movements. To be sure, there have been others, especially professional men, who shared a distaste for old politics, yet hesitated to
associate themselves with the more radical movements. Throughout
most of the 1960s, the continuing spread of education and its concomitant increase in popular awareness combined with the deterioration
of economic conditions to swell the ranks of this potentially sizable
group with latent yearnings for a "new politics." They exhibited little
faith in the ability of conventional democracy to solve the political
problems facing the Sudan, primarily because of the explicit behavior
of Sudanese politicians. Although it is doubtful that many opponents
of old politics appreciated the various theoretical implications of their
viewpoint, they were essentially correct in asserting that Sudanese
democracy appeared to follow some different behavioral patterns than
what is generally identified as Western democracy. This point is of
great importance to our concerns and needs to be amplified.

    The behavior of party leaders and representatives in the Sudan
cannot be adequately understood unless we examine the ways in which
both voters and candidates interpret the meaning of elections and the
relationship of the electoral process to democracy. This interpretation differs in certain fundamental ways from its Western counterpart.
This assertion is admittedly vague and general; moreover, I am not
certain at this time whether the stated Sudanese interpretation is in
fact limited to the northern Sudan, or to the Arab world, or to the
Muslim countries. Nevertheless, there does exist a fundamental difference in interpretation between the Sudanese and Western varieties,
(one of the consequences is the particular form that Sudanese factionalism takes). It manifests itself in the divergent concepts about
the bargain struck by voter and candidate and the kinds of responsibilities associated with that bargain. In essence, in the Western world
a delegate has clearly defined realms of independent decision making
and need not represent the views of his electorate on all matters. By
contrast, the ordinary Sudanese delegate represents the consensus
of power holders in his constituency beyond which he will not dare
act or speak out in public on any given issue, no matter how much he
may personally disagree with the substance of that consensus.[8]

    In order to appreciate the ramifications of this distinction, we
must ask ourselves what, in fact, constitutes the real and practical
meaning of the election of candidate X to the ordinary voter in an
average constituency? The answer is quite simple: X was elected
by his constituents as their most trustworthy delegate to the distant
capital, the man who, above all, was familiar to them and who could

be counted upon to return their favors in some small ways. He was
not really expected to bring fame and glory to his locality (national
decisions would be made by national leaders), but practical goods such
as schools, water wells, and some jobs for local school graduates.
Such was the nature of the bargain, and most parliamentarians as well
as the voting public understood this well and acted concretely upon
this understanding. It was within this framework that parliamentary
elections have become part of the Sudanese political process. To that
one might add that in practically all cases voters elected candidates
who were familiar to them, whether as local residents or as nationally
known figures. In several constituencies in Blue Nile Province, which
were observed for that purpose in April of 1965, voters preferred
locally known candidates to outsiders who were assigned to the particular constituencies by party headquarters, even if that party
(Umma) represented the political organization of the sectarian movement to which the voters belonged.

On the national scene the distribution of seats in parliament
tended to reflect rather accurately the approximate strengths of the
major parties in the country, although many nationally oriented observers felt that rural areas were overrepresented, a situation that
would tend to favor the sectarian parties. However, voting strength
in parliament did not reflect the relationships between local and national power in conflict situations, since parliamentarians in the Sudan
have normally been expected to support the policies of their party
leaders rather than regional or local objectives. Where party policies
conflicted with local interests, these conflicts tended to be resolved,
if at all, outside the parliamentary structure through bargaining between national and local leaders, as had been customary in the days
before the advent of parliamentary democracy. On this basis we may
conclude that, on the whole, elections have reconfirmed traditional
sources and positions of power on both the local and national levels
but do not reflect accurately the relationships between these levels.

One important exception to this generalization may be found in
the relative success of two groups of independents during the 1965
elections. Both groups managed to emerge victorious in all of the
nineteen constituencies that they contested save one, thereby under-
lining the extent of popular dissatisfaction with political developments,
and also opening up a potential alternative avenue for regional interest
groups. Yet their decline during the 1968 elections, despite credible
showings,* supports the earlier argument of relative inefficiency of

---

*The Nuba Mountains Federation saw both of its official candi-
dates victorious, and the three winning independents in Kordofan all
hailed from the Nuba area. The Beja Congress won three constitu-

local interest groups in the national political system. It may be interesting in this connection that until now southern politicians have been unable to exert effective regional pressure upon the central government through the democratic process, in part due to the inability of Southern leaders to merge their various political organizations into one unified front movement.

These foregoing observations should allow us to derive some conclusions about the relationships of the electoral process and of parliamentary democracy to the degree of political stability in the Sudan.

Because of the factional nature of Sudanese life and politics, voters tended to respond to candidates who delivered for them locally. This sort of behavior is well and good as far as it goes. But it does not help to solve fundamental and national—as opposed to local—problems. It does account for the undeveloped state of the national economy and the absence of any concrete efforts to respond positively to the demands of a changing world. For example, we may observe that up until the coup of May 1969, virtually none of the leaders of the major political parties had addressed themselves concretely—as opposed to paying lip service—to the large and pressing issues of economic revival, social change, and political modernization. When even such generally impressive figures as the Oxford-educated Umma president Sadiq el-Mahdi and the French-educated ICF president Dr. Hassan el-Turabi (former dean of the Khartoum University Law School) committed themselves to an Islamic constitution for such a heterogeneous country, then one was reluctantly left to conclude that the only politicians who seemed to have had a clear-cut plan for a Sudan integrated in the modern world were members of the extreme left. This may help to explain the prominence of leftists in the May Revolution government and their initial acceptance by a wide spectrum of Sudan's urban intelligentsia.

Military Rule

In the Sudan, as in other countries, the military does not exist in a vacuum; on the contrary, its political activities are mostly responses to a setting developed by civilian politicians and other nonmilitary factors. A main theme of the earlier sections in this book

---

encies outright and had a plurality of votes in a fourth in which two Congress candidates took votes away from each other; in three more losing causes Beja pulled more than 40 percent of the vote, and in only three constituencies did their candidates fare poorly.

has been to describe that setting in terms of a Sudanese variety of factionalism, which resulted among other things from multiple and reinforcing cleavages in society on one hand, and from destabilizing coalition tactics by poorly organized, traditional parties on the other. Any analysis of the two juntas in power, however, must first consider the argument that the mere malfunctioning of democratic politics need not necessarily lead to military takeovers.

On the basis of historical evidence it seems safe to assume that there was widespread disillusionment among the general public, and specifically among the intelligentsia about the deteriorating quality of parliamentary rule in the face of growing economic, political, and social problems in the late 1950s and again in the late 1960s. This disillusionment permeated the educational, civil service, professional, and journalistic establishments, and while demonstrable evidence of a quantitative nature is lacking, there is no reason to doubt the existence of similar perceptions among military officers. There were basically two alternatives to factional politics: a united national front or a grand coalition of political parties on one hand, or some sort of military intervention on the other.

The first alternative was unfeasible primarily because of the deepseated factional distrust among the three northern groupings, the depth of which became the major obstacle to effective coalition politics at those times when the NUP-PDP, NUP-Umma, and the Umma-PDP had, in fact, formed political alliances. A concomitant aspect of this situation was the absence of a universally acceptable and admired national figure, probably because the Sudan, unlike the Maghreb countries, won its independence without a militant and broadly-based nationalist movement under one strong leader. Thus, in the absence of a readily acceptable civilian strongman, and by a process of logical elimination, the military alternative seemed almost unavoidable, particularly in 1958.

Since that time the Sudan has experienced more than twelve years of military rule. One possibility for further evaluation of the political performance by these men in uniform is suggested by a comparison of several available scenarios. When the military came to power in 1958, and again in 1969, it theoretically could have pursued at least three options: one, it could have blamed civilian politicians for all the problems of stagnation and the general deterioration of the country's living conditions; consequently it could have outlawed all political parties and attempted to appeal to the populace on a nationalist rather than factionalist basis as symbolized by the national uniform. This policy, of course, required forging mass support where little or none existed, or where there was a measure of goodwill at most. Several questions remained: How would the population at large have reacted to the vilification and possible detainment of their civilian

leaders? Would such acts not have jeopardized whatever support and
popular goodwill the coup leaders enjoyed? And furthermore, in the
absence of a readymade political base, could the military have ruled
very long on the strength of the gun barrel alone?

The second basic option ran counter to the first. It would have
involved attempts to create an all party coalition or "united national
front" with some sort of military figure on top, but which would permit and actively seek channels for inputs from the existing traditional
power blocs. In effect, this alternative would have entailed military
cooptation of civilian groups, whereby the military sector would aim
to control factionalist excesses and to guarantee political activities
within a clearly defined parameter (perhaps similar to the Turkish
case during the past decade).

The third option would have required neither a crushing nor a
cooptation of all political groupings, but rather an association of the
military rulers with one particularly suitable political faction in an
alliance for the mutual benefit of both partners, coupled with attempts
to either control or destroy all other rivals.

This latter option was unfeasible because its strategy was based
on one or the other of two untenable premises. The first premise
would have required that one civilian faction pursue goals similar to
or compatible with junta policies in the fashion of a "natural ally."
Such was simply not the case; in the eyes of the various military
rulers the political behavior of all major factions was unacceptable.
The second premise would have stipulated that the junta was itself
factionalist in social composition like, for example, the recent Syrian
military rulers who have been almost exclusively Alawites, or alter-
natively, like the situation in some Latin American countries where
a particular regime is supported by one faction of the armed forces
and opposed by another. Neither of these conditions could likely be
replicated in the Sudan. Were Umma colonels as Umma colonels to
lead a revolt, they would be definitely opposed by khatmiyyah colonels.
This assertion does not by itself deny the existence of sectarian,
tribal, or geographic attachments among Sudanese military officers,
yet it alludes to the predominance of secular and professional values
over private sentiments in the armed forces.

Unlike this rather straightforward verdict about the third option,
conclusions about the first two are much more difficult. To be sure,
both the Abboud and Nimeiri regimes ostensibly associated themselves with the first option by outlawing all existing political parties,
detaining their leaders, and so on. Similarly, all evidence indicates
that military rulers in both regimes shared a righteous contempt for
the alleged incompetence as well as the duplicity of civilian politicians. Another commonality lies in the generals' perception of problems, which invariably emphasized technical over political aspects,

and in their methods, which stressed the military's penchant for organization, discipline, and output orientation over the subtle complexities of conflicts of interests and social-psychological predispositions. Yet, this observation should not surprise and we shall return to its implications in the concluding remarks of this chapter.

The Abboud and Nimeiri regimes differ in their ideological orientations with the former having been more conservative and the latter more "progressive-socialist." This may account for the fact that the Abboud regime initially maintained the political support of the three major civilian power blocs. In fact, within hours of the November 1958 takeover, the army had obtained endorsements from the two sectarian patriarchs.[9] Moreover, the composition of the first Supreme Council of State carefully reflected military representation of civilian factional interests at the highest level. It was not until after intramilitary disorders led to the dismissal of the pro-Umma Brigadier Ahmed Abd al-Wahhab, that effective control became more and more centralized, direct access by civilian interest groups became difficult, if not impossible, and the leadership of the major parties became increasingly suspicious and openly critical of the junta clique.

Ja'far Nimeiri by contrast was determined from the outset to destroy the conservative parties and particularly their sectarian bases. Of course, Nimeiri benefited not only from hindsight about civilian (misrule), but from the lessons of the Abboud period as well. He publicly lumped both groups together as reactionary elements and set out to consciously radicalize Sudanese affairs. He was convinced that there could be no progress unless the old politics were replaced by a new politics, which he envisioned as patterned on the Egyptian model of Arab socialism. He recognized that his major challenge would come from the conservative Umma party with its strong ansar organization; so he decided to take on that party at the outset of his rule. In the end, he wound up fighting the Communists as well.

On this level Nimeiri went considerably beyond Abboud. Yet he realized with time that the problem was not resolved after the destruction of political enemies, and that another institution had to assume the functions of political interest articulation and aggregation. For that purpose he proclaimed the Sudanese Socialist Union in May 1971 as the party to end all parties. The intricacies of ensuing political maneuvers has already been discussed in the preceding chapter. It remains to add that the Socialist Union could not develop into a viable organ until there was at least some accommodation with traditional power brokers such as the exiled Sayyed el-Sadiq el-Mahdi. It was not until Sayyed el-Sadiq had been brought back to Sudan and a few gingerly contacts had been made toward restoring an air of normalcy to military-civilian political relations, that ordinary Sudanese began to abandon their cautious reluctance to become "meaningfully" involved in the Socialist Union.

At this point, we may consider the relative merits of army rule. Several factors, characteristic of military regimes in general, are said to denote implicit advantages of this particular form of government: the direct chain of command that "gets things done;" the national rather than regional, tribal, or personal identification as symbolized by the uniform; the greater familiarity with technical matters; a more pragmatic outlook on life as reflected by the military training; the more effective and more authoritative elements of "persuasion" at their disposal; and finally, the previous example of civilian misrule. This line of reasoning is superficially intriguing. Moreover, recent events in Africa, the Middle East, and Latin America suggest that others accept its validity.

The difficulty, however, is that many observers seem to confuse the greater efficiency of military rulers with greater effectiveness. No reasonable person would doubt that military rulers can be and usually are more efficient than civilian ones, especially in administration and policy formulations. The evidence in the Sudan as elsewhere points this out quite clearly. But to contend that military rule is also more effective than civilian rule neither follows from the assertion nor is supported by recent events in many countries, for example the Sudan, where the military dictatorship under Major-General Abboud was overthrown by "the people" after six years in power.

Any effective and stable government regardless of its social base or elite structure has to be sensitive to existing or potential issues in the country. It has to create and/or maintain institutionalized processes by which politically important groups in society can communicate with one another and feel that they can participate, at least partially, in the formulation of policy and thereby legitimize the regime. In other words, those groups in society—tribal chieftains, religious or sectarian leaders, influential merchants, sectors of the armed forces, and so on—that hold substantial power regardless of who occupies the formal seats in government, must feel that their basic interests are, at a minimum, not threatened and, preferably, somewhat advanced in the overall scheme of things.

In practical terms all this comes down to the following: During the initial period of roughly one to two years in power, the military is normally tolerated (read: given a chance). Thereafter it faces one of two basic alternatives: One, it can civilianize itself by various means, such as the Nasser, Ayub Khan, and Ataturk regimes did; or two, if it retains its military character, it must also create political institutions and movements outside the military organization in order to enlist the active support of large segments of the population and to create the abovementioned institutionalized processes of communication and, at least imagined, participation in public affairs.

If the junta is unwilling to do either, it is likely to experience consequences similar to that of the Abboud regime: a loss of touch with what the general population considers to be the overriding issues of the day and, consequently, a rapid decrease of popular support for its measures. The regime of General Nimeiri had reached a similar stage in early 1971, and appeared ripe to be overthrown, when in the curious and fascinating style of Sudanese affairs, it was saved by an initially successful yet clumsily conceived coup against itself.

NOTES

1. Mohammed Ahmed Mahgoub, Democracy on Trial: Reflections on Arab and African Politics (London: Andre Deutsch, Ltd., 1974), p. 175.

2. For example, Francis M. Deng, The Dynamics of Identification: A Basis for National Integration in the Sudan (Khartoum: Khartoum University Press, 1973); Ministry of Foreign Affairs, Peace and Unity in the Sudan (Khartoum: Khartoum University Press, 1973); Cecil Eprile, War and Peace in the Sudan 1955-1972 (London: David Charles, 1974); Dunstan Wai, ed., The Southern Sudan and the Problem of National Integration (London: Frank Cass, 1973); also Muddathir Abdel-Rahim, "Arabism, Africanism, and Self-Identification in the Sudan," Journal of Modern African Studies 8, no. 2 (July 1970): 233-49; Oluwadare Aguda, "Arabism and Pan-Arabism in Sudanese Politics," Journal of Modern African Studies 2, no. 2 (1973): 177-200; Sam Sarkesian, "The Southern Sudan: A Reassessment," African Studies Review 16, no. 1 (April, 1973): 1-22. Also, the special Summer 1973 issue of Africa Today, entitled "The Sudan: A New Era." Earlier useful works include those by Mohammed Omer Beshir, Oliver Albino, Beshir M. Said, Robert O. Collins, William Deng and Joseph Oduhu, Muddathir Abdel-Rahim, and K. Henderson.

3. For details, see Mohammed Omer Beshir, The Southern Sudan: From Conflict to Peace (London: Barnes & Noble, 1975), pp. 29-30.

4. Democratic Republic of the Sudan, Ministry of National Guidance, Cultural Section, Policy Statement on the Southern Question, June 6, 1969, p. 2.

5. Note the official government pamphlet, Food and the Sudan, which was distributed to the participants of the United Nations World Food Conference in Rome, November 5-16, 1974. One substantive change has been a shift away from the earlier total dependence on cotton and cotton byproducts as chief cash earners, and toward greater diversification in the large agricultural schemes. The hope

is that the reorientation will yield self-sufficiency in cereal grains and sugar by the mid-1970s.

6. Middle East Economic Digest March 28, 1975, and May 2, 1975.

7. Democratic Republic of Sudan, The National Planning Commission, Economic Survey 1973, p. 126.

8. I am indebted to Manfred Halpern for these distinctions, which he has developed in greater detail in a work on "The Dialectics of Modernization," mimeographed.

9. Ruth First, The Barrel of a Gun: Political Power in Africa and the Coup d'Etat (London: Penguin, 1971), pp. 230-31.

10

THE TESTS OF
GOVERNMENTAL PERFORMANCE:
SUDANESE FOREIGN POLICY

The influence of foreign affairs on Sudanese political behavior has already been described in general fashion in an introductory section of that same title in Part I. It focused on the historical interactions between Sudanese and their African neighbors as well as the major powers, and on the ways in which these interactions contributed to Sudanese perceptions of public issues. One major conclusion was that Sudan's relations with her black African neighbors, Egypt, Great Britain, the United States and the Soviet Union, were all characterized by a certain ambiguity, which reflected on one hand the mixture of advantages and disadvantages in each case, and on the other a definite reluctance by the Sudanese to align themselves. What remains now is to describe the process of foreign policy formulation and the dominant trends in the foreign policy performances of the two civilian and the two military regimes.

FOREIGN POLICY FORMULATION

There has been a clear tendency in most newly independent countries for foreign policy formulation to be confined to a small group of individuals, irrespective of the official status of their positions. In some cases the president or prime minister, in others the foreign minister and a few trusted aides from within or without the cabinet, participate in the decision-making process, while the official machinery of the Ministry of Foreign Affairs is essentially charged with implementing those decisions, and with supervising the conduct of cultural and diplomatic relations.

This general pattern has persisted in the Sudanese case as well. The substance of foreign policy has been much more determined by such individuals as Ismail el-Azhari, Mohammed Ahmed Mahjoub, Ahmed Kheir, Mansour Khalid and Ja'far Nimeiri (and during briefer periods by Gamal Mohammed Ahmed, ex-Umma president Sadiq el-Mahdi, ex-PDP president Ali Abdel-Rahman, and ex-prime minister Babikir Awadallah) than by combined efforts of diplomatic representatives and Foreign Ministry employees. The latters' function was mostly limited to such bureaucratic activities as staffing personnel decisions for, and expediting communications with, overseas posts, absorbing and classifying data from the field, and facilitating the activities of foreign diplomats in Khartoum. The important point here is that Foreign Ministry employees have almost never contributed inputs to the actual foreign policy formulation in the manner of position papers by desk officers or section chiefs in the U.S. Department of State, for example. This, despite the presence of some senior Sudanese diplomats in the ministry, who had acquired considerable insights into foreign affairs during earlier assignments abroad. As a result, the working routine within the ministry centered around prospecting for attractive overseas appointments to a much greater extent than one encounters normally in, say, Western foreign services. However, once abroad, most Sudanese diplomats tend to restrict their activities to performing the bureaucratic and ceremonial functions of their offices, and are generally not as visibly engaged in diplomatic enterprises as their Egyptian or Kenyan neighbors, for example. This tendency can be explained in part by the general reluctance among Sudanese abroad to mingling with foreigners, and in part by the limited delegation of authority as negotiators or policy initiators.

In terms of substantive policies, all Sudanese governments have supported the objectives of the League of Arab States and the Organization of African Unity, of which the Sudan has been an active member, and have committed themselves to positions of "positive neutrality" in the cold war struggle, to resistance against neocolonialism and Zionism, and support for African self-determination in territories ruled by white minorities. Beyond these general terms, specific relations with individual nations have oscillated between estrangement and rapprochement with all major partners, as will be shown in the following analysis of foreign policy performances by the various civilian and military regimes.

THE FIRST PARLIAMENTARY PERIOD

The first parliamentary period lends itself to an easy division into the two pre- and postindependence segments. The former extended from January 1954, when the initial Constituent Assembly began its sessions, until December 1955, when that body opted unanimously for independence. During those twenty-four months most public debates centered on the future status of the Sudan, which was to be determined by the assembly in accordance with the Anglo-Egyptian Agreement of 1953 regarding the so-called "transitional phase" (see Chapter 1). For that reason, foreign policy considerations focused understandably on the relations between the two condominium powers and their colony.

The reader may recall that the NUP won the November 1953 elections on a "unity of the Nile valley" platform. At the time this victory was interpreted (especially in foreign circles) as an indication of strong anti-British and pro-Egyptian sentiments, particularly among urban, educated Sudanese. Such conclusions were quite erroneous. The only evidence for anti-British sentiments could be construed from the formation of the Sudanization Committee in February 1954, which was established for the specific purpose of replacing British civil servants with Sudanese as rapidly and as thoroughly as possible. By April 1955 the committee's work was completed, among residues of some bitter feelings on the parts of British specialists, who had devoted major portions of their lives in, and had much affection for, the Sudan. However, when the Union Jack was lowered on January 1, 1956, the British withdrawal was chiefly in the administrative and military sectors, but her strong commercial ties in the country remained. For at least the next ten years, Great Britain continued for many Sudanese to be the main focus for economic, cultural, and recreational activities.

By contrast, relations with Egypt deteriorated rather considerably, and much more rapidly than anyone would have anticipated. Many Sudanese, especially among the old Ashiqqah, had become sympathetic in part because the new rulers rescinded the monarchy's claim on Sudanese territory and contributed significantly to the effectuation of the Anglo-Egyptian Agreement that included the option of self-determination, and in part because they could identify with the new Egyptian head of state, who was half-Sudanese. Yet the air of mutual benevolence was to change within a very short period. First of all, during the arrival of General Naguib in early March 1954 many ansar congregated in Khartoum in a huge demonstration against the Nile unity policy. The demonstration led to violent clashes in which several persons lost their lives; the March events did impress on the ruling party that too close an association with Egypt might well yield further riots and possibly even civil war.

The pro-Egyptian elements received an additional jolt when Naguib was forced from power by Gamal Abdel-Nasser; but a more significant development occurred during the Bandung Conference in 1955, where Nasser and el-Azhari failed to hit it off,[1] and the latter was treated rudely during a stopover in Cairo on his return trip. It is difficult to gauge the precise effects of these and other factors (for an interpretation of el-Azhari's motives, see Chapter 5), but in any case Prime Minister el-Azhari rose in the assembly in December 1955 to introduce the motion opting for Sudan's complete independence, thereby not only reversing his previous position from the 1953 election platform, but also sending waves of shock and anger through the Egyptian capital.

The aftereffects of these events continued to dominate relations in the postindependence period. For one thing, the Egyptian government naturally resented the NUP about-face, especially in view of their financial investments in the 1953 elections. For another, Egyptian and other foreign observers began to recognize gradually that much of the electoral support for the NUP had been less a reflection of pro-Cairo leanings than a vote against the British influence in general and against the pro-British, rural and sectarian Umma and Socialist Republican parties in particular. Thus, with the British on their way out, the Egyptians had lost much of their earlier attractiveness to the Sudanese nationalists.

The resultant disappointment and bad feelings in some quarters only grew with the accession of the staunchly anti-Egyptian and anti-Nasserite Abdallah Khalil to the premiership. The fact that the latter indicated private approval of British and U.S. actions during the tumultuous events of 1958 in Jordan and Lebanon clearly did not endear him to the violently anti-British regime in Cairo. Whether it was simple retaliation for these postures, or a calculated gamble to affect the 1958 elections is not clear, but the Egyptian government did decide on the eve of these elections to reclaim Sudanese territory north of the twenty-second parallel, and sent a military unit into the Halaib area for that purpose. The results could not have been more disastrous from Cairo's point of view. Sudanese of all political persuasions rose in unison to meet the Egyptian challenge, a military detachment was successfully dispatched to the endangered region, and the traditionally anti-Egyptian Umma party won a resounding election victory.

This sequence of events is symbolic for the general pattern of Egyptian-Sudanese relations, because the Sudanese have always been wary of Egyptian designs on their country, and few (if any) events can galvanize the diverse Sudanese factions as successfully as evidence or suspicion of Egyptian interference.

Another important and immediate task for the Sudanese government after independence was to plan for future economic stability and growth. Toward that end a series of development schemes—mostly agricultural, including some dam construction and extension of irrigation systems—were devised, which required external funding. The United States was approached as the first choice prospective source because of its presumed capacity to give aid, but also because Great Britain (along with Egypt) for psychological reasons could not very well be "re-invited" into the Sudan so soon after independence. Initial contacts with the United States were made in May 1957, and an agreement was concluded the following March for aid amounting to 5.6 million dollars.[2] It should be noted that this aid agreement set off stormy debates in parliament and nearly caused the downfall of the coalition regime. The main opposition came from pro-Egyptian nationalists and an assortment of leftists, who were to resurrect the specter of Yankee imperialism via aid missions on and off during the next dozen years.

THE ABBOUD PERIOD

Among the first acts of the military regime was the announcement on November 29 reconfirming the aid agreement with the United States. Although many mistakes were made during the next six years in the implementation of this agreement that contributed to the eventual unpopularity of the Abboud regime, the aid program also produced several significant short-term benefits. Not only did a considerable amount of money and technical assistance flow into the country, but the prospects of a hospitable climate for foreign investors, coupled with a broad and ambitious development plan, gave the Sudan a strong credit rating with international agencies for probably the only time in the twentieth century.[3] The World Bank and West Germany combined with the United States as chief contributors to the giant Roseires Dam project, West Germany and Italy were prominent donors of technical assistance, and these two countries joined the United Kingdom at the head of a growing list of West European trade partners.

But the Abboud regime was careful not to project too one-sided an image at this time of cold-war rivalries. One of its first public acts was to extend diplomatic recognition to the Peoples' Republic of China and to exchange missions, followed by a gradual opening up to other selected Communist nations. A prominent role among these was played by Yugoslavia following President Tito's official visit in 1959. In the eyes of many Sudanese observers Yugoslavia was particularly attractive because of her skillfully designed neutral position in the East-West struggle, and because her brand of moderate socialism offered an apparently viable model for the development of countries like the Sudan. Yugoslav aid for such items as ship building, port construction, and technical expertise in the fields of health care was probably better received than that from any other socialist bloc state, and a steady exchange of educational and cultural programs

contributed to a close association between the two countries. Other
significant East European trade partners were Bulgaria and Czecho-
slovakia from 1963 on, whereby the latter gained a great deal of popular goodwill for its "lending out" of locally famous soccer coaches.

The Soviet Union entered the picture after the credit agreement
of 1961, but did not become very visible until February 1963, when
Soviet engineers examined factory sites at Wau and Karima for the
purpose of establishing fruit-canning and date-processing factories.
It was an ironic—some would say, symbolic—aspect of the foreign aid
scene in 1963-64, that Soviet technicians in Karima inhabited the
empty dormitory rooms of a technical school that had been built under
U.S. AID auspices.

In inter-Arab affairs the Sudan continued to enjoy its good reputation as an objective and skillful mediator of disputes, an image that
had first been built up by Foreign Minister Mohammed Ahmed Mahjoub
under the previous coalition regime. His successor, Ahmed Kheir,
played an effective role in bringing together the warring factions in
the Yemen civil war at the Sudanese resort of Erkowit, and his good
offices helped to ameliorate the dispute between Algerians and Moroccans in 1962.

The all-important relations with Egypt were on an upswing in
November 1958, when that country was the first to extend diplomatic
recognition to the new junta. The Sudanese leaders reciprocated in an
aura of goodwill, undoubtedly springing from a sense of identification
with fellow military rulers as well as the anticipation that the frosty
relations of the previous regime would be reversed, in accordance
with the apparent logic of Sudanese revolutions. The upswing manifested itself in an expansion of trade relations and in the conclusion
of a new Nile Waters Agreement in November 1959, which produced
the most favorable allocation of water for the Sudan to date, plus financial compensation for the relocation of Nubians whose dwellings
were to be submerged by the rising waters of new Lake Nasser. Alas,
what initially appeared to be a major accomplishment for Sudan's new
rulers was eventually received with rather mixed emotions, in part
because Sudanese experts had favored a series of smaller dams
against Nasser's vision of a High Dam, and in part because the dis-
placement of Nubians exacted a higher political toll than the apparent
economic gains of the agreement (for details, see Chapter 6).

Relations between the two countries cooled noticeably after the
Egyptian government's swing in 1961 to socialist-progressivist policies at home and away from conservative Arab and Western states
in foreign affairs. This affected the Sudanese regime, for it insisted
on maintaining a neutral position in these matters and refused to be
drawn into ideological disputes on such issues as the Congo Crisis
and the Yemen Civil War, in which its neighbor to the North had

become deeply involved. The two governments became further es-
tranged when the Abboud regime insisted that Egypt should pay off its
outstanding debt to the Sudan, and the rulers in Cairo, not illogically,
described this idea as unfair pressure emanating from imperialist
influences over Sudan that were aimed at undermining the Egyptian
struggle for survival and justice. In short, by the end of the Abboud
period, relations with Egypt had returned to a level comparable to the
last days of the previous civilian government six years earlier.

The deterioration of relations with the northern neighbor was
paralleled somewhat in relations with African countries to the South,
East, and Southwest, but for entirely different reasons. The mutiny
of some southern troops in 1955 had developed into a full-scale rebellion in the three southern provinces during the early 1960s, and the
heavy-handed response by the government in Khartoum drove many
southerners into neighboring countries. As horror tales about alleged
atrocities at the hands of the military spread among tribesmen in the
three southern provinces, the flood of refugees into neighboring states
continued to swell until it had reached several hundred thousand. This
development not only created a heavy economic burden on such relatively poor countries as Uganda, the Central African Republic, Congo
Kinshasa (now Zaire) and Ethiopia, but also produced sympathies
there for the anya 'nya cause, and, simultaneously, dissonance with
the "Arab" rulers in Khartoum. What probably saved the situation
from further deterioration was the sensible policy of the Sudan government in refusing to aid secessionist elements from those African
neighbors. In this sense, a thinly-veiled system of deterrence-by-
mutual-hostages kept the peace, such as it was; but this was no foundation on which to build good neighborly relations.

THE SECOND PARLIAMENTARY PERIOD

Like the first, the second parliamentary period can also be substantively divided into segments, namely the transitional period from
October 1964 to April 1965, the next two years until June 1967, and
the final two years. For the first two segments it seems fair to argue
that Sudanese foreign policy was a direct outgrowth, and reflection,
of domestic political struggles, while the final period was much more
characterized by the turbulent aftereffects of the June 1967 war between Israel and her Arab neighbors.

Under the influence of the Front of Professional Associations
(see Chapter 7), the transitional government of Prime Minister Sirr
el-Khatim el-Khalifah followed the basic rule of thumb of reversing
whatever policies the Abboud regime had cherished. Consequently,

there were loud demands—figuratively and literally, as in public chants "Down, Down, USA"—to eliminate the American AID (Agency for International Development) program, which over time was effectively reduced from a giant operation, whose administrative apparatus alone occupied one of the few tall buildings in Khartoum, to a smaller (and incidentally, much more effective) size. The technical assistance programs of West Germany were similarly curtailed, while others from Eastern European states were openly encouraged. As had been the case during General Abboud's inaugural address on November 17, 1958, the first official statement of the post-October regime pledged itself to a strong improvement of ties with "sisterly" Egypt; and indeed, for a short time Egyptian influence in the country was on the rise.

But perhaps the most dramatic reversal of foreign policy occurred with regard to two neighboring African states, when Prime Minister Sirr el-Khatim openly supported the Simba Revolution (Congolese Liberation Front under Christoph Gbenye) in the Congo and, somewhat more covertly, the Eritrean Liberation Front against Haile Selassie. Both groups were granted havens of refuge within the Sudan from where they could organize their activities, and the Sudan government permitted the transshipment of weapons (officially disguised as "medical supplies") to both groups from abroad. Not surprisingly, such actions disturbed the Ethiopian and Congolese governments greatly, who lost no time in a) protesting and b) retaliating by aiding southern rebel leaders in their respective capitals. One of the more grotesque consequences of the crazy-quilt pattern of country A/secessionist B alliances occurred in Equatoria Province, where anya 'nya rebels intercepted Chinese-made rifles on the way from Algeria via Khartoum to presumed CLF strongholds in Congo's northeastern Oriental Province, and proceeded to use them against Sudan government troops, while bands of Simbas raided southern Sudanese villages for food, women, and meyrissa beer.

The concrete effects of such unpredictable foreign policy adventures, combined with domestic instability, were a sharp drop of cotton purchases by Western consumer nations, and an understable reluctance to invest and/or commit themselves to aid programs. Because alternate sources for assistance were either unwilling or indecisive about moving into the newly created openings, a period of economic recession ensued as well as a noticeable decline in the overall volume of foreign trade.

After the April 1965 elections a more conservative coalition government came to power, but the reader may recall that the next four years were characterized by persistent factionalist intrigues (see Chapter 7). These inter- and intraparty machinations so preoccupied politicians in Khartoum that very little energy was left for formulating coherent economic, social, or foreign policies. As a result one could observe the opposition party PDP president Ali Abdel-Rahman intensifying personal ties with socialist leaders like Nasser, Ben Bella, and Castro, while the Umma chief Sadiq el-Mahdi maintained closer relations with Britain and the United States. (The NUPs, as junior partners in the government, remained in the background on this issue.)

With no clear policy forthcoming from Khartoum, some local festering sores came out in the open along border territories with Ethiopia and Chad. The latter became particularly serious in 1965 and 1966 when rebels and brigands from western Sudanese tribes decided to aid some of their consanguineous brethren in Chad, whom they perceived to be discriminated against. There have been reports that raids took place from sanctuaries within the Sudan with the apparent compliance of at least local Sudanese officials, and that Chadian forces made reprisal attacks on villages inside Sudan, during which approximately 300 Sudanese were killed.[4] Eventually the Khartoum government agreed to expel Chadian antiregime subversives, but tensions did not subside until 1968 following the mediation efforts of Niger's President Diori.

Foreign relations with extraregional nations were determined by Sudan's need for economic aid and favorable trade outlets for cotton. Thus, the Peoples Republic of China became the major purchaser of the 1964-65 cotton crop, replacing in essence West Germany and Great Britain (with whom diplomatic relations were severed over British policies toward Ian Smith's regime in Rhodesia). Trade and cultural agreements with East European countries increased substantially, but remained behind the volume of consumer goods imported from Western Europe. The two major Asian trading partners throughout the 1960s had become India and Japan, who had the advantage that their relations were totally unencumbered by political or ideological considerations.

As regards the traditionally important arenas of inter-Arab and East-West affairs, the Sudan government in the mid-1960s seemed to follow a line of strict neutrality, noninvolvement, lack of interest, or neglect, depending on one's point of view. The only marginally noteworthy development occurred with the increased commercial interaction with the Soviet Union in accordance with the 1965-67 Trade Protocol.[5]

All of this changed rather radically in June 1967, when the Sudan government responded to Egypt's plight by sending troops and other domestic resources to the Suez front, identified itself publicly with the Arab cause, and in July arranged for an Arab summit conference to be held in Khartoum. Trade agreements with Egypt increased, and in 1968 Sudan joined the Arab Common Market.[6]

In retrospect it seems fair to state that this sudden upsurge of
involvement in Arab affairs—quite unlike the response during the Suez
Crisis in 1956, for example—did not signify a dramatic change of
heart, but rather a quantitative and qualitative increase of politicization in the spirit of the October Revolution. Also, the regime's and the
masses' dramatic identification with the Arab cause helped to detract
ruler and the proverbial man on the street alike from the political and
economic woes of a dreary period by allowing their idealistic fervor
to identify with an "obviously just" struggle in which the lines were
clearly drawn, unlike the mess at home.

This sort of perception must have eased the decisions to break
diplomatic relations with the United States, West Germany, Romania,
and Great Britain (which had just been restored a few months earlier).
Although the Sudanese desired to separate the issue of political from
economic and cultural relations, the United States reacted by discontinuing its technical assistance program, and even moved to withdraw
AID-sponsored teachers from Sudanese classrooms only weeks before
the academic year ended. The situation was clearly tense. This atmosphere provided a welcome opportunity for enlarging political,
economic, and military ties with socialist bloc countries. Especially
in the latter category a complete change took place, when the Sudanese
armed forces, which had been equipped primarily with American,
British, and West German material, were now reequipped with Soviet
weapons, after the military aid programs with these three nations
were terminated in 1967.

THE REGIME OF JA'FAR NIMEIRI

Once again, the evolution of political events calls for a division
of this most current period into two segments, namely the years prior
to and after the July 1971 putsch. One dominant theme of Chapter 8
has been that the domestic political alliances and ideological postures
of the Nimeiri regime changed dramatically after that putsch; the
same can be said for the basic foreign policy orientations.

At the outset the new military rulers reaffirmed their desire to
retain and enlarge upon existing commercial and military aid ties
with progressive socialist countries, meaning Eastern Europe; and
by 1970 an estimated 2,000 Soviet and East European technical advisors were in the Sudan.[7] Such important areas as military assistance and economic planning were mostly provided by Soviet
specialists, while internal security affairs was now partly in East
German hands. This was accompanied by a remarkable increase in
trade with these countries, with the effect that Soviet bloc nations had

become purchasers of about one-fourth of the country's exports and supplied about 18 percent of all imports.[8]

Concomitant with these developments was the further deterioration of political and trade relations with the West. The Nimeiri regime lost no time in identifying itself with progressive Arab and African states and took public stances against "Western imperialism and Zionist intrigues." In fact, the volume and intensity of anti-Western and anti-Israeli statements has been unequalled in any other period of Sudanese history. The chief explanation for this posture can be found in the composition of the RCC and the cabinet, as already described in an earlier chapter; other reasons were the arousal of popular feelings throughout the Arab world after the June 1967 war, and the fact that there was concrete evidence of Israeli aid to anya 'nya rebels (apparently from military bases in Ethiopia and Uganda, which were receiving Israeli military assistance and technicians at that time, and also in air drops to rebels inside Sudan[9]). An additional factor was the program of nationalizing foreign banks and commercial enterprises in 1970 that negatively affected the relations with Great Britain.

The continuing rebellion in the southern Sudan, complicated by the Khartoum government's hard line tactics during much of 1970, was chiefly responsible for extending the already sour relations with African neighbors. This was especially true for Uganda, Zaire, and Ethiopia, who sheltered the largest contingents of refugees and who were all accused of intervention by means of aiding Sudanese insurgents.

By contrast, relations with the Arab neighbors in Egypt and Libya were unusually excellent during these two years. One reason has been the close identification among the three respective rulers, all fellow military officers of similar social background, and all committed to apparently identical brands of Arab socialism, who recognized each other as the first set of politically compatible rulers ever in the Northeastern corner of Africa after the overthrows of conservative regimes in Khartoum (May) and Tripoli (September) of 1969. Their newly-found sense of community was soon translated into concrete action during and after the Arab summit meetings in Rabat (December), and resulted in the signing of the Tripoli Charter on December 27, 1969, by Presidents Nasser, Nimeiri, and Qaddafi. The original purpose of the charter was to commit the three leaders to "cooperation and coordination" of their respective foreign policies, but in the end led to the formation of the Federation of Arab Republics (FAR). Although the Sudan never did join the FAR—the official announcement after the April 13, 1971, meeting in Cairo of the various heads of state spoke of a "postponement until circumstances in the Sudan permitted her to join"—she has participated in various technical consultations and ministerial arrangements within the framework of the charter,[10] and the government permitted the relocation of Egyptian army cadets to Jebel Awliyah on the White Nile during the "war of attrition" and made other military facilities available to her northern neighbor.

Chapter 8 already contains a discussion of the complexity of domestic issues that deterred the Nimeiri government from membership in the FAR, and that also led up to the abortive coup d'etat in July 1971. The outcome of these tumultuous days was that Ja'far Nimeiri was initially indebted to his Libyan and Egyptian colleagues. But he soon recognized the need to reorder his priorities from a Sudanese rather than Arab perspective, with the chief emphasis going to the rebuilding of domestic support bases and resolution of the conflict in the southern provinces. On the one hand, this brought about a slow but steady estrangement from the Libyan regime, which has been enthusiastically committed to Arab unitary movements. On the other hand, a marked strain in ties with Egypt ensued, after Nimeiri's crackdown on Communists placed Egypt's President Sadat in a temporarily embarrassing position vis-a-vis his Soviet patrons during his self-proclaimed "year of decision" in 1971, and after Nimeiri's further swing to the right led to the ouster of pro-Egyptian elements in the RCC and to resumption of diplomatic relations with the United States over Egypt's strong protests in 1972. Bad feelings between these two sisterly countries mounted through much of 1972, and finally exploded in the open, when President Nimeiri publicly attacked President Sadat for sparking bitterness between their countries in an interview with one of the Arab world's leading newspapers,[11] and affirmed publicly for the first time that Sudan would not join the FAR. Manifestations of that bitterness came in mid-September when the Sudanese branches of two Egyptian firms were liquidated, and in the final days of that month when mutual recriminations were publicly aired, including during anti-Egyptian demonstrations in Khartoum on September 28. Ten days later Egypt demanded that Sudan evacuate all her troops from the Suez front, and the following week withdrew Egyptian cadets from the Jebel Awliyyah camp.

Meanwhile, Mu'ammar al-Qaddafi's disappointments over rejections from Egypt, Algeria, and Tunisia in his various unification schemes seemed to have been taken out on the Sudanese leadership, which was remembered as the first to defect. Relations had been cool but correct for much of 1972 and 1973, but deteriorated rapidly in 1974 when Ja'far Nimeiri identified Libya as the one remaining haven of refuge for antiregime plotters. There were rumors and allegations about Libyan financing for anti-Nimeiri conspiracies; the conflict was finally aired during a radio address on June 10, during which the Sudanese president revealed the Libyan request for returning an earlier

loan of "seven million" that according to Nimeiri had been given
during happier days "from one fraternal revolution to another as a
loan which needn't be repaid."* Information Minister Omar el-Hajj
Musa termed this request a "national insult"[13] and announced the
formation of a new Committee for the Defense of Sudan's Dignity, designed to find ways for publicly collecting funds to repay the debt. The
president himself inveighed that "as we all know, we do not accept
charity nor do we accept superiority; we do not agree that bread should
deprive us of dignity, even if we have to starve to death,"[14] and disclosed that he had just received a check for one million dollars as a
contribution from "brotherly" King Hassan of Morocco, incidentally,
not one of Qaddafi's great admirers. This episode may have certain
comic overtones for some observers, but will undoubtedly be long
remembered by the Sudanese people, whose regard for dignity and
self-respect is second to none.

As the formerly close ties with Egypt and Libya began to fade,
other Arab states on the Arabian peninsula came more and more into
play. There had always been good relations with Kuwait, which had
awarded the first loan under the Kuwaiti Fund for Arab Development
to the Sudan, and with whom good trade ties continued. Comparable
relations developed with the rulers of the Lower Gulf sheikhdoms,
who were encouraged to invest huge sums in Sudan's considerable
agricultural potential and other development projects.† It should be
noted that President Nimeiri was the first Arab head of state to pay
an official visit to Lower Gulf states after the formation of the Union

---

*Actually on November 27, 1969, President Nimeiri reported that
Sudan had received a Libyan loan of 7.25 million Sudanese pounds at
2 percent interest.[12]

†In late 1972 the UAE presented Sudan with $1 million for reset-
tlement of Southern refugees, and $26 million in aid for the first stage
of the Port Sudan-Khartoum road. In January 1975 Qatar followed suit
with a similar $1 million gift for rehabilitation in the South. On June
27, 1975 Abu Dhabi extended a $20 million loan under its new develop-
ment fund, only weeks after the parallel Kuwaiti institution (KFAED)
had approved a loan of 12.7 million dinars, mostly for agricultural development. The KFAED had also pledged $50 million in March 1975
for the giant Rahad scheme, together with $9 million from the new
Kuwaiti-based Arab Fund for Economic and Social Development (and
$62 million from the World Bank). It should be noted that the Arab
Fund in its very first project had allocated $6,300 million toward a
scheme to establish in Sudan the future "breadbasket for the Arab
World" (MEED, August 23, 1975, p. 13). In addition, the AFESD
granted $16.8 million in January 1975 for telecommunications projects
in the Sudan.[15]

of Arab Emirates. Similarly, the formerly cool relations (after 1969) with Saudi Arabia began to warm considerably after the departure of leftist elements from the Sudan government. During a January 1974 address President Nimeiri spoke in the most glowing terms of the "wisdom and leadership of his elder brother King Faisal" who, coincidentally, had agreed to a 200 million dollar grant from Saudi Arabia for carrying out development projects in the Sudan.[16] In this connection it should be noted that a sizable reservoir of goodwill has generally existed on the peninsula for Sudanese, who have been valued there as highly qualified, well-educated, and honest civil servants and teachers.

Not surprisingly, the most complete reversal of relations after the 1971 putsch occurred with the major East-West powers. As already described in Chapter 8, the Soviet Union, East Germany, and Bulgaria were all accused of complicity in the abortive scheme, and President Nimeiri at one point threatened, but did not execute, a diplomatic break with the USSR. The Khartoum regime resented the relentless Soviet press attacks and "sanctioned" demonstrations against its Moscow embassy following the summary executions of CPS leaders, also the ensuing deterioration in trade terms and temporary unavailability of spare parts for military equipment. On August 11, 1971, a Sudan government spokesman complained that the USSR had sold Sudanese cotton at cutrate prices in markets that traditionally have bought from the Sudan.[17]

It is significant that relations with the People's Republic of China (PRC) were unaffected by the July events, in the sense that the PRC considered these to be an internal matter. This attitude gratified the foreign policy leadership, as indicated by repeated statements from Mansour Khalid, and encouraged it to intensify cultural and trade relations, especially after President Nimeiri's state visit to Peking in August 1971. The immediate payoff came in a series of trade, economic, and technical assistance and scientific and cultural cooperation agreements on an almost monthly basis through the remainder of 1971, in which the PRC had extended loans worth well over 100 million dollars in total. Incidentally, the former good relations with Yugoslavia were similarly unaffected by the July 1971 events, and the earlier severed diplomatic relations with Romania were resumed in December 1971.

In accordance with the pendulum concept of East-West relations, the Khartoum regime followed up on the estrangement with socialist nations by rapprochement with Western states, and resumed official ties with the United Kingdom (soon after the 1967 Arab-Israeli war), West Germany (December 23, 1971), and finally the United States in July 1972. In the former case the problem of compensating nationalized British firms was finally resolved to mutual satisfaction.

Meanwhile, West Germany had been periodically accused of aiding southern rebels because of the activities of the German Catholic relief agency CARITAS in the southern provinces, but this rather unfounded misunderstanding was removed, and West German aid was sought again for help in resettling Southern refugees.

Regarding the United States, the Nimeiri regime had undoubtedly hoped to combine the resumption of diplomatic ties with a substantial AID commitment, but this has remained little more than wishful thinking. The United States has funneled some contributions through the World Bank (especially for the Rahad Scheme) and through the office of the U.N. High Commissioner for Refugees, but aid has been small by former standards, and has been concentrated on southern relief, public health, and projects designed to increase basic agricultural production. Most unfortunately, the growing aura of goodwill was savagely disturbed by the assassination of two senior U.S. diplomats in Khartoum in March 1973 at the hands of Palestinian extremists, and by the eventual release of the eight defendants from Sudanese courts to PLO control in late June 1974.[*]

Relations with other West European countries were normal; even though Sudan would have desired stronger commercial ties, the opportunities were limited by the shortage of foreign exchange and the bleak prospects of the economy. Nevertheless, the government tried to involve as many neutral and friendly nations as possible in the development of the South, and achieved some success in obtaining commitments from Scandinavian countries.

It is, of course, always possible to argue about the merits of various policies; but few reasonable persons would dispute that the settlement of the North-South conflict has been a remarkable achievement by the regime of President Nimeiri. Not only had this conflict constituted a political powder keg and a drain on economic and military resources, but it also had been chiefly responsible for tensions with neighboring states. Particularly troubled areas had been Uganda, Kenya, and Ethiopia, whose governments had all been more or less sympathetic to the Southern cause. But once Ja'far Nimeiri had decided to reorder his priorities to bring about political stability and national unity first of all, this particular Gordian knot had apparently been cut. During mid-1971 the new rulers of Uganda returned the captured anya'nya mercenary Rolf Steiner to Sudanese authorities, and both governments made mutual declarations of noninvolvement in

---

[*]The Sudanese courts had sentenced the eight Palestinians to life imprisonment, but on June 24, 1974 President Nimeiri decided to commute the verdict to seven years each, and to hand them over to the PLO office in Cairo for carrying out the sentences.

each other's affairs. By the turn of the year diplomatic relations could be restored, and the borders were reopened on May 11, 1972, after having been closed since May 1969.[18] The same principle of mutual noninvolvement was applied to the Chad frontier and was subsequently strengthened by state visits of the two respective presidents.

The identical formula of state visits and nonsupport for each other's rebels bore fruits in a marked improvement in late 1971 of relations with Ethiopia, which had been strained for a long time despite recurrent diplomatic efforts by the respective heads of state. First, a boundary commission was set up to resolve a long standing border dispute. Almost immediately thereafter, the emperor used his good offices for the successful negotiations leading up to the Addis Ababa Agreement, which halted the Sudanese Civil War in March 1972. And it has been remarked that "without the help of Ethiopia in preparing for the difficult negotiations and the emperor's direct intervention when the talks appeared to be failing, peace in the South would have been difficult to achieve."[19] This was certainly no small accomplishment, and it seems appropriate that all due credit should be given to those who contributed so well. This same spirit of conciliation was to continue even after the overthrow of the monarchy in Ethiopia. The Khartoum government had an opportunity to return the earlier favor by becoming actively involved in mediation efforts between warring Eritrean and federal Ethiopian groups as early as February 1975, and at least for another half year thereafter.

Finally, when rising petroleum prices after the decisions of the Organization of Petroleum Exporting Countries (OPEC) in 1974 threatened to affect the anti-Israeli postures of poor African nations, the Sudanese government worked hard to maintain its "good African" reputation by forfeiting its 2-million-dollar share in price adjustment money from OPEC in favor of an OAU committee[20] that had been specifically set up to work on this problem.

But like a juggler on stage, dashing among several simultaneously rotating plates, the Khartoum rulers hastened to repair deteriorating relations with those Arab states that might have felt neglected or offended by the greater attention paid recently to the African continent and the Arabian peninsula. In early June 1973 both Khartoum and Cairo announced that relations had been "patched up," that the previous "summer clouds" had vanished, and that Sudanese troops would return to the Suez front. On February 12, 1974, a new Sudanese-Egyptian agreement was proclaimed, aiming at greater "political, economic, and cultural integration," and setting up appropriate committees for that purpose.[21] Even the sour relations with Libya had improved noticeably after President Qaddafi dispatched a series of emissaries to Khartoum in late 1974 on goodwill missions, and finally climaxed this new phase by making an unexpected personal visit to the Sudanese capital himself.

CONCLUSIONS

It remains now to consider what sorts of conclusions can be drawn on the basis of the records of the various Sudanese rulers in their conduct of foreign policy.

On the surface it appears that we can group together three sets of periods in terms of the foreign policy postures of their regimes. The first parliamentary and the Abboud military governments leaned somewhat toward the West, while the transitional period following the October 1964 Revolution and the first two years under President Nimeiri were characterized by a comparable tilt toward the Socialist bloc. The parliamentary regime of the mid-1960s and the post-1971 years of the Nimeiri junta exhibited the relatively most balanced posture vis-a-vis the major powers, albeit with the difference that the former administration arrived at that result much more by inactivity and the latter more by design. We should hasten to clarify that these three postures differ not fundamentally but in nuances, all of which reconfirms the earlier impression that Sudan's foreign policy has operated within a rather tightly defined parameter. Those variations that have emerged have been overwhelmingly a function of internal political events rather than external stimuli—quite unlike Egypt, for example.

A second possible criterion for comparison involves judgments about performance, that is to say, an evaluation of the effectiveness of the various regimes in managing the persistent issues of relations with neighbors and overseas political powers and trading partners. Such judgments are inherently difficult, first because they are inevitably subjective, and second because changing international conditions may require different responses and offer different opportunities. In this sense it seems unfair to criticize the first parliamentary regime, which was understandably preoccupied with the task of achieving independence and getting the country on its feet. The latter point was also invoked by all rulers after the 1958, 1964, and 1969 revolutions, but with much less justification. The record, as described in this chapter, reveals a rather poor performance in the middle 1960s, as contrasted by the quite imaginative foreign policy of the Abboud junta, which not only managed to establish good ties with East and West that soon yielded economic rewards, but also to avoid involvement in Arab or African problems that could only have hurt the Sudan's image.

Of course it is impossible to pass a final judgment about the current regime, yet one cannot help noting that its post-1971 policies seem to have been more successful than the earlier ones, not because of any antipathy toward Socialist bloc states per se, but because a policy of pragmatism has always suited Sudan's national interests better than ideological fixations.* Such pragmatism has enabled the Nimeiri government to receive some military aid and economic assistance from East and West, to increase trade with such diverse partners as India, China, Italy, and Scandinavia, and to develop equally good relations with Arab and African countries, thereby achieving the natural role of a bridging element for this, the largest country in both Africa and the Arab world.

NOTES

1. Henderson, Sudan Republic (New York: Frederick A. Praeger, 1965), p. 105.
2. Ibid., p. 117.
3. For details see Ruth First, The Barrel of a Gun: Political Power in Africa and the Coup d'Etat (London: Penguin, 1971), p. 250.
4. Area Handbook for the Democratic Republic of the Sudan (Washington, D.C.: Government Printing Office, 1973), p. 200.
5. Ibid., p. 204.
6. Ibid., p. 198.
7. Ibid., p. 204.
8. Ibid., p. 204.
9. Jerusalem Post Weekly, April 6, 1971.
10. For an extensive chronology of events see this author's "New Attempts at Arab Cooperation: The Federation of Arab Republics, 1971-?" Middle East Journal 27, no. 2 (Spring 1973): 154-58.
11. Al-Nahar of Beirut, reported by the Washington Post correspondent in that newspaper on October 25, 1972.
12. Arab Report and Record, 1969, p. 494.
13. Washington Post, June 6, 1974 (Khartoum dateline).
14. Foreign Broadcast Information Service, June 12, 1974.
15. Arab Report and Record, 1975, pp. 86, 173, 370 and African Diary 14 (1974): 7310.
16. Foreign Broadcast Information Service, January 26, 1974. This "grant" later turned out to be a Saudi bank guarantee. However, on June 24, 1975 an agreement was signed with the new Saudi rulers

---

*Some may object that pragmatism constitutes an ideology in itself; however, this denotation is not very useful for making distinctions. The point here is that a pragmatic policy permits greater flexibility than one tying a country to either a socialist alliance or anti-Communist camp.

on a $39 million loan for the Rahad project (Arab Report and Record, 1975, p. 370).

17. Arab Report and Record, 1971, p. 417.

18. Area Handbook, op. cit., p. 199, and Arab Report and Record, 1972, p. 238.

19. Area Handbook, op. cit., p. 201.

20. As announced by Foreign Minister Mansour Khalid and quoted on Radio Omdurman, August 17, 1974.

21. Arab Report and Record, 1974, p. 52. Since that time high-level Sudanese-Egyptian meetings have taken place periodically, and agreements about such joint ventures as improved river and road transportation links have been announced. The at least temporary "high" of relations has in a way been symbolized by the reappointment of the old (pro-Egyptian) RCC stalwarts Khalid Hassan Abbas and Ma'moun Awad Abu Zayd to important positions in the SSU Politbureau and additional functions as presidential advisors (Arab Report and Record, 1975, pp. 422-23).

APPENDIX: ELECTIONS IN
THE NATIVE CAPITAL—
THE CASE OF OMDURMAN SOUTH

In several previous chapters parliamentary elections on a nationwide basis were reported and analyzed in the larger context of democratic politics. By contrast, this chapter is devoted to a microstudy of the electoral process in 1965 in one selected constituency (no. 31) in the native capital of Omdurman.

The primary objective for its inclusion here is to enable the reader to receive insight into some details of Sudanese elections, such as the respective campaign tactics of candidates, the kinds of issues that concerned a local electorate, the popular response as indicated by the degree of voting participation, and an interpretation of voting results in the light of local issues and candidates—all this in a constituency where the outcome of elections had aroused great interest among Sudanese and foreign observers for a variety of reasons that will be discussed below. A further objective of this study was to investigate some relationships that could not be examined fruitfully on the nationwide level, such as the effects of sex, residence, occupation, income level, and, within limits, religious affiliation, on voting behavior in an urban area. This particular constituency lends itself well to an analysis of these variables through comparisons of voting results from various precincts in Omdurman South. Of course it is not the case that all wealthy Omdurmanis live in one area and all poor ones in another. Nevertheless, the distinctions between local quarters are sufficiently marked to enable the careful researcher to make generalizations about the socioeconomic status of their inhabitants.

The data for this chapter derive from two sources: a) research about the nine precincts that comprise the Omdurman South constituency, and b) counting and identification of every ballot cast in both elections. The latter was done by at first recording the marks on every ballot, then locating the polling station at which the ballot was cast, then determining the area that the polling station served, and finally identifying the delimitations of the nine districts. (This procedure might be relatively simple in some countries, but it consumed almost three weeks of concentrated work in the capital.)

We are very fortunate to be able to test the reliability of our results by comparing the outcome of the regular April elections with that of by-elections in the following November. The by-elections became necessary after the victorious candidate in the first election had to vacate his seat in the Constituent Assembly following his appointment as permanent head of the Supreme Council of State. This situation affords a unique opportunity for observing a repeated process under virtually constant conditions.

It should be emphasized that Omdurman South did not represent an average constituency in the Sudan, and any generalizations drawn from this case study do not necessarily apply to other parts of the country.

Constituency no. 31 was one of three that were reserved for what might be called, "Greater Omdurman". In contrast to the two others that included settlements outside of Omdurman proper, no. 31 was strictly urban. Its territory included most of the prominent features of Omdurman, such as the Khalifa's Square, the Mahdi's Tomb, the Town Council, the Graduates' Club, and the main mosque; in addition, the headquarters of the Umma party and the NUP, as well as the residences of almost all party leaders were located within its boundaries. If one were to rank constituencies by the prestige of their respective areas, Omdurman South would definitely lead the list in the Sudan.

No. 31 is bordered by the Nile in the East, by no. 33 in the North, by no. 32 and open dessert in the West, and by the southern edge of the Military Area in the South. For election purposes it was divided into nine precincts, of which eight form distinct geographic units. The ninth one, no. 7, was reserved for voters from the three western precincts, no. 4, no. 5, and no. 6, respectively, who registered late because of some administrative errors on the part of the original chief registration officer of the constituency (he was later replaced). A few words about the characteristics of the other eight are in order.

No. 1 is Beit el-Mal, one of the oldest sections of Omdurman. Its inhabitants are almost exclusively followers of the khatmiyyah sect; many are laborers and low-rank civil servants, although a few upper-income homes are sprinkled throughout the districts. No. 2 is Mulazimin, another old sector of Omdurman where the Khalifah Abdullahi had quartered his bodyguard. Today it is inhabited almost exclusively by middle and upper-level civil servants, including those retired who live in well-built government homes. This area gives the appearance of being by far the most affluent; many residents own automobiles and telephones and probably have the highest income average in the constituency. Mulazimin has always been a stronghold of the NUP. No. 3 is the so-called Hospital sector,* in which many

---

*In Arabic fariq al-ispitaliyyah.

official buildings are located but relatively few people live. Many of
these are well-to-do and own shops in or near the main suq (marketplace) that borders this precinct. For reasons unclear to this writer,
the three western precincts, no. 4, no. 5, and no. 6 all bear the same
designation, "Abu Kaduk plus Al-Abasiyyah plus Abu Anjah plus Hayy
al-Dubat," although they form distinct administrative units. No. 4
is the sector of Abu Kaduk that lies south of the Khor Abu Anjah and
is inhabited by relatively poor people, many of whom have moved
there from the western regions of the Sudan. No. 5 is situated just
north of the Khor and south of no. 6, the dividing line being Shari'
el-Funjur. These two were separated for technical reasons and in
accordance with local administrative subdivisions.* The residents
in the northern area are probably somewhat better off financially
and, perhaps, somewhat more fervent ansar than those living near
the Khor, but differences between the two precincts are only slight.
(No. 6 is part of the larger section called Abbasiyyah, most of which
is located in the adjoining constituency, and which is the stronghold
of the Umma party in Omdurman.) By contrast no. 8 forms a very
distinct section of Omdurman. It is called Muradah, and is inhabited
by two groups of people: Egyptians and their descendants who have
come to the Sudan in the early days of the condominium, and descendants of southerners who have settled in the North and have become
Muslims. Muradah is, perhaps, the most distinct of all precincts:
it has its own schools, own market, mosque, football stadium, and
so on. The residents of Muradah form one of the tightest communities in the capital, to which access for outsiders is very difficult if
not impossible. (This pattern persists in the famous Muradah soccer
club where, it is rumored, only players of a certain skin color have
a chance to make the first team.) No. 9 is physically the largest of
all precincts and includes Banat and the Military Area. The former
is inhabited mostly by poor people who live in fourth class housing
on the southern edge of Omdurman. The latter is a large military
installation near the White Nile; all military personnel and dependents who lived on base were assigned to vote in precinct no. 9.

   As we can see, at least seven of the nine precincts were populated by distinct groups of Sudanese who could be differentiated
either by religious affiliations or by income levels. To be sure, the
residents of Omdurman come from a great variety of backgrounds
and their financial standing spans the spectrum from very wealthy
to very poor. Nevertheless, Omdurmanis of similar socioeconomic

---

   *All of Omdurman is subdivided into units of rub' and harah
(both mean quarter or sector of a town) for purposes of local administration.

status tend to group together in compact residential sectors that can
be differentiated from one another very easily, much more so than
those in comparable large western cities.

THE APRIL ELECTIONS

Contestants and Issues

After the final date for withdrawing nominations for the April
elections, six candidates remained in the field to compete for the
Assembly seat. In the present analysis we shall be concerned only
with the four most successful ones; the others played very minor
roles in the elections and each obtained less than one percent of the
total votes cast. It may be interesting to note that one of these, Bedawi
Mustafa, was a PDP cabinet member who was prepared to challenge
Ismail el-Azhari in the NUP's home constituency rather than to select a safe electoral district. While this practice may be considered
odd by Western standards, it is even more astonishing that the sixth
candidate, Mahmoud Abbas Rahmtallah, was a member of el-Azhari's
own NUP, a matter that vividly underscores the absence of discipline
within that party. Nevertheless, it is still surprising that Mahmoud
received as many votes as he did: 91. On the other hand the electoral
"failure" of Bedawi Mustafa may be attributed to the PDP's decision
to boycott elections, a fact that apparently was either unknown to or
was objected to by 121 voters.

The four most successful candidates were the official nominees
of the NUP, Umma, the ICF, and the Communist party. By far the
most prominent of these was Ismail el-Azhari, the president of the
NUP since its founding, the acknowledged leader of the independence
movement in the late 1940s and early 1950s, and the first prime
minister of the Sudan. Along with most Sudanese observers, he considered Omdurman South to be his own constituency, not only because
he lived there (an important factor in Sudanese politics), but also because he had won handily there twice before. He considered election
victory to be automatic and spent rather little time campaigning in
the constituency[1] while concentrating his efforts on organizing the
election activities of his party throughout the northern provinces.
I cannot impress too strongly that anything but a sizable Azhari
victory at the polls was totally unthinkable for the vast majority of
those who constituted Sudanese public opinion.

The only people who took exception to this assumption were
the Communists. They nominated their most attractive talent,

Secretary-General Abdel-Khaliq Mahjoub, who likewise lived in the
constituency and was an intelligent and spellbinding orator. He welcomed the challenge of competing against the NUP leader because he
felt that he had nothing to lose. An electoral defeat could be ration-
alized as entirely expectable, whereas a respectable showing at the
polls, or especially a victory, would produce a greater propaganda
effect for communism in the Sudan than the winning of several rural
constituencies combined. Toward that end he campaigned hard in a
series of "political nights" (rallies), while his supporters mounted a
thorough registration drive, especially among women residents, who
were instructed in voting procedures by a cadre of female university
students.

The Umma party did not expect to emerge victorious in this
constituency. Consequently its president, Sayyed el-Sadiq el-Mahdi,
made no special efforts to support the Umma candidate, Abbas Da'
afallah Hamad el-Nil. Abbas was a pleasant and kind retired civil
servant, whose most notable asset was that he belonged to a prominent family in Omdurman. He seemed to have no illusions about
the prospects for victory[2] and limited his campaign activities accordingly to one political night during which he distributed mimeographed sheets containing his views and policies.

Apparently even less hopeful was the candidate of the ICF,
Mohammed el-Amin el-Sherif Barakat, who did not even bother to
stage political rallies or to send representatives to the vote count.
The objective of his party was most likely to determine at minimum
expense the approximate following that its movement could generate
in constituency no. 31.

The local issues confronting the voters of Omdurman South did
not involve the conventional claims of rival candidates to provide new
schools and hospitals, better roads, and so on. Such talk would not
have fired the voters' imagination, because the need for an increase
in the above services was not considered to be essential in Omdurman.
The real issues concerned personal and ideological commitments.
That is to say, voters who were strongly attached to any of the four
parties would cast their votes on that basis. There is nothing unusual
in that. What complicated matters somewhat in Omdurman South was
the split that many individuals must have experienced between their
ideological and their personal loyalties. The latter developed because
all candidates were local men, who lived practically all their lives
in Omdurman and whose personal relationships were bound to be both
numerous and far-reaching. During elections voters generally tended
to identify with the candidate's social background, such as his family,
if influential, his tribal affiliation, his religious orientation, and sometimes his residence. The latter form of identification resulted primarily from social activities. For example, a man who happened to

live near el-Azhari was likely to engage in frequent social visits with
his neighbor, thereby cultivating a relationship which made him automatically an el-Azhari man at the polls.

"Ideological" considerations also played an important role
in 1965. The reader may recall that prior to elections el-Azhari
had entered his party into a conservative alliance in order to combat
the influence of communism. Now he was about to compete directly
against the leader of this movement. The implications for most voters
were clear: those who felt inclined toward the new progressive forces
had an opportunity to demonstrate practically their displeasure with
the reactionaries. And conversely, those who perceived a Communist
menace—and this included Umma and ICF partisans—felt the need to
support el-Azhari, not necessarily because they agreed with his policies, but because they wanted to prevent a Communist victory. Incidentally, such considerations led the Umma party president to tour
Omdurman South on the eve of the second polling day (for women) and
to instruct his followers to support el-Azhari instead of the Umma
candidate, advice that does not seem to have been heeded by many,
as the voting results indicated.

The role of the People's Democratic party in this campaign
cannot be ascertained definitely, although it was widely rumored,
and probably correctly so, that the PDP leader, Sheikh Ali Abdel-
Rahman, had exhorted his followers to cast their votes for his recent
ally, Abdel-Khaliq Mahjoub. (This was apparently the only case where
PDP followers were asked to support a non-PDP candidate actively.)

Voting

The final registration rolls disclosed that 21,233 residents of
Omdurman South were eligible to vote; of these 13,577 were men and
7,656 were women. Table A.1 indicates the distribution of registrants
by precinct and sex.

A study of the relative sizes (in registered voters) of the precincts exposes the importance of nos. 9, 1, and 2, as compared with
3, 7, and 6. We may speculate, for example, that if a candidate could
do well among the relatively poor residents of 9 and 1, then he might
be able to carry the constituency on that basis. The distribution of
registration by sex indicates a fairly constant pattern throughout the
constituency with the minor, but noteworthy, exception that registration of women was lowest percentagewise in areas that were presumed to support the conservative parties of Umma and NUP, that
is, Mulazimin, Abu Kaduk, 'Abbasiyah, and the Military Area.

TABLE A.1

Registration of Voters by Sex and Precinct, 1965

Precinct		Men	Women	Total
1	a	2,499	1,497	3,996
	b	1,826	1,302	3,128
2	a	2,065	1,101	3,166
	b	1,810	1,058	2,868
3	a	299	200	499
	b	303	207	510
4	a	1,367	877	2,244
	b	1,297	879	2,176
5	a	1,583	985	2,568
	b	1,846	1,049	2,895
6	a	838	404	1,242
	b	829	415	1,244
7	a	600	225	825
	b	580	215	795
8	a	1,153	878	2,031
	b	1,145	853	1,998
9	a	3,173	1,489	4,662
	b	3,053	1,519	4,572
Total	a	13,577	7,656	21,233
	b	12,689	7,497	20,186

Note: a   Registrations for April elections
      b   Registrations for November elections
Source: Compiled by the author.

Polling was conducted on April 28-29; the first day was reserved for men and the second for women. Voting participation lay slightly above the national average at 61 percent; the percentage of women voters exceeded that of men by the small margin of 2 percent. Because the voting behavior of men turned out to differ considerably from that of women, it may be instructive to compare the figures of voting participation by sex and precinct as illustrated in Table A.2.

Four findings from this table deserve to be mentioned: 1. The unusually low turnout in precinct 7—the subdivision reserved for all late registrants in precincts 4, 5, and 6—may have been caused by the unwillingness of many registrants to walk considerable distances to the polling station in 'Abbasiyyah. (By comparison, all other voters lived within a short distance of polling stations in their own quarter.)

TABLE A.2

Voting Participation by Sex and Precinct
in April 1965 Elections
(in percent)

Precinct	Men	Women	Total
1	47	59	52
2	51.5	68	57
3	66	54	61.5
4	64	72.5	67
5	65	61.5	64
6	55	57	55.5
7	35.5	37.5	36.6
8	71	37	57
9	65	67	66
Total	60	62	61

Source: Compiled by the author.

2. As the voting analysis will demonstrate subsequently, the considerably higher turnout of women than men in precincts 1 and 2 affected the voting outcome measurably. 3. It is surprising that only little more than one-half of the men in the civil servant quarter of Mulazimin came to the polls, a fact that probably reflects the belief among many NUP followers that el-Azhari's victory was a foregone conclusion. 4. The degree of participation in all other precincts was normal except for the unusually low turnout of women in Muradah, a fact that I am at a loss to explain.

The vote count was conducted on April 30, 1965, under tight security in classrooms of an intermediate school in Omdurman. Anticipation among election staff and the candidates' official observers was equally great. Outside the guarded compounds a sizable group of newsmen and party members had gathered in the hope of catching some preliminary results; inside several policemen milled around near the open windows anxious to follow the developments. After twenty hours of counting and recounting, the Chief Returning Officer announced the following official results:

Ismail el-Azhari (NUP)	5,651
Abdel-Kaliq Mahjoub (Communist party)	4,590
Abbas Da'afallah (Umma)	1,764
Mohammed el-Amin (ICF)	499

Bedawi Mustafa (PDP)	121
Mahmound Abbas (NUP)	91
Invalid	240
Total	12,956

These were the only figures available to the Sudanese public, since it had not occurred to anyone, including election officials, to keep a separate tally for the returns from individual precincts.

The results caused considerable surprise to most observers, who had expected a much more comfortable victory by el-Azhari and no more than 1,500 to 2,000 votes at most for the secretary-general of the Communist party. Interpretations of these data and an explanation of the somewhat surprising outcome can be submitted much more fruitfully after an examination of the voting results by precinct and sex as illustrated in Table A.3.

Given the nature of the final score it seems instructive to focus special attention on the comparative results obtained by Ismail el-Azhari and Abdel-Khaliq Mahjoub on the one hand, and by the Umma and ICF candidates, respectively, on the other.

First, taking a look at the sum totals, we observe that Ismail el-Azhari obtained almost one-half of the total men's vote and about 145 percent of Abdel-Khaliq's male support; by contrast he was outpolled by the Communists in the women's vote. Regarding the also-rans, the Umma candidate fared much better than the ICF representative, as expected; it is noteworthy that Abbas found 44 percent of his backing among women as compared with only 18 percent by Mohammed el-Amin. The relatively good showing of Abbas and the relatively poor showing of el-Azhari among women is particularly interesting because of Sayyed el-Sadiq's appeal to Umma women on the eve of polling to support the NUP president. I shall present my explanations for the peculiar voting behavior by women in the concluding section of this appendix; for the moment I will confine myself merely to a description of voting patterns.

By examining the results of the individual precincts we may make the following interesting observations:

1. A study of the ratio of votes for el-Azhari to those for Abdel-Khaliq reveals that the NUP's comparative score among men was better in all nine precincts than his score among women.

2. In all precincts except Beit el-Mal, where the outcome was extremely close, el-Azhari won the men's vote by margins varying from comfortable to overwhelming.

3. In the numerically small districts 3, 6, and 7 the women's vote was virtually split among the two leading contestants, while in Mulazimin and Muradah, Abdel-Khaliq won the women's vote by a narrow margin and in Beit el-Mal by a huge margin.

TABLE A.3

Statistical Breakdown of Voting in Constituency No. 31, April 1965

District	1	2	3	4	5	6	7	8	9	Total
Ismail el-Azhari										
Men	477	578	87	472	390	196	81	388	1,129	3,798
Women	216	281	38	247	243	88	34	233	473	1,853
Total	693	859	125	719	633	284	115	621	1,602	5,651
Abdel-Khaliq Mahjoub										
Men	485	381	83	228	282	148	65	281	663	2,616
Women	518	310	50	171	197	70	30	249	379	1,974
Total	1,003	691	133	399	479	218	95	530	1,042	4,590
Abbas Daafallah Hamed El-Nil										
Men	77	99	17	149	252	68	38	88	199	987
Women	99	111	10	183	123	44	12	104	91	777
Total	176	210	27	332	375	112	50	192	290	1,764
Mohammed El-Amin Barakat										
Men	80	54	6	33	68	36	16	38	76	407
Women	12	15	3	11	20	13	2	9	7	92
Total	92	69	9	44	88	49	18	47	83	499

Source: Compiled by the author.

4. By contrast the Communist leader was defeated in precincts 4 and 5, areas in which the Umma candidate obtained his largest support among women. In this connection it is most interesting that ansar women apparently refused to endorse the Communist on a large scale, whereas khatmiyyah women in Beit el-Mal and NUP wives and daughters in Mulazimin gave Abdel-Khaliq a majority over el-Azhari.

5. More than one-half of the latter's margin of victory was obtained in precinct 9 where the NUP president overwhelmed his adversary in the men's vote and won comfortably in the women's. This result indicates that the relatively poor residents of Banat and the Military Area preferred el-Azhari to the Communist. To what extent ideological or personal considerations influenced this outcome is very difficult to assess without a special study. In view of the large margin of Sayyed Ismail's victory here it may be interesting to point out that the Military District Command had encouraged all resident soldiers and dependents in the area to vote by providing free transportation by truck to the polling centers. This was clearly intended to help the cause of the conservative candidates, as a high-ranking officer in the command confided privately. Given the nature of army "encouragement," this measure undoubtedly ensured a high voting turnout among registrants from the military area; but whether or not the enlisted men and their womenfolk voted as their superiors had intended remains questionable.

6. Despite the fact that women made up only 35 percent of all voters in Omdurman South, Abbas Da'afallah obtained more votes from women than from men in 4 of the 6 large precincts.

7. By contrast Mohammed el-Amin obtained less than 2 percent of the women's vote; his candidature was endorsed on no more than 20 ballots in any single precinct.

8. The ICF candidate's best showing was among male voters in a khatmiyyah area, a result that corresponds to the national findings.*

We may summarize these results by concluding that Ismail el-Azhari was the clear choice of male voters and obtained enough votes among the women to win the elections in Omdurman South. In view of his fame as a national leader and his position as president of a large political party it was not at all surprising that he emerged victorious. What did surprise most observers was the excellent showing of Abdel-Khaliq Mahjoub throughout the area, and especially among

---

*The ICF obtained its largest percentages of total votes in Northern, Kassala, and Khartoum Provinces.

women voters. Unfortunately, it was impossible to accumulate further data about the background of voters. Nevertheless, I am willing to speculate on the basis of my own observations and of various private interviews, that el-Azhari's support came mostly from middle-aged and older voters of both sexes, where Abdel-Khaliq was backed predominantly by voters of 25 years of age or less. Our collective data do suggest that age was a more appropriate criterion for identifying the voters' loyalties than income, for example. (El-Azhari did well among the wealthy and among the poor.) One explanation may be, of course, that the older people have been economically more secure than the younger. Another, and probably more important one, was that older voters could identify much more readily with el-Azhari's political achievements during the past twenty years, whereas the younger generation was more impatient with the ways of traditional politics and looked to those leaders who promised radical solutions for accomplishing rapid social and political change. As a result, quite a few young Omdurmanis who would normally identify with the NUP voted for the Communists. By the same token, there must have been considerable numbers of Umma supporters who backed el-Azhari at the April elections. Most of these patterns will become clearer after an examination of the November by-elections to which we turn now.

THE NOVEMBER ELECTIONS

Contestants and Issues

About one month after the April elections, the new government took office and Ismail el-Azhari was appointed permanent head of the Supreme Council of State.* This necessitated vacating his seat in the Constituent Assembly; consequently, by-elections were scheduled for the first weekend in November. El-Azhari's appointment resulted from a compromise between the two major parties, an action that was to become one of the leading issues of the campaign for the November by-elections. For this reason it seems worthwhile to describe very briefly the nature of and the reasons for that compromise.

---

*A body of five who assumed the functions of titular head of state after the October Revolution. Until Sayyed Ismail's appointment the chairmanship was rotated on a monthly basis.

The reader will recall that no single party had obtained an absolute majority of seats during the April 1965 elections. For a variety
of reasons the Umma and NUP decided to enter into a "grand coalition" in the Assembly. As the senior partner the Umma received
the premiership and five major cabinet posts, while the NUP settled
for nothing less than an equal number of ministerial seats—six—
and el-Azhari's appointment as head of state.

This development was viewed with great suspicion by all minority parties for fear that they might be legislated out of existence
by the grand coalition. (This fear was groundless, as it turned out,
because the coalition was unable to pass any major legislation despite
its overwhelming majority in the Constituent Assembly.) Moreover,
there were considerable misgivings among two groups within the NUP.
One was opposed to cooperation with the Umma party on traditional
and personal grounds; the reader may recall that the two parties had
been on opposite sides of Parliament since the days of the Legislative
Assembly in 1948. The other constituted the progressive, Arab Socialist oriented wing of the NUP, which considered Umma leadership
and following to be too conservative for their liking. In the process
the National Unionists experienced a serious split among both the
members of the Executive Council and the party followers over the
policy of coalition with the Umma. This split manifested itself when
a good many NUPs refused to support el-Azhari's hand-picked successor as party nominee in constituency no. 31, Ahmed Zein el-Abdein, who had endorsed the coalition.

Ahmed Zein, then 40 years old, was a lawyer and graduate of
Khartoum University and Cairo University, and had been imprisoned
by the Military Regime in 1961. He was thought to be a political
moderate and had some experience in business.* He campaigned
considerably harder than el-Azhari had in April and concentrated
on attacking his chief rival, the secretary-general of the Communist
party. By virtue of the grand coalition he received the official and
active endorsement of the president of the Umma party. He and
members of his camp were confident of an easy victory on the basis
of their electoral calculations, whereby they added the Umma candidate's 1,764 votes in the April elections to el-Azhari's margin of
1,061 over Abdel-Khaliq and predicted an election victory by between
2,500 and 3,000 votes.

---

*Later on, in June, 1967, he became minister of Industries
and Supplies under the new government of Mohammed Ahmed
Mahjoub.

Their optimism received only a very minor and hardly noticeable setback when the grand coalition collapsed on October 20, 1965,
following some rather infantile bickering between Premier Mahjoub
and el-Azhari over the right to head the Sudan's delegations to the
Casablanca conference of Arab states and the annual conference of
the Organization of African Unity in Accra. It was enlightening to
hear some leading NUP politicians, for example, the minister of
Communications, Nasreddin el-Sayyed, at a political night in Omdurman, denouncing the coalition after its collapse as a "grievous and
treacherous mistake, never to be committed again, of aligning the
party with the reactionary stooges of imperialism." When the coalition was restored a few days later on November 1, the same politicians spoke of the "wisdom of sacrificing individual desires for the
common good" by coalescing with "our brothers in the Umma Party."
This rhetoric may have satisfied some, but there can be no doubt
that a great many Omdurmanis, including followers and sympathizers
of the NUP, who were unhappy about the consequences of the coalition policy anyhow, were disgusted by this spectacle and either abstained from voting or supported the NUP's rival as a form of protest.

The rival was Abdel-Khaliq Mahjoub, incidentally the only candidate to contest both elections in Omdurman South. His campaign
strategy in October was similar to the one in the spring, except that
this time his attack on the "reactionaries" was given further am-
munition by the bickering among NUPs during the period of coalition
with the Ummas.

Our analysis of the November elections will be limited to the
activities of those two candidates, although five others contested the
election of whom three were NUPs, which further underlines the dis-
unity of that party. These five candidates together obtained less than
6 percent of the total votes cast; it appears that while some politicians
could not agree on one candidate for their party, the voters at large
were well aware that the real contest was between Ahmed Zein and
Abdel-Khaliq, and they virtually ignored the other five competitors.

Voting

Table A.1 reveals that registration in the nine precincts for
the November elections was almost the same as for the April elections. In November there were 1,047 registrants (or 5 percent) less
than in April; most of the drop can be accounted for by the lower
turnout of men in precinct no. 1 where, as the reader may recall,
the votes among men had been evenly split between the NUP and
the Communist candidates.

Polling took place during the weekend of November 5-6, 1965, at the same polling stations as were used in April. Again the first day was reserved for men and the second for women. The overall turnout fell below that of spring as only 11,441 registrants (or 56.6 percent) appeared at the polls compared with 61 percent in April. It is interesting that this drop resulted from the 7 percent decline of participation by men, whereas participation by women remained constant at 65 percent. Table A.4 contains the distribution of voting participation by sex and precinct. It is especially noteworthy that the percentage of women who turned out was greater than that of men in all precincts but the smallest (no. 3).

In light of the voting behavior by women in the April elections, this fact takes on added importance especially when we note that the largest differentials in voting participation are found in the six large precincts.

TABLE A.4

Voting Participation in November 1965 Elections
(in percent)

Precinct	Men	Women	Total
1	60	67	63
2	51	63.6	56
3	49	46	47.6
4	63.5	67	64
5	40.5	56	50
6	49	51	49
7	29	30	29
8	60	70.7	65
9	55	65	56.6
Total	53.3	62	56.6

Source: Compiled by the author.

A comparison of the voting turnout at both elections shows that the lowest figures emerge in precinct no. 7, which was reserved for late registrants and in which voters had to make greater efforts than elsewhere to get to the polling stations. Furthermore, in 15 of the 18 entries, participation figures were lower for the November than the April elections. The only exceptions are the women of Muradah, where the April figures had been unusually low (37 percent compared with 70 percent), and both men and women in Beit el-Mal. This pattern leads me to the conclusion that the Communists had intensified their registration and voting drives in their areas of strength (especially Beit el-Mal) and in the one precinct where participation previously was very low and a potential source of sizable support had been left untapped. On the other hand, the decline in voting participation was greatest in those sectors that would normally support Umma candidates, a development to be expected in the absence of an official Umma contestant. In addition, a sizable decline in voting participation was recorded in precinct no. 9, a phenomenon that may be attibuted, at least in part, to the transfer of many soldiers from the Military Area to the southern provinces. However, one should not underestimate the decline in voting turnout by NUP followers, a matter that was due primarily to the disagreement within the party about the candidacy of Ahmed Zein and about the policy of continued coalition with the Umma party.

Vote counting took place on November 8, 1965, in a large room of the Province Headquarters. Throughout the day the official NUP candidate was confident of a victory by at least 3,000 votes. However, when the results were announced past midnight, he could consider himself fortunate to have prevailed by one of the narrowest margins. The official tallies were:

Ahmed Zein el-Abdein (NUP)	5,357
Abdel-Khaliq Mahjoub (Communist party)	5,269
Zein el-Abdein (ICF)	231
Mu'tasam el-Taqalawi (NUP)	142
Tayfour el-Shayib Mohammed (NUP)	136
Abdel-Rahman Ismail (Independent)	105
El-Tijani Amer (NUP)	37
Invalid	163
Total votes cast	11,441[*]

*One ballot from precinct 1 was lost.

The close victory by Ahmed Zein came as a tremendous shock to the conservative alliance of Umma and NUP, whose members simply could not imagine that any Communist could hold his own against the combined resources of both parties. In the final analysis it was this shock, experienced in the by-elections of constituency 31, which set in motion a process that ended with the expulsion of Communist representatives from the Constituent Assembly in December 1965, after that body had passed legislation declaring the Communist party to be illegal.

The Communists themselves were initially pleasantly surprised
by the outcome, since they could not reasonably expect to gain a virtual
stalemate against the officially endorsed candidate of the nation's two
largest parties. However, when they realized how close they came
to winning the by-election, their attitudes changed from satisfaction
to disappointment over the narrow defeat. In the hope of deriving
additional propaganda value from the elections they charged at a
press conference that their candidate was cheated out of winning
by the combined machinations of the government and the Electoral
Commission. This charge was based on the one ballot paper that
was lost in Beit el-Mal; at a press conference the Communists spoke
of "numerous" lost ballots. However, in private, Communist delegates at the vote count admitted to the correctness of the election results.

These results can be interpreted most fruitfully by examining
the outcome of voting by precinct and sex as illustrated in Table A.5.

The most striking impression is that the competition throughout
Omdurman South was much closer than had been the case in April.
For example, Ahmed Zein defeated Abdel-Khaliq in the total men's
vote and lost to him in the total women's vote, by the identical ratio
of 52:48. Since more men than women voted in constituency no. 31,
Ahmed Zein was able to eke out a narrow victory. A glance at the
results in the individual precincts reveals that votes among men and
women were evenly split between the two leading candidates in the
numerically small precincts nos. 3, 6, and 7, just as had been the
case in April. By contrast, Abdel-Khaliq won impressively in Beit
el-Mal and comfortably in Mulazimin, while Ahmed Zein won impressively in Abu Kaduk and comfortably in Abbasiyyah and Muradah. Precinct no. 9 was the only large district in which one candidate took the
men's vote and the other the women's.

This slightly confusing picture becomes clearer if we examine
shifts in voting patterns by comparing the results of the April and
November elections. This procedure will also enable us to consider
some hypotheses about the effects of Ahmed Zein's candidacy and of
NUP policy during the intervening five months on the voters in Omdurman South. The figures in Table A.6 illustrate the voting trends in
the constituency, whereby the positive prefix denotes vote gains in
November from April, and the negative prefix correspondingly denotes losses in November as compared with the results in April.*

----

*This procedure is methodologically sound although the num-
ber of votes in both elections were not equal. As Table A.1 illustrates,
the number of male and female registrants in the nine precincts were

TABLE A.5

Statistical Breakdown of Voting in November 1965

Precinct	Ahmed-Zein			Abdel-Khaliq Mahjoub		
	Men	Women	Total	Men	Women	Total
1	402	285	687	637	557	1,194
2	409	284	693	468	344	812
3	70	49	119	71	43	114
4	443	323	766	279	200	479
5	475	285	760	315	251	566
6	188	94	282	184	100	284
7	82	27	109	71	25	96
8	342	299	641	305	269	574
9	858	442	1,300	696	454	1,150
Total	3,269	2,088	5,357	3,026	2,243	5,269

Source: Compiled by the author.

TABLE A.6

Voting Shifts between April and November Elections

Precinct	Ahmed Zein Ismail el-Azhari			Abdel-Khaliq Mahjoub		
	Men	Women	Total	Men	Women	Total
1	−75	+69	−6	+152	+39	+191
2	−169	+3	−166	+87	+34	+121
3	−17	+11	−6	−12	−7	−19
4	−29	+76	+47	+51	+29	+80
5	+85	+42	+127	+33	+54	+87
6	−8	+6	−2	+36	+30	+66
7	+1	−7	−6	+6	−5	+1
8	−46	+66	+20	+24	+20	+44
9	−271	−31	−302	+33	+75	+108
Total	−529	+235	−294	+410	+269	+679

Source: Compiled by the author.

The most striking feature of Table A.6 is contained in the sum totals, which indicate that both candidates achieved comparable gains in the women's vote, but that Ahmed Zein lost heavily among the men, while Abdel-Khaliq gained the equivalent of four-fifths of that loss. I interpret these results as being caused by three factors: One, Abdel-Khaliq's increased campaign activities, which were primarily responsible for his improved showing in the women's vote (witness the steady increase in the seven largest precincts); two, the reluctance of many NUP men to back the party's nominee, a factor that cost Ahmed Zein at least 800 to 1,000 "old" NUP votes; and lastly, Umma support for Ahmed Zein in accordance with the Umma president's appeal to that effect, which was directly responsible for the NUP candidate's improvement in the women's vote, and which also lessened the effects of NUP desertion among men.

These interpretations are supported by an examination of the statistics in the nine individual precincts, which enable us to make the following observations: 1. Ahmed Zein's most impressive improvements in the women's vote took place in precincts 4 and 8, that is to say, in areas where the Umma candidate had been most successful. This relationship holds in precincts nos. 1 and 5 as well, although to a lesser extent. 2. With respect to the men's vote, he suffered his greatest setbacks, both in absolute figures and in comparison to his rival's showing, in the traditional NUP districts of Mulazimin and Banat and the Military Area. By contrast, he did quite well in ansar territory and even improved upon el-Azhari's position in Abbasiyyah, the well-known center of Umma strength. 3. Although Abdel-Khaliq advanced in eight of the nine precincts, his most striking success took place in NUP and PDP territory, namely precincts 1, 2, and 9.

These observations lead me to the following conclusions about voting patterns in the November elections: One the one hand, Abdel-Khaliq Mahjoub's relative success was due to; a) his retention of previous support; b) ability to "get the vote out" in his area of strength; c) defection of a number of NUP followers, notably men, into his camp. On the other hand Ahmed Zein won the elections by retaining

---

nearly the same. Moreover, at this point we wish merely to study the relative gains and losses of the NUP and Communist candidates. For example, if both candidates found less support in November than in April because of a decline in voting participation, then knowledge of the relative losses may be instructive. If, on the other hand, less voters turned out, but one candidate gained support while the other lost, then we may interpret the decline in participation as disapproval of the second candidate.

the votes of the hard-core NUP's and, more importantly, by receiving considerable backing from Umma voters. If I were asked to speculate about the precinct that proved to be most important for Ahmed Zein's victory, I would select Abu Kaduk (precinct no. 4), where apparently many of the 183 women who had voted for the Umma candidate in April gave their support to Ahmed Zein, enabling him to defeat his rival by the considerable score of 323 to 200 votes.

CONCLUSIONS

It remains now to consider what kinds of generalizations we can make about factors influencing voting behavior on the basis of our analysis of elections in Omdurman South. More specifically, we will be concerned with examining briefly the nature of correlations between voting behavior and such criteria as locality, income level, religious affiliations, age, and sex.

The data at our disposal do not permit a clear-cut generalization about the impact of income levels on voting. While it seems true that the Communists (and Socialists for that matter) received the support of many laborers and unemployed people, it is also true that they were backed by a good number of professional people from upper-income brackets.

Religious affiliation seems to have been of some importance as evidenced by the results in precincts nos. 1, 4, 5, and 6, but the effects of religious affiliations were considerably less in Omdurman than in rural districts.

No bloc vote could be discerned on a geographic basis, although the Communist candidate was very successful in Beit el-Mal and rather unsuccessful in the Western precincts. However, these results are a function of religious, not geographic loyalties.

The age factor seems to have been fairly important in the April elections as already discussed, but less so in November. The reason for this change is probably that Ahmed Zein was not only considerably younger than Ismail el-Azhari, but also exhibited more empathy for the problems and aspirations of the younger generation than his predecessor seemed capable of.

Sex turned out to be the most distinguishing characteristic in both elections. This phenomenon and its root causes deserve a special investigation, since it surprised virtually all foreign and native observers.

It surprised those who a priori had entertained an assumption, which seems to hold in most countries, namely that to the extent that women vote differently from men, they tend to vote more conservatively.

It also surprised the vast majority of Sudanese men who were convinced that their womenfolk would vote exactly as they were told by their men. It is instructive to note that various Sudanese politicians and ordinary citizens alike felt certain of this outcome before elections. One Umma leader told me that "Umma women are going to support our candidate en masse, but I am not so sure about NUP and PDP women." A NUP official remarked similarly that there was "no doubt about the loyalty of NUP women to el-Azhari, but there was some doubt about the voting behavior of PDP and Umma women." And so on. These opinions persisted even after the elections, presumably because the interviewees were unfamiliar with statistics about voting patterns. After I presented my figures to NUP and Umma leaders for comment, the initial response was disbelief and surprise. It is significant that for several years I have not encountered any male Sudanese observer who has offered a plausible interpretation of this voting behavior by women. For example, President el-Azhari thought that most women who supported Abdel-Kahliq Mahjoub did so because of "PDP propaganda, not because they entertained any modernistic ideas." Others spoke incoherently of the role of faqis and such matters; none seemed even close to comprehending the fundamental reasons at work that caused so many women to back the candidate of the Communist party. These reasons were threefold: 1. The women remembered the opposition of the conservative parties to female suffrage and supported those who fought hardest to obtain it. 2. The Sudan Women's Organization was very active in the capital and instructed all women to "fight for their rights at the polls by backing the progressive forces." I have personally seen a number of female university students making repeated trips to homes in Omdurman, from where they picked up older women and brought them to registration and polling stations and instructed them carefully in the various voting procedures, leaving little doubt about the identity of the candidate whom they recommended to their protegees. 3. Most importantly, the women were receptive to the promises and demands by Abdel-Khaliq and Fatima Ahmed Ibrahim (president of the Women's Association), who called for a liberation of Sudanese women from the kinds of social restrictions described in the first part of this book. To be sure, not all women identified with these demands, but a sizable number did, as our data indicate. Most of these were young girls who had received considerable formal education, but not the freedom of movement and action to take advantage of it.

Nearly ten years ago this author wrote of his conviction "that the importance of the role of their women in private and public life has been greatly underestimated by nearly all Sudanese men, and that the issue of the place of the women in Sudanese society will loom larger and larger in the foreseeable future."[3] One vindication of this judgment occurred at the April 1968 elections, when women voters in Omdurman South constituency made major contributions to reverse the previous narrow defeat of Abdel-Khaliq Mahjoub by helping him to an equally narrow victory over his former opponent, Ahmed Zein el-Abdein.

NOTES

1. According to remarks made in a private interview on July 3, 1966.

2. Statement based on remarks by Sayyed Abbas during personal interview on April 30, 1965.

3. Peter K. Bechtold, "Parliamentary Elections in the Sudan," (Ph.D. diss. Princeton University, 1967), p. 18.

Arabic patronyms have been treated as surnames, despite the
Sudanese custom of addressing persons by their given names.

ABOUT THE AUTHOR

PETER K. BECHTOLD has been Middle East Specialist in the Reference Department of the Library of Congress since September 1975. Previously he had taught at the University of Organ and the University of Maryland, College Park. In 1971-72 he was a Senior Fulbright-Hayes Research Professor in Egypt. His articles and reviews have appeared in such periodicals as the <u>Middle East Journal</u> and <u>Africa Today</u>.

Dr. Bechtold holds an M.A. and a Ph.D. from Princeton University.

MILITARY RULE IN AFRICA: Dahomey, Ghana,
Sierra Leone, and Mali
                    Anton Bebler

THE ORGANIZATION OF AFRICAN UNITY
AFTER TEN YEARS: Comparative Perspectives
                    edited by Yassin El-Ayouty

THE POLITICS OF PARTITION, DIVISION, AND
UNIFICATION
                    edited by Ray E. Johnston

SMALL STATES AND SEGMENTED SOCIETIES:
National Political Integration in a Global
Environment
                    edited by
                    Stephanie Glicksberg Neuman

QUANTITATIVE TECHNIQUES IN FOREIGN
POLICY ANALYSIS AND FORECASTING
                    Michael K. O'Leary
                    and William D. Coplin

U.S. POLICY TOWARD AFRICA
                    edited by Frederick S. Arkhurst